Chapel Hill
An Illustrated History

by James Vickers — text
    Thomas Scism — illustrations
    Dixon Qualls — color photography

Barclay Publishers
Chapel Hill, N.C.

ACKNOWLEDGEMENTS

The purpose of the text of this book is to describe the events and the personalities that were responsible for placing the University of North Carolina in southern Orange County, thereby establishing the village of Chapel Hill, and to trace the development of the village thereafter. I have not attempted to condense, and certainly not to duplicate, the excellent histories of the university written by Kemp Plummer Battle, Archibald Henderson, Louis Round Wilson, William Powell, and others who have concentrated almost exclusively on the institution.

When I began researching in June 1983, I assumed I was undertaking a six-month job. I soon learned that I had underestimated my task and that I would have to turn to a detailed study of primary documents if I were to produce a worthwhile history. Information on the people connected with the university is readily available in plenty; little has been done on the people who resided in the area before and in the decades immediately following the founding of the university.

Tom Scism, who was collecting illustrations and information for captions, laid his work aside in large measure and assisted me with the research. Collectively, we consulted thousands of documents, housed primarily in the Orange County Courthouse in Hillsborough, the North Carolina Collection and the Southern Historical Collection in the Wilson Library on the UNC campus, and in the state archives. As a consequence of our time-consuming work, we had to delay publication by approximately 17 months, but we were able to fill in a background of events and personalities that, in our opinion, makes this a substantial history. We also gave Dixon Qualls an opportunity to photograph Chapel Hill in all seasons for his color section.

We could never have collected the information herein contained without the cooperation and assistance of many, many selfless individuals. The fine staff that Dr. H.G. Jones has assembled in the North Carolina Room was always prompt and pleasant. Jeff Hicks, Alice Cotten, Robert Anthony, and Linda Lloyd brought us hundreds upon hundreds of items, often with suggestions regarding related material. Director Carolyn A. Wallace, Richard A. Schrader, Lisa Meadows, Enola H. Guthrie, Michael G. Martin, and Rebecca McCoy of the Southern Historical Collection were equally helpful. Jerry W. Cotten and L.C. Scarborough of the UNC Photo Department patiently guided Tom Scism through their collection and assisted him with reproductions. In the Hillsborough Courthouse, Hilda Winecoff and the people in Betty Jean Hanes' Register of Deeds Office, especially Virginia Forrest, were very helpful.

As I began to complete drafts for the early chapters, I was fortunate to have knowledgeable Chapel Hillians volunteer to read the text for accuracy, completeness, and style. Roland Giduz took many, many hours away from a busy professional and private life to read each chapter carefully, correcting my errors and filling in gaps. Peter Wilson drew on his intimate knowledge of the "established families" of Chapel Hill not only to check the accuracy of the text but as importantly to point out errors of omission. Wallace Kuralt caught several stylistic errors of commission that should never have gotten to him.

The people in the Chapel Hill area who shared their photographs and their memories with us are simply too many to mention. However, Robert Eubanks, who died this year, was indispensable. Others who enjoy old connections to Chapel Hill were helpful from afar. They included Col. George Tilson and Ellen Henry of Leesburg, Va.; Maude Ashe of Bakersfield, Cal.; Prof. John Young of UCLA; Milton "Ab" and Minna Abernethy of New York City; Myra Champion and Lucille Caldwell of Asheville; Mrs. W.G. Polk of Nashville, Tenn.; Dr. Horace Kent Thompson of Wilmington; George Barbee and Teeny Dallas of High Point; Wilson Powell of Batesville, Ark.; Excell Gattis of Philadelphia; Jean Anderson of Durham; and Rowena Tull of Kinston. Lynn Magee of Chapel Hill edited most of the text.

Illustrations marked "DAH" have come from the Department of Archives and History in Raleigh; those marked "NCC" have come from the North Carolina Collection in Wilson Library on the UNC campus.

James Vickers

Chapel Hill, NC
6 April 1985

CONTENTS

Library of Congress Cataloging in Publication Data
85-071270

ISBN 0-9614429-0-5

First Edition, First Printing

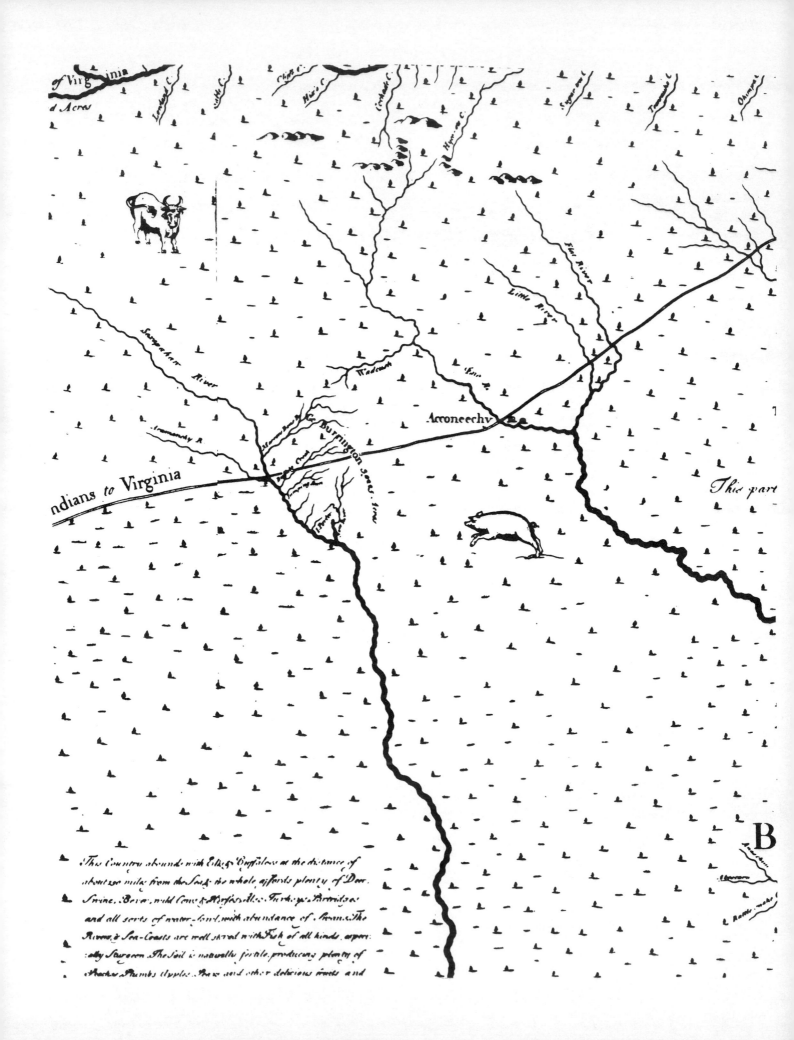

I
Before The Beginning
1729 to 1792

After a 66-year history of profitless invest-
ment, two generations of legal entanglements,
and decades of resistance to their authority in the
New World, in 1729 seven of the eight Lords
Proprietors sold their interests to the Crown, and
North Carolina became a royal colony. John Lord
Carteret, the first Earl of Granville, chose not to
sell and retained a one-eighth share of the original
charter, a 60-mile wide strip extending south of
the Virginia border, running west to the Pacific
Ocean, and including approximately one half of
the colony.

The first trickle of settlers into the Piedmont
region of the Granville District began in the
1730s, and as late as 1748 there were probably
fewer than 100 people living in the entire area. But
the trickle freshened around mid-century as settlers
flowed down the Great Wagon Road connecting
Philadelphia to the Yadkin River, with branch
routes dispersing the immigrants east and west.
Most of the arrivals were of Scotch-Irish, Welsh,
and German descent who were leaving New
Jersey, Pennsylvania, Maryland, and Virginia in
search of cheaper land to the south, relief from
overcrowded rural districts, and escape from the

*Chapel Hill lies at the boar's hind feet in this excerpt from
a map by Edward Moseley produced in London in 1733 for
the Lords Proprietor. Hillsborough today sits where
Acconeechy, an Indian village, is marked on the map. John
Lawson, an explorer for the Lords in 1701 visited what he
called "Occaneechi." Lawson was later captured by the
Indians, successfully argued for his freedom, but instead of
leaving the Indian camp he continued to argue the point.
The Indians soon tired of his rhetoric, tied him to a stake
and burned him. (NCC)*

incessant Indian wars of western Pennsylvania. A smaller number came directly from Europe.

In 1747 Mark Morgan, a Welshman and a Baptist, brought his wife Sarah and their children from Pennsylvania to set up camp a dozen miles south of the Eno on a creek that would later bear his name, on a site now occupied by the Finley Golf Course. While they were building a log cabin on the southwest bank of Morgan Creek, the family lived in a gigantic hollow sycamore log, reported to have been 10 to 12 feet in diameter. The Morgan children, whose birth dates are not recorded, were John, Hardy, Sarah, and Anne. Mark, John, and Hardy made further purchases which eventually gave them ownership of a large area encompassing most of the original boundaries of Chapel Hill plus territory to the east crossing the current Durham County line and to the south along and across Morgan Creek.

In 1755 Benjamin Bolin purchased a section on both sides of Bolin Creek a mile east of Chapel Hill. (Although Bolin Creek took its name from Benjamin Bolin, over the years it has been spelled variously as Bollengs, Bolling, Boiling, Boling, Borland, Bowlin, Bowling.) John Tapley Patterson purchased a tract in 1758 which would now include the western end of Franklin Street and a swath running south beyond Morgan Creek. In 1761 Henry Key bought the land on Bolin Creek lying directly west of Benjamin Bolin's holding.

William Barbee, of English descent, migrated with his wife Raichel and his sons John, Francis, and Christopher from Essex County, Virginia, and on 26 April 1753 obtained a grant for 585 acres lying east of Mark Morgan's homestead. Before he died in 1758 leaving John the guardian of Francis and Christopher, William had collected several other large tracts, and after his death his sons continued to buy land. Christopher, born ca. 1738-1742, went back to Essex County sometime between 1766 and 1777 to claim his bride Mary, surname unknown. They returned to the Piedmont, bought more land, and began a family whose progeny left prominent monuments on the landscape and on the spirit of the region.

In response to the sudden increase in the population, the General Assembly in 1752 created a new county extending from the Virginia border to the Granville line and including all of present-day Caswell, Person, Alamance, Orange, and Chatham counties as well as significant portions of Rockingham, Guilford, Randolph, Lee, and Wake. The new county of some 4000 to 4500 inhabitants was named in honor of King William III of the House of Orange, and Mark Morgan was named a justice of the peace for the first Orange County court, enjoying original jurisdiction and hearing cases appealed from magistrate courts.

Two years later William Churton marked off a county-

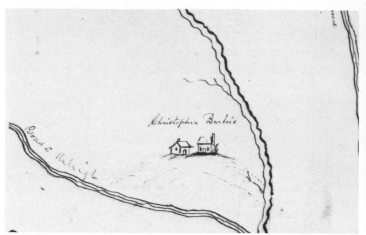

Christopher "Old Kit" Barbee, donor of 221 acres to the founding of UNC, built a homestead on his large farm three miles east of Chapel Hill. While this sketch shows only two buildings, Old Kit probably had slaves' quarters, a separate kitchen building, a stable and carriage house, a smoke house, and a privy on the property. He is buried on the farm, approximately one mile southeast of the present-day Landlubber's restaurant. (NCC)

seat site of 400 acres where the Great Trading Path crossed the Eno River, and Orange County officials designated it Corbin Town after Francis Corbin, land agent for the Earl of Granville. By the time the town incorporated in 1759, Corbin had been exposed as an unscrupulous fraud, guilty of collecting outrageous rents and fees, and townspeople took advantage of the occasion to rechristen their village Childsburg in honor of another of Granville's land agents, Dr. Thomas Child(s). However, when the doctor proved to be as disreputable as his predecessor, disgruntled residents looked abroad for inspiration and in 1766 named their town Hillsborough after the Earl of Hillsborough, the English secretary of state to the colonies.

The charter incorporating Childsburg named William Nunn as one of the five commissioners responsible "for designing, building and carrying on the said town." Three years later Nunn was coroner of Rowan County, and on 10 June 1765 Royal Governor William Tryon appointed him sheriff of Orange County.

By 1767, Orange County had become the most populous in the state with 3870 white male taxables, indicating a total population of 12,000 to 15,000; and the first settlers on Morgan and Bolin creeks had welcomed several new neighbors into their vicinity. Born in Pennsylvania in 1736, Thomas F. Lloyd, also a Welshman, received a grant for land near the headwaters of Morgan Creek in 1757. A year later he and his wife Margaret began building "The Meadows," a plantation three miles west of Chapel Hill at Calvander.

Lloyd was active politically, serving as a justice of the peace, a coroner, a militia general, and from 1761 to 1768 as an Orange County representative to the General Assembly. His daughter Margaret was to marry Adlai

Osborne of Rowan County and their decendants were to include three Adlai E. Stevensons: the Vice President of the United States during Grover Cleveland's second term; the Democratic presidential candidate in 1952 and 1956; and a U.S. Senator from Illinois. William Craig, Richard Caswell, and members of the Blackwood, Hogan, and Freeland families also set up homesteads in the area.

The early settlers fleeing from Indian wars to the north were surely relieved to find Orange County totally free of Indians. John Lederer observed a large tribe of Eno Indians during a June 1670 passage along the Great Trading Path, and John Lawson spent a night in February 1701 at an Occoneechee Indian village near modern Hillsborough. Two centuries later, university workmen collecting sand near Mark Morgan's original homesite, a few hundred feet behind the present-day Finley Golf Course Clubhouse, discovered in a single afternoon 150 sound arrowheads and a concentration of flint chips suggestive of a "weapons factory." The subsequent discovery of trading beads and burial grounds attests to the presence of an Indian village at some lost time.

However, the Occoneechee were in the process of a slow migration through the Piedmont when Lawson visited them, and by the time the first settlers arrived, there were

This photograph, itself nearly 100 years old, shows the house that Gilbert Strayhorn (1715-1803) built on his newly acquired land a few miles northwest of Chapel Hill. The oldest parts of the house were probably begun in the 1760's since Strayhorn acquired the property in 1759. Strayhorn is buried in the old graveyard just north of the New Hope Volunteer Fire Department on Route 86. (NCC)

This indenture for 570 acres of land in "the Parish of Saint Matthew" in Orange County was conveyed to Gilbert Strahorn (Strayhorn in the modern spelling) in 1759 by the Earl of Granville, with yearly payments to be 22 shillings, 10 pence. The land was located northwest of Chapel Hill in the vicinity of present day New Hope Presbyterian Church, a church that Strayhorn helped to found. (DAH)

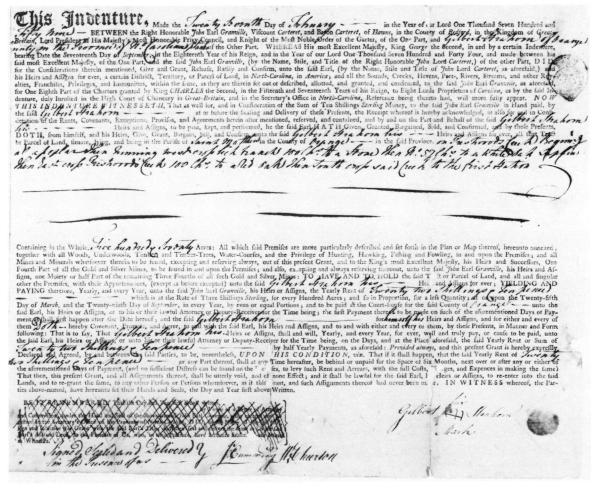

no Indians left in the region, permitting the Europeans to establish homes, farms, and villages unthreatened by human menaces not of their own creation.

The act creating Orange County in 1752 also created the Anglican Parish of St. Matthew within the same boundaries. During the next few years, the Church of England erected three churches within the parish: St. Matthew's in Hillsborough; St. Mary's a few miles to the northeast; and New Hope Chapel on the hilltop owned by the Morgans 12 miles to the south.

The latter plain log "chapel of ease" was at the northeast corner of the intersection of roads connecting Petersburg to Fayetteville and New Bern to Salisbury, on a spot now covered by the main parking lot of the Carolina Inn. The term "chapel" derives from the Italian "cappella," the diminutive of "cappa" or cloak, which in turn refers to the cloak of Saint Martin, fourth-century Bishop of Tours, who in church legend won Christ's admiration by sharing his cloak with a beggar. Consequently, a chapel is a subordinate place of worship, and a chapel of ease is a place of worship for parishioners living distant from the parish church. By the time of the Revolution, the prominence around New Hope Chapel had become known as New Hope Chapel Hill.

No one has left a description of New Hope Chapel, but the typical pre-revolutionary chapel of ease, popularly called the "church-house," was a simple, one-room log building with its ends facing north and south. A wooden

altar stood near the long east wall, opposite the entrance and separated from the congregation by a wooden rail. Behind the altar hung tablets inscribed with the Decalogue, the Apostle's Creed, and the Lord's Prayer. To one side of the altar, a communion table held copies of the Bible and the Prayer Book, supported in upright and open positions. Several rows of rough pews completed the interior, lit by windows cut into the two long walls. The New Hope Chapel rotted away with the demise of Anglican influence after the Revolution, and by the 1830s only a few decayed logs remained to mark its location.

Church records of the early years of St. Matthew's Parish have vanished, but one of the first ministers left a public record of activities before and after the Revolution. The Rev. George Micklejohn was born in 1717 at Berwick-on-Tweed, on the border of England and Scotland. He graduated from Cambridge University as an honorary Doctor of Sacred Theology, and he probably served as a chaplain with the Duke of Cumberland when he defeated Prince Charles Edward Stuart the Pretender at Culloden Moor on 16 April 1746. In March, 1766, the Bishop of London licensed Micklejohn to preach in North Carolina, and the Society for the Propagation of the Gospel sent him to Wilmington, where he arrived in July. Governor William Tryon liked Micklejohn, enjoyed his sermons, and assigned him to St. Matthew's Parish.

Micklejohn was small, but very strong, and possessed of somewhat unsettling features. He loved money, and would only accept golden doubloons, 33-shilling pieces, for his services. He loved whiskey, and on occasion would bribe a man to attend a sermon with a liberal draught, afterward taking a generous swig himself. He did not love women. Supposedly, while he was still in England his wife left him, leaving him with a lifelong distrust of the sex. He was tireless in his ministerial duties and undoubtedly preached many times at New Hope Chapel, although that assumption cannot be proven absolutely.

In September, 1768, Micklejohn was in Hillsborough when his friend Governor Tryon kept a promise to attend the trials of four Regulator leaders and Edmund Fanning, Tryon's hated register of deeds. The construction of an

Edmund Fanning (1737-1818), no relation to David Fanning, became Governor Tryon's private secretary in 1771. During the Revolutionary War he raised and commanded the King's Regiment of Foot, twice suffering battle wounds. In 1779 the General Assembly of North Carolina confiscated his property and when the British quit the war Fanning went to Nova Scotia where as Lieutenant-Governor from 1783-86 he assisted in resettling some of the North Carolina Loyalists who moved there. After a few years of further service on Prince Edward Island he moved to London. (NCC)

elegant governor's "Palace" far to the east in New Bern intensified resistance to the Crown in the western counties where dissidents, guided by leaders in Orange County, had collected under the banner of the Regulators.

The western counties were grossly underrepresented in the assembly, and even Governor Tryon conceded his administrators had received less than half the taxes collected in recent years. In Orange County specifically, the eight sheriffs serving between 1752 and 1770 were short 7820 pounds. Sheriff William Nunn was one of those who had been more assiduous in collecting than in turning over taxes. Patrick Creaton swore on 21 May 1768: "Last November William Nunn and Thos Hutchins sub:Sheriffs came to my House and broke open the roof of it and took a piece of linen cloath for one Levy tho' I offered to pay the money if they would goe about two miles to John Piles' who paid them fourteen shillings and relieved ye cloath." By 1771, Nunn's balance due the colony amounted to 1014 pounds, 11 shillings.

In response to such outrages, the Regulators declared they would pay no more taxes until they were satisfied that their money would go into the colony coffers and that local officials would be brought "under a better and honester regulation than any have been for some time past." In short, the Regulators were demanding accountable, representative government.

On 8 April 1768, about 70 Regulators entered Hillsborough to recover a member's horse that had been "distrained" by the sheriff for nonpayment of taxes. After rescuing the horse, the band marched as a mob to the center of town, fired shots into Edmund Fanning's house, and terrorized county and court officials. Afterward, Thomas F. Lloyd, newly commissioned a militia major general by Tryon, ordered the arrest of four Regulator leaders for confiscating the horse and "inciting the populace to rebellion." Colony officials indicted Edmund Fanning for charging fradulent fees. Christopher Barbee was among the pool of jurors who were to hear the cases.

This situation presented Rev. Micklejohn with an excruciating dilemma. His political and professional allegiances were solidly with the Tories, and he considered Governor Tryon a personal friend; but he was also a friend to his parishioners, and they in the majority supported the Regulators.

Regulator leaders knew of Micklejohn's ties with the established order, but they trusted him on several occasions to help draft documents and to deliver messages. Once at great risk he assisted Thomas Person, the Revolutionary War general after whom University of North Carolina trustees later named Person Hall. Person was confined in the Hillsborough jail awaiting trial for Regulator activities when Micklejohn persuaded the sheriff to release the prisoner at dusk so he could ride 30 miles east to his plantation, Goshen in modern Granville County, to conceal incriminating papers. Micklejohn loaned Person his prize mare, Person rode to Goshen, hid the papers, and returned by dawn. Micklejohn then took his customary morning ride, leaving no one to suspect his sprightly mare had traveled 60 miles during the night.

To keep order during the trials of the Regulators and Fanning, Governor Tryon brought four brigades totaling 1461 militia troops to Hillsborough. On Sunday, 9 September 1768, he had Micklejohn preach to the Orange and Granville County brigades while Presbyterian minister Henry Patillo addressed the Mecklenburg and Rowan brigades. Micklejohn chose as his topic "Let everyone be subject unto the Higher Powers," and in the course of the sermon he excoriated the 3700 rebels camped nearby as "wretched and unthinking men madly attempting to subvert the Laws of the Kingdom and foolishly bringing upon themselves Destruction here and Damnation hereafter."

Tryon succeeded in maintaining an uneasy peace during the trials. Christopher Barbee sat on juries which found Dennice Bradley innocent of burning the Granville County jail, but which convicted William Butler of recovering the horse and for "Rout" and assault. Two other Regulators were found guilty of recovering the horse and inciting rebellion. However, Tryon pardoned the Regulators in an effort to make peace, and Judge Richard Henderson fined his friend Fanning a single penny and costs.

When Regulator efforts to seek redress in the legislature ended with Tryon's dissolving the Assembly, they turned once more to violence. They took over the Orange County court on 24 and 25 September 1770, beat Fanning, dragged him through the streets, wrecked his house, forced Judge Henderson to flee, and held their own kangaroo court, humiliating their enemies and filling the records with profanity. Willian Nunn and Edward Fanning were two of 59 men who signed a petition condemning the Regulators for

In 1941, Thomas Person's desk with its seven secret drawers was given to the University. John Allcott (left) and Robert House are shown with the desk in this 1941 photograph. Thomas Person (1733-1800) was a sheriff of Granville County, a state legislator, and later a UNC Trustee. His $1050 contribution in "shining silver dollars" enabled the University to complete the second building on campus, which was then named for him. Person acquired land at a prodigious rate, making 69 purchases during the Revolutionary War alone, and he eventually owned 82,358 acres in North Carolina. (NCC)

their atrocities in Hillsborough.

The Regulator movement came to a sudden end on 16 May 1771 when Tryon in command of an army of 1452 militiamen soundly defeated 2000 Regulators in a two-hour battle at Great Alamance Creek west of Hillsborough. Six Regulator leaders died on the gallows, Tryon pardoned another six, and his promise of clemency brought forth 6409 former rebels who swore they would end their resistance and acknowledge the authority of the colonial government.

Meanwhile, the crude chapel of ease stood in near isolation at the crossroads atop New Hope Chapel Hill, although a continuous stream of immigrants flowed into Orange County. Included among them in 1774 was the individual ultimately most responsible for providing the *raison d'etre* for Chapel Hill. James Hogg was born in Caithness County, Scotland in 1729. Married to McDowell Alves, a second cousin to Sir Walter Scott, James Hogg himself was related to the Scot poet James Hogg, "the Ettrick Shepherd." In 1772 Hogg became involved in a clannish feud when he helped recover bounty plundered from a shipwreck by some of his neighbors. They retaliated by breaking into and burning his house. Since the arsonists were members of the sheriff's clan, Hogg was able to have them prosecuted only at great personal expense, and they continued to harass him by stealing his property and produce.

His brother Robert had migrated to North Carolina in 1756, where he had become a successful merchant. During

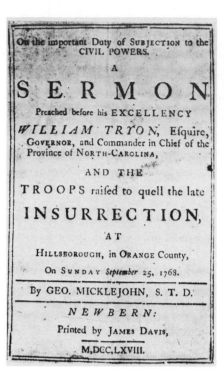

Rev. George Micklejohn (1717-1818), at Gov. Tryon's urging, privately printed the sermon he had delivered to Tryon's troops in 1768 during the Regulator period. In December Assembly Speaker John Harvey notified Tryon of the Assembly's approval of the sermon and of its resolve to reimburse Micklejohn for the cost of printing, a move Micklejohn welcomed because his salary from the Church of England was only £133 annually. Tryon sent a copy of the sermon to Lord Hillsborough in England, complimenting Micklejohn on his "assiduity" in carrying out his duties. (NCC)

Governor Tryon (1729-1788) confronts the Regulators in this old illustration. The artist portrays the Regulators as a ragtag bunch of rabble, but for the most part in Orange County, the center of the activity, the group was composed of enfranchised planters, farmers, and merchants. (NCC)

James Hogg (1729-1805) was the central figure in locating UNC at the site destined to become Chapel Hill. Because his wife was the last of her line, in order to preserve her family name, Hogg legally changed the last name of his two sons to Alves, thereby causing some unknown wag to write, "Hogg by name / Hogg by nature / Changed by Act / of Legislature." His children remained closely associated with Chapel Hill, buying and selling property and marrying local belles.

This silhouette is the only known likeness of Hogg. (NCC)

a 1772 visit to Scotland, Robert convinced James to follow him to America. James later wrote he "easily determined to leave a country, where, for want of police, and due administration of the laws, I had found it impossible to defend my goods from being stolen; . . . and where the thief, the robber, the murderer, and willful fire-raiser, never hitherto wanted a gentleman, or rather a part of gentlemen to patronize them."

When James Hogg announced his intent to emigrate, 280 of his neighbors asked him to become a "tackman" and arrange passage for them. Charging commissions far below the going rates, he arranged passage with James Inglis, Jr., owner of the "Bachelor," and the immigrants sailed from Thurso, Caithness County on 14 September 1773. But foul weather and a storm-induced shipwreck delayed their arrival at Wilmington until late summer 1774.

Supposedly, members of the McCauley, Strayhorn, and Craig families sailed with Hogg and continued their journey directly inland to Orange County, in some instances to join relatives. The absence of their names on Hogg's head-of-families list has spurred speculation that they may have traveled as servants. Hogg himself briefly joined his brothers Robert and John in their mercantile business at Cross Creek, now Fayetteville, before moving on to 1600 acres he had purchased at Hillsborough, where he quickly became a prominent man in the community.

In January 1775, Hogg became a partner in the Transylvania Company, organized by Judge Richard Henderson to purchase western lands from the Cherokee. For $50,000 the company bought most of modern-day Tennessee and Kentucky, an area explored for them by Daniel Boone. James Hogg attended the Second Continental Congress in Philadelphia in September to petition for recognition of Transylvania as the fourteenth American

colony. However, Virginians Patrick Henry and George Rogers Clark succeeded in having the petition denied in order to protect Virginia's claim to a portion of the Transylvanian territory. Unlike his brothers who remained loyal to England, during the Revolution James was an ardent patriot.

The brothers Matthew and William McCauley came from County Antrim, Ireland before the Revolution. According to family tradition, the British had placed a bounty on Matthew's head and had forbidden him to leave Ireland. To evade authorities, William hid his brother in a whiskey barrel, loaded the barrel aboard ship, and kept Matthew's presence secret during the voyage to America. The brothers stopped off briefly in South Carolina before moving on to the vicinity of New Hope Chapel Hill.

In response to demands by westerners that they be given greater representation in the Assembly, Orange County began to lose large blocks of territory during the Regulator movement. The legislature created Guilford County in 1770, taking from Orange a narrow strip running from the Virginia border to the Granville line. Also in 1770, the southern portion of Orange went into the new Chatham and Wake counties. In 1777 the northern portion became Caswell County, leaving what is now Alamance, Orange, and Durham counties inside Orange borders until Alamance broke off in 1849 and Durham in 1881.

The American Revolution was well underway when the Rev. George Micklejohn read a prayer opening the Third Provincial Congress in Hillsborough in August 1775: the First Provincial Congress had met a year earlier in New Bern in defiance of Governor Josiah Martin; William Hooper, who had moved from Massachusetts to Wilmington in 1767, and other delegates who had attended the First and Second Continental Congresses; Minutemen had fired "the shot heard round the world" on 19 April 1775; and Governor Martin had fled to a British warship

William Hooper (1742-1790), was an ardent patriot who signed the Declaration of Independence. After the Revolutionary War he moved, with his wife Ann (Clarke) and three children, from Wilmington to Hillsborough where he was known as 'The Signer.' His name is closely linked to Chapel Hill: his grandson was a professor at the university; his daughter-in-law Helen Hogg Hooper married Joseph Caldwell, President of the University, after the death of her husband, William Hooper, Jr.; a grandnephew, John DeBerniere Hooper became a professor at the university later. (NCC)

Lord Charles Cornwallis, (1738-1805) used Hillsborough as a staging area in 1771. On 21 February 1771 a number of Loyalists were on their way to join Cornwallis in Hillsborough when General Nathanael Greene ambushed them, killing 300, forcing Cornwallis to withdraw to Deep River.

After the war, Cornwallis became Governor-General of India, 1786-94, then ambassador to France, 1801. In 1805 he accepted reappointment as Governor-General of India, but died within a month after his arrival in Calcutta. (NCC)

General Horatio Gates (1726-1806) led his army from Hillsborough to Camden, South Carolina, on 16 August 1780 where he fought Cornwallis' army and lost. His flight from the lost battle did not end until he reached Hillsborough some three days later, without his army. His superiors sent him to New York and he left his dying wife behind, never to see her again. After she died in 1783, Gates married Mary Vallance, a woman worth $500,000. He lived the rest of his life on Manhattan Island on a farm near the present Madison Square Garden. (NCC)

on the Cape Fear in June. The 184 delegates at Hillsborough pledged their allegiance to the Crown and unanimously adopted an empty resolution submitted by William Hooper declaring their readiness to die in defense of the rule of King George III. More substantially, they established an interim government and provided funds to support an army of 10,000 men to fight for independence.

At the beginning of the war, a significant portion of the Orange County population supported the loyalists, among them Robinson York, Dr. John Pyle, James Hunter, Michael Holt, and the Rev. Micklejohn. The early support in the county encouraged Tory leaders who for years sustained the belief that the former Regulators would join them en masse, a belief they retained even after neutrals and erstwhile loyalists such as James Hunter, Michael Holt, and the Rev. Micklejohn had pledged their allegiance to the patriots. However, from the beginning rebel sentiment dominated the New Hope Chapel Hill area.

John Hogan lived in what became Randolph County, but he owned land on New Hope Chapel Hill, and he married Mary Lloyd, the daughter of General Thomas F.

Lloyd. Hogan rose to the rank of colonel in the Continental Line, leading troops in the central Piedmont against Lord Cornwallis.

Reportedly, Mark Morgan joined the rebels. If so, his service had to have been short because early in 1778 the Orange County court ordered an inventory of the estate of "Mark Morgan, dec'd." Later in the year, his son John had to appear in court to answer charges that he had hidden his father's will. Evidently he had a convincing story because when his mother died in 1787 she included a bequest to her "beloved son John" along with bequests to her son Hardy, her daughters Mrs. Anne Hartbone and Mrs. Sarah Yeargin, and her granddaughter Charlotte Yeargin. Hardy Morgan was listed in a General Assembly act of 1783 "to liquidate and fully settle the accounts of the officers & soldiers of the Continental Line, of the State of North Carolina," but Hardy's rank, his length of service, and his duty assignments are unrecorded.

Matthew McCauley joined the 10th N.C. Regiment on 19 April 1777 as a lieutenant and spent the next several months recruiting and training the men who made up the unit. The regiment received only a few supplies when they moved on to Halifax. In November, Matthew McCauley and 19 other regimental officers were marching north of Halifax when they sent a curt note to Governor Richard Caswell insisting that they be supplied since they were ill-prepared either for winter or for battle. Matthew served for 25 months, three months as a prisoner of the Tories; he received a bounty of 761 acres of Tennessee land for his service; and after the war the General Assembly raised his rank to captain. Naturally, he was "Colonel" McCauley to his neighbors at New Hope Chapel Hill.

James Hogg was secretary of the Orange County Committee of Safety, the board which took over local authority for the militia and government, and he served on the first Hillsborough board of commissioners in 1777. Even though he did not serve in the patriot army, reportedly a group of veterans met at his home on 23 October 1783 to form the North Carolina Society of Cincinnati, a fraternity of officers and descendants of officers who served in the Continental Line. William McCauley was a justice of the peace in 1777 and afterward, an Orange County representative to the House of Commons for four terms between 1778 and 1782, a state senator from 1783 to 1788, and sheriff of Orange County in 1789-1790.

William Nunn, whose loyalty to the Crown during the Regulator troubles was never a question, was a fanatical rebel during the Revolution. After the war he went by the name "Captain" Nunn, but since his name does not appear among the rosters of Continental Line officers, he must have served in a militia unit. In 1770 Richard Simpson had given a tract on the Haw River to "my son-in-law William Nunn." Evidently, Nunn's first wife died,

David Fanning (1756?-1835) is escaping from one of his dozen or so captures by the Patriots during the Revolutionary War. He is astride his horse, Bay Doe. After the war, Fanning and his 16-year-old bride Sarah Carr moved to Nova Scotia where he served in the provincial assembly of that Canadian province, 1791-1800. He became the first member expelled for a felony after he was convicted of rape and sentenced to death. He received a pardon because of his war service and he went into exile across the bay in Digby, where he acquired several hundred acres of land, became a merchant, a shipbuilder, and a land speculator, living in apparent peace until his death. Fanning submitted a bill of £1625 for his war services, but the crown paid him only £31 of that sum, although later he received an annuity of £91. (DAH)

because during the war he met and married Elizabeth Copeland, a young woman who shared his enthusiasm for the ideas of Thomas Paine and the French liberals.

Clashes between Tories and Whigs occurred sporadically in the region around New Hope Chapel Hill until the summer of 1782 when the tide of battle had shifted irreversibly to the rebels. Hillsborough was a focal point for both armies. The rebels used the area primarily for staging and foraging; the loyalists hoped to use it for recruiting as well; and, with the coastal region under Tory control, the first state governors used Hillsborough and Halifax for the seat of government.

The Rev. Micklejohn's tour of duty as a chaplain for Tory General Donald McDonald was unexpectedly brief. He was among the 850 prisoners captured when McDonald's 1600 Highlanders were ambushed by 1100 patriots at dawn on 27 February 1776 at Moore's Creek Bridge. At the Provincial Congress meeting in Halifax a few weeks later, the Rev. Henry Patillo had the unpleasant duty of sentencing his fellow divine to exile in Perquimans County for the duration of the war. But after seven months of unaccustomed tedium, Micklejohn had a change of heart and on 23 November took the oath of allegiance to the American cause.

Gen. Horatio Gates assembled his patriot army in Hillsborough before marching to defeat at the hands of Lord Cornwallis at Camden, South Carolina in August 1780. Lord Cornwallis occupied the town for five days in February 1781 before marching to his Pyrrhic victory at Guilford Courthouse, all the while dogged by small but fierce detachments of militia and Continental Line troops. In 1781 the most savage of all Tory commanders also made his presence felt in the Eno-Haw-Deep River region.

In the intervening two centuries, "David" has become the de facto middle name of the "Notorious" David Fanning. Born about 1755 in what is now Wake County, Fanning was an outcast as a child and a young man because of his affliction with "scald head," a disease of the scalp that made him repulsive to others. He wore a silk cap to hide his malady, took his meals and slept alone to spare the timid, and became an Indian trader for lack of better prospects.

At the beginning of the Revolution, a party of Whigs robbed Fanning, who swore vengeance, and kept his word. He gained a commission in the Tory militia and set about recruiting enough men in Orange, Chatham, and Randolph counties to make up three regiments. Operating out of headquarters at Cox's Mill on Deep River in modern Randolph County, he pillaged Whig-owned farms and plantations, slew scores of people in isolated attacks, and hanged rebels in retaliation for the punishment of loyalists. Along the way he garnered a reputation for leading a band of heartless murderers and rapists. But he denied being anything but an efficient soldier and emphatically denied unwarranted attacks on women. Captured well over a dozen times, he always escaped, often astride his favorite mare "Bay Doe."

Daunted not the slightest by Cornwallis' departure into Virginia, Fanning turned the summer of 1781 into a spectacle of daring. On 14 July he strategically placed 73 of his followers in ambush along the roads leading into Pittsboro, setting a trap for the officials who were to try captured loyalists the next day. His ploy took the Whigs totally by surprise, allowing him to capture 53 patriots, including a Continental Line captain, three legislators, and every militia officer in the county. He paroled the majority, but sent 14 of the ranking prisoners to the Tory command in Wilmington. Pleased with Fanning's coup, his British superiors rewarded him with a colonel's commission, a brilliant red uniform, a sword, and a set of pistols. Encouraged by his flamboyant success, Fanning picked up the pace of his attacks on farms and fortified plantations, often hanging the Whigs he captured.

Governor Thomas Burke in September set up headquarters in Hillsborough and selected a Captain Allen to lead a company of infantry and cavalry against Fanning and other Tory bands harassing the district. Christopher Barbee was a member of Allen's command and reportedly fought in several skirmishes. When Fanning learned of Burke's location, he joined his smaller force with Col. Hector McNeil's 500 men and moved toward Hillsborough, arriving during the morning fog of 12 September. The attack began as well organized as the raid on Pittsboro two months earlier. The Tories captured Governor Burke, his secretary John Huske, and some 200 other rebels. They freed about 30 loyalists prisoners, one scheduled for execution that day, and filled the empty jail with patriots, including the guards.

Fanning and McNeil certainly had no scruples against plundering enemy homes and businesses, but they realized the danger of their position within hostile territory when their men broke into Whig rum stocks and began rioting merrily. Two of the invaders rode to James Hogg's house, stripped his shoes of their silver buckles, took his watch and keys, and looted his residence. Hogg appealed to Col. McNeil, a fellow Scot, and McNeil posted a guard on Hogg's house. In the early afternoon, Fanning and McNeil reestablished order and set off with their prisoners.

Notified of the raid, Gen. John Butler stationed his men to ambush the Tory column at Lindley's Mill on Cain (Cane) Creek, 20 miles west of New Hope Chapel Hill in what is now southeast Alamance County. Butler's initial fusillade felled McNeil with mortal wounds and panicked his followers, who would have fled in a rout had not Fanning regrouped them, moved the prisoners onward, and led a counterattack. By the time the battle ended, Butler had lost 24 dead, 90 wounded, and 10 captured; Fanning lost 27 killed, 60 wounded so seriously they had to be left behind, 30 walking wounded, and seven captured. Fanning's left arm was shattered by a musket ball, forcing him to remain in hiding while others delivered the

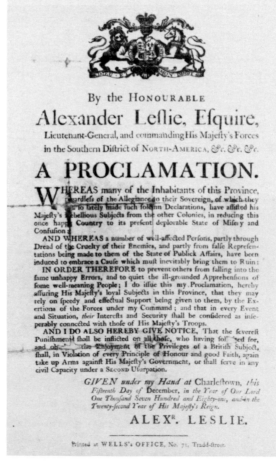

Thomas Burke (1747-1783) was Governor of North Carolina during the Revolutionary War. After his capture by David Fanning, he gave his word not to try to escape and was paroled to James Island, South Carolina. He broke parole after serious threats and attacks on his life, and he returned to Hillsborough to resume his duties in late January 1782. Unfortunately, his reputation was somewhat tarnished because he had broken "a Gentleman's Word," he began to drink heavily, and he died soon after. (DAH)

In 1781, Loyalists were beginning to have second thoughts about the wisdom of supporting the King of England, leading Alexander Leslie to issue this proclamation declaring that "speedy and effectual" support would be given to all Loyalists as if they were in His Majesty's Service itself. (DAH)

prisoners to Wilmington.

Since the trial of the captured Tories was held in Hillsborough, attorney Alfred Moore no doubt had the easier task in prosecuting than young William R. Davie had in defending in this, his very first case. After due deliberation of the facts presented in court, and after appropriate consideration of Fanning's threat to hang 10 Whigs for every one of his men executed, the jury returned a verdict of guilty, and Judge John Williams sentenced the seven to hang. Three of them died on the gallows on 1 February 1782. The remaining four chose the alternative of serving a hitch in the Continental Line.

Fanning increased his attacks during March and April 1782, threatening an unprecedented reign of terror, but the fortunes of war had abandoned him. Cornwallis had surrendered in October 1781, and Gen. Nathanael Greene had rid inland North and South Carolina of significant organized resistance. In April, Fanning and his 16-year-old bride Sarah Carr Fanning anticlimactically slipped into British-held territory in South Carolina. Afterward they lived in St. Augustine, Florida, before leaving in 1784 for Nova Scotia, where David Fanning died in 1825 after writing a lively memoir of his experiences as a guerrilla leader.

Even in the midst of an uncertain war, the delegates to the Fifth Provincial Congress meeting in Halifax in late 1776 acted on the need to provide advanced educational facilities for the new state. Although records are incomplete, historians generally cite Waightstill Avery, one of the founders of Queen's College at Charlotte in 1771, as the person most responsible for the inclusion of Article XLI in the state constitution adopted on 18 December: "A school or schools shall be established by the legislature for the convenient instruction of youth, with such salaries to the masters, paid by the public, as may enable them to instruct at low prices; and all useful learning shall be encouraged and promoted in one or more universities."

Although the colonial legislature passed an act incorporating Queen's College in 1771, King George III refused to approve the bill. Without official sanction, Presbyterians operated the school until 1777, when the General Assembly chartered it as Liberty Hall and the church ceased its administration. The depression accompanying the Revolution forced the school to close in 1780. The Rev. Samuel Eusebius McCorkle, a trustee of Liberty Hall, headed a successful movement to have the school rechartered as the Salisbury Academy and moved to Rowan County in November 1784.

Hoping to have the Salisbury Academy receive the "promotion" of Article XLI, Rev. McCorkle and Salisbury borough representative Spruce Macay drafted a bill to establish "a University in this State" that Rowan County representative William Sharpe introduced in the House of Commons on 8 November 1784. The bill passed its first

By JOHN HAMILTON, Esq.
Lieut. Col. Commandant Royal
North-Carolina Regiment of Infantry.

All colonials who had served in the British army's Royal North Carolina Regiment received honorable discharges "at the King's Order" in 1783. The crown held the loyalists of North Carolina in the army to protect them until the new government guaranteed that they would not be punished if they remained as civilians in the new state. (DAH)

reading on 11 November, but the next day the House delayed further action until the next session of the General Assembly. No further official action occurred in fact for five years, but the matter did not lie dormant. Political, social, and economic leaders were determined to establish an institution to train the future leaders of the state, and they were equally determined to model it after Princeton College, where many had received their education, McCorkle and Macay included.

The legislators of 1784 faced stubborn economic and political problems. The depression that had forced Liberty Hall to close remained in effect. The state treasury was empty, and politicians were divided over the economic ramifications involved in the ceding of territory west of the Smoky Mountains to the national government. A great division was also growing between the conservative Federalists and the liberal, sometimes radical, Jeffersonian Republicans. The Republicans feared conservatives would control the university and use it as a means to create an elite class. In one of the great ironies of North Carolina history, when the university finally came into being it was the conservative Federalists responsible for its founding who complained loudly of the democratic sentiments of the early faculty.

William Richardson Davie was born in Egremont, County Cumberland, England on 22 June 1756. After arriving in America as a youth, he attended Queen's College and the College of New Jersey, later Princeton, before reading for the law under Judge Spruce Macay in Salisbury. Although a Continental Line officer at one time serving under his father-in-law General Allen Jones, Davie became a master of guerilla warfare leading small bands of partisans in harassing Lord Cornwallis. In the "hornets' nest" at Charlotte on 26 September 1780, Davie at the head of 20 cavalrymen briefly stopped the entire British army.

He finished his reading for the law while recovering from a wound, obtained a license to practice in time for the Hillsborough trial of the men captured in Fanning's raid, then completed the war as commissary general to General Nathanael Greene. After the war, he was a Halifax County representative in the House of Commons, a delegate to the Continental Congress in 1787, and a member of the North Carolina constitutional conventions of 1788 and 1789.

After the failure of the 1784 bill, Davie mounted a campaign to underscore the advantages of a public university, and his persuasive arguments coincided with a sharp shift in political sentiment within the new state. Influenced by powerful Republicans, the constitutional convention at Hillsborough in 1788 had voted 184 to 84 against ratifying the U.S. Constitution until it contained a Bill of Rights. But when the second constitutional convention and the legislature met in Fayetteville in November 1789, the Federalists were firmly in control.

To Davie fell the distinction of introducing both the bill to establish a university and the successful motion to ratify the Constitution. With supreme confidence he submitted the University Bill on 12 November. The legislature chartered The University of North Carolina on 11 December with the provision that it not be located within five miles of the new state capital or of any court, thus eliminating county seats.

The preamble to the charter noted the social value of "a University, supported by permanent funds and well endowed," but Davie and his allies knew the economic and political realities of their time. To encourage gifts, the articles of the charter offered anyone donating ten pounds the privilege of educating one student tuition-free and promised "the public hall of the library and four of the colleges shall be called severally by the names of one or another of the six persons who shall within four years contribute the largest sums towards the funds of the University."

Trustees moved quickly, and in their first meeting on 18 December, Davie announced that Col. Benjamin Smith had donated his Revolutionary War land bounty of 20,000 acres of Tennessee land to the new institution. James Hogg represented Orange County at the meeting, and Thomas Person represented Granville.

As encouraging as the gift of Col. Smith was, it provided no immediate money, and the trustees needed ready cash to begin actual work on building a campus. The charter appropriated no funds for construction or operating expenses. It only gave the university arrearages due the state from 68 state and county officials before 1 January 1783 and property reverting to the state when owners died without heirs. Attorneys for the trustees raised $7362, but the treasurer had to turn over all principal to the state, which allowed the university to spend only the six percent interest. Facing those obstacles, William Davie and James Hogg headed efforts to raise subscriptions and donations,

William R. Davie (1756-1820) was the last Federalist Governor of North Carolina and a tireless worker for the creation of a university. As North Carolina became less federalist and more republican, his political fortunes declined although his interest and influence in the university remained strong. In 1803, he was handily defeated in a race for the Congressional seat for Halifax, and he moved to his plantation "Tivoli" on the Catawba River in South Carolina. Davie received the first honorary degree awarded by UNC. (NCC)

James Iredell (1751-1799) was a member of the first UNC Board of Trustees in 1789. He was an ardent supporter of education and his immense prestige was a boon to the efforts to create a state university. He resigned as a trustee in 1790 to become a Justice of the United States Supreme Court, a post he held until his death. Iredell's dissent in the case of Chisholm vs. Georgia(1793) led to the adoption of the Eleventh Amendment to the U.S. Constitution in 1797. (NCC)

Benjamin Smith (1756-1826), Governor in 1810, was well-known for his quick temper and fought a number of duels. A quarrel with his brother James at the Orton Plantation in Wilmington led to James' move to South Carolina where he took his mother's maiden name, Rhett, and founded that now famous family.

Benjamin married Sarah Dry, a wealthy woman, but by the time of his death, he was so far in debt that his body was the object of creditors' searches. Smithville, renamed Southport in 1887, was named for the old advocate of public education. (NCC)

but their efforts fell short.

Governor Alexander Martin, who was also president of the trustees and a graduate of the University of New Jersey, strongly supported state funding of the institution. Opponents argued that the state should spend money only for the functions essential for orderly government, such as a police force and a court system. Following a passionate appeal by William Davie in late December 1791, the General Assembly reluctantly approved a loan of $10,000 -- and just barely. The House passed the measure 57-53, the Senate 28-21. When legislators converted the loan into a gift early in the next century, the action constituted the only direct appropriation to the university between its founding and Reconstruction when state money was needed to pay faculty salaries.

Meeting in Hillsborough in August 1792, the trustees voted to select an appropriate site for the university within a 15-mile radius of Cryprett's Bridge across New Hope Creek on the Raleigh-Pittsboro road. They also appointed a committee to submit plans for the first university building and instructed an eight-man site-selection commission to meet in Pittsboro on 1 November to begin a search for a desirable tract of 640 acres for a campus near to or adjoining another 1400 acres for a farm and a source of timber and firewood.

Commissioner James Hogg did not wait idly for his associates to make an objective decision. He wanted the university in Orange County, and he went to work persuading property owners in the New Hope Chapel Hill area to make offers of land and money too substantial for the commissioners to ignore. He and five other commissioners met in Pittsboro on the assigned date, and on 2 November began their job in earnest, visiting four nearby sites and entertaining additional offers. Moving in a northerly direction, they inspected two tracts on the third of November, two more on the fourth, and another on the fifth. According to their journal, they "then proceeded to view New Hope Chapel Hill, in Orange County."

Mrs. Cornelia Phillips Spencer, whose personal efforts on behalf of the university have entered the realm of legend, helped to inspire the myths surrounding the selection of New Hope Chapel Hill as the seat of the University of North Carolina. She wrote of the commissioners' visit to the hilltop: "They stopped at Chapel Hill to lunch, taking their refection, as I have been told, at the foot of the great poplar which now stands in the campus. They fell in love under these benignant circumstances with the beauty of the spot."

Another account has William Davie accompanying the commissioners and sticking his riding switch into the ground as he dismounts, and from that fortuitous planting sprang the tree now bearing Davie's name. Other versions attribute the commissioners' entrancement to the liquid they consumed with their open-air repast: in one they succumb to the delectable waters dipped from a spring near the chapel of ease, in another they mellow following wholesome libations to Bacchus. Induced into a restful nap, they awake refreshed and unanimously agree with Davie's pronouncement that they are in the midst of the ideal and idyllic campus. In point of fact, they did not arrive unannounced.

James Hogg's efforts had succeeded. Local property owners had conditionally promised 1386 acres and 798 pounds, "or thereabouts," with the provision that the university be located on New Hope Chapel Hill. The commissioners spent three days collecting subscription pledges and accepting deeds from Col. John Hogan, Benjamin Yeargin, Matthew McCauley, Alexander Piper, James Craig, Christopher Barbee, Edmund Jones, and Hardy Morgan. John Daniel signed a bond promising to convey property; Thomas Connely and William McCauley each promised to convey deed for 100 acres. John Hogan contracted to produce 150,000 bricks at 40 cents per hundred, and Edmund Jones agreed to supply lumber.

This notice was sent out in April 1791 to all members of the UNC Board of Trustees. However, the site-selection committee chosen at the July meeting failed to act, and the trustees chose a new committee in August 1792 which later that year recommended that the university be located at New Hope Chapel Hill. (NCC)

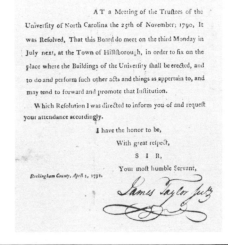

SIR,

AT a Meeting of the Truftees of the Univerfity of North Carolina the 25th of November, 1790, It was Refolved, That this Board do meet on the third Monday in July next, at the Town of Hillfborough, in order to fix on the place where the Buildings of the Univerfity fhall be erected, and to do and perform fuch other acts and things as appertain to, and may tend to forward and promote that Inftitution.

Which Refolution I was directed to inform you of and requeft your attendance accordingly.

I have the honor to be,
With great refpect,
SIR,
Your moft humble Servant,

Rockingham County, April 1, 1791.

James Taylor Jun.

Alexander Martin (1740-1807), served as Governor of North Carolina in 1789-1792, during which time the Assembly passed the bill establishing the university. He thus became the first head of the Board of Trustees. Martin had very close ties to Chapel Hill: his nephew by marriage, Pleasant Henderson, one of Chapel Hill's most respected and influential citizens, 1800-1830, had been his private secretary 1782-85 and Pleasant's brother Thomas married Martin's daughter. Pleasant named his youngest son Alexander Martin. (NCC)

Legends are lovely, but the discerning Archibald Henderson had no doubt about who was responsible for placing the university on New Hope Chapel Hill. He concluded in *The Campus of the First State University*, "Credit for the location is attributable both to the generosity of the donors and to the shrewdness, assiduity, and indefatigable labors of James Hogg in personally soliciting the gifts."

Eight men gave most of the land later occupied by the campus. Christopher Barbee donated the 221-acre "Old Chapel Tract" that now includes Polk Place, much of McCorkle Place, the area north to Cobb Terrace, and land west along Cameron Avenue. Known universally as "Old Kit" in his later years, he already owned large amounts of Wake County land in 1778 when he purchased the 800 acres three miles east of New Hope Chapel Hill on which he built his plantation "The Mountain."

Apparently, Old Kit never learned to read or write (he registered his "mark" with the Orange County Court of Pleas and Quarter Sessions in November 1785), but he thrived and continued to accumulate property. By 1787 the Orange County tax files list him as the largest land-holder in the immediate region with 2145 acres. Because his nearest land was two miles to the east of the hilltop, when James Hogg asked him for a contribution, Barbee purchased the "Old Chapel Tract" of 225 acres from Hardy Morgan for 95 pounds and donated 221 acres to the trustees for a nominal five shillings (50 cents). The "missing" four acres undoubtedly resulted from surveyors using different reference points in measuring the land for the two transactions.

Hardy Morgan, who by 1790 owned 13 slaves on his Bolin Creek farm, gave 205 acres including areas now occupied by Carmichael Auditorium, grounds to the east, the cemetery, Gimghoul Road and Evergreen Lane. Hardy Morgan died in 1795 and left his estate to his sons Lemuel and Allen.

Benjamin Yeargin donated a 50-acre, wedge-shaped section entering the modern campus from the north and coming to a point approximately at Old West. He retained possession of property extending north and east to Bolin Creek containing slave quarters and a house he built about 1791 on what is now Tenny Circle. Yeargin was the son of Andrew Yeargin, a Methodist preacher prominent in Virginia and North Carolina. In addition to teaching country students, Benjamin ran a grist mill at the small gorge on Bolin Creek known as Glenburnie slightly more than a mile north of the chapel, near the current Airport Road bridge. The mill dated back to pre-Revolution days, and it was the earliest recorded mill operating in the New Hope Chapel Hill area.

After the death of her first husband John Tapley Patterson in 1781, Mark Morgan's daughter Sarah married Benjamin Yeargin in 1782. She had two children by Patterson—Mann and Milly, and four by Yeargin—Charlotte, Bartlett, Harriett, and Mark Morgan Yeargin.

John Morgan's son Mark, named for his grandfather Mark Morgan, signed a bond giving the trustees 107 acres that includes Pittsboro Street, South Columbia Street, and much of the Medical Center; but Mark was still a minor and died shortly afterward. His brothers John and Solomon, as his heirs, honored Mark's pledge and formally deeded the 107 acres to UNC in 1806, Solomon's signature being certified by his guardian Chesley Page Patterson. In 1795 when Edmund Jones purchased a portion of the Mark Morgan estate from John Morgan, Jr., Benjamin Yeargin was listed on the deed as "Guardian to John Morgan on account of his lunacy." Solomon married late in life, like his father became mentally unstable, and begat a daughter who would leave the old Mark Morgan homestead, known under her ownership as Mason Farm, to the university.

John Daniel donated an adjacent 107-acre square

containing the land occupied by Kenan Stadium and reaching southwest to Manning Drive. For a payment of eight pounds, Daniel surveyed the land and drew a map delineating some of the donations, a map used in 1792 by James Hogg during his solicitation drive. In 1792 Daniel lived between the chapel and a section of land on Morgan Creek which he later sold to Old Kit Barbee.

Edmund Jones gave a 200-acre, L-shaped tract wrapping around south campus to the west and south. A Revolutionary War veteran, Jones lived on a farm south of the chapel with his wife, the former Rachael Alston. He also operated a saw mill below Yeargin's mill on Bolin Creek. Soon after he gave the land, he sold out and moved to a farm near Siler City.

James Craig donated five acres west of the chapel of ease which lay across what is now Cameron Avenue. Craig, who lived farther to the west, had a reputation for being a reserved, generous, but very absent-minded man.

Matthew McCauley, generously referred to as Colonel McCauley on Daniel's map, donated 100 acres directly north of the chapel across Bolin Creek on what is now known as Mt. Bolus. Even though the first deeds recorded by Matthew and William McCauley date to 1779, both brothers probably owned property on Morgan Creek before the Revolution. In any event, when Matthew purchased 100 acres from the State of North Carolina in 1782 the property adjoined "his own land at the foot of Piney Mountain," another name for New Hope Chapel Hill. Matthew set up a blacksmith shop, accepted 10-year-old orphan Thomas Kee as an apprentice in 1785 as directed by the Orange County court, and won a reputation for his industry—and his ingenuousness.

In his *History of the University of North Carolina*, Kemp P. Battle cited an oft-repeated story. Having been blessed with an ignorance of serpents thanks to St. Patrick, early after his arrival from Ireland, Matthew carried a rattlesnake to an elderly lady and inquired, "What is this pretty beast?" He threw the reptile to a safe distance when the woman informed him it was poisonous.

In 1785 Matthew obtained a license to operate a tavern out of his house, and he may have been operating a mill by that time, although as late as 1797 Jesse Neville owned a mill in the vicinity. A land purchase by Matthew McCauley from Alexander Piper in that year used "Neville's mill" as a reference point. However, if Neville's mill and Matthew's are not the same, it was Matthew's which enjoyed the greater reputation and which remained in operation for over a century. He ground the best flour and meal in the area, and by the turn of the century roadsigns on the Hillsborough-Pittsboro road gave the distance to "McCauley's Mill," by that time a well-known landmark. In 1793 the mill was 1.25 miles southwest of the chapel of ease; today it would be near the Smith Level Road crossing.

William McCauley purchased several hundred acres farther up Morgan Creek and established his plantation "Great Meadows" three miles to the west of the chapel of ease, on what is now the site of University Lake. When he left the sheriff's office in 1790 to concentrate on farming "Great Meadows," he owned 10 slaves.

Alexander Piper, who lived on a farm a few hundred feet north of Matthew McCauley's mill, donated 20 acres one mile west of the chapel. Later he moved to a farm in Fayette County, Tennessee.

About the only sign of civilization in the immediate vicinity of the chapel of ease in 1792 was an inn some two hundred yards to the north. Run by James Patterson, probably a brother or nephew of John Tapley Patterson, the inn catered to travelers on the main roads intersecting at the chapel of ease and to drovers herding cattle, sheep, and hogs to distant markets.

The site-selection commissioners unanimously recommended New Hope Chapel Hill at a trustees meeting in New Bern on 3 December 1792. Three days later the Board of Trustees approved the recommendation and named a new commission to erect buildings for the university and to lay off "a Town adjacent thereto."

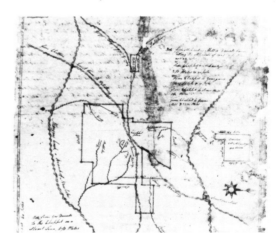

John Daniel, a Chapel Hill area resident and surveyor, drew this map of the area in 1792, probably because James Hogg wanted it for his presentations to the University site-selection committee and for Hogg's solicitations for land donations. Almost in the dead center of the map are the words "Chappel Place" that locate the crossroads where the Chapel of Ease was situated and where today the Carolina Inn stands. The roads were probably built in the 1770's and 1780's.

Roadbuilding meant that first the Orange County Court of Pleas and Quarter-Sessions would appoint a jury of land owners and county officials to lay out the right-of-way, and upon receiving their report, the court would appoint a group of "Hands" to build the road, "Hands" usually meaning the landowners along the proposed stretch of road. Slaves and hired men would do the actual work. For example, the August 1777 session of court ordered a number of men, including Thomas Lloyd, John Hogan, William Strowd, Jesse Neville, John Morgan, and William McCauley, all of whom, together with their descendants, would play large roles in Chapel Hill's development, to "be a jury to lay out the best and nearest way to Hillsbro' from Chatham Court House over Haw River at a place known by name Morgan's Mill." (NCC)

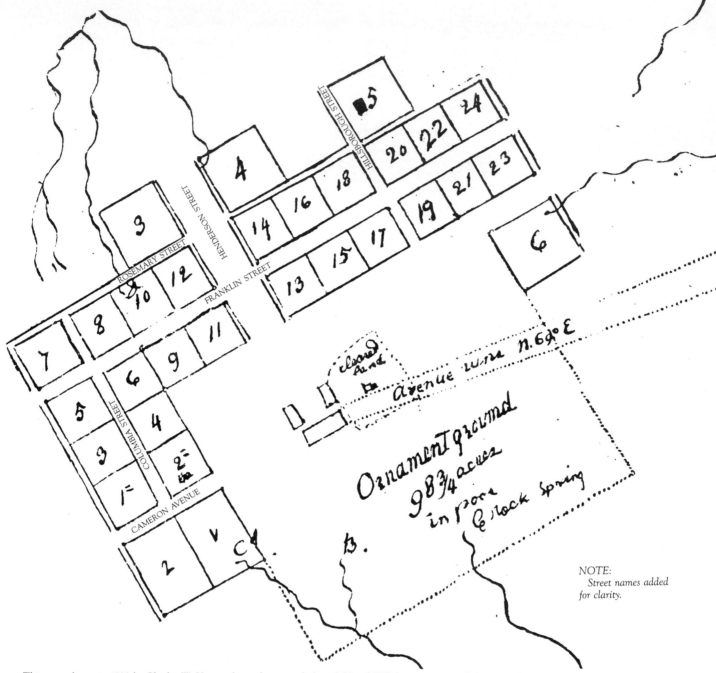

This map, drawn in 1798 by Charles W. Harris, shows the original plan of Chapel Hill that was prepared for use at the 1793 auction. The smaller lots were approximately 300 feet square and contained two acres. The six larger lots contained four acres each.

John Grant Rencher, the auctioneer, sold all of the four acre lots and sixteen of the two-acre ones, according to deeds filed in Orange County. Purchasers of four acre lots: Edward Jones bought no. 1; Christopher "Old Kit" Barbee, no. 2; Andrew Burke, a Hillsborough merchant, nos. 3 and 6; William Hays, a planter, no. 4; Rencher bought no. 5.

The two-acre lot purchasers: James Patterson, planter and tavern owner, bought lot nos. 4 and 5; John Carrington, farmer, nos. 8 and 9; Daniel Booth, merchant and planter, no. 10; George Johnston, farmer, no. 11; Hardy Morgan, planter, mill owner, and original land donor, no. 12; Jesse(e) Neville, later a Chapel Hill merchant, no. 13; Samuel Hopkins, later postmaster, no. 14; John Daniel, planter and civil engineer, no. 16; William Henry Hill of Hillsborough, no. 18, which he sold to John Taylor before the deed was recorded; Rencher, nos. 19 and 20; Chesley Page Patterson, planter and guardian of Solomon Morgan whose descendants gave "Mason Farm" to UNC, nos. 21 and 22; and John Caldwell, planter, no. 24.

The remaining lots were sold later. For example, Charles Collier bought no. 17 in 1803; J.W. Carr, whose family name is preserved in Carrboro, bought no. 7 in 1847.

Reference points: Lots 7, 8, 10, and 12 are bounded on the south by Franklin Street and on the north by Rosemary Street, then called Back Street. The Carolina Inn sits on four-acre lot no. 2. The University Baptist Church is on two-acre lot no. 5. First Citizen's Bank and Trust Company and the Methodist Church are at the west and east ends of lot no. 9. Lot no. 12 is the post office corner.

The proposed "Grand Avenue," shown on the map running northerly from Franklin between lots 12 and 14, then between four-acre lots 3 and 4, was never built. Owners of lot 14 gradually built westward toward lot 12 until only a narrow passageway remained, present-day Henderson Street. One of the first buildings to so encroach on the Avenue was the Preparatory School built by the university. (NCC)

II
The Early Years
1792 to 1832

The first concrete move to build a physical campus began on 10 August 1793 when a trustee commission met in Chapel Hill to survey the university grounds and "to lay off and survey adjacent thereto a town containing 24 lots of two acres each and six lots of four acres each." The original boundaries of the campus constituted a rough square marked approximately by the present Battle Lane, South Road, Columbia Street, and Franklin Street. The original plan for the town contained six streets, including a proposed 290-foot-wide Grand Avenue running out of the campus and through the area now occupied by Cobb Terrace. Both the campus and the town were tilted 21 degrees to the west.

On 17 July 1793, James Patterson had signed a contract witnessed by George Daniel, to build the "North Wing" of a projected three-structure complex, the building that is now Old East. George Daniel had agreed to deliver 350,000 bricks at forty shillings ($4) per thousand.

Seven members of the site-selection commission, other trustees, land speculators, and a large contingent of university supporters formed ranks at James Patterson's inn at the southwest corner of Franklin and Columbia on 12 October before moving off to lay the cornerstone for Old East and to auction off the town lots. The Eagle Lodge Masons of Hillsborough organized the formalities and led the stately noontime procession from the tavern to the campus, assisted by Masons from Chatham, Granville, and Warren County orders.

With great solemnity, North Carolina Grand Master William Davie, assisted by six other Masonic officials, laid the cornerstone on the southeast corner of the three-foot thick foundation. The ceremony continued with an address by the optimistic Rev. Dr. Samuel Eusebius McCorkle. "May this hill be for religion as the ancient hill of Zion; and for literature and the muses, may it surpass the ancient Parnassus!" he asked in blessing the institution. His expectancy for the town was somewhat more mundane, but—considering the character of the inhabitants of the backwoods North Carolina in 1793—perhaps no less quixotic: "Ere long we hope to see it adorned with an elegant village, accommodated with all the necessaries and conveniences of civilized society."

Following a closing prayer, John Grant Rencher of Chatham County proceeded to auction off the village lots. Several of the men who had donated land to the university purchased property, most as speculators. John Daniel bought the current Presbyterian Church grounds; Hardy Morgan paid $150 for the tract now occupied by the post office; Christopher "Old Kit" Barbee purchased the Carolina Inn lot. James Patterson bought the plot containing his inn and a lot diagonally across Columbia Street.

Patterson, a resident of Chatham County, lived in his Chapel Hill inn while building Old East and added to his holdings in 1793 by purchasing 10 acres of the old Hardy Morgan tract on Bolin Creek from Edmund Jones. In 1795, for 275 pounds Patterson sold his inn and some adjoining property to former Orange County sheriff William Nunn and his wife Elizabeth, called "Betsy" by all who knew her. William enlarged the facility, creating a drinking-and-dining room and a loft for lodging, and by October 1795

This apron, now the property of the Temple of the Grand Lodge of Masons in Raleigh, was worn by William McCauley at the ceremonies to lay the corner stone of what is now Old East. The 14½ inch by 16½ inch, white lambskin apron is covered with symbols of McCauley's Masonic Lodge. (Courtesy of the Mason Lodge)

he was advertising "a house of Entertainment, where James Patterson lately lived." On 16 July 1796, Nunn paid the trustees eight pounds, 13 shillings "for 4000 Bricks lent him," no doubt used for the additions to the inn.

The Nunns continued true to the principles they had adopted during the Revolution. Mrs. Cornelia Spencer observed that William Nunn was "soaked in the unbelief of the Revolutionary armies, taken by induction from the French Liberals." When he preached Betsy Nunn's funeral in 1851, Professor Elisha Mitchell still felt impelled to apologize for her "carelessness about religious matters."

The Nunns moved their growing family into the inn in 1799, unsuccessfully applied to purchase additional land from the university, and bought a lot from Archibald Campbell directly across Columbia Street in 1801. The aging William died early in the nineteenth century, leaving the very capable Betsy to run the inn and to care for their five children: David, Ilai, Hugh, Sally, and Edith.

Andrew Burke entered winning bids for the Battle lot and another four-acre lot north of Rosemary off Grand Avenue. George Johnson purchased the land now occupied by the Battle-Vance-Pettigrew complex. Another James Hogg, this one from Wilmington, bought that lot a few years later and erected a large frame house there when his son Gavin entered the university. Gavin graduated in 1807 and moved on to Raleigh to begin a distinguished law career. His parents remained in Chapel Hill, where his father ran into financial difficulties.

When three New York creditors forced James Hogg into a sheriff's sale in 1810, Gavin bought the house and property for $501, thus enabling his parents to remain in their home. They continued to live there after Gavin sold the property to Benton Utley for $400 in 1832. Two factors were responsible for the decrease in value: James Hogg had allowed the house to deteriorate, and a regional economic depression was in its second decade.

Also in 1832, Benton Utley signed a series of notes for $2500 each in which he agreed to pay John Newton a total of $19,715.54 over a period of two years for his dry goods business and stock. He then either built a storehouse

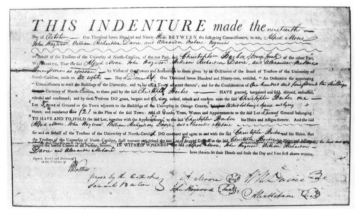

This indenture states that "Old Kit" Barbee purchased the four-acre lot no. 2 for 105 pounds and 10 shillings sterling. He sold it soon after to Samuel Holmes, a member of the UNC faculty. (NCC)

beside the house or an addition onto it, moved in with the Hoggs, and ran the store, but not successfully. In 1834 he announced he was selling off an estimated $25,000 in stock "contemplating a new arrangement in business," and in 1837 he sold the property and what remained of his stock for $1800 to Ezacariah Trice, who had no better luck than Benton as a storekeeper.

Auctioneer John Rencher, who through his wife Anne Nelson Rencher was related to British naval hero Admiral Horatio Nelson, bought three lots, including those now occupied by the president's house and the Sam Phillips law office. During the sale, Rencher disposed of 23 of the 30 lots for a total of approximately $3100, leaving a tidy profit for the trustees after deducting his $20 auctioneer's fee and a $16 surveyor's fee for John Daniels.

Although speculators failed to realize quick profits, trading in Chapel Hill property was brisk during the early years. Transactions involving Lot 8 at the northeast corner of Franklin and Columbia are typical. On 17 October 1793, John Carrington paid 55 pounds ($110) for the lot. However, when he could not meet his debts, James Carrington bought the property in a sheriff's sale. James Carrington sold it to Matthew McCauley for 60 pounds on 13 November 1797. In 1819, for $100 Matthew McCauley sold James Thompson and George Trice a 20' by 30' section fronting on Franklin Street a few paces from Columbia on which they built a small store. When Matthew died in 1821, the remainder of the lot passed on to his son William who sold it for $500 in 1822 to Dr. Charles R. Yancy for a home site. In 1824, Yancy sold .7 acres between Thompson and Trice's store and Columbia Avenue to Old Kit Barbee, who had operated a blacksmith shop there for several years. Old Kit sold the blacksmith plot to his son William in 1831; Dr. Yancy sold his house and property to merchant Jesse Hargrave in 1840.

By 1818 the village contained at least thirteen residences, four stores, two "hotels," and a blacksmith shop, in addition to the grammar school and four university buildings. Early in this century, when J.D. Webb and Herbert Lloyd were preparing the foundation for the building now housing the Carolina Coffee Shop, they discovered sawdust which suggested the presence of a sawpit dating to about the time the village was founded. Merchant records from a store begun in 1813 by William Barbee and William Watson indicate that they furnished a good deal of the lumber used in village construction after that time.

On 10 January 1794, the trustees elected David Ker "Presiding Professor" and set 15 January 1795 as the opening date for the school. David Ker was born to Scotch-Irish parents in Ireland in 1758, and he supposedly attended Trinity College in Dublin before emigrating with his wife Mary to Fayetteville in 1791. However, the only

Abram Rencher (1798-1883), son of John Grant Rencher who was the auctioneer at the village auction in 1793, was a Congressman, Minister to Portugal, and Governor of the Territory of New Mexico. After graduating from UNC he married Louisa Mary Jones, sister of Johnston Blakeley Jones, a Chapel Hill physician who helped to found the N.C. Medical Association. Abram's son delivered a senior speech at the 1862 commencement before joining the Confederate army. (NCC)

David Ker (1758-1805) resigned as UNC President, had his name stricken from Presbyterian church rolls, moved first to Lumberton and then to the Mississippi Territory where he settled down as a cotton planter, a lawyer, and, after 1801, a territorial judge appointed by his idol Thomas Jefferson. When he died in 1805 from pleurisy, his widow Mary (1757-1847), a schoolmistress left with five children, burned all his manuscripts so that he could not corrupt others from the grave. (NCC)

David Ker on record at Trinity matriculated in February 1765, when Professor Ker was only six. In any event, Ker had built an excellent reputation as a preacher and as the master of a preparatory school in Fayetteville, but observers in 1794 were unaware that he had abandoned his Presbyterian faith while evolving into a passionate republican, at a time when conservative Federalists controlled the Board of Trustees.

On that rainy 15 January 1795, Governor Richard Dobbs Spaight headed a delegation of trustees, legislators, and interested private individuals who came to Chapel Hill to inspect the campus and to open the university formally. Ker was there, Old East and the president's house were ready for occupancy, but no students were present.

During the opening ceremonies, officials also broke ground for a chapel—what is now the east wing of Person Hall, built by Samuel Hopkins, Chapel Hill's first postmaster in 1795-1799. Until Gerrard Hall was completed in 1837, Person Hall served as a hall for commencements and as a chapel both for the university and the village. Thereafter, it continued as a center for campus activities and an auditorium for public meetings and entertainment. Mrs. Cornelia Spencer recalled its use by "all itinerant preachers, lecturers, showmen, ventriloquists, Siamese twins, and the like," and she remembered one event in Person Hall perhaps too clearly for comfort: "There I once saw a conjurer slip a glass pepper-castor into his mouth and proceed to chew it up. I have not got over it to this day."

Ker moved his wife Mary and their two sons into the unpainted president's house—and waited. It was not until 12 February 1795 that the first student arrived. Custom has it that 18-year-old Hinton James walked the 150 miles from Wilmington to Chapel Hill, arriving footsore to occupy Old East alone for a fortnight until his classmates began to trickle in. One of the earliest was John Taylor, the great-grandfather of Louis Graves, founder of the Chapel Hill *Weekly*.

Ker and mathematics tutor Charles Wilson Harris soon realized that the average student was ill-prepared to succeed with the ambitious curriculum drawn up primarily by the Rev. Samuel E. McCorkle. The trustees faced a critical choice. They could abandon their lofty goals, or they could remain faithful to the university emblem—Apollo, the Greek god of eloquence, and his symbol the rising sun, signifying the dawn of a new age of education in North Carolina. They stood by Apollo and voted to add a Preparatory Department, or grammar school, which for several years utilized space available on campus or rented in the village.

Richard Simms, the first honor student, headed the grammar school in its formative months. Then in December 1795 when Nicholas Delvaux and Samuel Allen Holmes became tutors, David Ker could enjoy the company of two kindred spirits. Delvaux was a former Catholic Priest who had renounced his religion, and Holmes ceaselessly derided the most sacred tenets of Christianity. At a cost of £159-12-1, in 1801 or 1802 John M. Goodloe built a grammar schoolhouse, a 30-foot-square, two-story frame building which sat in a woods on the proposed Grand Avenue, a few feet west of the main sanctuary of the present Presbyterian Church.

Ker visited each student's room twice daily, the tutors roomed with their pupils, and the entire faculty diligently and enthusiastically punished those they believed deserving. The more conservative students complained of Ker's religious skepticism and republicanism; almost all were displeased with his vigor as a disciplinarian. Ker survived an effort by the trustees to replace him in late 1795, but an outright student rebellion in the spring of 1796 left his superiors no choice but to request his resignation and to replace him with Charles Harris.

Not surprisingly, the students' displeasure with Ker was matched by their annoyance with the stewards who fed them in the white frame, green-shuttered Steward's Hall

Richard Dobbs Spaight, Sr. (1758-1802), as Governor, attended the university's opening ceremonies in 1793. While still very young he inherited a fortune, and from 1764 to 1778 he lived in the ancestral home in Scotland, eventually graduating from the University of Glasgow. His son, Richard Dobbs, Jr., graduated from UNC in 1815; in 1834 he, too, became Governor.

Spaight, Sr., died in a duel with Congressman John Stanly. Stanly declared that former Congressman Spaight had used the pretext of illness to avoid votes on important issues such as the Alien and Sedition Acts. Spaight defended himself in a caustic pamphlet, Stanly challenged him, Spaight accepted, and he was killed on the fourth exchange of shots. (NCC)

that would now face west in the center of Cameron Avenue in front of Bynum Hall. In January 1795, John "Buck" Taylor contracted to serve three meals per day for $30 per student per year, all the downed campus wood he needed, and the use of a ten-acre "old field" east of Steward's Hall as a pasture.

Buck was the father of John Taylor. He owned a plantation three miles west of the village, and in August 1796 he paid Jesse Neville 28 pounds for Lot 13, the Graham Memorial site. The tough-minded old Revolutionary War veteran's problems as steward began almost immediately. Students wrote letters home complaining of his cooking skills and of the poor quality of his food, mentioning specifically maggoty meat, offensive tea and coffee, and inedible bread. Taylor endured three years of constant abuse before resigning as steward to manage his plantation and to run a tavern he built on the land he had purchased from Jesse Neville.

In 1803 the trustees sold Charles Collier the lot at the southwest corner of Franklin and Raleigh streets, now occupied by Spencer Dormitory. Collier sold the land to Buck Taylor's brother Tom, who either built onto an existing log cabin or erected a log cabin that eventually became the core of a much larger frame house. Undocumented rumor has the cabin existing as far back as the Revolutionary War and being the scene of a suicide by hanging.

Tom Taylor also built a small gambrel-roofed store across Franklin Street from the Morehead Planetarium parking lot. The building survived until the Civil War. A.H. Patterson remembered hearing that before the war "a crazy negro woman" living there believed she was perpetually stalked by a large black bear. When the chimney fell from the dilapidated old store one night, she swore the bear had torn it down trying to get her. Tom Taylor left Chapel Hill in 1829 after swapping his home site to the trustees for a section of Tennessee land escheated to the university. Taylor's store was not the first in the village, however. John Scott had a store somewhere on Franklin Street as early as 4 July 1798, the date the faculty purchased $2 worth of stamp paper there according to university records.

Buck Taylor was followed as steward by Major Pleasant Henderson, also a veteran of the Revolutionary War. The brother of Judge Richard Henderson, Pleasant had been a companion of Daniel Boone in explorations of the Transylvania Colony territory. He had also gained immense popularity as reading clerk of the House of Commons (a position he held from 1789 to 1830) and as private secretary to Governor Alexander Martin, the uncle of his wife Sarah Martin Henderson. Henderson moved to Chapel Hill in 1797, built a seven-room house where the post office now stands, and opened a store in his front yard. But the Major's excellent reputation stood him in poor stead with the students, who could detect no improvement over the food served previously by Buck Taylor.

Responding to continuing complaints, a trustees' committee once declared that Henderson's consistent service of mutton and fat bacon had almost starved the students. Henderson defended himself with spirit and statistics, pointing out that the first student to the table usually stripped all the lean from a slab of bacon and insisting he had served mutton no more than "12 or 13" times in a year when chicken, beef, and fresh pork were in short supply. The trustees accepted his arguments, but the students were more obdurate. At one point, they vented their outrage by stoning his home, overturning his outhouse, and depositing his gate on the chapel pulpit in Person Hall. Henderson retired as steward in 1801, refused to become a trustee although unanimously elected, but remained in Chapel Hill as a merchant and a justice of the peace.

Major Samuel Love of Virginia replaced Henderson, purchased a 132-acre farm on Bolin Creek from Jessee Riggsbee and Alexander Strain, and resigned as steward in 1805. Buck Taylor then returned for five more years as steward, while continuing to operate his tavern where Graham Memorial now stands. Students again protested, but the trustees backed Taylor and as a further demonstration of their confidence named him the first superintendent of buildings and grounds. When Taylor died, in accordance with his wishes his family buried him on a hilltop on his plantation, so he could watch over his slaves to ensure they were working.

The poor quality of food on campus led to increased student-townsfolk interaction, not always congenial. Breakfast usually consisted of bread, butter and coffee; luncheon staples were coarse corn bread, fat bacon, and coleworts; dinner was seldom more than coffee and corn bread without butter. "You will wonder not, if, after such a supper," Dr. William Hooper submitted as a defense for the nocturnal pursuits of his youthful colleagues, "most of the students welcomed the approach of night, as beasts of prey, that they might go a prowling, and seize upon everything eatable within the compass of two miles."

Students determined to have more delectable and substantial meals took advantage of several local boarding houses. The widow Jane Puckett's was popular early on; Major Henderson consistently boarded and housed almost a dozen students; Betsy Nunn provided meals; and by the time the student population topped 100 in 1819 the young men were dining and rooming with a dozen other villagers, including Joseph Caldwell, William Barbee, and the widows Sarah Mitchell and Sarah Morgan Yeargin, Benjamin Yeargin having died in 1812. The practice altered the landscape of Chapel Hill by causing homeowners to build extra rooms, a custom still beautifully preserved in the large houses that line Franklin Street.

Mrs. Jane Puckett began serving meals to students as early as 1796, and in January 1798 she advertised she could "accommodate a number of boarders." However, the location of the Puckett residence in the 1790s is an abiding mystery, but it was probably not the Franklin Street house now occupied by Chancellor Robert House. Long after the death of her husband John in 1802, the widow Puckett purchased that property from John Craig for $40 in 1817. She sold it to Professor Denison Olmstead in June 1820 for $1300, a sound indication that she had built a house on the lot in the interim.

Students could look forward every school day to an almost unrelieved regimen of study, prayers, and an 8 p.m. curfew bell tolling mandatory confinement to their rooms until daybreak. Any entertainment they could fit into their tight schedules was almost exclusively of their own making. Most of them enjoyed hunting in the game-laden woods surrounding the village, and it was natural for young men so confined to turn to sports for recreation and release.

The most popular games were "knucks" and bandy. "Knucks" was the generic nickname for a variety of marble games in which the winner's reward was the option of striking the loser's knuckles either with his own or with a marble. In the same family with field hockey and lacrosse, bandy involved players using a stick shaped somewhat like a golfer's wood to strike a hard ball, or a round stone when no playable ball was handy; and hard-fought matches routinely produced lumps, bruises, disjointed limbs, broken bones, and assorted discomforts.

Of course, there were the clandestine sports. The trustees outlawed card playing, and the faculty tried to enforce the prohibition strictly, but imaginative young men could easily fabricate an alarm system. Students who stabled horses in the village raced over the public roads, and in the 1820s villagers built a racetrack just west of the future location of the depot in Carrboro. The faculty decreed the track out of bounds to students, thereby encouraging them to master the art of disguise or to place bets by proxy. Cockfighting was always popular, and always forbidden.

Charles Harris resigned in December 1796 after the trustees had followed his advice to engage Joseph Caldwell, who had graduated a year ahead of Harris at Princeton. In a letter to Caldwell commending the university, Harris complained of the "very uncultured" society of Chapel Hill while observing that agreeable company could be found a short ride away in Hillsborough.

Charles Harris went to Halifax to practice law with William Davie and to manage the firm when Davie became governor in December 1798. He sailed to the West Indies in 1803 when his health failed, but after it became evident that he was terminally ill, he returned to Halifax, rejoined the Presbyterian faith, and died on 15 January 1804 from consumption, nine years to the day after the university opened.

Caldwell was born in 1773 in Lamington, New Jersey, two days after his physician father died. He graduated from Princeton in 1791, worked four years as a teacher, and returned to Princeton as a mathematics tutor in April 1795. Encouraged by Harris, he accepted an offer of $600 annually to teach mathematics at UNC and began the long jouney south, stopping to preach in Philadelphia at the invitation of Dr. Ashbel Green and performing well enough to be offered a vacant pastorate in the City of Love. He soon questioned his wisdom in turning down a ministry among God-fearing Philadelphians to administer a state university among folk more attuned to the secular.

Caldwell was a bachelor when he came to Chapel Hill, and he may have built a log cabin shortly after his arrival. In any event, future Congressman Carl Durham bought what he assumed to be Caldwell's old cabin in 1928 and moved it to his backyard at 805 East Franklin Street. Caldwell moved into a modestly more substantial house just east of the present president's house and equipped it with an astronomical observatory on the roof which he and a few upperclassmen used almost every clear night.

Caldwell was of small stature, but wirily strong and fleet of foot, and the stories of his chasing down and subduing students by sheer strength are legion. In recognition of those determined efforts, students nicknamed him "Diabolus" (Latin for "devil") and shortened it to "Bolus" and later "Old Bolus"—a cognomen retained in Mount Bolus, the hill rising north from Bolin Creek to the east of Airport Road.

But Caldwell was not happy as presiding professor and

Joseph Caldwell (1773-1835) was the first person officially titled President of the University of North Carolina. He was a scholar devoted to astronomy as an avocation and built an observatory near the village cemetery. He recorded his observations in detail in hard-cover journals, one of which Cornelia Phillips Spencer used during the Civil War as a scrapbook to paste in articles on the war, thus obliterating Caldwell's careful notations. (NCC)

resigned in the fall of 1797, citing his inability to get along with grammar-school instructors Nicholas Delvaux, "a feeble-minded monk," and Samuel Holmes, "an apostate and skepticized preacher, whose little mind is fruitful in every kind of villainy which envy can suggest." The trustees then named James Smiley Gillaspie "principal of the university," retaining Caldwell as professor of mathematics.

The highlight of Gillaspie's relatively uneventful first year occurred on 4 July 1798 when the first seven graduates received their diplomas and tutor William Augustus Richards directed members of the literary societies in a dramatic presentation. Not everyone in the audience approved the initial Thespian endeavor at a university that is today proud of its reputation for innovative excellence in dramatics. William Davie pointedly warned, "If the faculty insist on this kind of exhibition the Board must interfere. Our object is to make the students men, not players." Richards was an Englishman who had jumped ship in Norfolk to join a band of strolling players, which he left in Warrenton to join the grammar school faculty. After the commencement, he returned to Warrenton to help Marcus George run an academy, and there the first "playmaker" died in December 1798.

In the spring of 1799, triggered by some now forgotten incident, the students rebelled in a week-long riot during which they beat Gillaspie, harassed Caldwell, stoned language professor William Edwards Webb, and threatened tutors Andrew Flinn and Archibald Debow Murphey. Caldwell reluctantly resumed his old post, and Gillaspie left for the less demanding occupation of ministering to Presbyterians in Kentucky, where he settled with his wife, the former Fanny Henderson. The niece of Pleasant and Richard Henderson, Fanny was the daughter of their older brother Samuel and his wife Elizabeth Calloway Henderson. Reportedly the first Caucasian child born in Kentucky, Elizabeth as a child had been rescued from the Indians by Daniel Boone.

Two of UNC's most illustrious alumni attended during the period of troubles under Gillaspie. Thomas Hart Benton, the U.S. Senator from Missouri from 1821 to 1851, was a student in 1798 and the early weeks of 1799. In the spring of 1798, student Archibald Lytle announced that he would whip the "rascal" who had beaten his younger cousin, a student in the grammar school. Benton answered the challenge, set a date to fight, and arrived armed with a horse whip. When Lytle pulled a pistol, Benton got his own, and Lytle backed down. Nonetheless, the faculty suspended Benton.

He returned in January 1799, joined the Philanthropic Society on 5 February, and roomed with William Cherry of Bertie County, later a lawyer, a university trustee, and a member of the House of Commons; Fleming Saunders of Rocky Mount, Virginia, a future Virginia legislator and judge; and Marmaduke Baker of Gates County, whose accomplishments, if any, are obscure.

A few weeks into the term, all three were missing cash, including a marked bill belonging to Baker and a newly minted federal dollar belonging to Cherry. Hugh Nunn, a clerk in John Scott's store, saw the coin in Benton's possession, he informed the roommates, they discovered the missing money in Benton's possession, and he confessed when confronted with incontrovertible evidence. The faculty expelled Benton from the university, and the Philanthropic Society expelled him by a unanimous vote on 19 March.

Among Benton's many duels in later life, two were fought with U.S. District Attorney Charles Lucas of St. Louis, who is believed to have referred unkindly to Benton's university experiences. Benton wounded Lucas on 12 August 1817 and killed him six weeks later. The Philanthropic Society readmitted Benton on 9 May 1827; his biographers and other partial observers have either ignored his troubles at Chapel Hill or dismissed them as having resulted from misunderstandings. The facts, however, are well documented.

Another famous eighteenth-century alumnus gained

Thomas Hart Benton (1782-1858) and Francis Blair (1821-1875) both became U.S. Senators from Missouri, and when Congress in 1864 established a Statuary Hall to hold two statues from each state, Missouri chose these two men as its representatives. Both men were students at UNC. (NCC)

Johnston Blakeley (1781-1814) was lost at sea, and after his death the North Carolina General Assembly honored his widow by appropriating $500 for a 352-ounce sterling silver service for her. In 1968, Mr. and Mrs. Charles Lee Smith, Jr., of Raleigh, donated the silver service, which they had discovered in England, to the North Carolina Museum of Art in Raleigh. At the same time the James G. Hanes Foundation along with Edgar D. Baker and Dr. G. Fred Hale, both of Raleigh, gave the museum a Thomas Sully portrait of Blakeley's daughter Maria. (NCC)

fame in savage combat at sea. Johnston Blakeley of Wilmington had been born in Seaforth, Ireland in 1781. After the death of his father, he enrolled at UNC, living on income from buildings rented in Wilmington and the largess of N.C. Solicitor-General Edward Jones of Chatham County. He was a popular, fun-loving student, a member of the Philanthropic Society, and one of the first of hundreds of students who carved their initials on a beech tree at the Meeting of the Waters. His initials were still legible in the late 1930s, but the Meeting of the Waters now occurs underground southeast of Kenan Stadium, and the historic tree is gone.

During the 1799 rebellion, Caldwell entered Blakeley's room demanding the names of rebel leaders. When Blakeley denied knowing who they were, Caldwell threatened to throw him out the window. Blakeley, exhibiting a coolness that would later contribute to his military glory, calmly answered, 'I beg, sir, you will not attempt it, or it will necessitate my putting you out." Caldwell pursued the questioning no further.

When his Wilmington property burned, Blakeley left

UNC, joined the U.S. Navy, and attended the Naval Academy. As captain of the 14-gun brig *Enterprise*, early in the War of 1812 he captured the British Privateer *Fly*. While waiting for the *Wasp* to be launched, Blakeley married Anne Hoope of Boston, and neither knew she was pregnant when he sailed on 1 May 1814. In the next five months Blakeley captured or sank 15 British warships, including the 18-gun man-of-war *Reindeer*. Then on 9 October, the Swedish ship *Adonis* spotted the *Wasp* sailing unmolested in smooth waters off Cape Verde. Neither the *Wasp* nor Blakeley was ever seen or heard from again.

Even before Blakeley's death was suspected, Congress struck a gold medal recognizing his defeat of the *Reindeer*, and in December the N.C. Senate gave a bejeweled sword to his widow. When his death became a certainty, the United States issued a bronze medal carrying his likeness, and the General Assembly adopted his posthumous daughter Maria Udney Blakeley, appropriated money for her education, and voted $500 for a 352-ounce silver service for Mrs. Blakeley. Maria used the scholarship, married Baron Joseph Von Brettan in 1841, and in 1842 died along with her infant in childbirth, ending the direct line of descendants from her hero father.

The U.S. Navy has since honored Blakeley by giving his name to three ships. Both the *Wasp* and the *Enterprise* lent their names to aircraft carriers that won distinction in the World War II battle for the Pacific. Coincidentally, during the days of its most intense and successful action, the fast carrier *Enterprise* was commanded by another UNC alumnus—Captain, later Admiral, O.B. Hardison, Sr.

To combat overcrowding, the trustees voted in 1798 to build what would be called the Main Building until about 1830, when it became known as South Building. Contractor Samuel Hopkins completed a story and a half by 1800, but then money ran out and the open structure sat exposed to the elements for over a decade. Students, driven both by desperation and resourcefulness, built leantos, tents, and even relatively secure cabins within the abandoned and roofless Main Building. Finally, Joseph Caldwell toured the state in 1809 and again in 1811, raised some $8000, and John Close finished the job in 1814.

Excessive measures adopted by the trustees in 1805-1806 to maintain discipline and mass expulsions in 1808 following violent protests over food quality reduced the number of graduates to 10 in 1809, to three in 1810, and to only one in 1811. William Barbee, son of Old Kit, relieved the faculty of a portion of their worries in 1810 when he took over Steward's Hall. During his decade of tenure, students seem to have had fewer complaints. A Mrs. Burton, recently widowed, rented Steward's Hall in 1819 with the understanding that she would provide board at no more than $9 per month per student the first year and $10 the second. A Mr. Moore took over from Mrs. Burton in 1827 and repaired the building. He was followed by John B.

Robert Hett Chapman (1771-1833) married Hannah Arnette about 1797. After his UNC Presidency he went to Winchester, Virginia, for 12 years, then spent two years in Asheville, and in 1829, he moved to Covington, Tennessee, on the Mississippi River. His wife died in 1845, leaving 12 children, 7 of whom survived their father, and one of whom, William Smith Chapman (1804-1836) graduated from UNC with highest honors in 1823. (NCC)

William Biddle Shepard (1799-1852), after he was expelled from UNC, attended the University of Pennsylvania and then began a career as a lawyer and as a Congressman, earning a reputation as a bitter opponent of Andrew Jackson and of slavery. Plagued with poor health, he retired from public life after losing to George E. Badger in a try for the U.S. Senate in 1844. In Chapel Hill, Shepard was remembered as the orator who had a "voice like a bugle." (NCC)

Tenney, original settler William McCauley's widow Raichel, merchant John Scott's widow Caroline, and Miss Sally Mallett before Steward's Hall was dismantled in 1847.

Joseph Caldwell had remained a bachelor until he married Susan Rowan in Fayetteville on 9 July 1803. Susan died in January 1807, and on 17 August 1809 Caldwell married Helen Hogg Hooper. Helen was the daughter of the James Hogg who had solicited land for the university, the widow of William Hooper II of Hillsborough, and the mother of three sons—William, James and Thomas. When he married Helen, Caldwell moved into her house, a few hundred feet east of his own.

The trustees had designated Caldwell the first president of the university in 1804, but by 1812 he had grown thoroughly tired of his administrative responsibilities, and he resigned when the trustees reluctantly followed his recommendation and selected Robert Hett Chapman, D.D., as his successor. Born in Orange, New Jersey in 1771, Chapman graduated from Princeton in 1789. He later toured the South as a Presbyterian missionary, stopping off in Chapel Hill to visit his "old friend" Joseph Caldwell, and in 1812 he was minister of a Presbyterian church in

Cambridge, Massachusetts.

Chapman was as devout a Federalist as he was a Presbyterian, but by the time he became president of the university, the Federalist party was out of favor because of its opposition to the War of 1812, and the majority of the students in Chapel Hill were strongly Republican and highly supportive of the war against Britain. They registered their objection to Chapman's pro-peace stand and his introduction of Bible studies into the curriculum by attacking him and his property ferociously.

Chapman's stay in the original president's house was unpleasant in other respects. His eldest daughter Margaret Blanche Chapman died there from typhus fever on 25 November 1814, as did Charles A. Brewster, a visitor from New York, in April 1815.

Chapman's troubled tenure reached its climax on 18 September 1816 when William Biddle Shepard of New Bern continued to read a very partisan Republican speech after Chapman had ordered him to stop. Students demonstrated vigorously in support of their comrade, the trustees expelled Shepard and his leading advocate George C. Dromgoole, they suspended two other students, and Chapman resigned. With a well documented sense of relief, the trustees installed Caldwell once more as president on 14 December 1816.

Of course, student unrest did not cease with Chapman's departure. At least one bitter conflict between a faculty member and a student grew out of their competition for the affections of a local belle.

The trouble began one Sunday in 1819 when tutor Simon Jordan and student William Anthony collectively escorted Betsy Puckett to Mount Carmel Church. Believing the tutor had insulted him repeatedly on the trip, Anthony armed himself with three pistols, a knife, and a club and assaulted the smaller Jordan, but students broke up the row before injury occurred. Following a faculty hearing, in which Anthony called Caldwell a liar, the enraged youth again attacked the tutor with a club. Jordan fought him off with a walking stick, then beat him in a rousing fist fight cheered on by partisans—the Di's for the tutor, the Phi's for the student. Anthony, still swearing revenge, fled the country to avoid arrest.

In 1829, the faculty expelled Spencer Reeves for hosting a drinking and card-playing party. Reeves later killed his sister in a dispute over family property and died on the gallows—the only UNC graduate to achieve that distinction.

While the university proper was establishing itself firmly, the Preparatory Department was fading into nonexistence. After graduating in 1809, Abner Wentworth Clopton remained for a decade as a tutor in the grammar school, resigning in 1819 to practice medicine and to continue in the ministry after having been ordained at the Mount Carmel Baptist Church in 1818. By then several excellent preparatory schools were operating within the state, and

the trustees chose to end the program in Chapel Hill.

Former grammar-school student William Hooper, by then a professor, agreed to pay Clopton $2500 for his log cabin on what became the Battle lot, but when his friends informed him he had overbid for the property he in turn notified Clopton the deal was off. Clopton, not one to be intimidated by a bookish professor, retorted that in his opinion an agreement had been struck and the deal was on. He won the point, along with the payment.

In 1821 the trustees rented the grammar school for use as a residence to Peyton Clements, who as a professional hunter provided stewards and boarding-house operators with much of the game they served the students, and who as the father of three lovely daughters with willing dispositions supplied those same students with fare equally as pleasing. For a price, the daughters lived with young men of their choice in arrangements not blessed by clergy. "The youngest girl was pretty and modest and several good ladies endeavored to keep her straight," Kemp Battle sadly relayed, "but she finally fell." Desperate for money to complete Gerrard Hall, in June 1832 the trustees sold the grammar school and an acre of land. But no record of the sale exists, and the amount raised is unknown.

After he received an A.B. degree in 1809, Joseph Caldwell's step-son William Hooper stayed on as a tutor, earning an M.A. in 1812. In 1814 he married Francis Pollock Jones, daughter of Edward Jones and Mary Curtis Mallett Jones of Rock Rest Plantation in Chatham County. Mary Jones was the daughter of Dr. Peter Mallett, a prominent physician in Fayetteville. Edward Jones, Solicitor-General of North Carolina from 1791 to 1827, had assisted the orphan Johnston Blakeley Jones when he was a student, and he had built a school named "Kelvin" in

Chapel-Hill Academy.

THE exercises of this institution will commence on the twentieth of July next, under the superintendence of the undersigned. The course of studies in this Academy will be (as usual) so arranged as to render it in every respect preparatory to the University. Elocution, correct pronunciation according to the rules of Prosody; Scanning and the derivation and composition of words will receive particular attention. Due regard will also be paid to those pursuing the lower branches of Education, and every exertion used to stimulate them to emulation. The moral conduct and good deportment of the pupils will receive special attention.

The local situation of this Academy must always afford advantages to those preparing for the University. The terms of Tuition will be as usual. The sessions and vacations will be regulated by those of the University.

JAMES A. CRAIG.

Chapel-Hill, May 1st 1820.   21-7ts.

J. A. Craig will keep on hand a supply of School Books.

James Alexander Craig (1790-1840) ran this ad in the Raleigh Star, promising that the course of study "will be (as usual) so arranged as to render it in every respect preparatory to the University." Craig later studied medicine and practiced in his home county, Lincoln. (NCC)

Chatham County. Francis and her sisters constituted the faculty at "Kelvin." Hooper built what is now known as the "Kay Kyser House" for his bride, who brought cedar seedlings from Rock Rest to plant along Franklin Street.

After additional studies at the Princeton Theological Seminary, William Hooper taught ancient languages at UNC from 1817 to 1822 when he resigned to become rector of St. John's Episcopal Church in Fayetteville. He returned for the years 1825-1837, during which time he left the Episcopal Church for the Baptist after a dispute with Bishop John Stark Ravenscroft over a point of theology. After he left Chapel Hill the second time, he was an active preacher and educator for another half century, including terms as president of Wake Forest College and Chowan Female Collegiate Institute. Among the seven children of William and Fanny Hooper, sons William and Edward became physicians, daughter Mary married UNC professor John DeBerniere Hooper, and son DuPonceau died from wounds received at Fredericksburg in the Civil War.

Three other young professors left telling marks on Chapel Hill during the Caldwell era.

In the fall of 1817, the trustees engaged Denison (Dennison) Olmstead and Elisha Mitchell, both Connecticut natives and Yale graduates in 1813. Before arriving in Chapel Hill in January 1818 to teach mathematics, Mitchell hurriedly obtained a license from the Theological Seminary of Andover, Massachusetts, allowing him to preach in the Congregational Church. After a year of additional study, Olmstead moved into the president's house and began teaching chemistry and mineralogy in the fall of 1819. Although he was from Connecticut, he hired several black servants for his growing family and purchased one slave girl for $350.

Mitchell returned to Connecticut in the late fall of 1819 to marry Maria S. North. The newlyweds began the arduous 815-mile trip south from New York on 20 December, traveling overland to Baltimore, sailing on the *United States* to Norfolk, and continuing by coach to Raleigh, where they arrived too late to catch the scheduled stage to Chapel Hill. Mrs. Mitchell recorded their dramatic last leg from Raleigh to Chapel Hill in a 1 January 1820 letter to her mother: 'We hired an extra stage, and I heard Mr. Mitchell tell the driver to drive us well, for he was armed. He then whispered to me that the driver was strongly suspected of being a murderer, and with this comfortable assurance we plunged into the woods leaving all civilization apparently far behind us, and taking the whole day for the twenty-eight miles, reaching Chapel Hill December 29.'

The Mitchells moved into the president's house, paying Olmstead $288 per year for room and board. In 1820 Olmstead purchased the Widow Puckett house for $1300, spent another $900 for additions and restoration, and moved in, leaving the Mitchells to occupy the president's

house for almost four decades. When he left to join the Yale faculty in December 1825, Olmstead sold the Widow Puckett House to the university for what he had invested in it.

The indefatigable Mitchell propelled himself into a variety of jobs for the university and the state which would establish him as the most famous faculty member of the nineteenth century. Along with his duties as professor of mathematics, chemistry, mineralogy, and geology, he was also university bursar, superintendent of grounds, a practicing preacher, and, when occasion required, acting president of the university. He progressively widened his area of study and influence in scientific expeditions that carried him from the Outer Banks to the peaks of the Smoky Mountains.

Mitchell's increased load of science courses left the mathematics professorship vacant, and Joseph Caldwell knew from previous correspondence with Dr. Robert Adrain of Rutgers College that James Phillips was the man he wanted. As a young man in Plymouth, England, James Phillips had watched the Emperor Napoleon walking on the deck of *HMS Bellerophone*, the ship that carried him to St. Helena. In 1818 at age 26, he emigrated with his brother Samuel to New York City, where they established a classical school in Harlem. James married Judith Vermeule, descended from a French-Dutch family long prominent in New York, and their three children were born in Harlem, two sons Samuel and Charles, and on 20 March 1825 a daughter Cornelia.

On their arrival in Chapel Hill, the Phillips moved into the "Widow Puckett House," and their children were soon fast friends with merchant Tom Taylor's daughters Nancy and Jane, Betty Hooper, Julia Anderson, Mary, Ellen and Margaret Mitchell. In later life, Cornelia Phillips Spencer complained that she got only the "crumbs" from the educational program the Phillips sons studied at home and under the tutorage of William Hooper. Nonetheless, alongside her brothers and many of her playmates, Cornelia by age 11 was studying mathematics, moral principles, Greek, Latin, and Roman history.

Appreciating their success in teaching their own and neighborhood children, and appreciating as well an opportunity to supplement a professor's income, James and Julia established the Phillips Female Academy in their home in January 1837 and advertised statewide that a classical curriculum was available at $225 per year. The next year classes in French, drawing, and music taught by "Mons. Maret" were available for extra fees. Young Cornelia would nibble on those crumbs as well.

Judith Phillips joined Mrs. Hooper and Mrs. Mitchell in conducting a Sunday school on the campus, the first in Chapel Hill, and her husband progressively became a more devout Presbyterian. In 1832 he accompanied William Hooper to Virginia to hear well known evangelist

Asahel Nettleton (1783-1844) was the most prominent of many evangelists who visited Chapel Hill and vicinity in the ante-bellum years. A Congregationalist minister, Nettleton's unique religious tenets put him in disfavor with even the Theological Institute of Connecticut which he helped to found in 1833, but his evangelical style was quiet and his sermons were reasoned arguments rather than "Bible-thumping." (NCC)

James Phillips (1792-1867) had a singular peculiarity: he thought that asking questions in class signified laziness. Students were occasionally perplexed by the fact that if they asked a question they chanced receiving a lower grade. (NCC)

Asahel Nettleton. After studying theology at Yale, Nettleton (1783-1844) had long been prominent in New England by 1829 when ill health forced him to start spending his winters in Chapel Hill, Hillsborough, and elsewhere in the South. Bennett Tyler, who attended Yale with Nettleton and later served as president of Dartmouth, wrote in 1844 that Nettleton had become known as the "Grand Old Man" of evangelism but that his "intransigence in the theological controversies of the 1830s has earned for him...the reputation of a crabby old man who stubbornly defended an obsolete system of Calvinism."

During a great revival led by Nettleton in Chapel Hill in the fall of 1832, Phillips professed to having been saved and began to preach with all the fervor of his mentor anywhere he could find an audience. When preacher and educator Dr. William McPheeters of Raleigh insisted that he either become licensed or cease preaching, Phillips dutifully got a license from the Orange Presbytery, became ordained, and began traveling the state as an evangelist. According to Elisha Mitchell's granddaughter Hope Chamberlain, "He was so earnest and so sincere in seizing

a word in season, that he served a parish as wide as his acquaintance." Chamberlain also recorded another effect of his propensity to preach to everyone on every occasion—Chapel Hillians made a practice of giving him an unobstructed path whenever he walked the byways of the campus and village.

Phillips' religious convictions did not, however, stop the former New Yorker from purchasing two slaves, the Uncle Ben and Aunt Dilsey so dear to his daughter Cornelia.

Every Washington's birthday, Fourth of July, and commencement week, Chapel Hillians had opportunities to enjoy public spectacles and village-wide festivities. Other than that, organized entertainment was scarce. Each Washington's Birthday and Fourth of July started with pomp and patriotism, and invariably ended with inebriation and tested tempers. The sedate formalities of the official commencement programs dissolved into evenings of relaxed fun and boisterous joviality as visiting alumni and guests remade old acquaintances and returned to old haunts in the village and on campus, usually accompanied by John Barleycorn.

The scant professional entertainment that had been available in the village shrunk drastically in 1825 when a company of traveling players left town with $400 taken in during a one-week run in the second story of a village store. Incensed at the "waste," the faculty asked for and got permission to restrict all theatrical performances not meeting their approval. Had there been no restriction, the fare available would hardly have stimulated studious minds or satisfied desires for cultural enrichment. On rare occasions, traveling players on the Raleigh/Wilmington/Fayetteville/New Bern circuit might stop off for a performance in Chapel Hill, but fundamentalist opposition to the theatre in North Carolina was strong and effective, and popular taste ran to farce and sentimental drama rather than to the classics.

The 22 November 1820 Hillsborough *Recorder* notified readers that a Mr. Bartle would perform in Chapel Hill the following Friday and Saturday and promised that handbills would give details, but Mr. Bartle's specialty is a mystery. The paper advertised that Siamese twins "will be happy to see company" on 15 and 16 October 1835, probably the Siamese twins Mrs. Spencer saw in Person Hall and certainly Chang and Eng Bunker, who were touring the South at the time.

On 9 November 1836, Aaron Turner brought his Columbian Circus to town for a single 1 p.m. performance in a gigantic tent 90 feet in diameter. P.T. Barnum and his protege Signor Vivalla, "the Italian Professor of Equilibrium and Plate Dancing," had traveled with Turner for several months but had left him a week prior, thus denying Chapel Hillians a glimpse of the master showman of the future. However, they did get to see Joe Pentland, whom Barnum judged to be the "wittiest, best, most

Chang and Eng Bunker (1811-1874), the original Siamese Twins (in fact, they were of Chinese descent), charged 50 cents per person when they appeared in Chapel Hill on 15 and 16 October 1835. The brothers became wealthy and in 1843 they married sisters Adelaide and Sarah Yates of Wilkesboro; they retired from show business in order to till lands they bought near Mt. Airy. Chang and Eng built separate houses and maintained separate households, moving from home to home on a three-day cycle until financial troubles caused by the Civil War forced them on the road again, this time with P.T. Barnum. Chang, a rather heavy drinker, was the first to die, and Eng, a near teetotaler, died two hours later.

In this Matthew Brady photograph are (left to right) Sarah, Eng, Chang, and Adelaide. In front are two of their 22 children, one of whom, Chang's son Albert Lemuel (right), went to UNC 1878-80. (NCC)

original of clowns."

On the whole, ante-bellum Chapel Hillians enjoyed an almost miraculous freedom from infectious diseases of the body. In matters of the mind, many were not so fortunate.

When Chapel Hill was founded, there was no public school system in the state and little demand to create one. Parents concerned with the education of their children either provided instruction at home, used the services of a neighborhood tutor, or sent their children to the few private academies then operating. Before 1800 Benjamin Yeargin taught children living on the farms scattered around Chapel Hill, and in the years immediately following 1800 an Englishman, "Old Father" Hughes, offered classes to village youngsters. About 1820, Baptist preacher William H. Merritt built a one-room schoolhouse approximately a mile south of town near his mill on Morgan Creek. One of his first "dropouts" was his son William H., Jr., who ceased attending after becoming enamoured of a neighborhood lass.

Abner Clopton accepted area students while he was directing the grammar school, and when he left in 1819 James A. Craig, a Lincoln County native and a graduate of the class of 1816, advertised widely for private students. His success is unknown, but it must have been slight since no records of his efforts remain. William Hooper taught his own children along with several from the growing number of faculty and merchant families in the 1820s, and he later assisted the Phillipses with their female academy, the most ambitious private school in Chapel Hill before the Civil War.

While matters of education may have lagged except for those in the immediate vicinity of the university, matters of the spirit never flagged. Journeying from his base on Gen. Thomas Person's plantation at Goshen, the Rev. George Micklejohn held occasional Episcopal services in Chapel Hill after the Revolution. Micklejohn moved to Mecklenburg County about 1801 and continued to preach until his death in 1818, at age 101. Years later, an Orange County farmer remembered being baptized along with Paul Cameron by Micklejohn. The son of Duncan Cameron, Paul became the richest man in North Carolina

William Gaston (1778-1844) was a former Congressman and one of the most respected attorneys in North Carolina when he delivered the UNC commencement address on 20 June 1832 and made a now famous, then jarring, speech against slavery: "Disguise the truth as we may, and throw the blame where we will, it is Slavery which . . . keeps us back in the career of improvement."
He went on, telling the assembled group, "Perils surround you," because "on you will devolve the duty too long neglected . . . the ultimate extirpation of the worst evil that afflicts us." (NCC)

Aaron Turner's circus used this ad in the Hillsborough Recorder to promote its Chapel Hill visit in 1836. Despite the lavish description of the events only six people made up the circus, and two of those were Turner's young sons. There was no menagerie and only two or three horses. Turner operated the circus until 1850. (NCC)

Unparalleled Attraction!!
THE OLD
COLUMBIAN CIRCUS.
Under the management of A. Turner & Co.

WILL be opened in Hillsborough, on Thursday and Friday, the 10th and 11th inst. Performances to commence at 1 o'clock in the day and at half past 6 in the evening, when will be offered a variety of attractions unsurpassed in America. For particulars see bills.

In addition to the many other performances, the proprietors have, at an enormous expense engaged the services of SIGNOR VIVALLA, the Italian Professor of Equilibrium and Plate Dancing, whose apparently impossible feats have been witnessed by crowded and admiring audiences in the principal Theatres in the United States. Mr. PENTLAND from Boston, will exhibit his celebrated CHINESE GAMES, with Cups, Balls, Rings, Daggers, &c &c.— The Equestrian Company is led by N. B. & T. V. TURNER, whose wonderful feats of Horsemanship on one and two horses, are unequalled in America.

☞ Admittance 50 cents, Children under 10 years of age and servants half price.

MUSICAL PAVILLION.

At the termination of the performances in the Circus, the entertainments will commence in this appartment: They consist of a variety of Comic Songs by the celebrated Mr. PENTLAND, and a variety of Negro Songs, and Extravaganzas, by Mr. WHITE of the New York and Boston Theatres, whose representations of the Negro Character are allowed by all to surpass those of the far famed Rice.

☞ Admittance to the Pavilion 25 cents—Children and servants 12½ cents.

☞ The above performances will be exhibited at CHAPEL HILL on the 9th inst. to commence at 1 o'clock.

November 3. 43—

when he inherited his father's vast holdings, including the family plantation Fairntosh northeast of Durham. The farmer succinctly evaluated the efficacy of the baptism, "It tuck on Paul, but never done me no good."

The Methodist Society organized the New Hope Circuit in 1778 and appointed James O'Kelley minister over the 500-plus members in 1780. When O'Kelley converted to Methodism in 1775, he burned his fiddle, destroyed his still, and diligently followed the dictates of his faith and conscience thereafter. The fervent Irishman was a leader in calling for a general conference of Methodists in Baltimore in 1792 opposed to the increasing power of bishops. Joined by 36 other ministers and approximately 10,000 laymen, O'Kelley broke from the established church to form the Republican Methodist Church, "a republican, no slavery, glorious church," later called the Christian Church.

O'Kelley bought a farm in Chatham County, formed a congregation in 1794, and built a church some ten miles southeast of Chapel Hill on what is now highway 751. Then in 1797, when Matthew McCauley, Jesse Neville, and John Wilson organized the Damascus Congregational Church four miles southwest of Chapel Hill, O'Kelley was their first pastor, and he continued to preach in the Chapel Hill area until his death in 1826.

The great Methodist bishop Francis Asbury participated in at least one service in Chapel Hill in the year 1800. His associate Nicholas Snethen preached; Asbury baptized several children. His degree of intimacy with Joseph Caldwell is perhaps best revealed in a diary entry noting he had been "treated with great respect at the University, by the president, Colwell, and the students, citizens, and many of the country people."

The Baptists built Mount Carmel Baptist Church in 1803 two miles southwest of the village at the fourteenth mile marker south of Hillsborough, near the university lake, but fire has destroyed almost all early records. Grammar-school director Abner Clopton was ordained there in 1818; William Hooper was baptized there in 1832 when he converted from the Episcopalian to the Baptist faith; William Barbee was a mainstay of the church for decades. The Mount Carmel congregation formed an "arm" of their church in town in 1854 and moved to their present location on Mount Carmel Road in 1873.

Of the families who donated land to the university or who were living in the area when the university was founded, the Barbees were to have the most significant and the most lasting influence. Old Kit and Mary Barbee had five children. Several of the children and their descendants joined the great migration to the west; others remained in Orange County. Daughters Elizabeth and Nancy married Orange County men and moved to Tennessee. A third daughter, Susanna, married Baptist preacher William H. Merritt.

In February 1794, Old Kit's son Francis married Jesse Neville's daughter Elizabeth, a woman who had eight children on her way to attaining a weight of 500 pounds. "For love and 5 shillings," Francis "purchased" 500 acres of the family plantation from his father on 22 September 1804 and spent his life there as a successful farmer, owning 14 slaves by 1830. Four of Francis' children went west, including Allen Jones Barbee who graduated from the university in 1825, studied medicine, and practiced in Tennessee. The other four stayed in Orange County. William married Mary Norwood in 1818 and settled into farming 213 acres on Caswell Creek; Neville married Sally Hopson in 1821 and left her a widow with four children and a mountain of debts in 1828; Betsy married John M. Craig in 1831; and Susannah married Sidney S. Lloyd in 1830.

Old Kit's second son William was more successful and left the greater imprint on Chapel Hill. After marrying Ghaskia Jones of Wake County in 1800, William purchased a lot on the west side of Columbia Street half-way between Franklin and Cameron, erected a two-story frame house, and in partnership with William Watson became one of Chapel Hill's leading merchants and probably the richest man in the village as the owner of several plots of land and 69 slaves by 1830.

William Watson had come to Chapel Hill to work on the South Building. He married an Orange County woman and fathered Jones and John H. Watson, who were to become prominent figures in the village. Existing records indicate that Barbee and Watson's store opened about 1813 and numbered among its early customers nearly every resident in the area. However, its location is unknown.

In addition to managing the store and dealing in real estate, William was the university steward from 1810 to 1819, at one time the custodian of the university property, a successful farmer, the village postmaster from 1816 to 1820, and a member of the House of Commons in 1819. Although the students generally appreciated his performance as steward, during one of their many riots they stoned his home, breaking several windows and shutters. But William did not take the offense as lightly as those before him. He obtained warrants that ultimately led to the dismissal of one offender and the suspension of three others.

On 28 May 1804, Old Kit gave William 504 acres "on the west of Boland's Creek and on both sides of the road leading from Raleigh to the University;" on 6 October 1830 he sold William the remainder of the family homestead, "The Mountain," for $2500; and on 11 March 1831, he sold William the .7-acre blacksmith property at Franklin and Columbia for $350. When Old Kit died in 1832 at or about age 90, he still owned 26 slaves.

In December 1831, William's daughter Emily married Ilai Nunn, the son of William and Betsy Nunn, the village violinist and dancing master, and a fixture at all well-attended festivities. A second daughter Adelia, or "Delia," married Dr. Hudson M. Cave of Virginia on 25 September 1823. Delia inherited Barbee's Mill on Morgan Creek at the foot of Upper Laurel Hill. Built by Old Kit about 1800 on land he had purchased from surveyor John Daniel, it was known as Cave's Mill under Hudson Cave's management and later as King's Mill, Bennett's Mill, and Oldham's Mill after Henderson Oldham, a Negro, purchased it late in the 19th century.

In 1827, Dr. Cave purchased from his father-in-law a long strip of land fronting Franklin Street about where the Carolina Theatre sits today and running south almost to Swain Hall, a tract that had been the eastern halves of Lots 4 and 6. William Barbee had bought the plot in 1814 from Elias Haws, who had purchased it from David Nunn, who had received it from his father William Nunn. Dr. Cave built a house deep in the property facing Franklin Street.

A small, secluded meadow one-half mile upstream from Cave's Mill is a firm part of Chapel Hill's romantic heritage. It was there that James Hervey Otey, a graduate of 1820 and a tutor in 1820-1821, retreated from the world to study his books—and to woo Miss Bessie Pannill. Otey succeeded in both endeavors, and when he left Otey's Retreat behind he took Bessie away as his bride and entered a religious career that culminated with his lengthy tenure as the Episcopal Bishop of Tennessee, but he maintained his ties with Chapel Hill and the university. He delivered the baccalaureate sermon at the commence-

Public Sale.

THE subscriber, in compliance with the last Will and Testament of Christopher Barbee, Senr. deceased, will offer for sale, on Wednesday the 22d inst. at the late residence of said deceased,

A number of Horses, Cattle, crop of Corn, Fodder, Farming Utensils, Household & Kitchen Furniture, &c.

The sale will continue from day to day until all is sold. A credit of twelve months will be given, the purchaser giving bond with approved security.
WM. BARBEE, Senr. Ex'r.
Orange county, Jan. 2, 1834   19 ut

When Christopher "Old Kit" Barbee died his will made his son William his executor. This notice appeared in the Harbinger in 1834. Old Kit's later years were scarred by serious mental impairment—he was 90 or more when he died—and he spent some of those years living in a house near his son William in the vicinity of the Columbia and Cameron intersection, according to an old deed. (NCC)

This 1890's photograph depicts the house that stood near the present Carolina Inn. It was built between 1818-19 by William and Martha Pannill, who bought the lot from William E. Webb in 1817 for $450; they sold it for $2000 in 1825. While they lived in the house, the Pannills offered room and board to students as did nearly all of the house's subsequent occupants, including famed geologist Elisha Mitchell's son-in-law Richard Ashe who led Chapel Hill's first Civil War troop into battle. (NCC)

candidates had to own at least one acre of village property and to have been a resident at least six months, 12 months between 1825 and 1851. The board appointed a constable, a clerk, a treasurer, and a magistrate of police (viz., mayor) who acted as chief executive, oversaw the constable, and heard minor court cases.

The laws governing Chapel Hill strongly reflected the presence of a growing number of university students, all male and all at a mischievous age. The sale of spiritous drink and the operation of games of chance, even the gentlemanly sport of billiards, were forbidden within a five-mile radius of the university. Firing a gun within the village except during public celebrations, working at an occupation on Sunday except in emergencies, and selling goods on Sunday were all offenses punishable by fines. Merchants had to have the permission of the faculty before they could legally sell to students.

Slaves were liable to either 10 lashes or a fine of $1 if they were apprehended abroad without their owner's permission after 8 p.m., 4 p.m. on election days. Slaves were also forbidden to hire out their services or to live alone, but that restriction was seldom, if ever, enforced. All white men between the ages of 21 and 50 served on night patrols to guard the village and to apprehend slaves at large, and all males—whites between 18 and 40 and slaves between 16 and 50—could be recruited for work on streets and roads.

Like the vast majority of ordinances in all times, the early Chapel Hill laws sound more harsh in the abstract than their enforcement was in fact, and except for the predictable student rowdiness there was little tension between the citizens and the village authorities. Postmaster Henry Thompson did see the need to notify the public on 14 March 1822 that problems arising from "the mode of transacting the business of this office" had forced him to change his operating hours and payment methods. In the

ment of 1857, he preached the funeral oration when his old professor Elisha Mitchell was entombed atop Mount Mitchell in 1858, and he received an honorary LL.D. at the commencement of 1859.

Bessie Pannill was the daughter of William and Martha Pannill, who purchased the Carolina Inn Plot on 7 April 1817 from Willam E. Webb. Webb had paid Samuel Holmes "$320 Spanish Milled dollars" for the property in 1797 after Holmes had bought it from Old Kit Barbee. The Pannills either moved into or built a house on the lot and began taking in students for room and board; however, they sold part of their property to Elisha Mitchell in December 1818 and left for Petersburg, Virginia, in the early 1820s, apparently after a struggle to make a living.

William Barbee's daughter Margaret in February 1843 married Jesse Hargrave, who had come to Chapel Hill from Davidson County as a bankrupt in 1835. William's youngest daughter, Mary Carolina, did not marry until January 1858, when she became the second wife of James N. Patterson, who had two children from a previous marriage. William's bachelor son Willis lived on a farm east of town and practiced as a country doctor.

Throughout the present century, long-time residents have lamented the passing of "the village." In one sense the village vanished in 1819 when the General Assembly established a municipal government for Chapel Hill with a bill naming Joseph Caldwell, Pleasant Henderson, Ezekiel Trice, William Barbee and Thomas Taylor commissioners empowered to set down limits, enact ordinances, and appoint town officials. Between then and 1851, when the town incorporated, freeholders elected a board of five commissioners annually, seven in 1824 and 1825. Eligible

Willie Person Mangum (1792-1861) of Hillsborough graduated from UNC in 1815 with his brother Priestley, and while Priestley remained in Chapel Hill as a tutor for several years, Willie became a lawyer, married Charity Alston Cain in 1819, and embarked on a career that would eventually make him a powerful U.S. Senator. He was bitterly opposed to industrialization, and it was his influence that kept Orange County free of such institutions as "banks, railroads, and stock companies" because they were "inconsistent with the true spirit of liberty." (NCC)

9 July 1823 *Recorder* Sheriff Thomas D. Watts warned that, in an effort to avoid customary delays in the yearly tax collection, "The prevailing cry of hard-times will not be received as a good excuse." On relatively rare occasions, the town constable did have to deal with serious crime and criminals.

Of course, Chapel Hill remained relatively isolated for decades, and just when the school and the village were beginning to expand in the 1820s an extended drought accompanied by a lengthy depression hit central North Carolina and effectively halted any hope for significant economic expansion until the recovery from the great national depression of 1836-1843. Mail carriages passed through Chapel Hill only once per week in 1795, and for years afterward administrators used express riders when they had to contact trustees or state officials swiftly. By the late 1820s, the stage coach came through town every day, stopping at Pleasant Henderson's store at Franklin and Henderson streets. Another indication that Chapel Hill was entering the mainstream occurred around 1820 when merchants replaced the pound sterling with the dollar as the standard monetary unit.

The people attracted to wash clothes, chop and deliver firewood, furnish meat and produce, and provide other menial services in a new university village were hardly sophisticated. Mrs. Cornelia Spencer remembered those outside the university community proper as being plain, rough, and vicious, quick to resort to violence. Her biographer, Hope Chamberlain, was equally negative in assessing the working-class people residing in and near the village: "In the early years of the last century horse racing, cock fights and gambling, hard drinking, and here and there a murder were the usual accomplishments of the lives of the common folk around Chapel Hill."

The large lots, approximately 300' by 300', gave villagers room for a granary, a carriage house, stables for a milk cow and one or more horses, and a privy, as well as ample space for vegetable and flower gardens. The nearby woods yielded an abundance of game and wild fruit in season. The passenger pigeon was still present in profusion, and twice yearly their migratory flights gave North Carolinians an opportunity to slaughter so many of the tasty birds that the excess was routinely used as fertilizer and as feed for swine.

The great western human migration of the 1820s and 1830s greatly affected the area and the state. Between 1820 and 1830, the population of Orange County—then consisting of modern Alamance, Orange, and Durham counties—rose only 1.8% from 23,492 to 23,908; and the white population actually declined 5.1% from 16,777 to 15,916. The 1840 census records 16,771 whites, 631 free blacks, and 6954 slaves in Orange County, a total population of 24,356, or only 864 more than in 1820.

Wagon trains of 100 or more families heading west were common, and Chapel Hill was on one of the main arteries.

Mrs. Spencer wrote in adulthood: "Another of my earliest recollections is that of frequently seeing long processions passing through town; of white covered wagons, full of beds, buckets, and babies, with lean men and women, tow headed children and dogs walking beside. 'Movers' we children called them. We always made a rush for the front door or gate to stare at the exodus. 'Going out West,' was the invariable reply to all queries. Something pathetic about their appearance still lingers in my mind as I recall them." The trustees had to borrow money to pay salaries during the depression.

Chapel Hill merchants were able to survive for several years on savings and their staple clientele of students and faculty, but by the end of the 1820s the hard years had

This ad appeared in the Harbinger near the end of its brief life. Sally Mitchell ran a well-known boarding house near the present Carolina Coffee Shop; Elizabeth Nunn and her husband William had operated Chapel Hill's first tavern, and at the time of this ad the widow Nunn was running a tavern and boarding house about where the Baptist Church is today at the corner of Columbia and Franklin streets; Mary Watson was the wife of William Watson, well-known merchant and farmer; W.H. Thompson was a farmer and merchant, as was John McGee; Isaac Patridge was postmaster, printer, and editor of the newspaper; Alexander Martin Henderson was a physician and the youngest son of Pleasant Henderson. (NCC)

This ad appeared in the Columbian Repository in 1836. Chapel Hill was on the western trail for thousands of North Carolinians who left the state in the 1820's and 1830's. The subsequent dearth of people left Chapel Hill with no shoemakers, no plasterers, no bricklayers, and no saddle nor harness makers. Villagers had to ride 12 miles to the nearest saddle and harness shop in Hillsborough.

There were two Christman families in the area at the time of this ad, and Thomas Christman was no doubt related to one or both of them, although his name does not appear in any extant records. (NCC)

begun to take their toll.

Major Pleasant Henderson was still prosperous on 9 July 1820 when his lovely daughter Eliza married attorney Hamilton Jones, and at the time it was not axiomatic that the daughter of a respected merchant had made a fortuitous match in a lawyer, a member of a profession then not held in the highest esteem. For example, UNC graduate and future Secretary of the Navy John Young Mason wrote a friend two months before Eliza's wedding, "I have taken a most invincible distaste to the practice of Law, and nothing but hard necessity should ever compel me to open my lips in another court of Justice." Although he realized the profession "is becoming daily fashionable," he was convinced, "It is, the dernier resort, in this State of every s—o—b, who fails in every other attempt at subsistence."

But within a few years Major Henderson was bankrupt. Soon after he arrived in Chapel Hill in 1797, he had begun to purchase village and farm properties. His slave work force had increased to 27 by 1820, and he had become a reliable, mutually acceptable arbiter in disputes involving students and university administrators, often arguing successfully for the readmission of expelled students. In the early 1820s, rising debts forced him to begin selling his property. In 1822 for $1314 he sold merchant Benjamin Rhodes a house and lot on or near the present location of the NCNB Franklin Street office. The next year he sold Rhodes another tract he owned jointly with Joseph Caldwell, Nathaniel King, and William Barbee.

Henderson's financial plight continued to worsen, to a considerable degree because he had guaranteed surety for Nathaniel King, whose inability to meet his financial obligations forced Henderson, Lemuel Morgan, and others to sell their own property to honor notes they had endorsed or shared. In 1827 attorney William McCauley, the son of Matthew McCauley, began to handle the Major's estate, which had dwindled to a house and 2.25 acres in Chapel Hill, 16 slaves, 192 acres on Morgan Creek

purchased from Samuel Hopkins, two other nearby tracts, horses, cattle, store goods, and household furnishings. His combined debts stood at $6400.

When it became evident that he could never pay his debts, Henderson on 25 February 1828 turned over all of his property to William McCauley on the condition that McCauley pay the State Bank of North Carolina $1260, the Bank of New Bern $3500, the Bank of Cape Fear $600, the Bank of New Bern in Raleigh $250, a Greensboro newspaper $700, and Sampson Moore an undisclosed amount. The Major stayed on in Chapel Hill until 1830, then left for Carroll County, Tennessee. Attorney John Norwood, representing Henderson's creditors, continued to press the Major for a settlement as late as August 1841, and every indication is that Henderson escaped the hounding only with his death on 10 December 1846.

Benjamin Rhodes fared little better. Just after Henderson sold out to McCauley, Rhodes fled the village to escape unpayable debts, but he carried with him Susan Price, the wife of Washington Price of Raleigh, who advertised he would no longer be responsible for Susan's debts because she had run off "with Benjamin Rhodes of Chapel Hill." On 8 October 1828, Orange County Sheriff Thomas D. Watts sold Rhode's house and lot on Franklin Street, at which time it was the residence of John Hutchins, Anderson Blackwood, and Abraham Craig's widow Jane.

Of the two sons of Hardy Morgan who reached maturity, Allen led a life of debauchery until he and his impoverished family joined the western migration; Lemuel married Mary Shaw in 1805 and prospered for several years, until he too was left deeply indebted by Nathaniel King. In November 1827, Lemuel, Major Henderson, and George Johnson had to sell an acre of original Lot 4 to clear a debt of $782 they jointly owed the Bank of North Carolina. Lemuel later sold off the remainder of his

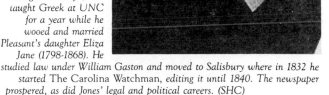

Hamilton Chamberlain Jones (1798-1869) was the stepson of Col. James Martin. He attended UNC, living in the home of Pleasant Henderson who had married Col. Martin's daughter Fanny. Jones taught Greek at UNC for a year while he wooed and married Pleasant's daughter Eliza Jane (1798-1868). He studied law under William Gaston and moved to Salisbury where in 1832 he started The Carolina Watchman, *editing it until 1840. The newspaper prospered, as did Jones' legal and political careers. (SHC)*

holdings, most of them to Jesse Hargrave. However, Elisha Mitchell, who picked up several pieces of choice property in the depression-ridden 1820s and 1830s, bought the four-acre Carolina Inn lot and a 34-acre tract bordering the campus on the west, and a slave trader purchased some of Lemuel's slaves.

One of them, Tom, went into hiding in a cave on Morgan Creek rather than go to the cotton fields of the southwest. For several years area residents left Tom alone, but when he started to break into village stores for food, a posse chased him down, shot him in the leg, and sent him south to be sold. After selling out, Lemuel and Mary Morgan moved to Raleigh where they lived on Lemuel's income as a potter until Mary inherited enough money to allow them once more to live in relative comfort.

There were other changes in the business district during President Caldwell's tenure. William D. Kirksey became the village blacksmith in the 1830s. Isaac J. Collier and Jones Watson opened a cabinet-making business in the summer of 1833, which Collier ran with Kendal Waitt after March 1836. W.H. Grimes purchased Henderson's old store.

Buck Taylor's son John advertised that his father's old "Tavern House...with necessary and usual servants and furniture" would be available 1 January 1822. Attorney David B. Alsobrook took over the establishment, which sat on the current Graham Memorial site, and turned it into a popular gathering place for political and ceremonial occasions.

On 4 July 1826, faculty and villagers celebrated the National Jubilee. Major Pleasant Henderson read the Declaration in Person Hall, and attorney William McCauley delivered the keynote address. The assemblage then repaired to Alsobrook's hotel for an afternoon lunch prior to an evening ball at which couples danced to the fiddle of Ilai Nunn. The commencement ball was held at Alsobrook's on 26 June 1828.

Mrs. Alsobrook had the misfortune to be in the hotel one spring day in 1830 when the notorious Anne Royall thundered into town. A small-statured, homely woman, Mrs. Royall had written a remarkably bad novel, *Tennessean*, and a bitingly provocative travel journal, *Black Book*. Recently, a Washington, D.C. court had convicted her of being a "common scold" for having publicly abused members of a Presbyterian church near her home with some imaginatively scurrilous invective.

When Mrs. Royall dismounted from the public coach unattended, Mrs. Alsobrook was surprised at a flagrant breach of current custom and asked, "Have you no man with you?" Almost any question could have raised the ire of the Presbyterian-hating, self-confident Mrs. Royall, and she responded with a sharp retort and an immediate dislike for her hostess that quickly radiated to include everyone in the room. She described one woman as an

Archibald DeBow Murphey (1777-1832) graduated from UNC in 1799 and remained in the village as a tutor of Ancient Languages for two years. He became an attorney and was instrumental in recovering UNC's escheats money from Tennessee in 1822, money which UNC depended on for its finances up to the Civil War. Murphey's personal finances were less happily conducted and he died a pauper. Historians today consider him North Carolina's most progressive public figure of the early 19th century. (NCC)

"old, sly Presbyterian, who, as I afterward learned, was very goodly, and went to church and made a long face, but sold whiskey to the students, every chance she had, the hypocrit." Another "was an old maid...small, and ugly enough to tree a wolf.—The students call her *Greasy Monkey*." She journeyed onward to Raleigh, but the angry aging woman, whom President John Quincy Adams had called a "virago errant," wrote a scathing account of her short visit in the first volume of *The Southern Tour*.

She found the university "a most delightful situation, sitting upon an eminence, in the midst of a handsome grove—but to the disgrace of the State, is under the influence of a WOMAN, the president's wife. She is ruled by priests, the priests are ruled by *money* and she rules the university." The result, Mrs. Royall believed, was that the university did little more than disseminate religious propaganda, and she asked "any man, not a Presbyterian" to visit Chapel Hill to see for himself.

She accused Mrs. Helen Caldwell of "fleecing the last cent of pocket money" from unsuspecting young men to purchase religious tracts and of punishing students who "happen to smile" during compulsory religious services, and "not a step, dare the hen-pecked president take without apprising this tyrannical woman."

Kemp Battle, who was 15 when Mrs. Caldwell died in 1846, defended her vigorously, with just enough hint of her forceful character to suggest that Mrs. Royall's perceptions may not have been totally tainted by prejudice: "Mrs. Royall was either a malicious, untruthful woman, or demented. Mrs. Caldwell was a woman of talent, of polished manners, and excellent heart. She naturally dominated and gave tone to the village society, but her husband was distinguished for his independence of character and inflexible will."

Sheriff Thomas D. Watts left office in 1832 and in 1834

took over Alsobrook's hotel. Within a year he had competition, directly across Franklin Street. In January 1833, postmaster Isaac C. Patridge established Chapel Hill's first newspaper, *The Harbinger*. It was an ambitious project intended "to diffuse" information on literature, science, agriculture, religion, politics, education and any other topic submitted by contributors. Elisha Mitchell and William Hooper in particular encouraged Patridge and joined scores of writers who sent in articles, but few newspapers survived for long in early 19th-century North Carolina, where subscribers and advertisers were notorious for not paying their bills, and *The Harbinger* ceased its cry in 1834. Hugh McQueen, a university trustee and a Chatham County legislator, tried his hand with the *Columbian Repository* in 1836, but with no more success than Patridge.

When *The Harbinger* failed and left him penniless, Patridge decided he would make his fortune in the hotel business. He persuaded Elisha Mitchell to sell him for $1400, on credit, a building and lot on Franklin Street opposite Watts' Hotel. To raise capital to build stables and make other improvements, he signed over the lot to Dr. Hudson Cave for $500 cash, with the provision that if Patridge did not pay Mitchell the $1400 the lot would revert to the professor. In a 30 December 1834 advertisement, Patridge announced the opening of the University Hotel and assured "the travelling public...that every exertion will be made by him to please as well as accomodate."

Patridge struggled with the floundering hotel until 1837, when he left for New York City, leaving Mitchell in possession of the property and Dr. Cave holding a note for $500. Patridge later worked on the Norfolk *Beacon*. When he applied for a teaching job in North Carolina in 1856, he listed Jones Watson and T.C. Watson of Chapel Hill as his references, an indication that Chapel Hillians harbored no ill will for a popular former neighbor who had been caught in the crunch of the depression.

Once in the early 19th century, university trustees found themselves in the embarrassing position of having to auction off slaves escheated to the university. The public sale of slaves—invariably advertised as "Likely Negroes"—was a periodic but not routine practice in Chapel Hill. As instructed in a deed of trust, on 24 February 1821 the widow Jane Craig sold nine slaves. "Six Likely Negroes" from the estate of original settler William McCauley were sold in January 1836, and some 20 "Likely Negroes" from the estate of William L. Durham were sold in October 1839. In the summer of 1828, Major Pleasant Henderson sold the slave "Sawney" to Thomas McGehee of Person County, but Sawney did not approve of the transaction and ran away. By October, McGehee was offering a reward of $20 for the capture of his "property."

The subject of slavery in general received a surprisingly reasoned treatment in Chapel Hill, even after the Nat

The Harbinger *was edited by Isaac Patridge during its short life. Patridge, as postmaster, received nearly all the newspapers published on the east coast, and he would publish what he considered the most newsworthy items on pages two and three of the four-page weekly, reserving page one for essays written by university professors and articles from other sources. (NCC)*

The Columbian Repository *was Chapel Hill's second newspaper. Advertisements in its pages, as in the* Harbinger, *took up less than 20% of the available space. Chapel Hill's commercial community, even when it paid its bills, was not large enough to support a newspaper at this time.*

Page one of this four-page weekly was always devoted to scholarly essays, such as the two articles on page one of the issue illustrated here: one-half of the page is given over to a discussion of Sir Walter Scott's trip to Greece, and the other half to a scholarly discussion of the life of Samuel Johnson. (NCC)

Turner rebellion of August 1831. At the turn of the century, students had debated the topic, "Resolved, that Africans have as much right to enslave Americans as Americans to enslave Africans." The affirmative team won.

By 1818, Chapel Hill had a thriving chapter of the American Colonization Society, organized nationally in 1816 to purchase slaves and transport free blacks to Africa. Joseph Caldwell, Pleasant Henderson, William McCauley, William Hooper, Tom Taylor, and Robert King were local officers. In 1819, Episcopal minister William Meade of Virginia stopped off in Chapel Hill on his way to Georgia to purchase 34 slaves for the society. During his stay with Joseph Caldwell, he raised over 200 pounds sterling in the village. Near the end of the century, Rev. Meade's grandson William H. Meade came to Chapel Hill as the rector of the Chapel of the Cross, bringing with him his daughter's family, including the young William Meade Prince.

But ultimately Chapel Hillians reacted as those throughout the slave belt to the increasing din of abolitionist propaganda—they cited staple biblical evidence of divine approval of the "peculiar institution." And after emancipation members of the established community liked to remember the loyalty of slaves to their masters and to the university in ante-bellum days. Kemp Battle wrote of the slaves Dave Barham and November Caldwell, who worked on campus, "They were irreproachable in the performance of duty." He related that "Barham was a good moral man" and that November failed "only on the side of unchastity." Indeed, it was clearly obvious that the dignified November greatly enjoyed driving Dr. Caldwell's carriage, and he spoke often of having served governors, senators, and a president of the United States.

William H. Meade (1789-1862), Episcopal Rector of Virginia, was a fund-raiser for the American Colonization Society, a group that bought slaves in order to free them by shipping them back to Africa.

One official of the Society was Elias B. Caldwell, and Caldwell's sister, Eliza, was married to the head of the Society, Robert Finley. These New Jersey Caldwells were probably related to UNC President Joseph Caldwell, which would explain the Society's and Rev. Meade's easy access to Chapel Hillians when Meade came through town in 1818. (NCC)

Caroline Lee Hentz (1800-1856) befriended George Moses Horton, the slave poet, when she lived in Chapel Hill in the early 1830's. When she died, he penned his sorrow in a poem: "Deep on thy pillar, thou immortal dame / Trace the inscription of eternal fame; / For bards, unborn must yet thy works adore, / and bid thee live when others are no more." (NCC)

November Caldwell (1791-1872) was a slave in the household of UNC President Joseph Caldwell when he was a young man. In 1869 he bought a half-acre lot on Cameron Avenue for $300 from Green Cordal and lived in peaceful retirement with Chaney Caldwell, probably a daughter. Ms. Lucille Caldwell, great-granddaughter of November, says that he chose his first name in accordance with the custom of his west African tribal ancestors.

This sketch, made by Caddie Fulghum about twenty years after November's death, used November's son, Wilson, as the model, but authorities at that time reported that the two men were "dead ringers" for each other. (NCC)

Dave Barham belonged to Elisha Mitchell, who he claimed never spoke harshly to him.

Remembering days gone by, Mrs. Spencer painted a social portrait reflective of the old-guard spirit common to the post-war era: "Much of the high aristocratic feeling of the community found its home among the old slaves who had been in their places for half a century. It made them proud to see themselves untouched amid changes and upheavals. They considered themselves the *Patres Conscripti* of Chapel Hill."

Nicholas Marcellus Hentz fled war-ravaged France for the United States in 1816 at age 19. He met Caroline Lee Wright while teaching in Northampton, Massachusetts, and married her in 1825. The next year he came to UNC to teach modern languages and moved into a small house on the Battle lot. He was an expert on spiders, and while in Chapel Hill he wrote a book on arachnology that was

considered the definitive work of the age. Once after a violent thunderstorm, Nicholas protected his house with lightning rods, a curious innovation to Chapel Hillians who already considered the Frenchman a harmless eccentric.

Caroline Hentz wrote poems, many of which are preserved in the scrapbooks of Mary Louisa Jones, the daughter of Edward Jones, the sister of Dr. Johnston Blakeley Jones, and the future wife of Abram Rencher. Mrs. Hentz also encouraged the literary efforts of George Moses Horton, a slave off a Chatham County Plantation who had taught himself to read and write and who had gone into the "business" of writing love poems for students to send to their girl friends.

The students usually paid Horton 25 cents per poem, up to 75 cents for difficult assignments; they gave him old clothes and books by the literary masters; and they also gave him the liquor he had drunk in excess since childhood. In his memoirs Horton confessed they had "flattered me into the belief that it would hang me on the wings of new inspiration, which would waft me into the regions of poetical perfection." Instead it had encouraged his dependence on alcohol.

Assisted by Joseph Caldwell, Joseph Gales & Sons of Raleigh published a collection of Horton's poems in 1829, *The Hope of Liberty*. Horace Greeley published his poems in the New York *Tribune*, abolitionist papers in Boston printed others, and Horton began to hope that he would realize enough income from his compositions to purchase his freedom and passage to Liberia. Such was not to be. The book sold poorly, and with Caroline Hentz gone and Caldwell dead, after 1835 no one in the village took the drunken poet seriously any longer.

When federal troops arrived in 1865, "the colored bard of Chapel Hill" met them and begged to follow them north. Michigan Ninth Cavalry Captain W.H.S. Banks looked after Horton, oversaw the publication of his third volume, *Naked Genius*, in Raleigh, and escorted him to Philadelphia, where Horton lived until his death in 1883. The Chapel Hill Historical Society issued a new edition of

After he returned to Chapel Hill in the 1840's, Dr. Charles "Bullet" Yancey lived in this house on Pittsboro Street, on the site of the present Carolina Inn parking lot.

At the time this 1933 photograph was made, Louis MacMillan, Chapel Hill's Chevrolet dealer, was living in the house. The child is Josephine MacMillan, his daughter.

(Courtesy of Mrs. Josephine MacMillan Killeffer)

Elisha Mitchell (1793-1857) engaged in an 1824-25 feud with John Stark Ravenscroft (1772-1830), Episcopal Bishop of North Carolina presiding at Christ Church in Raleigh. Ravenscroft, proud of his First Family of Virginia status, given to "visions" as a child, was apparently dismayed by the Presbyterian influence at the university and said so, causing Mitchell to engage him in a bitter exchange of letters. Mitchell answered one Ravenscroft charge on 11 April 1825 writing, "I was not aware that there was anything dictatorial in my letters but supposed that as it respects calmness, moderation and candour the advantage was decidedly with me." (NCC)

Naked Genius in 1982.

After Carolina Hentz left in 1834, she wrote *Lovel's Folly*, the first novel by a Chapel Hillian and a book containing characters based on November and Venus Caldwell, slaves she had known in the village. According to Cornelia Spencer, after they had left Chapel Hill, Caroline and Nicholas Hentz "seem to have suffered from an attack of the same homesickness that all experience who have left the place."

During the late 1820's when religious fervor was sweeping the state and the nation, a number of students formed the Students' Bible Society of Chapel Hill, which in 1829 distributed between 200 and 300 Bibles in the neighborhood, a number that would have provided at least one copy per household for a wide radius. That year students also formed a temperance society, and in 1831 they solicited Elisha Mitchell to speak on the evils of intemperance.

He responded with a rousing damnation of hard liquor in which he argued that the ancient Greeks and Romans had been content with libations made by a natural process of fermentation. Mitchell assured his impressionable audience that "the lips of Moses, the Jewish lawgiver—of David, the sweet singer of Israel—of the holy and sublime Isaiah—of the Redeemer of mankind, were never polluted by the products of distillation."

Such was not true of the lips of many Chapel Hillians. Old Kit Barbee and his son William, Asa and Leroy Couch, Mrs. Jane Puckett, and William Watson were just a few of the regular purchasers of brandy and whiskey in the local stores. Those who lived in town routinely bought spirits by the quart, at four shillings, four pence (42 cents) per bottle during most of the 1820s. Those who had to travel in from the countryside usually purchased by the gallon, or gallons.

One of the most inveterate tipplers in the area was Dr. Charles "Bullet" Yancy, born in Virginia about 1801. Dr. Yancy was known far more for his intemperate habits than for his healing powers. Called Bullet because of his single, jet-black eye, Dr. Yancy was undeniably the "town character" for decades even though he was quite well-to-do, and over the years his neighbors grew used to hearing him singing the virtues of the patriots and of "corn-cob whiskey" as he rode through the streets, late into the night.

In 1822 Bullet purchased what was originally Lot 8 at Columbia and Franklin, except for the 20′ by 30′ section on which Thompson and Trice had their store. He sold the corner blacksmith shop to Old Kit Barbee in 1824 and used the remainder as a homeplace, on which he built a house, a barn, a carriage house, a smokehouse, slave quarters and a kitchen. His deaf-mute brother Lemuel, also something of a town character, lived with him, and they were joined on 11 February 1827 by Bullet's bride, 21-year-old Mary Merritt, probably the eldest daughter of Rev. William H. and Susanna Barbee Merritt. Mary died on 10 June 1829, and the next year Bullet married Martha Merritt, probably Mary's younger sister.

About 1833 Yancy moved his household (which included nine slaves by 1840) to a 325-acre farm on the Orange-Chatham County border he had purchased from Edmund R. Pitt in 1824 while Pitt was experiencing financial difficulties. The depression had worsened, and Yancy could not find a buyer for his Chapel Hill house and lot until he sold them to Jesse Hargrave for $800 in 1840. The 1850 census lists Frances Yancy, age 36, as living with Bullet and Martha Yancy in a house on Pittsboro Street a few paces south of the Carolina Inn parking lot. Frances no doubt was Bullet and Lemuel's younger sister.

Martha died soon after the census, and on 3 October 1851 Bullet took a third wife, Charlotte Creel of Chapel Hill, in a civil ceremony unmatched in macabre humor by any other, ever, in the village. Bullet had only one eye; Justice of the Peace Thomas Long had only one eye; Charlotte Creel's father was totally blind; one of the witnesses, Bullet's brother Lemuel, was a deaf-mute. Dr. Yancy was 50 years old, his wife about 29. To insure that she would have a means of income after his death, Bullet bought Charlotte a 156-acre farm south of the village, and when Bullet died in 1860 Lemuel and Frances "Fannie" stayed on in the Pittsboro Street house.

Charlotte married Washington Caudle in 1862 and moved onto the farm Bullet had provided for her. Caudle died shortly thereafter, and in February 1864 Charlotte married Thomas Pickett, a man 10 years her junior, but only after Pickett had signed a marriage contract to be administered by Jones Watson which allowed Charlotte to keep complete control of her property. Charlotte and Thomas Pickett lived into the 20th century as the parents of a single child, a daughter Elizabeth born in 1868.

William Barbee's son Willis was more reliable as a healer but less acceptable socially. He attended the university briefly in 1818 before studying medicine privately and settling on a farm to the west of "The Mountain" which his father had purchased from John Morgan. For over 40 years he was the archetypal "country doctor," caring for black or white, rich or poor, and living the rustic life of a modest planter. However, his romantic attachment to one of his female slaves, Harriett Barbee, made him *persona non grata* in polite Chapel Hill society.

Although expert practitioners were rare and in great demand in ante-bellum North Carolina, country doctors were commonplace, and most of them depended on other sources of income to support themselves and their families. Such was Dr. Hudson Cave, who after his marriage to Delia Barbee devoted the majority of his time to operating Cave's Mill on Morgan Creek, while living on Franklin Street.

Dr. Walter A. Norwood began practicing in Chapel Hill during the 1820s and set up a "medicine shop" across Franklin Street from the Alsobrook/Watts Hotel. He also advertised "printing and printing materials" for rent in 1828, and he was the recording secretary of the N.C. Institute of Education from its creation in Chapel Hill on 22 June 1831 until he moved to Hillsborough in 1834. He worked consistently for the improvement of education in North Carolina.

Near the end of Caldwell's tenure, the most persistent legend of 19th-century Chapel Hill had its origin with scant basis in fact. Peter Dromgoole of Virginia came to Chapel Hill in 1831 to attend the university. However, he grew angry over some comments by a professor, refused to submit to a preliminary examination, and never matriculated. A few days later he left town, to the mystification of some who knew him.

Soon a rumor spread that he had died in a duel at Piney Prospect and had been buried under the stone on which he fell, known thereafter as "Dromgoole's Tomb," located on the slope below Gimghoul Castle. Supposedly, Peter's sweetheart Fanny arrived just in time to clasp her dying lover to her bosom. Naturally, she lost her senses and died of a broken heart, leaving a new name for a nearby landmark—Miss Fanny's Spring. The tellers of the tale could point for verification to the "bloodstains" on the "tomb," in reality nothing more than rusted traces of metal in the stone.

Peter Dromgoole's uncle George C. Dromgoole,

suspended for supporting William Biddle Shepard in the troubles of 1816 and a Congressman from Virginia from 1841 until his death in 1845, came to Chapel Hill to learn if any truth lay behind the rumors. He could discover nothing to substantiate the intriguing stories, and his nephew's short-term roommate John Buxton Williams tried to end the gossip with a public letter which denied that Peter had been involved in any sort of violent affray and insisted that he had simply left on a public stage. Edwin W. Fuller drew on the myth in his 1873 novel *Sea Gift*.

A distinct period in the history of Chapel Hill ended on 27 January 1835 with the death of Joseph Caldwell. Caldwell's awareness of the seriousness of his illness is poignantly apparent in a 15 April 1834 letter to Judge William Gaston. Referring to a slight improvement, he ended with a note of despair, "Life had nonetheless been prolonged, but my health is very infirm. My journey to the springs had little or no influence in any way."

When Caldwell's health went into a decline, Elisha Mitchell had taken over most of the president's duties, and the trustees named him chairman of the faculty when Caldwell died. The general assumption was that Mitchell would be named the next president, but the post was far from being divorced from politics, and a young politician old in experience got the nod, a gentleman with a disposition sharply different from that of his predecessor.

Caroline Lee Hentz (1800-1856) executed this painting of the first home built for UNC Presidents. The house was located on Cameron Avenue approximately where Swain Hall is today. Elisha Mitchell and his family lived there for almost four decades, using part of the lot as a family cemetery. (NCC)

This painting depicts the university in 1854. The population of the village was about 730, rooms in the village rented for $30 per year, UNC President Swain's salary was $1600 yearly, and there were about 1000 living alumni. Left to right are Gerrard Hall, South Building, the Playmaker's Theater, and Old East. The theater was built in 1849 by Captain John Berry, who had recently built a new court house in Hillsborough.

In 1854, there was a shooting that shook the school. James H. Evans (1834-1890) and Edwin Smith Sanders (1837-1863) were freshmen, staying at the time in Old East, although they later moved into the home of Richard and Mary Ashe. Suspecting that they were about to be hazed by upperclassmen, they armed themselves with pistols, and when the seniors entered the room, Evans shot, hitting and breaking the arm of one student. The other students pummeled Sanders, seriously injuring him. The shot student was expelled. Sanders was killed in the Civil War.

The decade of the 1850's was eventful for students in other ways. In 1851 an order of Delta Kappa Epsilon became the first secret society sanctioned by the school's authorities since the establishment of the Dialectic and Philanthropic Societies in August, 1795. The Beta Theta Pi was active from 1851, Sigma Alpha Epsilon began in 1857, and the Zeta Psi in 1858.

In 1856, students playing with fireballs made from kerosene-soaked rags either accidentally or deliberately burned the belfry in the North Quadrangle. A trustee committee futilely attempted to collect evidence to prosecute.

A historic first occurred on 19 January 1857: a blizzard crossed the Piedmont and the faculty suspended classes for the first time due to inclement weather. (NCC)

III
Lotus-Eating Years and Battlefields
1832 to 1865

David Lowry Swain was born in Asheville to parents of English descent on 4 January 1801. His father George Swain had come to Buncombe County from Roxboro, Massachusetts; his mother, the former Caroline Lane, was the sister of the Joel Lane who had sold the state the land on which Raleigh was founded.

David Swain attended the university in 1821 and roomed with another famous nongraduate, Leonidas Polk, "the Fighting Bishop" who as a Civil War lieutenant general died on Pine Mountain during the futile defense of Atlanta. Swain left the university, studied law under Judge John L. Taylor in Raleigh, began a law practice in the capital, and on 12 January 1824 married Eleanor White, a granddaughter of Richard Caswell, the first governor of the State of North Carolina.

Swain then rose rapidly to the pinnacle of North Carolina politics, from the state legislature in 1824, to the state supreme court in 1831, to become the youngest North Carolina governor in

David Lowry Swain (1801-1868), almost universally admired during the ante-bellum years, made a strong impression on Charles Force Deems, Chapel Hill's Methodist minister and a university professor. In his autobiography, Deems wrote, "That great and good man, judge, governor, president of the university, has accompanied me to the cabins of sick servants and knelt humbly on the sanded floor while I prayed."

Swain's cousin, Joseph Lane (1801-1888), who grew up with Swain in Asheville, became the governor of the territory of Oregon and then became that state's first U.S. Senator when it joined the Union in 1859. Lane ran as the vice-presidential candidate on the Southern Democrat ticket with Breckenridge in 1860. (NCC)

history in 1832. During three one-year terms as chief executive, he won a host of lasting admirers. One of them, Duncan Cameron, thought the sitting governor would make an excellent president for the university. Swain actively lobbied for the position, and the trustees selected him to succeed Caldwell effective 5 December 1835. Although he would remain president for nearly 33 years, he was always "Governor" Swain to the villagers.

Governor Swain did not wish to move Elisha Mitchell out of the president's house, Eleanor did not like the old Caldwell house, so they chose to reside in the Tom Taylor house. In an age of nicknames, students quickly dubbed their new president "Old Bunk" in reference to his county of origin and "Old Warping Bars" in reference to his ungainliness. His general appearance prompted Phillips Russell to designate him "a very prince of ugliness." From the beginning, he was popular with the students, the faculty, and the people most likely to send their children to the university. Under his administration, enrollment grew until UNC was nationally second in size only to Yale by the outbreak of the Civil War.

But Swain's popularity did not interfere with the students' expressing their independence in unbridled outbursts that often ended in outright riots. A particularly rambunctious group formed the Ugly Club in 1838, an informal organization dedicated to resisting all forms of regimentation. On the first Saturday night of the fall term of 1838, a routine hazing party by "club" members erupted into a village-wide rampage with black-faced young men intimidating faculty and citizens, turning over privies, and happily defying all attempts to restore calm. The faculty dismissed one student for riding a horse through Old West and forced 19 more to sign pledges of obedience, but the

Ugly Club thrived until the Civil War.

In 1840 the Whigs were at the crest of their power in North Carolina, and they unleashed their enthusiasm for their presidential candidate William Henry Harrison and his popular running mate John Tyler in the infamous "log-cabin-and-hard-cider" campaign during which rallies were enlivened with copious servings from barrels of hard cider. Recognizing the dangers inherent in the combination of volatile students, a volatile political situation, and barrels of volatile spirits, Swain forbade the students from participating in the emotional canvass. As usual, they exercised their own prerogatives, but at least one of their unsanctioned efforts to aid "Tippecanoe and Tyler Too" backfired. They purchased 50 acres in the name of Edward "Old Blind" Pendergrass to qualify him for the ballot. Pendergrass accepted the deed, and then voted for Democrat Martin Van Buren.

When wits failed, students could always turn to their staple pranks. They placed so many calves in the arena in Gerrard Hall that it became known as the "Bull Pen." They never tired of ringing the college bell at all hours, of stabling Swain's white mule "Caddie" in the upper stories of the dormitories and the South Building, of taking gullible underclassmen on snipe hunts, of dragging a fox skin through the village churches early on Sunday mornings before releasing the hounds in time for the services, of faking duels.

From the modern perspective, the ante-bellum decades may seem to have been dominated by the widening divisions that would culminate in the Civil War. Yet, the great preponderance of private correspondence, diaries and journals of the period focus on personal and routine matters. Cornelia Phillips' letters and her journal are not the exception.

The only extended period Chapel Hill was without students then was the long winter recess, and Cornelia captured the sense of their absence succinctly in a 1 December 1844 letter to Ellen Mitchell: "The students melted away as imperceptibly as usual, and by Saturday everthing was settled down to the ancient quiet of the

The exact identity of this E. Hunt is unknown. During his three years in Chapel Hill (he left in the summer of 1859) he housed students, some of whom he photographed. Among the students who roomed in his house near the east corner of Franklin and Henderson were two UNC tutors who were killed in the Civil War, Robert Anderson and George B. Pettigrew, plus the "boy Colonel of the Confederacy," Henry K. Burgwyn (1841-1863). An Ellery J. Hunt was later a photographer in Camden, New Jersey, 1878-90. (NCC)

MAN

Behold Thyself,

BY VISITING E. HUNT'S GALLERY opposite the Union Hotel and getting a Superior Ambrotype, Melainotype, Photograph, Pearl, Ambrotype, or Cameotype (raised picture) neatly set in lockets pins &c.

Having seven years experience in the art, and arrangements for receiving all the new discoveries as soon as they are issued, I do not deem it necessary to say what I can do. Ladies and gentlemen are requested to call and examine my specimens. Cloudy weather as good as sunshine.

E. HUNT.

winter vacation." With the routine broken and time on their hands, Cornelia and her mother Julia could stroll leisurely over their beloved countryside, and Cornelia struck another theme as alive today as in 1844--opposition to change: "Ma and I took a long walk the other day to Glenburnie--Glenburnie no longer."

She described the scene on Bolin Creek west of the Hillsborough Road: "Mr. Waitt has had the barbarity to clear the stream of those picturesque rocks, and the large one stands alone in the midst of the most insipid flat creek that every rippled over a bed of fine gravel, and he has cut a road all along there, and so completely changed the face of nature that the place was hardly recognizable."

But even with the students present most of the year, Cornelia remembered the 1840s and 1850s as a lotus-eating time for reading and leisurely enjoying the natural beauty of a village in which on summer afternoons "the very cats and dogs languidly stretched out under the shade of some pleasant bush."

The Mr. Waitt who ran the mill on Bolin Creek was Thomas Waitt of New England, who signed on as superintendent of grounds and buildings early in Swain's tenure and who never completely pleased administrators with his management of money. His son Kendal Waitt was the university carpenter, locksmith, blacksmith, and jack-of-all-trades, who moonlighted as the village coffin maker and undertaker. The Waitts had a workshop on the bottom floor of a barn-like structure that would now be located behind Phillips Hall. Kemp Battle described Kendal as "a Northern man with the usual Yankee ingenuity and industry." Part of his ingenuity consisted of preparing imaginatively itemized bills, which Battle defended, with some effort, as "probably not exaggerated."

After graduating from the university in 1841, Cornelia's brother Charles studied medicine briefly before studying mathematics and theology at Princeton. He returned to Chapel Hill to teach at the university and to preach to Presbyterian congregations. On 8 December 1847 he married Laura Battle, who was then living in Chapel Hill with her brother Judge William Horn Battle. Charles contributed generously to the *University Magazine* and undertook further studies at Harvard in the mid-1850s when he was named professor of engineering.

Samuel Phillips graduated from the university with his older brother Charles in 1841. He studied law under Judge Battle, assisted Battle in his law school, joined the editorial staff of the *University Magazine* when it formed in 1844, and earned a master's degree that year. He and his brother Charles were charter members of the Alumni Association at its organization on 31 May 1843, and for a generation thereafter Sam Phillips took a leading role in the activities of the Alumni Association and the university at large, culminating with his work as a trustee in 1864-1868. In 1848 he married Frances Lucas, a granddaughter of North

Carolina Governor David Stone. They lived contentedly in Chapel Hill until 1868 when Sam's Republican affiliation made him a pariah in the eyes of most Chapel Hillians, and he moved on to a very successful career in state and national government.

One cold January day in 1852, Cornelia was passing the frozen natural pond where the Horace Williams House now sits when she came upon a group of skaters. One of them was a student James Monroe Spencer, nicknamed "Mangus" and "Longus" because of his height. Cornelia and Mangus fell into conversation, and after a stroll on the ice he accompanied her home. A decade later she wrote in her diary, "I can recall our talk, and his looks and tones, so vividly. It seems but yesterday, instead of ten years." On 30 April 1853, near the end of his junior year, Mangus proposed. The 28-year-old Cornelia and her younger fiance did not rush to the altar. After graduating with honors in 1854, Mangus returned to his native Alabama for a year, set up a law practice, and returned to Chapel Hill to claim his patient bride on 20 June 1855.

After an extended honeymoon, the couple settled in Clinton, Alabama. It was there on 1 June 1859, that Cornelia gave birth to Julia James Spencer, appropriately nicknamed "June." Mangus wrote Mrs. Phillips, "Cornelia is a little disappointed about the sex of the little stranger. She had labeled it James Phillips. As for myself, a girl is as good as a boy any day."

On 24 June 1861, Mangus died after years of intense pain from a spinal lesion. Cornelia stayed in Alabama to collect her belongings and her thoughts, then returned to her family. In Chapel Hill, she could share her deep misery with her childhood friend, Professor Mitchell's daughter Mrs. Eliza Mitchell Grant. Eliza and Richard Grant were raising a young family in Texas in 1858 when a notorious gang of rustlers killed Richard during a raid. A man named Wash Garner was apprehended, tried and condemned for the murder. As he was being led to the gallows he asked for whiskey. His guards gave him a glass, he gulped it down and bolted, the guards shot him in the back. In a 25 August 1858 letter Mrs. Grant expressed satisfaction in knowing that Garner had died slowly and painfully. All of Mrs. Grant's children died young, and she had lost a son to diphtheria the year after Cornelia returned to Chapel Hill.

Mrs. Spencer would soon discover that very much remained for her to do. As the fortunes of the South declined in war and Reconstruction, she rose to defend southern honor, and when the very existence of the university was in peril, she rose to rescue it. But life never lost its tragic overtones for her. In 1905 she wrote to Dr. J.J. Summerell, the widower of Elisha Mitchell's daughter Ellen, "I have been musing a good deal on the Mitchell family--the Summerells, Ashes and Grants. They pass and turn and pass again like the shadows on the grass. I have survived them all and I find that old age is lonely and to recur to the past is like walking over a battlefield."

For several decades essentially nonsectarian religious services were held in the university chapel and in the Union Church, a small frame structure that sat on the current Presbyterian Church lot. William Mercer Green, Elisha Mitchell, and James Phillips generally divided the preaching chores, abetted by a generous flow of visiting ministers and circuit riders.

The Mason's University Lodge #80 held regular religious celebrations, often in conjunction with the Eagle Lodge of Hillsborough. During the Civil War, University Lodge became Caldwell Lodge #80, named in honor of Joseph Caldwell. In the mid-1830s, University Lodge secretary John B. McDade was also the secretary and the most energetic member of the Chapel Hill Temperance Society, which organized area residents for the battle against alcoholic consumption that raged with increasing passion throughout the nation in the 1830s and 1840s. Excessive tippling was common in all levels of ante-bellum North Carolina society.

The elite enjoyed their potations in respectable taverns and in well furnished libraries or dining rooms. Working men, students, and -- illegally but routinely -- slaves found abundant, cheap supplies in grog shops, or "doggeries."

John McDade organized a combined meeting of Temperance Society chapters from Chapel Hill, Antioch, and Sandy Field at Mount Carmel Church in February 1836, and for years he oversaw annual conferences in the area. The success of the movement in Chapel Hill can be measured to a degree by the observations of a *Recorder* reporter at the Chapel Hill Festival in September 1840. He deemed the substitution of hard cider for whiskey at the

John Calvin McNair (1823-1858), class of 1849, became a Presbyterian minister and later moved to Scotland to preach until his death. This picture shows his tomb in Glasgow, Scotland.

McNair built a sizable fortune in the United States, and in his will he specified that after his mother's death his slaves and his land should be sold and that the proceeds from the two sales should be given to the trustees of UNC to establish a course of lectures designed to "prove the existence and attributes of God (as far as may be) from nature." The McNair Lectures began in 1908; educator John Dewey was one of the early participants in 1915. (NCC)

event "a blessing to the community." Editor Dennis Heartt added, "We learn from our informant (and he is an administration man too) that he has seldom seen better order prevail even at a camp meeting."

The local order became affiliated with the New York based Sons of Temperance after that organization expanded into North Carolina in 1843, and the crusade continued. Patterson H. McDade, Charles and James Phillips, Elisha Mitchell, and others joined John McDade in delivering lectures in and around Chapel Hill. In April 1849 the ladies of Chapel Hill presented the Sons of Temperance with a banner saluting the group's good work.

In response to a temperance lecture on campus in October 1850, "Four faculty members and 16, or more, students joined." But the movement failed to make major inroads into the student body, and it languished into local insignificance as public apathy increased and national problems occupied more attention.

Well into the 19th century the various denominations in the village were content to participate collectively in Sunday services, but "after awhile," wrote Mrs. Spencer, revealing a bias then common against "enthusiastic" religions, "the methodists began their own, where they could shout if so inclined."

During the 1830s, those Methodists who preferred to meet exclusively with members of their own faith joined the Orange Church congregation, which built a church three miles out on the Hillsborough Road in 1838. Early in 1840, the American Bible Society sent the Methodist preacher, Charles Force Deems, from his Asbury, New Jersey, ministry to North Carolina. He and Peter Doub held a series of camp revivals that summer, and Governor Swain left one Raleigh meeting so impressed with Deems that he arranged for the minister to be named an adjunct professor of logic and rhetoric at the university. The Methodist Conference was happy to assign Deems to the fledgling Chapel Hill congregation, then meeting in Miles Davis' house across Rosemary Street behind the present Presbyterian Church.

At first Deems preached at the campus chapel, the Union Church, Orange Church, and Miles Davis' house. When the congregation grew too large for the Davis home, the Methodists moved to a room above Jesse Hargrave's Franklin Street store. The pulpit consisted of a cloth thrown over a table, the congregation sat on plain pine benches, and members named their church Bethesda -- the House of Mercy.

By 1843 Bethesda had 72 members, 64 white and 8 black. Then growth slowed, and after Deems left in 1847 the church had no regular preacher until the Rev. J. Milton Frost arrived from Mocksville in 1851 to attend the university. Frost and the Chapel Hill Methodists yearned for a church to accommodate both an increasing roll and a growing student body, but the local members could not afford the costs of a respectable structure. Frost solved their problem by touring the state on a fund-raising mission that collected approximately $5000, and a "Mr. Horn of Pittsboro" designed and build a church in the Greek Revival style which still stands at the northeast corner of Rosemary and Henderson streets. Rev. Rufus T. Heflin dedicated it on 3 July 1853.

When Frost moved to a ministry in Fayetteville in 1854, several preachers, including Peter Doub and Miles Davis' son-in-law L.S. Burkhead, filled in until the arrival in 1855 of the Rev. Adolphus Williamson Mangum, later a university professor. The congregation reached 148 whites and 40 blacks before the Civil War, but membership declined during the war before rebounding to 216 whites and 58 blacks by 1869, when most of the black members joined the Negro Methodists, who had withdrawn from the Methodist Evangelical Church, South.

The withdrawal of the Methodists from the Union Church set off a chain reaction. Rev. William Mercer Green, the rector of St. Matthew's Church in Hillsborough from 1822 to 1837, moved into the old Caldwell house in 1838 after signing on to teach rhetoric at the university. He purchased that part of the old Benjamin Yeargin plantation in and around Tenny Circle, he became the leader of the few Episcopalians in the community, and he organized a congregation that was admitted into the Episcopal Union on 20 May 1842.

During his sermons in the university chapel, Green incurred the wrath of Elisha Mitchell, who believed his Episcopalian colleague had introduced sectarianism by reading the Lord's Prayer. Mitchell also objected to Green's role in building the Episcopal church, and he attacked him publicly for administering Holy Communion to a sick young girl. At the time, Mitchell was overseer of roads in the area, and he insisted that Green replace him. Then when Green began work redirecting the Raleigh Road, Mitchell charged him with gross incompetence. The discord between the two men grew so pronounced that Bishop Levi S. Ives rose to defend Green at the 1843 Episcopalian Convention and, by inference, denounced Mitchell as a "pious fraud."

Green provided slaves, horses and equipment, lumber, bricks from his own kilns, and his own inexhaustible labor in an effort to complete the church as soon as possible. He was so sincere in his piety that he once allowed a kiln-load of damp bricks to ruin before he would add fuel on a Sunday. By May 1844 the chapel was three-fourths complete, but money ran out and work stopped. Green anonymously loaned money to continue construction, but even then progress remained slow for the next four years. The Episcopalian Union assigned the Rev. Aaron F. Olmstead to Chapel Hill in January 1848, Green and his helpers completed the church a few months later, and Bishop Ives consecrated the Chapel of the Cross on 19 October 1848.

William Mercer Green (1798-1887) of Wilmington, an 1818 UNC graduate, became Chancellor of the University of the South and served as the Episcopal Bishop of Mississippi after he left Chapel Hill. He engaged in a long-running dispute with Elisha Mitchell; Green had probably developed a strong distaste for Mitchell even before the two men met because of Green's earlier friendship with Bishop John Stark Ravenscroft, who had a serious disagreement with Mitchell in 1825. Charles Force Deems, the Methodist minister who began teaching logic in place of Green in 1842, wrote that he had replaced the logic textbook because Green's choice was "a most absurd and contemptible little treatise." (NCC)

Green had become so exasperated with Mitchell that he was preparing to resign from the university and retire to a life of farming when he received word that he had been named Bishop of Mississippi. He gladly left Chapel Hill, but he left a legacy in the Episcopalian community yet to be exceeded. The Rev. Thomas F. Davis replaced him as rector in 1849, to be followed in 1851 by professor of Latin F.M. Hubbard, D.D., and in 1853 by professor of rhetoric and logic John Thomas Wheat, D.D., both of whom served later terms as rector.

In the late 1840s, the trustees built a new president's house where the current president's house stands on Franklin Street. After Swain moved into the new house, Professor Wheat and his family occupied the old Tom Taylor house from 1849 to 1859. In the late 1850s, Mr. and Mrs. Henry Thompson lived diagonally across Franklin Street from the Wheats. The attractive Mrs. Thompson had been born Cornelia Graves. In 1834 she had married Alexander Morrow, and she was the mother of several children when Morrow died in the early 1850s. She then married Henry Thompson, a widower with a son also named Henry Thompson. In 1857, Mrs. Thompson's daughter Salina Morrow married the younger Henry Thompson.

In a 1931 reminiscence, Charles Phillips' oldest daughter Mrs. Mary Phillips Verner recalled that as a young girl she had heard her parents and neighbors whispering of a romantic scandal involving Professor Wheat and Mrs. Henry Thompson. Professor Wheat moved to Little Rock, Arkansas, in 1859 to become rector of Christ Church and to serve as a chaplain in the Civil War. He lost two sons in the war, Mrs. Thompson lost three. Lucy Phillips Russell remembered that even into the 1870s Mrs. Thompson was "a dainty, dressy old lady ... using rouge freely at a time when that cosmetic was held to be the badge of the demimonde, with her hair in flat curls on each side of her face and lace mitts on her slender hands."

The Presbyterians had dominated the faculty from its early years, and by consequence they commanded respect within the village. James Phillips, his son Charles, Elisha Mitchell, and David Swain were the leaders in organizing a Chapel Hill congregation of less than a dozen on 8 June 1845. Charles Phillips drew the plans and James Phillips oversaw the construction of a simple, rectangular, columned church topped by a square belfry.

Following a procedure diametrically opposite to William Mercer Green's, James Phillips would not begin work until a total of 142 donors, most from outside Chapel Hill, had honored $3644 in pledges and until Charles Phillips and Governor Swain had purchased the Union Church lot from the university for $200. Governor Swain gave $450, Elisha Mitchell $300, James and Charles Phillips $300 each. The Union Church was moved backward for use as a village schoolhouse. The Rev. John A. Gretter of Greensboro formally dedicated the church on 23 September 1849, assisted by Dr. Drury Lacy of Raleigh, who had come to Chapel Hill to preach to the Methodists the night before.

Charles Phillips had designed the church with utility, not comfort, uppermost in mind. There were no facilities to provide heat, a deficiency which encouraged the cold-natured to bring their own dutch ovens during the winter. The ladies of the Presbyterian Sewing Society made cushions for some of the plain wooden pews, but they removed them when more ascetic members complained that such luxuries led to indolence and laxity during sermons. Likewise, those who petitioned for heat as early as 1854 gave way to majority opinion.

The small congregation could not afford a salaried preacher, but James Phillips and others willingly volunteered to lead services. The Presbyterian Church had 12 members in 1851, 17 in 1852, and it accepted its first black members on 21 October 1855 when "Aggie, a slave of James Watson, and her husband, Martin, slave of Mrs. Freeland, were received into the church on certificate from New Hope Church." The black membership grew to include the slaves "Uncle Ben" Craig., Jenny Anderson, and Lucy Rainey and the free Negro women Caroline Bennett and Sallie Brooks. No congregation in Chapel Hill has struggled more over matters of conscience than the Presbyterian, and the primary concern that ultimately led to a difficult schism in the 1950s had a parallel antecedent a century earlier.

The Rev. Daniel Baker, president of Austin College in Texas, came to Chapel Hill in 1856 and delivered a spirited series of daily sermons to the Presbyterians. His enthusiasm spurred the congregation into a long search for a permanent minister that ended on 3 November 1858 with the unanimous election of the Rev. John B. Shearer. Shearer owned slaves and brought them with him, and that was the rub. Benjamin S. Hedrick and his wife Ellen left the church to signal their disapproval of Shearer's

Merritt's Mill was built by Rev. William Henry Merritt. After his death in 1850, his son-in-law Rev. G.W. Purefoy ran it until he died in 1880. The old mill was finally closed about the turn of the century and, along with King's Mill, was washed away when Morgan's Creek flooded in early August 1923. The mill was located near the intersection of present-day Pittsboro Road and the Route 54 by-pass. This photograph was made in the late 19th century. The people are unidentified. (NCC)

owning slaves and of the church's condoning slavery. White membership rose to 37 in 1862, but black membership fell to three, and Shearer left on 6 June of that year when the small congregation could no longer pay him an adequate salary. Afterward he was president of Davidson College.

The Rev. William Henry Merritt, the Rev. George Washington Purefoy, and William Barbee led the Baptists in establishing an "arm" of the Mount Carmel Church in Chapel Hill proper. William Merritt was the son of a Chatham County Methodist-Episcopal preacher. In 1803 he married Old Kit Barbee's daughter Susanna, and they moved into a new house where the Pittsboro road then crossed Morgan Creek. Merritt began to acquire what eventually amounted to thousands of acres, and after several years of farming he built a modern mill near his house that immediately became known as the best in the region. Steel purchases from Tom Taylor in 1815-1816 and the payment of $400 to Bryant Kittrell in 1817 for land flooded by the dam indicate that Merritt built the mill in that period.

In recognition of Merritt's deep religious convictions, in 1823 the elders of Mount Carmel Church ordained him a Baptist minister. From then until his death, he and his brother-in-law William Barbee helped form a half-dozen Baptist congregations in Chatham County, and they were laying plans for a congregation in Chapel Hill when Merritt died in 1850.

He left land to Wake Forest College which trustees sold for over $2000, and then lost by investing it in Confederate bonds. Several of Merritt's children died before him, including a son Pleasant Henderson Merritt. Of those who survived him, William Henry Merritt, Jr. was so mentally unstable that the Rev. Merritt provided in his will for George Wynn to manage William Jr.'s estate, which included the Merritt homeplace on Morgan Creek. William, Jr.'s son James "Jimmie" Yancy Merritt later served with Robert E. Lee's Army of Northern Virginia in the great battles of the northern front, returning after the war to continue the Merritt line in Chapel Hill. Rev. Merritt's daughter Lucy had married Baptist preacher George Washington Purefoy.

Born in 1809 to a French Huguenot family, G.W. Purefoy settled on a farm a mile south of the village after his marriage and became a major influence in the religious life of Chapel Hill. He preached at Mount Carmel and other Baptist churches, and he engaged in a long-running theological duel with neighborhood ministers of opposing faiths, most notably Methodist preacher Orin Scoville. Debating such questions as whether Judas had ever been a Christian, the ministers flayed each other mercilessly in sermons and pamphlets, often equating their opponents with the anti-Christ and calling down the most dreadful divine punishment on their antagonists. Kemp Battle

This 1925 photograph depicts a birthday party for James Yancy Merritt (1846-1926), grandson of Rev. William H. Merritt, at the family home about one mile south of Chapel Hill on the Mt. Carmel Church Road. Rev. Merritt built the house soon after 1803 for himself and his bride, Susanna Barbee. The building in the background was the detached kitchen; out of the photograph on the right was the smoke house.
Rev. Merritt died a wealthy man and his will specified that all his bacon be sold; the executor, son-in-law Rev. G.W. Purefoy, weighed the bacon and discovered that it amounted to 10,000 pounds. (Photo courtesy of Mrs. Ruby Merritt).

Rev. George Washington Purefoy (1808-1880) was a controversial preacher in the Chapel Hill area. In one notable 1852 encounter, new Wake Forest graduate and minister Orin Scoville noted that Purefoy's "propensity to meddle with the affairs of others is not excelled by the Ape." Scoville went on, "But for him, the people of God in all our section would enjoy uninterrupted peace." Reverend Purefoy withdrew from the quarrel in this manner: "With such an opprobrious and scurrilous writer, as Mr. S. has shown himself to be, we decline all further controversy." (NCC)

credited Purefoy for being largely responsible for introducing into Chapel Hill "the ghastly doctrine" that the unbaptized would go to hell.

But in spite of his harsh religious beliefs, Purefoy was a respected member of the community, numbering among his close friends business leaders John Wesley Carr and Dave McCauley. After Lucy inherited her father's mill, her husband operated it successfully as Purefoy's Mill, demonstrating his affection for his father-in-law by burying him in the Purefoy family graveyard, located near Watts Hotel on US 15-501 south.

Before Rev. Merritt died, the Baptists in town recognized the need to build a local church, both as a convenience to themselves and as an accommodation to the Baptist university students who might otherwise be tempted to attend churches of other faiths. G.W. Purefoy, William Barbee, Brantley J. Hackney, and traveling missionary John J.

The first Baptist church in Chapel Hill is pictured here about 1890. The congregation hired Norvell W. Wilson (1834-1878) of Halifax, Virginia, as its first paid pastor. He arrived in January, 1862, with his pregnant wife, and they moved into a room in the home of Jesse Hargrave's widow Margaret. In his first year, Norvell earned his pay: he preached 181 times, gave 11 "expositions of scripture," attended 35 Sunday schools, held 32 prayer meetings, presided at 16 conferences, made 154 pastoral visits, held 14 singing sessions, and presided at a number of births, deaths, marriages, and baptisms. In 1866, Wilson left for New Orleans and more money; he died there of yellow fever.

Norvell's brother, Eugene H. (1837-1905), came to Chapel Hill in 1865 after his service under Stonewall Jackson, and he married Rev. G.W. Purefoy's daughter Emily (1845-1941). Eugene stayed in Chapel Hill until his death, serving as singing master at the Baptist church and giving private lessons; his wife was a music teacher also. (NCC)

James were instrumental in organizing a congregation which met for the first time on 14 August 1854 in the home of W.G. Weaver, where James P. Mason signed on as the first member. Deacon John R. Hutchins built a temporary meeting room; the Rev. Purefoy delivered the first formal sermon on 26 August and completed the inaugural services by baptizing five of William Barbee's slaves at Purefoy's Mill; and the congregation separated from Mount Carmel on 15 September 1954. There were 38 members, divided equally by sex, 28 whites and 10 Negroes.

The Rev. Merritt left the Baptists a church site at the northwest corner of Franklin and Church streets, $300 in cash, and additional land to be sold, the proceeds to be applied to the building fund. Judge William Horn Battle's wife Mary had Dr. Francis Wayland of Brown University draw plans. She, Rev. Hackney, and former Governor William A. Graham's wife Susan led a drive to add to the $1200 realized from Rev. Merritt's bequests. G.W. Purefoy and William Barbee gave $100 each; church clerk P.H. McDade recorded donations of $1 to $200 from as far away as Smithfield, Raleigh, Fayetteville, and Richmond. Work

progressed rapidly on the two-story, 60' by 35' structure fronted by a 45'-high bell-tower.

Members then began collecting money toward the purchase of a $210.10 bell. When they had raised $140, merchant William Morgan donated the remainder so that the bell would be in place for the 6 May 1855 dedication conducted by Rev. J.J. James. When completed at a total cost of $3425, the unpartitioned church had a seating capacity of 250, sufficient to serve the Baptists of Chapel Hill for three-quarters of a century.

In 1857, G.W. Purefoy built a schoolhouse beside the church. Jonathan Lafayette Steward of Monroe County, Mississippi, who received an A.B. from the university in 1857, was the first teacher; Miss Jennie Fuller taught there for several years; and the church added a residence to the schoolhouse when she married John Blackwood. Dr. William B. Harrell, author of *Ho for Carolina*, and Locke Craig, future governor of North Carolina, were teachers before the entire building was converted to a parsonage in the 1880s.

From the beginning the Chapel Hill Baptists required

strict adherence to church rules. In February 1855, elders expelled a white member for adultery. Later in that year a black member sought forgiveness by confessing to the same offense, but the elders dismissed him anyway "for the purity and honor of the cause and church," later reinstating him. Members could miss a limited number of Sunday services for a fine of 6 ¼ cents per service, but any who missed roll-call two consecutive Sundays had to "appear and answer for his delinquency." For the remainder of the 19th century, members were expelled routinely for moral turpitude, poor attendance, visiting other churches, and -- on at least one occasion -- for distilling and selling liquor.

Levi Thorne signed on as preacher in February 1857 for $800 per year, but subscribers were slow in fulfilling pledges, and Thorne resigned in December, refusing to preach until his salary was paid in full in advance. Elders assessed all 154 members in January 1858, and Thorne returned, only to leave again in arrears. Various pastors shared the preaching duties, G.W. Purefoy whenever his health allowed, and in spite of the lack of a permanent minister membership increased rapidly by Chapel Hill standards, topping 200 in 1860.

In areas other than the religious, Elisha Mitchell continued to maintain a prominent presence in the village long after the trustees passed him over for the presidency, although as the university bursar there were times when he questioned if the extra income were worth the burden.

He was equally perplexed in dealing with the women who ran boarding houses or provided laundry and other services for the students: "I should do better if I had to do with men—knowing what the rules and properties of business are, but the Petticoat has the ascendancy at the Hill. My principal customers are women, some 15 in number—married women, widow and maid—to say nothing of those that are neither—and such a time as I have!"

However, Mitchell was not a humorless man. He enjoyed leading students on treks around the area studying geological formations and the flora and fauna, and the students enjoyed his instruction and his ability to take and to return jokes. Mitchell's colleagues believed he had too many interests to excel at any, but he had written profusely on a variety of scientific subjects in his 39-year tenure, and by the time of his death he was certainly the most respected geologist in North Carolina. A challenge to one of his assertions, however, led directly to his death in the summer of 1857.

After questioning Mitchell's figures showing a peak in the Black Mountain range to be the highest in the state, State Senator Thomas L. Clingman produced findings supposedly taken from a higher point. Mitchell returned to the mountains to take new readings and on 27 June set off alone to climb the mountain now named in his honor. When he had not returned after several days, friends organized a massive search, which ended on 8 July with the discovery of his body in a pool beneath a 40-foot cliff on the Cattail fork of the Caney River.

He was buried temporarily in Asheville, and on 16 June 1858 Bishop James Hervey Otey preached the funeral oration when the body was placed in a mausoleum atop Mount Mitchell. The trustees voted to give his widow his salary for the remainder of 1857, free rent for six months, and $4500 for his books and scientific apparatus. They also belatedly paid him for the construction of rock walls on campus by giving her a two-acre home site on Cameron Avenue.

Other faculty members and villagers in the ante-bellum decades left marks on Chapel Hill and the state. John DeBerniere Hooper remained first as a tutor and later as a professor of Latin after his graduation in 1831. He was the son of Archibald M. Hooper of Wilmington, the great-nephew of William Hooper "The Signer" and Edward Jones of Rock Rest, and the brother of the humorist Johnston J. Hooper who gained fame with his Simon Suggs stories. In Chapel Hill he met and married his second cousin Mary Hooper, the daughter of professor William Hooper. He left in 1848 to run a series of private schools for almost thirty years, returning to the university in 1875 to teach until his death in 1886.

In 1838 Manuel Fetter, a native of Lancaster, Pennsylvania, brought his bride to Chapel Hill when he contracted to teach Greek. He lived happily in the village, raising a popular family, until the ruinous years of Reconstruction.

In 1857 Catawba College President Hildreth Hosea Smith arrived as the first professor of modern languages. Originally from New Hampshire, Smith had married a North Carolinian, Mary B. Hoke, daughter of an unsuccessful Democratic candidate for governor in 1844 and sister of Civil War General Robert F. Hoke. In spite of his marriage to a southern belle, the students remained suspicious of "Old Tige's" sectional loyalty, especially

William Horn Battle (1802-1879), a Chapel Hillian, played a key role in a unique case when he served as a justice of the North Carolina Supreme Court. Willis Hester, who lived near Chapel Hill, stole slaves and resold them for a living. He was caught, tried, and sentenced to hang for stealing "Dick," a slave who belonged to John U. Kirkland, a county official. Relying on an opinion written by Judge Battle, the North Carolina Supreme Court rejected Hester's appeal and the thief was hanged at Pittsboro 5 May 1855, thus becoming the only North Carolinian ever to suffer capital punishment for stealing slaves. (NCC)

when he remained on duty after hostilities began, living comfortably in the Horace Williams House which he had purchased from its builder Benjamin S. Hedrick. Smith also ran a preparatory school, numbering among his students his son Hoke, who was later owner of the Atlanta *Journal*, Secretary of the Interior in 1893-1896, twice governor of Georgia, and a powerful U.S. Senator from Georgia.

Even the trustworthy doctors who served the village in the ante-bellum period rivaled their maverick colleague Bullet Yancy for singularity. Dr. Johnston Blakeley Jones was the son of Solicitor-General Edward Jones and the former Mary E. Mallett of Fayetteville, daugher of physician Peter Mallett.

Named in honor of the naval hero, Johnston Blakeley Jones developed an intense love for literature during his studies at the Episcopal Classical School for Boys in Raleigh and at the university, from which he did not graduate. He entered medical college in Charleston, S.C., studied two years in Paris, where he was known as "the handsome American," and returned to Charleston to graduate. In 1841 he married Mary Ann Stuart of Halifax County, began a practice in Chapel Hill, and over the years with his partner Dr. George Moore trained several university students in a small frame building on Franklin Street that may have been Dr. Walter Norwood's old "medicine shop." Their students visited the slave graveyards occasionally when they needed corpses for dissection.

Although he and Mary Ann were charter members of the Episcopal congregation, Dr. Jones swiftly earned a reputation as a mild eccentric. He would deliberately avoid patients if they interfered with his study of the classics, particularly *Don Quixote*. He did not, however, care for Lord Byron, whom he considered immoral in practice and in poetry. That dislike carried its misfortune for Dr. Jones, who closely resembled the great romantic but who disliked hearing mention of the resemblance, which was frequent. Dr. Jones prospered both as a physician and as a farmer, investing his entire fortune in slaves and a Lenoir County plantation. However, the war devastated him. He lost his son Edward in the Battle of the Wilderness, and emancipation coupled with the destruction of the southern economy bankrupted him.

Dr. Jones' partner Dr. George Moore was descended from South Carolina Governor James Moore and Sir John Yeamans, the first governor of the Colony of Clarenden on the Cape Fear River. His grandfather George Moore had 27 or 28 children by two wives, the first of whom was Mary Ashe, the sister of North Carolina Governor (1795-1798) Samuel Ashe and the mother of Dr. George Moore's father James. James Moore married Margaret Lloyd, the daughter of a British Army surgeon who migrated from Massachusetts to Wilmington. James Moore lost every-

thing by going bond for a member of the Ashe family, and when he died about 1880 he left a destitute wife and five children: Anna, George, Lloyd, Mary "Polly," and Rebecca. Poverty forced the widow Moore and her children to live with relatives and prevented the children from receiving formal educations.

About 1814, Anna Moore married her cousin Richard Davis Ashe, a wealthy grandson of Governor Samuel Ashe and the owner of a plantation on Cane Creek in Orange County. By June 1821, Anna had given birth to four children, each of whom died in infancy. In June 1821, Richard died of a fever, and five months later, Anna gave birth to a posthumous son, Richard James Ashe. She moved to Hillsborough, where she lived until Richard reached the age to enter UNC. She then purchased Pleasant Henderson's old home in Chapel Hill from Pleasant's son Dr. Alexander Martin Henderson.

Her brother George had remained in Wilmington as a rice planter and had then joined an unsuccessful venture to raise sugar crops in Louisiana. He too married a cousin, Polly Moore, several years his elder. George and Polly also moved to Chapel Hill so their sons could attend the university, and apparently they and George's brother Lloyd were living in the Henderson house when Anna Ashe bought it. After Richard graduated in 1842, Anna returned to Hillsborough. The Moores remained in residence, with Polly earning money by running a boarding house while her husband, then in his 40s, read medicine under Dr. Johnston Blakeley Jones. Dr. George Moore went to Philadelphia briefly, probably to further his education, then returned to join Dr. Jones as a partner in practicing medicine and in teaching medicine to university students.

Dr. Moore's was not a contented life. He and his older wife did not get along well; his bachelor brother Lloyd, described by a relative as "a fanatic in politics and religion" who "had little manners and no conversation," died about 1850; and Dr. Moore was a deeply pious but frustrated Christian who refused to join an organized church and who openly questioned the literal interpretation of the Bible. On his death bed in 1857, he asked his nurse Sally Williams, "Miss Sally, do you think that a man will go to hell for not believing all that is in the Bible." Hopefully Miss Williams did not learn her bedside manner from her employer, because she answered in the affirmative. Dr. Moore's response were his dying words: "Well, I don't, I can't. I have never to my knowledge lied or cheated. I have been charitable to the extent of my means. I never was a coward. I have paid my debts as far as I possibly could. Now if they send me to hell, I will go a grumbling."

If "Bullet" Yancy was a bit too elevated in society to qualify as the town drunk, then that distinction certainly fell to another on the fringe of the medical profession.

Leroy Couch lived just east of the village limits on Franklin Street in a section that became known as "Couchtown" when others built nearby. Couch earned his meager income as a nurse, often caring for students confined to The Retreat, a small building behind the Tom Taylor house which was used as the campus infirmary. Even though he was habitually inebriated, as a nurse he was gentle, trustworthy, and careful to follow doctors' orders.

A notice in the 12 May 1875 Hillsborough *Recorder* inserted by "Dr. Lee Couch" stated that he had "watched by the bedside of sick students through the long hours of many weary nights at Chapel Hill." Now he was "old and in want," and he begged assistance. However, in response to a rising tide of complaints caused by his chronic drunkenness, in 1876 the village commissioners paid Arley Andrews $4 to carry "Old Couch" to the county poor house, where he died.

The doctors of Chapel Hill were well assisted by druggists and drugstores. In the 1830s and 1840s, James B. McDade dispensed medicine. Jones Watson and Company were in the business in the late 1840s, and in 1851 J.S. Lucas, an in-law of Sam Phillips, was advertising several brands of patent medicine and sarsaparilla by the quart at his "place" on Franklin Street. In the spring of 1855, "Dr." Lucas sold his stock to R.B. Saunders, who announced he was ready to fill "prescriptions compounded at all hours of day or night."

Saunders' specialty was "Blue Mass," a purgative which he produced in the basement of his drugstore on the northeast corner of Franklin and Henderson streets. Village children, including Sophia and Eliza Mallett, earned change by collecting the rose petals which Saunders ground and mixed with metallic mercury to produce "Blue Mass." He joined the Confederate States Army in 1861, but when the Civil War cut sharply into the importation of medical supplies from the North, authorities released him so he could return to Chapel Hill to make his purgative both for civilians and the military.

Saunders was back in business by October 1862 and

Richard Benbury Saunders (1834-1890) graduated from UNC in 1854 and in April 1855 bought out the J.S. Lucas drugstore. The following April he was instrumental in effecting an agreement among town merchants whereby no credit would be issued to students without written permission from their parents. Saunders was joined by two other young merchants, partners Thomas Long and David McCauley who had recently taken over the Jesse Hargrave store, and by older merchants J.W. Carr and J.R. Hutchins, among others. Saunders moved to Durham in 1868. (NCC)

asserting in advertisements, "The Blue Mass now made by me is warranted to be one-third MERCURY and equal to any made in England, and much superior to most of that now brought into the Confederacy from the United States (as nearly all of that is deficient in Mercury)." He cited assurances by State Geologist Ebenezer Emmons that his product was at least 33% mercury, he included a letter from North Carolina Surgeon General Dr. Edmond Warren testifying to its quality, and he promised "orders for any quantity can be filled, and it can be sent by Express to almost any place in the Confederacy."

Saunders carried a wide line of products other than medical supplies, including general merchandise, veterinarian supplies and at one time 11,000 cigars. Responding to a demand created by the severe shortage of manufactured cloth during the war years, in April 1864 he and the Rev. G.W. Purefoy obtained exclusive regional rights "to make, use and sell *Kendall's* family Hand or Power Looms."

After James Knox Polk's inauguration as president in March 1845, the trustees voted to grant him and John Young Mason, his new Secretary of the Navy and a UNC graduate of 1816, honorary LL. D. degrees, which were given *in absentia* in June. Two years later, Polk accepted an invitation from Governor Swain to attend the commencement of 1847.

President Polk left a detailed account of his visit in his diary. Accompanied by Mrs. Polk, her niece, Secretary Mason, and a host of others, Polk left Raleigh at 9 a.m. on Monday 31 May, stopped for lunch at Morings Tavern, and reached Chapel Hill about 5 p.m. A large crowd greeted him outside the village and conducted him to a new apartment which proprietor Nancy Hilliard had built onto the Eagle Hotel (formerly the Alsobrook/Watts Hotel) especially for the occasion. Governor Swain extended an official welcome, Polk and Mason addressed the crowd, and Swain performed the necessary introductions. Polk ended his long day with a visit to the Chapel of the Cross to hear a sermon by Bishop Levi S. Ives.

On Tuesday and Wednesday, the President toured the campus, visited the room he had occupied as a student in the southwest corner of the third floor of the South Building, and attended the scheduled events. On Thursday, commencement day, hundreds of additional visitors crowded the village and the campus, seemingly all eager to shake the President's hand before the 10:30 a.m. exercises. An uninformed observer would have hardly suspected that in the presidential election seven months earlier Chapel Hill and area residents had voted 210 to 118 in favor of Polk's Whig opponent, Henry Clay.

During the lunch break, Polk returned to the Eagle Hotel for lunch, and an expectant crowd again gathered in McCorkle Place. He shook hands and spoke to several hundred well-wishers after he had eaten, and then all who could enter once again filled Gerrard Hall, this time to see 37 seniors receive diplomas and to hear James Johnston Pettigrew of Tyrrell County deliver the valedictory. President Polk was so taken with Pettigrew that he offered the 19-year-old a position at the Naval Observatory.

Pettigrew accepted and spent two years in Washington before turning to the study of law, setting up a practice in Charleston, and serving in the South Carolina legislature. In 1859 he was on his way to join Sardinia in her war with Austria when fighting ended. He was not long disappointed in his search for a noble cause. In April 1861, he joined the 1st Charleston Rifles and soon afterward became colonel of a North Carolina regiment. He refused to accept promotion to brigadier-general until he had proven himself in battle, which he did dramatically on 1 June 1862 by leading a charge in the battle of Seven Pines. Rendered unconscious by a wound and captured, he remained an invalid prisoner for two months. Then the Yankees agreed to exchange him, assuming he would never fight again.

But by the fall of 1862 Pettigrew had returned to active service in command of a brigade battling federal raiders in eastern North Carolina. In the spring of 1863 he defended Richmond during General George Stoneman's raid into northern Virginia, and in the summer he joined General Henry Heth's division and followed Lee to Gettysburg. Leading his brigade in a murderous charge against General John Buford's division on 1 July, he played a leading role in establishing the field of battle for the two fateful days to follow, becoming division commander when Heth received incapacitating wounds.

On 3 July, Pettigrew achieved immortality by riding to the left of General George Edward Pickett in the famous charge that momentarily gave the Rebels control of Cemetery Ridge, but at a grievous price in dead and wounded. Pettigrew was among those seriously wounded. Nevertheless, he commanded a rear guard contingent in the agonizing retreat back into Northern Virginia. On the morning of 14 July, he and his men were attacked by a cavalry raiding party, and Pettigrew received a second wound, this one mortal. He died three days later near Winchester, Virginia.

From the beginning of his tenure until the dark, depressed days of the Civil War, Governor Swain struggled with the meager means available to improve the appearance of the campus. While designing Smith Hall in 1848, architect Alexander Jackson Davis also drew plans to landscape the grounds, and Swain engaged gardeners to carry them out. A 26-year-old Englishman, John Loder (also spelled Loader), had letters of recommendation from the Duke of Northumberland, but it was his willingness to work for only $400 per year that got him the job.

Loder and his wife Jane probably moved in with William and Mary Watson, who lived on the current Peabody Hall

In addition to his job as university gardener, Thomas Paxton earned extra money by operating Chapel Hill's only nursery. Roses were ubiquitous in the village, and young Sophie and Eliza Mallett found it easy to collect rose petals for young and handsome druggist R.B. Saunders, who used them in making his "Blue Mass."

lot. After the birth of his son Charles in 1848 and his daughter Mary Ann in 1850, Loder could no longer afford to work for so little and gave his notice. In 1847 Robert Loder of England had married William and Mary Watson's daughter Frances and moved in with her family. John Loder was probably the older brother of Robert Loder, who joined William Watson in running a dry-goods store near Franklin and Columbia.

John Loder was followed as campus gardener in late 1851 by another Englishman, Thomas Paxton, a relative of the master gardener-architect Sir Joseph Paxton, who had been knighted that year by Prince Albert for having designed the Crystal Palace. Thomas Paxton moved in with William and Mary Watson, and he raised a few eyebrows among the local gentry on 30 June 1852 when he married the Watson's 15-year-old handmaid Mary Ann Johnston. Paxton had to make do with an annual budget of $1000 which covered his own $500 salary and costs for Negro laborers, draft animals, plants and shrubberies, and the maintenance of a nursery. Under his guidance, young Wilson Swain (later Caldwell) and other black workmen became expert gardeners.

Swain was also responsible for the first stone walls in Chapel Hill, built by slaves following a prototype section put up by Elisha Mitchell from his memory of rock walls in his native Connecticut. As a direct result of their ancestors' work on the walls, even today Chapel Hill blacks monopolize stonework on campus, as they monopolized bricklaying in the village until the mid-20th century.

Even though the General Assembly provided for public schools in 1839, local systems were contingent upon referenda, and the quality of early education remained in general a matter of private concern. The children of Chapel Hill were fortunate enough to live in a society which valued education. James and Julia Phillips closed their academy after their children passed school age, but they continued to take in a few students. Elisha Mitchell also tutored a few young scholars, the Baptists operated their school after 1855, and during the war Cornelia

By the 1850s Chapel Hill had several private schools, including the two represented by these advertisements that appeared in the Chapel Hill Literary Gazette in 1857. J.L. Steward (1835-1923) was from Centreville, Mississippi. He lived in the home of Dr. Hudson and Delia Cave while he was a student at the university, graduating in 1857. He later became a lawyer, then a Baptist minister, and then he moved to Clinton where he founded the Clinton Female College. He was a trustee of UNC 1881-1897.

Henry C. Thompson (1835-1901) was a Chapel Hill native who also graduated in 1857. A few years later he began a lifetime career in the U.S. Treasury Department. (NCC)

Spencer taught several children from the neighborhood and from families who had fled the eastern counties seeking refuge in Chapel Hill.

There were always plenty of recent graduates willing to teach private students in the village while they searched for permanent positions. William Hooper's son William, prior to becoming a physician, taught preparatory courses in English in 1841. When Kemp Battle arrived in 1843, his first teacher was Richard Don Wilson, studying for the law under Judge Battle. Wilson served in the Confederate Army and later committed suicide.

Battle's next teacher was Ashbel Green Brown, whose performance was inhibited by his chronic melancholy, which approached insanity. When he once severely chastised young Jim Jennings, the boy's mother Mrs. Sidney Jennings—a husky widow weighing 200 pounds—angrily confronted Brown and forced him to look at her son's injuries. Brown apologized to his formidable antagonist, "Madam, I never whipped any one before, and I did not understand the effects. I punished more severely than I intended and I am sorry for it." The widow accepted the apology, but her son did not return to Brown's classes. During the Civil War, Jim Jennings contracted yellow fever and died on his way home from Wilmington.

The General Assembly on 29 January 1851 ratified the "Charter of the Town of Chapel Hill, N.C. — An Act for the better regulation of Chapel Hill." Covering slightly more than two narrow pages, the charter named Manuel Fetter, Jesse Hargrave, Patterson H. McDade, Elisha Mitchell, and Jones Watson to the first board of commissioners and granted the board "all the powers and privileges necessary for the proper government of said village." Citizens elected five commissioners annually, and after each election the commissioners chose a treasurer, a constable, a clerk, and a magistrate of police who presided over board meetings with the right to vote in case of ties.

The charter authorized the commissioners to establish town boundaries, to assess taxes on persons and property, excluding students and trustees, and to apply public funds "to the construction, improvement and repair of the streets, and to such other purposes, as they may deem conducive to the prosperity of the village." The commissioners were also responsible for the adoption of "proper ordinances," for the suppression of "nuisances," for the regulation of shopkeepers, and for the "exclusion of itinerant vendors of spiritous liquors" and other contraband. Those citizens who owned a lot valued at $500 or more and who had lived in town for a minimum of six months could vote. The commissioners set boundaries enclosing a rectangle 2622 yards long from Boundary Street to Merritt Mill Road, and 1549 yards wide from North Street to Kenan Stadium.

Constables in ante-bellum Chapel Hill had little crime to contend with beyond the usual peccadilloes of rambunctious students, although there was some. In March 1853, a mail stage on the Chapel Hill route was robbed. Envelopes and other items from the stage were later found in New Hope Creek, but the outlaws escaped detection. In April 1853 with a single blow from a set of tongs, a slave belonging to Jesse Hargrave killed a slave belonging to John Berry of Hillsborough.

Just before the Civil War, a slave belonging to Jones Morgan named Asgill was hanged for killing another slave. Students made a holiday of escorting the body back to Chapel Hill, and some medical students sent the head in a bag late one evening to John B. Tenney's teenaged son, Abdel Kader, who worked as the night clerk in a drugstore. Their slave messenger told the boy it was a watermelon. Probably the most sensational crime of the 1850s occurred in March 1854 when Joseph Brockwell cut the throat of James Davis during a drunken brawl. Attorneys Sam Phillips, J.W. Norwood, and Josiah Turner, Jr. represented Brockwell and succeeded in getting a change of venue to Chatham County, but to no avail. Hugh Waddell of Chapel Hill prosecuted and won a conviction for manslaughter. The presiding judge sentenced Brockwell to branding and a six-month jail term.

Each summer there were three great gatherings in Chapel Hill: commencement, the Fourth of July, and tax-collection day. Commencement and the Fourth were occa-

The average price of a slave on the Chapel Hill market in the 1840s and 1850s was $750. This ad appeared in the Literary Gazette of January 1858. Walter A. Thompson was a Chapel Hill butcher and the grandson of William and Elizabeth Nunn, who had operated Chapel Hill's first tavern and rooming house. Andrew Mickle was a merchant, postmaster, and UNC bursar. John R. Hutchins was a village merchant. (NCC)

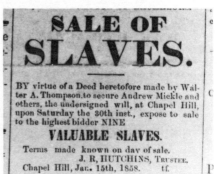

John Wesley Carr (1814-1889) was one of the most successful merchants in Chapel Hill history. Between 1835 and 1889 he ran a general store, a blacksmith shop, a cotton gin, a sawmill, a brick-making plant, and he engaged in over 100 real estate transactions. His children were uniformly successful, leading The University Magazine to eulogize him in 1890, "Mr. and Mrs. Carr certainly raised their children well, and that is a crown to both of them. It was a hard thing to do in Chapel Hill."
This photograph was made in the 1880's long after Carr's health had begun to fail in 1874. (NCC)

sions for formal pomp and ceremony, ending with spirited balls. Tax-day was the occasion for heavy eating and hard drinking by the citizens and for earnest speechification by politicians. Until the 1840s, orators harangued the public from atop a large rock at the northwest corner of Franklin and Columbia. After John W. Carr removed the rock to prepare a store site, they shouted to crowds beneath the large chestnut trees lining Franklin Street in the business district.

The more stable businessmen of the ante-bellum period were John Wesley Carr, Jesse Hargrave, Richard B. Saunders, partners George M. Long and Benjamin McCauley, J.R. Thompson, F.A. Davies, H.L. Owen, William Watson, John Loder, and Andrew Mickle.

John Wesley Carr of the New Hope community moved to Chapel Hill in 1834 to work for merchant Nathaniel J. King. Soon after his arrival, he purchased a substantial quantity of household goods, undoubtedly to furnish a house on the farm he acquired from original-settler Matthew McCauley's youngest son Matthew, who was experiencing financial difficulties that would lead to his bankrupcy in October 1842. Carr became King's partner in 1836, and after King fled to Tennessee to avoid his debts, Carr had a succession of partners, including Jones Watson, W.M. Davis, and Capt. J.F. Freeland.

On Christmas Day 1839, the Rev. William Mercer Green officiated at the marriage of Carr to Elizabeth Bullock. Elizabeth had come to Chapel Hill with her widowed mother Martha in 1837. Martha had purchased Mrs. Sarah Mitchell's former residence near the Carolina Coffee Shop from the Mitchell estate. In the spring of 1841, John and Elizabeth moved in with Mrs. Bullock, and in February 1843 John bought his mother-in-law's house.

In the mid-1840s, the trustees, needing money for campus construction, sold some of the residential property they had collected over the years. Gabriel Utley bought a home site on Rosemary; William Hogan purchased one on

Columbia; Sally Mallett bought the land at Cameron Avenue and Wilson Court on which she built the house that still stands; Judge Battle bought property adjoining Battle House; Andrew Mickle and a partner purchased a tract west of the Presbyterian Church; the trustees built a house for Professor Fordyce Hubbard at Cameron Avenue and Pittsboro Street; William Mercer Green paid $64.67 for the lot east of the Widow Puckett House, built a house on it, and sold it to Charles Phillips for $1200 in 1849; and John Carr paid $300 for what originally had been Lot 7 at the northwest corner of Franklin and Columbia.

Carr blasted away the large rock on the corner and built a storehouse in its place and a home to the west, approximately where He's Not Here is now located in The Village Green. In 1852, Carr joined Dr. Bartlett Durham and James Matthews in opening what is considered to have been the first bona fide store in Durham. However, after a few years, Carr once more focused attention on his extensive Orange County real-estate ventures and his commercial interests in Chapel Hill. He and Elizabeth had named their eldest son William Mercer Green in honor of the man who had married them. William died in 1860 in his third year at UNC.

The younger Matthew McCauley stayed in the area after going bankrupt, but, understandably, he was not happy. In July 1848 he wrote his nephew, attorney R.D. McCauley of Tennessee, that he was thinking of coming to Tennessee and asked if R.D. could find him "a nice girl for a wife." Noting that Matthew had failed to state whether he wanted a young or an older woman, the nephew assured him that he would certainly enjoy the welcome in Tennessee because the young girls "have the utmost confidence in us and will believe anything we tell them about you."

Sidney Mulholland Barbee, distantly related to Old Kit Barbee, and his bride the former Frances Winifred Hardee of Halifax County visited Chapel Hill on their honeymoon

Sidney Mulholland Barbee (1806-1881) eventually became one of Chapel Hill's most successful citizens, active in university affairs and serving the village as one of its leading merchants and as father of one of its most successful families. (Photograph courtesy of Mrs. W.G. Polk)

In 1846, John W. Carr bought original lot no. 7, the northeast corner of Columbia and Franklin Streets, from UNC, built a house on it, and erected a general store just east of the house.

The Carrs used the upstairs of this house to room students, housing eight or nine in some years before the Civil War in addition to raising their own large family. This photograph was made shortly after Mr. Carr died in 1889. The people in the yard are unidentified. (NCC)

in 1839. They fell in love with the village and stayed. Barbee and L.S. Tower of Pittsboro bought the old James Hogg home from Zachariah Trice, who like Benton Utley before him had failed as a storekeeper. Barbee moved into the house, ran the store, and bought out Tower in 1844. Barbee made the store profitable and used his profits to purchase additional properties that eventually gave him control of most of the north side of the business block of Franklin Street. He built an imposing residence immediately west of the post office lot and established three stores on that side of the block, two immediately west of his new house and the other a few paces from Columbia. Meanwhile, Frances was giving birth to four children, each of whom would play a leading role in the economic development of Chapel Hill in the recovery from Reconstruction. Daughter Frances Adele suffered her personal tragedy in the Civil War.

In 1859 when Frances Adele Barbee was a student at St. Mary's in Raleigh, she met Felix A. Tankersley of Alabama, a student at the university. Tankersley joined the Confederate Army while emotions were running high in the spring of 1861. He returned to Chapel Hill on leave in 1862, married Frances Adele, and returned to the war. When he visited Chapel Hill for the last time in 1864, he left a will and a pregnant wife; and after he died on 4 April 1865 Frances Adele gave birth to a son William. When her father died in 1881, Mrs. Tankersley inherited the family

John Jenkins, carpenter and cabinet maker in the 1850s, regularly ran this ad in the Literary Gazette 1857-58.

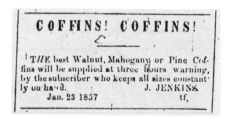

home and a significant portion of the business property on Franklin Street. She and William managed the real estate, and William ran the family business very successfully until his death in 1931. In 1927, Mrs. Tankersley left Chapel Hill to live with her granddaughter Mrs. F. Earle Rives in Greensboro, where she died on 14 October 1942 at age 100.

Benjamin McCauley, the grandson of the first William McCauley, married Cynthia Neville, the granddaughter of the first Matthew McCauley. From his farm west of the village, Benjamin hauled in produce which he and George M. Long sold in their general store on Franklin Street, but it was Benjamin's son Dave, born 20 May 1832, who would restore the family fortunes in a business career spanning over half a century that would make him the richest man in Chapel Hill long before his death in 1911.

In 1850, Dave McCauley and his close friend Thomas A. Long went to work in Jesse Hargrave's store near the present location of the Varsity Theatre. Hargrave had done well in Chapel Hill, both in business and in marriage, but he was spending more time on the 935-acre plantation off the Raleigh Road he had purchased at public auction for $4300 in 1845 when Lemuel Morgan could not pay his debts. Hargrave was quite content to turn the management of his store over to McCauley and Long, two popular young bachelors.

When Hargrave died in 1854, his widow Margaret sold the Franklin Street business to McCauley and Long. The men sunk all their savings into the venture, but business was good in Chapel Hill in the 1850s when the student body grew from 230 to over 400, and by the outbreak of the Civil War McCauley and Long were well established.

In April 1861, Private Dave McCauley left Long in charge when he enlisted for six months in Capt. R.J. Ashe's volunteers. After fighting at Big Bethel, Virginia, on 10 June, McCauley saw little additional action before returning to Chapel Hill when his enlistment expired in November. Three of his four brothers were less fortunate. James McCauley died while serving with a Texas regiment; Benjamin died in a Southern offensive at Malvern Hill in 1862; and George, a captain, received mortal wounds in the last Rebel charge at Appomatox.

Dave McCauley was best man for Thomas Long when he married Zoa White on 31 December 1861, and Long returned the honor when McCauley married Mary Elizabeth Rogers 23 days later. McCauley then ran the store during Long's military service, which ended with his health broken in a prisoner of war camp. After the war the men remained partners until McCauley bought Long out in 1872. Mary McCauley died in 1872, and the next year Dave married Mary Wheaton Barbee, the daughter of Sidney M. and Frances Barbee. Future UNC President George Tayloe Winston had been a suitor to Miss Barbee, and he gave her the Bible in which she and her descendants were to record important family events for generations.

As sole owner of one of the few businesses able to survive during Reconstruction and as husband of a woman who was heir to prime property, Dave McCauley was

David McCauley (1832-1911), pictured here at the turn of the century, was the great-grandson of brothers William and Matthew McCauley. (Courtesy Mrs. W.G. Polk)

ideally situated to buy when property prices bottomed out after the war and to sell both real estate and merchandise when the economy went into an upswing in the late 1870s.

One merchant's sacrifice on the home front reached legendary proportions. Andrew Mickle's selfless generosity during the war went far in keeping the financially strapped community going. Inflation raged after early 1862, but Mickle refused to raise the price of his stock, even though the cost of replacement greatly exceeded his list prices. He was equally generous with his time and labor. For example, in the fall of 1862 he scoured the region for the corn necessary to keep villagers and their livestock fed. He collected 1921 bushels at a cost of $1897.95 plus $677.27 for transportation by train to Durham Station and by wagon to Chapel Hill. He accepted payment only for his expenses, which amounted to $172.35. Livery-stable keeper John H. Watson purchased 50 barrels (or 383 bushels), David Swain took 33 barrels, William Battle bought 24 and so on down to those who could afford or who needed only two barrels.

Mickle also at one time owned and occupied one of the most treasured houses in Chapel Hill. Cabinet maker and contractor Isaac J. Collier bought the lot at the northwest corner of Hillsborough and Rosemary streets about 1853. He built a house there and sold it to Andrew Mickle and Richard J. Ashe in 1856, apparently for $1850. Then on 3 January 1857, Mickle and Ashe sold the house and lot to Mickle's brother-in-law John W. Norwood for $1850, and Norwood transferred the deed to Mickle alone on 14 February 1857 for the same $1850.

Mickle emerged from the Civil War deeply in debt, and on 15 May 1867 George Laws exercised his right of lien and sold both Mickle's residential and business property at public auction. Mickle's father-in-law the Rev. William Norwood, William Bingham, Robert Bingham, and John Norwood bought everything and collectively paid George Laws a total of $1784.27 "it being their purpose that said property should be settled on Helen Mickle wife of Andrew Mickle and sister of John W. Norwood." Andrew and Helen remained in the house until they left to join their son Joseph in Texas in 1882. In 1885, Joseph sold the Rosemary Street residence to Professor Adolphus W. Mangum; Mangum's heirs sold the house in 1944 to Betty Smith, who purchased it with royalties from her best seller, *A Tree Grows in Brooklyn*.

For the first third of the nineteenth century, hotel accomodations were sparse in Chapel Hill. After the death of Captain William Nunn, his widow Betsy kept their old and increasingly delapidated hotel-tavern-boarding house operating until mid-century. Mrs. Nunn died 20 December 1851 at age 91, still proud of her early patriotism, bragging she was "as good a Whig as ever hopped," and still careless "about religious matters." Noting that she was leaving her son Ilai the nine slaves he "alleges" she had given him, she

The Literary Gazette, four pages long, was Chapel Hill's third ante-bellum newspaper. James M. Henderson started the paper in Concord in March 1854 as a staunch advocate of the America First, or Know-Nothing party. After three controversial and financially strapped years, he moved to Chapel Hill and published the first issue 18 April 1857. The paper folded within two years. Dennis Heartt, publisher of the Hillsborough Recorder, reported that Henderson had died of pneumonia while in military service in Pennsylvania in 1863. (NCC)

willed her estate to butcher Walter Thompson, the son of her daughter Edith, the widow of Richard Thompson.

The most fondly remembered hotel keeper in Chapel Hill was Miss Ann Segur Hilliard, better known as Nancy Hilliard, probably because of a corruption of Ann to "Nan" and "Nan" to "Nancy." Nancy came to Chapel Hill from Granville County about 1814 with her parents William and Lucy Hilliard. Apparently William died soon thereafter, because in 1819 Lucy paid William Webb $160 for two acres across Cameron Avenue from the Carolina Inn. Lucy died in 1820, leaving property and no doubt some debts to Nancy, who was ordered by the courts to sell the corner lot in 1825. She sold it, paid Elisha Mitchell $129 for two acres across Columbia Street, sold part of that plot to Tom Taylor in order to pay Mitchell, and apparently built a house on the remainder. She began to board students, and over the years she bought more land, including a farm on Bolin Creek and part of what became the Chapel of the Cross grounds.

In 1839, Thomas Watts' widow Lucy bought the Watts Hotel property and adjoining land to the east from James Webb, the area now occupied by Graham Memorial and the Morehead Planetarium parking lot. Lucy Watts moved to Cumberland County and in 1846 sold the hotel and adjacent property to Nancy Hilliard for $1250. Nancy named her new purchase the Eagle Hotel and began operating it as an inn and a boarding house, assisted by her sister Martha and Martha's husband Benton Utley, who had never recovered from his failure as a storekeeper in the old James Hogg house across McCorkle Place from the Eagle Hotel.

In spite of her inability to refuse credit to any student, and in spite of students' habitually carrying pocketsful of fried chicken away from her tables, Nancy made the Eagle popular and profitable, serving over 100 students daily within a year of taking over. She built the Polk extension onto the hotel for the President's use during his 1847 visit, she made other improvements, and in 1853 she sold the hotel to Major Hugh B. Guthrie for a reported $10,000.

She used part of the money to erect a large, two-story house immediately east of the Eagle, which the students dubbed "The Crystal Palace" because of its oversized windows. Nancy ran a guest house on the upper floor and continued to serve meals in the large basement. She had earned such an excellent reputation for her meals that in 1856 the North Carolina Railroad hired her to operate a restaurant in Company Shops, now Burlington. She rented the "Crystal Palace" while she was gone, and although she could not then know it, her days of prosperity were nearing their end.

A strong unionist both before and after the war, Major Guthrie changed the name from the Eagle to the Union Hotel and enjoyed a popularity approaching that of his predecessor. He was a town commissioner in the 1850s, a Whig member of the House of Commons in 1860, sheriff of Orange County in 1862-1864 and 1865-1867, the magistrate of police in 1869-1872 and postmaster of Chapel Hill on two occasions in the 1870s. During Reconstruction, he was also an unabashed Republican "scalawag," detested by most of his old-guard Democratic neighbors. His gravestone in the village cemetery carries the defiant inscription, "Born a Whig and died a Republican."

In 1856, the university and the village received a dramatic introduction to the angry, irreconcilable political passions which in the coming years would consume all reason and hurl the nation into bloody civil war.

Benjamin Sherwood Hedrick was born near Salisbury in 1827. He graduated from the university with distinction in 1851 and continued his studies at Harvard. After marrying Mary Ellen Thompson of Orange County, he returned to Chapel Hill in 1854 to teach analytical and agricultural chemistry and to build what is now known as the "Horace Williams House." Hedrick was a gentle, shy man who in his youth had been appalled by the sight of slaves marching south and who had grown to share the western

Nancy Hilliard built this large house in 1854 on the site of what is now the Morehead Planetarium grounds. She boarded up to 100 students and provided housing for several more, including nearly all the law students. The house belonged to Algernon Barbee, Chapel Hill mayor, when this picture was made in the 1890's (NCC)

Joseph A. Engelhard (1832-1879) (left) was the author of the letter signed "alumnus" that appeared in W.W. Holden's Raleigh Standard 29 September 1856, a letter that started a chain of events that eventually forced Benjamin Sherwood Hedrick (1827-1886) (below) off the UNC faculty.

Engelhard, who lived at Nancy Hilliard's while a student, was an honor graduate of 1854 when this portrait was made. Later, he was editor of a Wilmington newspaper and after the war became a lawyer. He and W.W. Holden married sisters. After he left the university and the south, Hedrick became an officer in the "Red Strings," officially the Heroes of America, in 1864. The "Red Strings" were a collection of men and women who were anti-slavery and pro-union during the Civil War. (NCC)

farmers' general abhorrence of slavery.

In August 1856 while voting in the state election, a student asked Hedrick how he intended to vote in the November national election. Hedrick at first evaded, but upon being pressed admitted he would vote Republican should the state ticket include John C. Fremont, the son-in-law of Thomas Hart Benton. The reaction was calm until 13 September when William Woods Holden, at that time the most powerful Democrat in the state and the editor of the Raleigh *Standard*, attacked Hedrick savagely, if indirectly: "If there be Fremont men among us, let them be silenced or required to leave. THE EXPRESSION OF BLACK REPUBLICAN OPINIONS IN OUR MIDST IS INCOMPATIBLE WITH OUR HONOR AND SAFETY AS A PEOPLE. If at all necessary, we shall refer to this matter again. Let our schools and seminaries of learning be scrutinized; and if black Republicans be found in them, let them be driven out. That man is neither a fit nor a safe instructor of our young men who even inclines to Fremont and black Republicanism."

Two weeks later the *Standard* printed a letter from "An Alumnus" castigating Hedrick and asking for his dismissal. Perhaps unwisely, Hedrick answered — admitting to being

the target of "An Alumnus" and to supporting Fremont; citing opposition to slavery by western North Carolinians and by Washington, Jefferson, Madison and other patriots; and denying he had ever lectured on political matters. Confessing he was not infallible, he ended with the plea, "I think I should be met by arguments, and not by denunciation." Holden countered that it was absurd to expect debate "with a black Republican" and called for the trustees to take action.

Swain called a faculty meeting on 6 October to consider the matter. A committee consisting of Professors Mitchell, Phillips, and Fordyce M. Hubbard reported that Hedrick's political opinions "are not those entertained by another member of this body" and that the committee "sincerely regret the indiscretion into which he seems in this instance to have fallen." The faculty approved the committee resolutions by a vote of 12 to one with only Henri Harrissee voting in the negative on the grounds that the matter was personal to Hedrick. The students responded by burning Hedrick in effigy to the slow tolling of the school bell.

Holden continued the attack, and on 11 October the Executive Committee of the trustees "Resolved, That in the opinion of the committee, Mr. Hedrick has greatly if not entirely destroyed his power to be of further benefit to the university in the office which he now fills." On 17 and 18 October, the New York *Herald* and the New York *Tribune* ran articles announcing the de facto dismissal of Hedrick.

Hedrick's ordeal was not over. He barely escaped mobs in Salisbury and Lexington, and the newspaper attacks continued. In a letter to the Wilmington *Commercial*, he charged that "the trustees have never been able to assign any reason for my dismissal, except that Holden and the mobocracy required it, and Holden and the mobocracy must be obeyed or the stars might fall, of some other equally great calamity happen to the State." The *Commercial* dismissed Hedrick's defenses as the statements of an untrustworthy man and apologized for having printed such offensive references to Holden and mobocracy.

Understandably, Hedrick left the South. He worked for a time as a clerk for the mayor of New York City, in 1861 he became an examiner in the Patent Office Department of Chemistry and Metallurgy in Washington D.C., and from 1872 to 1876 he was a professor at the University of Georgetown. He died in Washington in 1886, and he remains the only professor ever fired from UNC because of his political beliefs.

During commencement week of 1859, a second incumbent president of the United States visited Chapel Hill. Governor Swain had asked Jacob Thompson, a UNC graduate of 1831 and the current Secretary of the Interior, to invite President James Buchanan. Student marshalls

Richard James Ashe (1821-1899), Captain of the Chapel Hill Confederate army troop, grew up in a family divided over the slavery question. His aunt, Mary "Polly" Moore, lived in the Ashe house and was a bitter opponent of slavery; in the 1820's she freed all the slaves she inherited from her mother's estate.

Richard Ashe's granddaughter Mary R. Ashe remembers her grandfather as an irreligious man in a religious family. Richard's mother, Anna Moore Ashe (1795-1880?), once rebuked him for his religious laxity, quoting, "Search the Scriptures, Richard, search the Scriptures." Richard replied that the scripture she cited was directed at Jews who doubted the divinity of Christ, and he, Richard, did not entertain such doubts, therefore he was not under the injunction.

Mary Phoebe Mitchell Ashe (1822-1903), daughter of Elisha Mitchell and wife of Richard James Ashe, became the matriarch of one of California's most respected pioneer families after she and her family settled in Kern County. Mary was well loved by her children, but her grandchildren considered her a martinet. (Photographs courtesy Maude Ashe, of Bakersfield, Calif.)

met the President at the eastern town limits at 1 p.m. on Wednesday, 1 June and escorted him to Swain's house.

Governor and Eleanor Swain hated to entertain and escaped the unpleasantness of an indoor luncheon, which inevitably would have offended those not invited, by serving a gargantuan meal to several hundred guests seated at tables arranged on their lawn. That afternoon in Gerrard Hall, William Hooper delivered his address "Fifty Years Since" to a delighted audience and to a particularly delighted Buchanan. That evening after the sophomore declamations, the President presented the English composition prize to Elisha E. Wright of Memphis, who would die in the Battle of Murfreesboro in January 1863. Buchanan also addressed a few words to the evils of intoxication, a problem currently being investigated by a trustee committee.

At 3:30 p.m. on Thursday, a crowd of 2500 assembled in Gerrard Hall to hear four more student speeches and to applaud as Swain gave diplomas and Bibles to 89 graduates —26 of whom would die in the approaching war.

Both in Raleigh and Chapel Hill, Buchanan had pleaded for a compromise of sectional differences, and he had expressed hope that both the Union and peace could be preserved. But when the southern firebrands split the Democratic party in 1860 rather than see Illinois Senator Stephen Douglas elected president, and after Republican Abraham Lincoln won without receiving a single vote in the deep southern states that had not carried his name on their ballots, the lame-duck Buchanan saw his hopes vanish utterly on 20 December 1860 when South Carolina left the Union.

On 28 February 1861, North Carolina voters rejected a referendum calling for a convention to consider secession. But on 15 April when President Lincoln responded to the attack on Fort Sumter by calling for 75,000 volunteers to

put down the "insurrection," North Carolina unionists instantly became secessionists, and military units formed across the state long before a convention meeting in Raleigh formally carried North Carolina out of the Union on 20 May.

In Chapel Hill, they did not wait even until Fort Sumter. On 6 April, Capt. Richard James Ashe, the son of Anna Ashe and the nephew of Dr. George Moore, began accepting six-month volunteers into the Orange Light Infantry. A graduate of 1842, Ashe was a charter member of the Alumni Association and later a member of its executive committee. In 1845 he married Elisha Mitchell's daughter Mary. He was the administrator of Mitchell's estate, he was a partner with Andrew Mickle in several business and real-estate transactions, and he worked for the railroads. In the spring of 1861, Ashe was living in the old Pannill house with his wife, their eight children, his widowed mother-in-law Maria Mitchell, Eliza Mitchell Grant, and Mrs. Grant's young son.

By 22 April, the Orange Light Infantry had grown to include 107 men. James Jennings, Richardson Mallett and druggist R.B. Saunders were lieutenants. The enlisted men included William F. Strowd of Chatham county, William C. Tenney, Jones Watson, Ilai Nunn's son William, Prof. Manuel Fetter's sons Frederick and William, and scores of other eager young Chapel Hillians. On 26 April 1861, Baptist minister Norvell W. Wilson directed a joint-denominational mass service to call on divine support of the Confederacy and to bid farewell to Capt. Ashe and his men, who marched to Raleigh to become Company D of the 1st NC Regiment.

After adding nine more volunteers, Company D and the 1st Regiment moved on to engage in the first significant battle of the war on 10 June at Big Bethel, 13 miles below Yorktown, Virginia. Compared to other actions of the war, it was a minor affair. The Federals suffered 76 casualties, the Rebels lost eight men. But the southerners carried the day overwhelmingly, deflating the sense of invincibility that had begun to infect the northern army and confirming the southern belief that their opponents lacked the grit to risk life and limb for an unpopular cause. Three of the eight Rebels killed at Big Bethel were members of the Orange Light Infantry, Company D: William Baldwin, William Chisenhall, and James B. Moore.

The students also departed the campus in large numbers to enlist in home-county companies long before the firing on Fort Sumter. On 27 April, the underclassmen petitioned the trustees to suspend classes, but the trustees, eager to preserve the institution, refused. All five tutors volunteered in the spring of 1861; only Frederick Fetter among them survived the war. Captain Robert Anderson of New Hanover County was killed at Wilderness Creek; Captain George Pettigrew Bryan of Raleigh fell at Richmond; Captain George B. Johnston of Edenton died in Chapel Hill

Frederick Adolphus Fetter (1838-1910), the son of UNC professor Manuel Fetter, was the only UNC tutor to survive the Civil War. He went to war with Captain Richard Ashe's troop in April, 1861, returned with the troop six months later and resumed his teaching duties at UNC, staying until 1866. He spent most of the rest of his career in Reidsville as an Episcopal minister. (NCC)

from illnesses contacted in a prison camp in Sandusky, Ohio; Iowa Michigan Royster of Raleigh died instantly at Gettysburg, shot while leading a charge singing "Dixie." Captain Elijah Graham Morrow of Chapel Hill, who had been a tutor a year earlier, also died at Gettysburg.

Of the 1592 UNC alumni alive when the war began, 1060 served in the Confederate forces. Lieutenant General Leonidas Polk attained the highest rank, followed by Major General Bryan Grimes. Of the 13 who rose to brigadier general, four died from battle wounds: J. Johnston Pettigrew, Lawrence O'B. Branch, Isham W. Garrott, and George B. Anderson, the brother of tutor Robert Anderson.

In Chapel Hill during the first months of the war, the primary difficulty for residents, other than concern for their loved ones in the military, was to adjust to life without the students. John W. Carr, Nancy Hilliard, and several others had housed 10 or so students each. That income, and a corresponding volume of business for merchants, was lost.

The women of Chapel Hill, like their compatriots throughout the South, threw themselves into the war effort, knitting socks and sweaters, sewing trousers and jackets, preparing edibles to send to the troops. Nathaniel Brooks Tenney thanked the ladies for the "Patriotic Kindness" in a letter from Yorktown. Dave McCauley, R.B. Saunders, and John H. McDade signed a notice printed in the Hillsborough *Recorder* of 17 July thanking the women for their gifts. Matthias M. Marshall, a student from Pittsboro still in class, attended a Gerrard Hall fund raiser on 9 October and left his impression in his diary: "The young ladies of the village gave a concert at night in the chapel for the benefit of the soldiers. It was very good but rather too long. Paid 50 cts for ticket."

The Orange Light Infantry saw little further action after Big Bethel, suffering only two further deaths, Sidney B. Atwater in action and Joseph McCullum at home in Chapel Hill from an illness contacted in Virginia. Matthias Matthews described their triumphant return to

PROCEEDINGS
OF A
PUBLIC MEETING
IN
CHAPEL HILL, NORTH CAROLINA.

On 6 February 1861, Chapel Hill's notables met in "the village school house," located behind the Presbyterian church, and elected UNC President David Swain and former Governor William A. Graham to be Orange County's delegates to the proposed state convention on secession. (NCC)

Chapel Hill on 14 November at the end of their six-month enlistment: "The Orange Light Infantry came home at night at 10 o'clock. Triumphal arches were erected across the street opposite Prof. Fetters by the ladies, who were out in numbers. Bon fires were burning & the Bells rang. Gov. Swain made a short speech which was replied to by Capt. Ashe after which they partook of a supper prepared for them at Miss Nancy Hilliard's house by the ladies."

Captain Ashe had escaped injury in action only to encounter personal tragedy in seemingly safe Chapel Hill. In mid-January 1862, a fire in Robert Loder's dry goods store, which was well stocked with military clothing, destroyed the building and spread to John W. Carr's store on Franklin Street before being contained. Ashe's teenage son Richard was helping the firefighters when he stepped on a nail. He developed lockjaw and died on 20 January. His parents buried Richard in the Mitchell family graveyard behind the original President's House on the current Swain Hall grounds, a graveyard that would later in the year receive Eliza Mitchell Grant's young son Richard. Captain Ashe returned to battle.

In 1868, Capt. Ashe moved his family, including his mother Anna and his aunt Mary "Polly," to Bakersfield, California, via train to New York City, boat to Panama, train across the isthmus, and boat to California. In Bakers-field, he became a licensed lawyer, practiced as an assistant district attorney, and won election to the California state legislature. He was a member of the state constitutional convention that liberalized California law in 1879, he died a prominent man in 1889, and he now has a street named after him in Bakersfield.

During 1862 villagers began to suffer increasingly severe privations brought on by the war. Medical supplies and manufactured goods from the North and Europe were cut off by the blockade; there was no graduation ball that summer when only 24 seniors received diplomas, many *in absentia*; inflation began to drive prices of scarce supplies out of the reach of many families. The price of a pound of bacon, for example, rose from 33 cents in 1862, to $1 in 1863, to $5.50 in 1864, to $7.50 by the end of the war. In the same period a pound of sugar rose from 75 cents to $30.00; a barrel of flour from $18 to $500; a pound of coffee from $2.50 to $40.00; and a bushel of corn from $1.10 to $30.00.

In May 1862, the village learned that Professor John Thomas Wheat's son, John Thomas, had died at Shiloh; the next month his second son, Robateau, fell at Gaines Mill during the Battle of the Seven Days. Professor Wheat's former neighbor Cornelia Graves Morrow Thompson lost her son Alexander on 13 December 1862

In 1822, Dr. Charles R. "Bullet" Yancy built the house shown here on a portion of the lot he purchased from the estate of Matthew McCauley, between East Rosemary and East Franklin, bordering on Columbia. He rented rooms to students, then sold the house to Jesse Hargrave and his wife Margaret (Barbee) in 1840. The Hargraves continued to rent to students, and at the time of this 1860 photograph Mrs. Hargrave had 14 student roomers, some of whom can be seen around the house. One of her roomers was James N. Thompson, brother of the Jacob Thompson who was implicated in the Lincoln assassination. Seven of the 14 died in the Civil War.
Mrs. Hargrave died in 1863, and the house burned at the end of the Civil War. (NCC)

at the Battle of Fredericksburg, and she would lose another, Captain Elijah Graham Morrow, in the battle that delivered the most devastating blow of the war to the village and the university. Twenty alumni died in the 1-3 July 1863 struggle at Gettysburg, among them eight villagers: Captain Morrow; Captain William S. Durham; Thomas W. Howard; Lt. John H. McDade; Lt. William Norwood Mickle; Lt. Nathaniel Brooks Tenney; Lt. James W. Williams; and Judge Battle's son, Wesley Lewis, whose brother Junius had died in September 1862 at South Mountain in a skirmish preceding the great battle at Antietam Creek. Mrs. Thompson would lose a third son at Atlanta in 1864.

The early lists of the dead at Gettysburg included Major Joseph H. Saunders; and Saunders was among those mourned at memorial services conducted by the University Lodge Masons on 5 August and by the Rev. Norvell W.

The father of Chapel Hill's Dr. Thomas J. Wilson distributed this broadside in 1865. Several old-time residents of the area identify the "Walter Scott" who is accused of horse stealing with the Scotts of Haw River, the family that produced Governors W. Kerr Scott and Robert Walter Scott. There is, however, no documented evidence. (Courtesy of Peter Wilson)

STOP THIEF!
$25 Reward.

Stolen from the Subscriber, living near Hillsborough, on Tuesday the 4th inst., a bay Horse, saddle and bridle. The horse is a racker or pacer, has a light mane and tail, the mane lays on the wrong side; has some saddle marks, but no collar marks; the horn of the saddle was broken, but still there; the bridle was a double rain bridle, passing round a roller on each side the bit. The horse was stolen by a certain Walter Scott. The last heard from he was at the Shops in Alamance county; it is supposed he has or will sell the horse to get money. The above reward will be given for the apprehension of the thief and horse, or $12:50 for either, if delivered, the horse to the subscriber, and the thief to the Jail of Orange or Alamance counties.

THOS. WILSON.

Hillsborough, N. C., July 11, 1865.

Wilson on 8 August at the Baptist Church. However, Major Saunder's family learned before the end of the month that he was alive and in excellent health.

Governor Swain, who had been released for reasons of health after volunteering, wrote President Jefferson Davis in October asking that the 63 students currently enrolled be exempted from conscription. Davis assured the Governor that he did not intend to use up the "seed corn," but only upperclassmen were exempted, later only students under 18 were exempted, and the great majority continued to volunteer when they reached military age. Of the 376 students who enrolled in 1860, only J. Buxton Williams, Jr. of Warren County graduated in 1864. Williams then served in the Confederate army; afterward he practiced as a physician in Oxford until his death in 1887.

More than 30 men from Chapel Hill had died as a result of the war, and all hopes for a southern victory had vanished when the men of the village met on 22 February 1865 to draft a resolution affirming their support of the Confederacy and condemning those who wanted North Carolina to negotiate a separate peace. Jones Watson chaired the meeting attended by Governor Swain, Drs. William P. Mallett and Johnston Blakeley Jones, Andrew Mickle, the Rev. Norvell W. Wilson, and others. No one had invited Sam Phillips, the most vocal local advocate for a separate peace, but he got wind of the meeting and walked in after the resolution had been drafted. He voiced his opposition and submitted a substitute resolution calling for a convention of the people of the state. After long and heated debate, the diplomatic Governor Swain reworded the preamble in an effort to appease Phillips while leaving the spirit of the document intact.

Near the end of the war, Ilai Nunn's son Willis was killed at Petersburg. Col. Edward Mallett died in battle on 22

Right to left in this painting by W.G. Randall (1860-1905) are Zebulon Vance (1830-1894), Henry King Burgwyn (1841-1863), and John R. Lane (1836-1905?). Randall, from Blowing Rock, graduated from UNC in 1884, returning to his alma mater to teach before tuberculosis forced him to move to Texas. Lane, from Chatham County, was an active campaigner for native Chapel Hillian Julian Shakespear Carr in his unsuccessful try for the U.S. Senate in 1900. Burgwyn was a brilliant student at UNC, became the "boy colonel" of the Confederate army, and was killed at Gettysburg. Vance spent most of the war as Governor of North Carolina, then he became a U.S. Senator. Gutzon Borglum, creator of the Stone Mountain, Georgia, memorial, sculpted the statue of Vance that State authorities placed in the U.S. Capitol's Statuary Hall in 1916. (DAH)

Needham Bryan Cobb (1836-1905), center, and his brother John Probert (1834-1923), right, both lived at the home of Dr. Hudson Cave during their years at UNC, 1851-1854.

Needham was so impressed by a sermon of Methodist minister Jesse Cunninggim that he decided to become a preacher. He considered the Episcopal, the Universalist, and the Methodist faiths before settling on the Baptist. He served as a chaplain in the Confederate Army, then was the Baptist minister in Chapel Hill in 1880-1881. His first-born child was famed UNC professor Collier Cobb, left.

John Probert Cobb (1834-1923), wounded three times during the Civil War, led 32 North Carolinians at the Battle of the Wilderness in May 1864; only two of them survived the fight. He lost a leg at Cold Harbor in June 1864. He later moved to Florida and made a career in the citrus fruit industry and in politics.

Collier Cobb (1862-1934) grew up to become one of Chapel Hill's most famous citizens. Cobb's father, Needham B., first married Martha Louise Cobb, a relative. After her death he married Ann de Lisle Fennell. Collier was the son of Martha. When he was born, his then Confederate army chaplain father wrote, "He was a very funny-looking specimen of humanity with scarcely any flesh on his poor little bones." (NCC)

March. Col. Mallett had joined the army in his home town of New Bern and had sent his wife and five children to spend the war with relatives in Chapel Hill. After escaping harm in Northern Virginia and in the extended action against Sherman in Georgia and South Carolina, he was in Chapel Hill on leave on 15 January when he learned of the fall of Fort Fisher, which meant that Sherman's army would be united for the push north. Mallett rushed to rejoin his command and to lead his men in the southern defeat at Bentonsville 19-21 March, the greatest battle ever fought in the state. A day later, he was riding by a thicket when northern sharp-shooters shot him out of the saddle. A few hours later he died. A servant wrapped the body in muddy blankets, placed it in a crude coffin, and transported it to Chapel Hill. Col. Mallett's once affluent estate had been lost, and he left an impoverished widow in failing health. She lingered until the fall, and after she died Miss Sally Mallett took on the responsibility of raising the five Mallett orphans.

After Bentonsville, Confederate General Joseph Johnston resumed his retreat. By early April, with Johnston's army quickly losing its ability to fight effectively, little stood between Sherman and the essentially undefended symbols of North Carolina: Raleigh, the state capitol; and Chapel Hill, the seat of the state university. With no means to control their fate, the only thing that Chapel Hillians could know for sure about their future was that it would be dark.

Julian Shakespeare Carr (1845-1923), son of John W. and Elizabeth Bullock Carr, grew up in Chapel Hill. Although he never rose above the rank of private during the Civil War, he became "General Carr" to the Confederate veterans and wore his dress uniform frequently on public occasions. He became wealthy by marketing "Bull Durham" smoking tobacco after he moved to Durham during Reconstruction. (NCC)

The story of this house, located at what is now University Square and pictured here in a 1900 photograph, illustrates the bleak financial life of Chapel Hill during the period the university was closed. The builder was Mary Southerland, who bought the property, a 5½ acre tract, for $1000 in 1851 from Dr. Johnston Blakeley Jones. She sold it for $5500 to A.J. De Rosset in 1862. DeRosset sold it to Caroline Frederica Baudry for $3500 in 1867, and she, in turn, sold the 5½ acre property intact for $1525 to Chapel Hill druggist Seaton Barbee during the depressed days of 1873. Baptist minister Needham Cobb later occupied the house. (NCC)

IV
An Old University Busted and Gone to Hell
1865 to 1875

Following the defeat at Bentonville, Confederate Gen. Joe Johnston resumed his retreat, with Gen. Joe Wheeler fighting delaying skirmishes against Sherman's vanguard under the command of Gen. Hugh Judson Kilpatrick. On Saturday, 8 April, Governor Swain and former Governor William A. Graham exchanged letters in which they agreed they should confer with Governor Zebulon Vance.

Swain went to Hillsborough on Sunday, visited Graham, and caught a 7 a.m. train to Raleigh on Monday, 10 April. Governor Vance asked Swain to join Graham on a five-man commission to meet with Gen. Sherman to arrange for the peaceful surrender of Raleigh. Swain wired Graham, Graham arrived in the capital at 3 a.m. on Wednesday; and, while Joe Johnston was moving his army on to Hillsborough, the commission left Raleigh at 10 a.m. on a train headed toward Goldsboro. Fate was a mischievous playfellow that day. Among the many delays the commissioners encountered, one was occasioned when they were stopped by a cavalry unit under the command of Brig. Gen. Smith Atkins, who would become Governor Swain's son-in-law four months later after a sensational courtship that would shake the social and educational foundations of North Carolina.

Yankee troops escorted the commissioners to Gen. Kilpatrick, who pointedly informed them they were his prisoners of war before sending them on to Gen. Sherman. Sherman agreed to spare Raleigh if he encountered no resistance, and the commissioners returned to Raleigh early on Thursday, 13 April, after spending the night in Sherman's camp. Believing the commissioners were prisoners of war, Vance had left for Hillsborough, leaving the keys to the state capital with a servant, who gave them to Governor Swain. Swain surrendered the capital to a Federal officer and delivered the keys to Gen. Sherman, who asked him to deliver a message to Hillsborough requesting that Vance return to Raleigh. Vance chose instead to go to Greensboro to meet President Davis and Gen. Johnston, and Swain returned to Chapel Hill on Friday afternoon to await the inevitable.

After the summer of 1863, southerners in general and North Carolinians in particular had grown increasingly disillusioned with the Confederate States government and its policies. However, with defeat a certainty in the spring of 1865, southerners were beginning to give way to a romantic fatalism in their lament for the glorious Lost Cause. Mrs. Cornelia Spencer's journal is a representative example of the value of myth as a salve for debilitating spiritual depression.

While Sherman was approaching Raleigh, Mrs. Spencer pondered, "I do not know but that the strong arm of the United States law and authority would be preferable to the miserable prospect in store for us under Jefferson Davis and his bankrupt, reckless crew. I have no confidence in them. I believe General Lee is the only man in whom I do place much confidence. But I do love the SOUTH." Nonetheless, she awaited Yankee military rule with the greatest dread. "If the Stars and Stripes wave again over our unhappy land, I for one should want to leave it forever," she wrote, believing that for "many of us death would be far preferable." If Mrs. Spencer's logic is less than consistent, we have only to remember that the ordeal she and her neighbors were facing was one then unique in the American experience — military defeat and occupation.

While southern troops were falling back on Raleigh and Hillsborough, an advanced unit of Joe Wheeler's cavalry passed through Chapel Hill. "Our whole town turned out to feed them," Mrs. Spencer observed. "The streets were lined with girls, offering smiles, food, and flowers. It gives me a cheering sensation to see so many gallant fellows — eager to fight and hopeful." But once the euphoria passed, harsh reality interposed, and she admitted, "But we fear

Cornelia Phillips Spencer (1825-1908) is credited with being the person most responsible for publicizing the plight of the university and the village in the early 1870s. Referring to the desolation visited on Chapel Hill, she wrote, "People who before the war had lived up fully to incomes of $2000 a year, were reduced to less than one tenth of that sum, and are fully qualified to give an answer to the question of how little one can live on." A 10,000 ton Liberty class merchant ship, launched at Wilmington, N.C. in April, 1943, bore her name. The Germans sank it in the North Atlantic six months later. Both UNC-CH and UNC-G named buildings in her honor. (NCC)

they will be greatly outnumbered. In a few weeks they may all be retrograding in despair." It was a matter of days.

Writing to his son Charles Beatty Mallett in Wilmington, Chapel Hill bookstore owner Charles P. Mallett noted that on Sunday the ninth of April artillery units were already retreating through the village, and on Monday rumors of Lee's surrender sharply hastened the pace of retreat. On Tuesday a drove of 300 mules and a train of wagons and artillery pieces rushed by, and the next day companies of infantry eight abreast marched through, "all in good condition and spirits."

On the day Raleigh capitulated, 13 April, Gen. Hugh Judson Kilpatrick continued his hot pursuit of Wheeler and pushed onward to Morrisville, where he stopped after an intense skirmish at dusk. That evening one of Wheeler's officers, James P. Coffin (UNC class of 1859), requested permission to station a guard at his alma mater — not against marauding Yankees, but against Wheeler's own notorious "bummers" who were already filtering into the village. Wheeler complied, allowing Coffin to pick a guard.

Earlier that Thursday afternoon, Gen. Benjamin Franklin Cheatham had led his soldiers through Chapel Hill, and Baptist minister Norvell W. Wilson recorded his diary that Gen. Robert Hoke's brigade was passing. C.P. Mallett reported that Hoke refused to believe the rumor of Lee's surrender but was very anxious over Johnston. Mallett's sons John and Herbert were with the retreating army, and they had the comfort of sleeping that night in warm beds at home. (Mallett's son Richardson had been killed attempting to round up southern deserters in Saltville, Virginia, in August 1863.)

Capt. "Billy" Overman of Durham had eaten only wild onions since Tuesday, and he was overjoyed to see a group of young women passing out flowers and biscuits beside a large honeysuckle patch at the corner of Franklin and

Raleigh Streets. His joy dampened, however, when the young ladies honored him as an officer with flowers, while bestowing the less noble biscuits on his enlisted men.

Gen. Joe Johnston knew that Lee had surrendered, and on Friday, 14 April, he sent Sherman a letter requesting a ceasefire to allow civilian leaders to negotiate a final peace. Sherman agreed to meet Johnston to discuss "the suspension of further hostilities," and he promised to halt his main column at Morrisville and his cavalry at the university so long as Johnston maintained his position. Responding to Sherman's orders to halt at Chapel Hill or at "a point abreast of it," Kilpatrick turned his main force toward Durham Station, and sent Gen. Smith Atkins on to occupy Chapel Hill. That night John Wilkes Booth assassinated Lincoln, thereby making North Carolina native Andrew Johnson President.

Without question the most perilous hours in the existence of Chapel Hill were those between the afternoons of Friday, 14 April and Easter Sunday. There are conflicting versions of when Wheeler actually arrived on that rainy Friday, but there is no doubt that he briefly contemplated making a stand when he had two regiments dig in on the slopes below Piney Prospect.

According to C.P. Mallett, early in the morning while his sons John and Herbert were leaving to rejoin their command, Wheeler rode up, asked for directions, dismounted, and spread a map on the ground. Mallett judged the general to be a pleasant, "little" gentleman "roughly clad with a small faded wool hat upon his head, that no man at first sight would have classed him above a private." The little gentleman and an aide accepted Mallett's invitation to dinner that evening. Rev. Wilson helped to place the wounded temporarily in private homes.

According to Mrs. Spencer's more popularly accepted account, Wheeler arrived in the afternoon. In any event, he set up headquarters at the Franklin Street home of Kendal Waitt, and villagers looking in could observe the general and his aide Capt. John DeRosset in consultation, over maps. Not absolutely sure Lee had surrendered, Wheeler was looking for routes to link up with the Army of Northern Virginia. Lt. McBurney Broyes, of the 5th Tennessee Cavalry, searched for Governor Swain to get instructions for relieving Coffin's guard on the university. When he learned Swain was in Raleigh, he called on Charles Phillips and in effect placed himself under Phillips' command.

Then Swain returned with bad, but not unexpected, news. He had seen the correspondence between Lee and Grant, and he confirmed the rumor of Lee's surrender. "At that news," Mrs. Spencer remembered later, "our hopes for the Southern Confederacy died out." It was clear that Johnston's surrender was a matter of when, not if, but the villagers and Confederate foragers were still left with the necessity of caring for an army. "The whole town was

busy night and day cooking and feeding the men," Mrs. Spencer reported. "My heart yearned toward every one of them, though they carried off many horses and mules from the country road." Indeed, Wheeler's loosely disciplined men had become almost as infamous as the Yankees for leaving havoc and bare country behind them.

Eight miles east, Wheeler's rear guard destroyed a bridge crossing New Hope Creek and left a cavalry unit to delay Gen. Atkins. Atkins sent a unit of the 9th Ohio Volunteer Cavalry under Gen. W.D. Hamilton upstream to ford the rising New Hope, and Hamilton had little trouble dislodging the Rebels, who lost four men killed in the last significant skirmish of the war. Atkins threw up a new bridge Saturday morning while his force gathered for the last push to Chapel Hill. That night, however, the flooding waters carried it off, delaying his advance by a day.

On Saturday, C.P. Mallett kept an appointment with Wheeler, and together they went to see Swain, who spent 90 minutes detailing his experiences in the surrender of Raleigh. Although Wheeler was not yet ready to cry quits, the morale of the southern soldiers had finally broken. In *The Last Ninety Days of the War*, Mrs. Spencer tells of a Tennessee lieutenant who cried upon hearing of Lee's surrender. He had no money, his wife and children were homeless after their house had been burned, and he was as hungry, as ragged, and as desperate as the majority of his comrades in arms.

Dawn of Easter Sunday, 16 April, brought relief from the rains that had drenched the region. Afterward, people would remember the bright sun, the stillness of the air, and the scents of spring. Following their inspection of the positions on Piney Prospect, Wheeler and an aide lunched with C.P. Mallett, who urged the general not to endanger the village and the university by making a determined

James Park Coffin (1838-1930), Confederate guardian of the university grounds, graduated from UNC in 1859. As a student, he lived first with William Barbee, the son of Old Kit Barbee, then with William's daughter Margaret Hargrave, the grandmother of William Rand Kenan, Jr. Four of Coffin's six roommates in the Hargrave home died in the Civil War.
At the end of the conflict, Confederate Gen. Joseph Johnston paid Coffin one Mexican silver dollar for his war services. Coffin settled in Batesville, Arkansas, as a banker, and the silver dollar is still in the family. Union General Francis Blair, also a UNC alumnus and later a U.S. Senator from Missouri, set the Federal guard over the university a few days after Coffin's Confederate contingent left. (Courtesy of Mrs. Harry Carter of Batesville, Ark.)

stand. The hopelessness of his situation more than Mallett's plea caused Wheeler to withdraw his pickets and move on toward Hillsborough at about 2 p.m., leaving James Coffin in charge of a rear guard to protect the university from southern stragglers and bummers. By 3 p.m. all the Confederates had left.

Most residents had long ago hidden their valuables; those who had not taken the precaution quickly found hiding places. Charles Phillips hid his in a horseradish patch, where his wife later watched uneasily as Union soldiers helped her dig. James Phillips hid his watches in Joseph Caldwell's old telescope. Judge Battle buried his valuables under a maple tree in Battle Park, and forgot which tree. He also hid some of the gold and silver he was protecting for his son Kemp in a well, which was used several times by Yankees who did not notice the hidden treasure. Dr. William Mallett also used his well for a safety vault.

Several people entrusted watches, coins, silver, gold, and other articles to William A. Wright, a Wilmington lawyer and president of the Bank of Cape Fear who had sought haven in Chapel Hill. (Dr. Armand J. DeRosset of Wilmington and Dr. Samuel I. Johnston of Hertford County were among others who had migrated to Chapel Hill for the duration of the war.) C.P. Mallett had buried his cured pork on 8 April as a precaution against both southern and northern foragers, and by the time the Yankees arrived he was beginning to wonder if any could ever be salvaged following the drenching rains. After the Confederate foragers left, there were few supplies left to hide, a circumstance that prompted Mrs. Spencer to muse, "The sight of our empty store-rooms and smoke-houses would be likely to move our invaders to laughter."

In the stillness of the afternoon, the villagers selected a committee to treat with the Yankees, who were sure to come. Led by Governor Swain, Judge Battle, John W. Carr, Manual Fetter, Andrew Mickle, C.P. Mallett, and accompanied by the freedman Wilson Caldwell and other villagers, the group nervously walked out the Durham and Raleigh roads to meet the first arrivals, but no one came. Fortunately for the villagers, they were unaware, as were Sherman's men, that Abraham Lincoln had died a day earlier, killed by a well known southern sympathizer. After repeated trips, the peace commissioners followed the example of their neighbors and retired to their homes to endure the tension.

Finally, at dusk, Capt. J.M. Schermerhorn of the 92nd Illinois Cavalry led 12 men into town. Swain met him, and the captain reported that he had orders to protect the university, greatly relieving the anxiety that had been building all afternoon. He then pulled his small force out of town after insuring that none of Wheeler's stragglers remained. (According to C.P. Mallett, there were 40 to 50 men under the command of a lieutenant, and some of the men began robbing citizens until their officer stopped them. Rev. Wilson recorded simply, "some Yankee scouts reached the town this evening.")

At 8 a.m. on Monday, Gen. Atkins rode up the Raleigh road at the head of soldiers from the 92nd Illinois, 9th Michigan, 9th Ohio, and 10th Ohio cavalry units who would occupy the town. Mrs. Spencer estimated their number at 4000, and her figure has been quoted without question hundreds of times. However, the Regimental Daybook kept by the Federal officers reveal that the units occupying Chapel Hill contained 21 commissioned officers, 410 enlisted men ready for action, 220 absent on leave, 215 sick, 66 assigned to special duties, and 29 otherwise accounted for. In short, Mrs. Spencer's figure was either a slip of the pen or about a sixfold exaggeration.

Observing the devastation already wreaked on local food supplies, Atkins moved quickly to limit additional confiscations by issuing orders on 19 April forbidding further foraging for "horses or other property." If forbidden articles were absolutely essential, a commissioned officer would oversee and "enough shall always be left for support of the family." He also ordered his subordinates to "treat the citizens and soldiers of our late enemy with courtesy and kindness." The Union officers set up headquarters in the most prominent homes and in the university buildings; the enlisted men established a camp running west from Tenney Plantation (Tenney Circle) to about where the Orange Savings and Loan building now sits on Rosemary Street. Lucy Phillips Russell also remembered seeing tents and campfires in Battle Park.

C.P. Mallett learned of Lincoln's assassination from a captain of the guards on the morning of 18 April. He and his neighbors were again relieved when Atkins assured them that no reprisals would be tolerated. Still, they spent a very uneasy night, serenaded by barking dogs and much bustling movement. The next day they learned that most of the Negroes had left to follow the Yankees north, to go to urban centers, or just to get away from their former masters. Mallett, who learned of Johnston's initial surrender while writing his son of the flight of the Negroes, confessed, "I feel conquered but not subdued. Might has overcome right — My opinions and feelings are the same and will go down with me to the grave."

Curiously enough, after an advance group of Union bummers ransacked Mary Ruffin Smith's isolated home on what is now Smith Level Road, very few if any other Chapel Hill residences were thoroughly looted, though experienced soldiers gathered booty from the usual hiding places — wells, chimneys, floor bases, vegetable and flower gardens, outhouses. Atkins placed a guard on each house, and on Tuesday, the 18th, he told Judge Battle that he intended to return to Illinois with nothing to show that he had traveled through the south except for his commission. On 19 April Sherman announced an armistice, with the line of demarcation running through "Tyrrell's Mount, Chapel University, Durham's Station, and West Point on the Neuse River." It was at this time that another of the enduring legends of Chapel Hill was born.

The Union soldiers stabled their horses in Smith Hall, the university library. After the fact, student Peter Mitchel Wilson of Warrenton saw humor in their callousness: "The alcoves of the college library were filled with straw bedding and stable litter left by the detachment of Federal cavalry recently departed, which converted the alcoves into stables for their horses. In ultra Roman histories we had read of the horse that was made a consul. But never before, surely, had a horse been a student." The Yankees also saw humor in their iconoclastic stabling and laughingly claimed they rode the best educated horses in existence. Old West was also a stable, and as late as April 1874 a trustees committee reported that the South Building retained the "ordure of cattle and horses."

But on the whole, Atkins rather admirably enforced his orders to protect the university and the town. After the occupiers left, Swain assessed their damage to the campus and the buildings at no more than $100. In addition, in 1874 a trustee committee inspected the campus and reported that neglect and exposure had left the grounds and buildings in deplorable condition, but they detected no signs of flagrant destruction left by the Yankees.

The enlisted men guarding the university buildings and private homes caused some discomfort, mentally and physically, by their forced lodging in homes in the village, but their care in protecting property encouraged Mrs. Spencer to label them "a decent set of men . . . who behaved with civility and propriety." And after a few days of observing Yankee officers and men mingle freely with the conquered civilians, she judged their behavior to be "in all respects like other human beings."

Atkins supported the inhabitants of his theatre of operations when they used force to protect their property from Union soldiers who defied his orders. Mallett wrote his son on 30 April, "Capt. Ramsey with a number of citizens from Pittsboro crossed Haw River and detected five of the Yankees pillaging a house on this side — and attacked them, killed two and wounded three." Atkins's reponse to the vigilante-like action was simply to send a detail to bury the dead and return the wounded. The next day he sent a detachment to C.P. Mallett's house to get wood, thinking him a woodseller. After Mallett corrected the misconception and sent word that all the wood he had left was for his own consumption, Atkins left his supply untouched.

Mallett's bacon and valuables had not fared so well. On 24 April he told the captain of the guard where they were buried in a nearby wood, and it is fortunate he did, because he and the officer arrived just as men were digging up the previously discovered cache. The food was spoiled, papers and books were soggy, and several watches were full of water. Mallett soaked the watches in a vat of peanut oil to prevent further rust.

The most sensational aspect of the Federal occupation of Chapel Hill was the whirlwind courtship of Gen. Atkins and Eleanor "Ellie" Swain, the headstrong daughter of Governor Swain. As might be expected, there are various accounts of their meeting.

After leading the attack against Wheeler's rear guard at New Hope Creek, Brig. Gen. W.D. Hamilton arrived in Chapel Hill on 18 April. According to his contribution to a later Ohio military history project, Hamilton introduced Atkins and Ellie at a village social.

Almost 40 years after the event, Hamilton remembered that "Miss Swain was as brilliant and original as she was elegant and attractive." At the party, she chided him for the ruin left behind by Sherman's army and asked what he proposed to do with southern women. Hamilton suggested that the conquerers follow the example of the Fabians and marry the women who had been so woefully deprived of fit male consorts. After this exchange he claimed to have introduced the general to the president's daughter, concluding his tale poetically: "It was the old, old story. A feathered arrow from an ancient bow had pierced the heart the modern bullet failed to reach." In the Hamilton version, Atkins called on President Swain, and the romance followed a natural course.

Mrs. Spencer's is the generally accepted version. In it, Atkins called on Governor Swain as a good-will gesture and during their conversation Swain mentioned having recently consulted Lord Cornwallis' order book. When Atkins asked if he might look at the document, Swain left to ask either a maid or Ellie to get it. Ellie, anxious to see the general, either took the book from the maid or got it herself. In any event, the determined young 21-year-old defiantly walked into the parlor to confront her father's visitor. But her demeanor altered instantly when she saw Atkins, and "they changed eyes at first sight." Atkins was as stricken with Ellie, "and a wooing followed on that first meeting which greatly incensed all who looked on, including the Federal army, and gave governor Swain and his wife as much uneasiness as anything short of a death in the family."

Reaction to the romance was immediate. Mrs. Spencer wrote after Swain's death, "I have never seen any man so deeply concerned and agitated as Governor Swain at this unexpected denouement." After weeks of strenuous preoccupation with his duty to the state and the university, he was suddenly saddled with an unexpected family problem which immediately became the talk and the curse of the town. Mrs. Spencer believed that Lincoln's assassination had a great deal to do with tempting Swain to receive Atkins so pleasantly: "Our heads were in the lion's mouth, and it behooved us to be careful."

Confronted by her parents' objections to her very public

Eleanor "Ellie" Swain (1844-1881), left, and her husband Gen. Smith Dykins Atkins (1835-1913), right, had a daughter, Eleanor Hope, who in 1891 married Raleighite Needham Cobb, brother of UNC professor Collier Cobb. In 1906, Needham and his family moved to Freeport, Illinois, where he edited the Journal, *a newspaper owned by his postmaster father-in-law.*

Between the end of the Civil War and her death in 1883, Ellie's mother lived a life of almost unrelieved tragedy. First her daughter Annie died, then her husband, then her physician son Richard in a train accident in Illinois in 1872, then Ellie. (Eleanor, NCC; Gen. Atkins, courtesy of the Illinois State Historical Society Library, Springfield, Illinois)

behavior, Ellie declared she was in her majority and free to do as she pleased. Mrs. Spencer blamed Mrs. Swain for being too lax in rearing her independent-minded daughter, as well as her other children: "She had many peculiarities; but her great weakness, and her failure in their training was signal. She spoiled them all systematically, being unable to see any faults in them or to allow the least criticism of them from others."

Governor Swain gained at least a modicum of relief when he checked into the general's background. Born in Horseheads, New York, in 1836, Smith Dykins Atkins had moved west with his family and had attended school at Rock River Seminary in Mount Morris, Illinois. Admitted to the Illinois bar in 1854, by 1860 he was a prosecuting attorney. He enlisted as a private in the 11th Illinois Infantry on 17 April 1861 in answer to Lincoln's call for volunteers, and 13 days later he was elected captain of his company. He rose to the rank of major in March 1862, to colonel the following September, and on 12 January 1865 Sherman named him a breveted brigadier general "for gallant and meritorious services" in the Georgia campaign.

Others in Chapel Hill were quick to condemn Ellie's "collaboration." C.P. Mallett informed his son on April 23, "Miss Ella Swain sent to Cassie to borrow her side saddle to ride out with some officer — Several other ladies — or I would rather call them women — have been riding out with them." Two days later he wrote that one of Professor Manuel Fetter's daughters was planning to marry a captain, and he declared, "Certainly those girls with Beck Ryan and Ella Swain have lain themselves open to much scandal."

A student asked his diary, "Who can sympathize with or even pity a young lady who willingly throws herself into the arms of a Yankee General, while his sword is yet reeking with the blood of its victims, her own relations or at least her own countrymen?" Even the tolerant Kemp Battle objected in a letter to a young relative in Raleigh, "Some of them seem to have made good friends with the Yankees, and like their horses, go to see the 'parade' and all that sort of thing: Do you know it is even said Miss Ellie Swain is going to marry the Yankee General (Atkins)! Well! every one to her own taste!"

Battle's mention of the "horses" alluded to the horse Sherman sent Governor Swain and the horse Atkins gave Ellie. Incensed critics very logically pointed out that in all likelihood both animals had been taken from southerners. Swain said that he had taken the horse as a symbol of reconciliation, but the animal was a lasting torment for him. People freely heaped the vilest criticism on him for accepting it, three times he recovered it from thieves, and he died from injuries received in an accident caused by the uncontrollable beast.

Atkins also drew undeserved criticism because of the courtship when angry southerners blamed him for the preponderance of Sherman's devastation. Far and wide, people suddenly accused him of thievery, even in areas he had never entered. For example, suspicion that he had stolen silver plates from the residence of Mrs. Rebecca Jones in Hillsborough persisted long after Atkins had left the region and was laid only partially to rest when John W. Graham, writing for Mrs. Jones' son Dr. Pride Jones, assured Swain on 11 June 1866 that "no silver was taken the night General Atkins stayed at the house."

But the gossip continued and became legend. In 1951 Atkins' granddaughter Mrs. Eleanor Hope Swain Cobb Newell was in Chapel Hill when she learned that the Durham *Morning Herald* was preparing an article on her visit. "I don't care what you print in such an article," she laughed, "but please say that my grandfather General Atkins did not steal all the silver in North Carolina, for I know that he did not."

Atkins later convinced Swain that he was innocent of the outrageous charges, and while admitting his army was often undisciplined and that some in it had been guilty of abhorrent crimes, he insisted he could return to any house he had occupied "in North Carolina and be sure of receiving a courteous welcome." Afterward, Mrs. Spencer wrote Zeb Vance that she believed Atkins' denials, but she still deprecated him for his lack of education, his Yankee-like "sense and smartness," and his nasal speech which "was artificial in manner." Mrs. Spencer could not let the past die easily.

Atkins' men were almost as upset as their erstwhile enemies. The popular general was a fine stump orator, and they missed his speeches. Also, he repeatedly sent the regimental band ostensibly to serenade Governor Swain, but all knew who the real audience was. Mercifully, the disapproving Mrs. Spencer was spared the ordeal of hearing the offensive music. By that time she was almost deaf, and she was amused with the concern of her Yankee guard when he learned she could not hear the band. "Well, I declare, I hate to think about it," he consoled her. "I'd give two hundred dollars if you could have your hearing."

One evening, after having played in front of Swain's house, the band members asked Atkins to grace them with a few words. He stepped onto the porch to say simply, and shortly, "Soldiers, I am making a speech to a young lady here tonight, and I have no eloquence to waste — she requires it all. The War, as I told you it would, at Mount Olive, has played out, and in less than the ninety days I then named, I think speech making has played out also, except to the young ladies. You must go to your quarters."

Gen. Hamilton also made friends in Chapel Hill. After dining with Professor and Mrs. Fordyce M. Hubbard and their family, he praised Mrs. Hubbard's biscuits. She frankly told him that she had scraped the bottom of a barrel the family could not afford to refill. When his men later confiscated 18 barrels of flour labeled "C.S.A.," according to Hamilton, "I directed my commisary lieutenant, who was rather an elegant fellow, to black his boots, put on a white collar, if he had one, and trim himself up, and take a barrel of flour down to Mrs. Hubbard with my compliments." He considered himself amply repaid with an invitation from a Hubbard daughter to attend a second social and with "a beautiful specimen of the fragrant magnolia in full bloom."

No matter that Atkins sympathized with the conquered Chapel Hillians and tried to restrain his men, he still had to have supplies. Mrs. Spencer remembered, "They remained two and a half weeks, and in that time the surrounding country was completely stripped of everything. Houses were ransacked and plundered: corn, oats, fodder, flour, meat, everything eatable carried off. My soul sickened to see the marauders coming in day after day from every road, loaded with spoils."

The confiscations prompted Swain to appeal to Sherman as early as 19 April. He explained that foraging by both Wheeler and the northerners had left villagers and farmers without provisions and without means to sow new crops. He briefly delineated the plight of Baptist minister G.W. Purefoy, who was responsible for "a family of more than fifty persons (white and colored)." He praised Atkins for executing "his orders with as much forbearance as he deems compatible with a proper discharge of his duty," but he still hoped that Sherman could "relax the severity of the orders under which General Atkins is acting."

On 22 April, Sherman thanked Swain for the kind words about Atkins and promised that "the moment war ceases, and I think that time is at hand, all seizures of horses and private property will cease on our part. And it may be that we will be able to spare some animals for the use of the farmers of your neighborhood." But the pragmatic general also promised to remain prepared to resume hostilities should negotiations fail.

When the Union army established supply lines to Chapel Hill, Atkins did in fact reverse the flow of goods and supplied any person, black or white, who requested rations. However, Kilpatrick answered Atkins' request for draft animals with the stern reply that he had no intention of dismounting Union soldiers to please southerners. Meanwhile, Rebel soldiers began to flow through town on their way home from the Virginia battlefront, and their plight was heartbreaking to those who once had so enthusiastically cheered their young men off to war.

On 2 May Atkins left one company in Chapel Hill and moved his command to Lexington. The brigade which replaced him two days later repeated his measure of posting guards on each house in the village. Mrs. Spencer recorded in her journal on 7 May, "I walked this evening

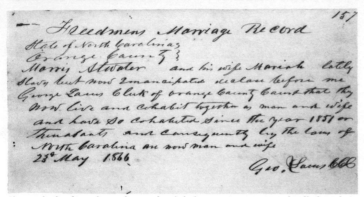

Slaves who lived together as man and wife before emancipation were legally bound as man and wife after 1866 through a device known as the Cohabitation Certificate. Chapel Hillian Morris Atwater and his wife Mariah already had four teenage children when this document was executed. One son, Albert, was destined to play a major role in a sensational burglary case in 1878-1879. See Chapter 5. (DAH)

alone, all over the hill back of our house, where a regiment lately encamped. Not a blade of grass, nor leaf of any kind is to be found there." She also noted, "The whole framework of our social system is dissolved. The Negroes are free, leaving their homes with very few exceptions, and those exceptions only for a time." But her despair was not shared so deeply by Ellie, who on 11 June dressed in lavender with pink ribbons and a pink oleander blossom to receive Gen. Atkins when he drove in to town. He was mustered out, with honor, on 21 June.

On July the Fourth, Governor Swain volunteered to deliver a speech, but the feeble response discouraged him, probably for the better. He was aging rapidly and his cognitive powers were fading, causing him to underestimate the animosity directed toward him and to assume incorrectly that Ellie's forthcoming nuptials were of a type by then calmly accepted in the South. The freed slaves held a wild Fourth of July celebration in Hillsborough, but for the time most Chapel Hillians were content simply to endure.

During the summer, Swain showed Mrs. Spencer notes Ellie and Atkins had exchanged. Distressed at her father's indiscretion, Ellie wrote Mrs. Spencer, "As for myself, but one voice can prevent this affair, and that is higher than man." The marriage remained scheduled for 23 August. On the back of Ellie's letter, Mrs. Spencer penned the poem "General Atkins' Surrender," containing the lines: "The wisest soldier and perchance the boldest/ Yields to a pair of blue eyes and a bow-and-arrow."

Governor Swain sent out invitations galore, hoping to attract a respectable number of guests. Most declined, and some were reported to have spat on the invitations, but Swain's old friend William A. Graham came with his wife, along with several Confederate veterans and a sprinkling of villagers. The students tolled the bell in front of South Building during the entire ceremony and hanged Atkins and Swain in effigy.

No doubt many of those present, and more who heard of it, were offended that the bride, groom, and parents had

dared to display "a large and handsomely decorated cake" sent by the freedmen. When Ellie left with Atkins for Illinois, gossip had it that her wedding dress was bounty taken by Atkins and that the couple's baggage included "confiscated" gold, silver, jewelry, and other finery. Whenever Mrs. Spencer intimated to Swain her desire to write an account of the wedding for the newspapers, he would always retort, "When I am dead, you may."

The same week of Ellie's wedding, the few students in town got into a row with a group of freedmen assembled to elect delegates to a civil-rights convention in Raleigh. Several people were injured in this the first of Chapel Hill's two race riots, and villagers assumed that a Negro guard would be placed on the university. That in fact later came to pass.

Ellie and Atkins settled in Freeport, Illinois, where he became editor of the *Daily Journal*. Mrs. Spencer wrote later, "This marriage was of ill omen to Governor Swain. The blight that immediately fell upon the University was directly attributable to the fact that he not only permitted his daughter to marry an invader, but that he gave her a fine wedding." Many other factors played a role in the difficulties the university faced in the next few years — depression, party politics, conflicts of personality. But Mrs. Spencer was correct — Ellie's courtship and marriage greatly limited her father's ability to manage the faltering institution.

Ellie and Smith returned to Chapel Hill in September 1866 after the death of Ellie's sister Annie, but residents resented their visit, especially at a time when things were going so poorly. Afflicted with mental instability and debilitating headaches, Annie had raised her own poppies during the war when her supply of opium had been shut off. Her death drove her father deeper into depression. When Sam Phillip's son Charlie died, Governor Swain told the grieving father, "Mr. Phillips, when you come to be as old as I am, you will not look upon this loss as being such a great misfortune." The Governor buried Annie in his back yard and visited her grave daily for the remainder of his life.

On 11 August 1868, Swain and Professor Manuel Fetter drove into the country to visit a farm the governor had recently purchased in a mortgage foreclosure. On the return trip, the spirited horse Sherman had given Swain ran wild, wrecked the buggy, and injured both men, Fetter slightly, Swain seriously. He seemed to be recovering, but on 29 April he died.

Afterward, Mrs. Swain went to live with Ellie and Smith Atkins, and supposedly never sat at a table with her son-in-law. Apparently the marriage was a happy one, producing a daughter, also named Eleanor Hope. Atkins returned to Chapel Hill in April 1882 on the anniversary of the occupation of the university and the village by Union troops. He saw Mrs. Spencer, and although Ellie had died the year before, the stern lady had little sympathy for a man she still considered plain. The younger Eleanor Hope Atkins attended St. Mary's in Raleigh, and completed a cycle of sorts by marrying Raleighite Needham Tyndale Cobb.

While he was imprisoned in Washington, D.C., in the autumn of 1865, Governor Vance asked Mrs. Spencer to write an account of what North Carolinians had experienced in the final weeks of the Civil War. Charles F. Deems, who helped found the Methodist congregation in Chapel Hill, promised to print it in *The Watchman*, his New York City newspaper. Vance, Swain and Mrs. Spencer sought to counter northern demands for revenge by showing the extent to which Southerners had suffered.

She worked on *The Last Ninety Days of the War* for over a year, completing it in October 1866. On reading the manuscript as an editor, Vance predicted, "I am sure it will be read greedily by North Carolina at least. For my own part I shed tears freely over some of it." On 9 December, Mrs. Spencer received her first copies along with word that *The Watchman* was about to fold. Three weeks later, after recording flattering praise in her journal, she added pragmatically, "All this, however, is the merest chaff. I want to know that the book SELLS." By the end of the year she was in utter despair. "What will the new year bring?" she asked, and answered forlornly, "Who can even guess." It did not bring increased sales of her book.

Like the village, the university was also suffering from a lack of income. Only 22 students enrolled in the fall of 1865, and only three graduated in June 1866, when the students threw the faculty into a quandary by electing as their honorary ball managers Jefferson Davis, Zeb Vance, Robert E. Lee, and three other southern generals. The faculty desperately called on the trustees, and the trustees — fearing reprisals from the military government — declared the election invalid. The next year commencement difficulties were primarily logistical, at least initially. The special guests included President Andrew Johnson, Secretary of State William H. Seward, Postmaster General Alexander W. Randall, and General Daniel E. Sickles — the military governor of North and South Carolina.

The President had come to North Carolina to attend the dedication of a monument in the Raleigh city cemetery to his father. Governor Swain had delivered the keynote address at the dedication and had invited the President to be his guest during the upcoming commencement exercises. The President heard two students from Chapel Hill deliver orations to the celebrity-packed audience. Winfield S. Guthrie spoke on "The Love of Money," and Albert G. Carr delineated "The Achievements of Hannibal." The President accepted an honorary membership into the Dialectic Society. Secretary of State Seward, Postmaster Randall, and Col. J.W. Bomford joined the Philanthropic Society. Minorities in each society blocked the admission of Gen. Sickles, charging that he was the symbol of north-

James Selby ran this notice in the 24 June 1824 Raleigh Star when his two apprentices ran away. Andrew Johnson fled to Chapel Hill and recalled later that he had spent a night with James Craig, son of the James Craig who had donated land to UNC in 1793. Johnson soon returned to Raleigh, but could not find work and left for Tennessee to make his fortune. In this ad, Selby mistakenly reversed the descriptions of the two boys. (NCC)

ern suppression.

Seward stopped the initiation ceremony when he was asked never to divulge Phi secrets. Long opposed to the Masons and other secret societies, he protested, "Mr. Secretary, I must have that understood—I am principled against joining secret societies." When assured that the Phi's had nothing to do with the Masons, he allowed the induction to continue. Seward also accepted an honorary Doctor of Laws, Johnson having received the honor a year earlier. However, many in town resented Seward's criticism of the shabby condition of the campus and the town, believing he was overlooking the invasion, the occupation, and the economic depression.

Perhaps by oversight, more likely by design, Governor Swain and the trustees failed to invite former Governor William Woods Holden to the commencement. It was not good politics. The disenfranchisement of those who had served the Confederacy had left blacks and unionists with the balance of power within the electorate, and the Freedman's Bureau and the Union League had succeeded in gathering the newly enfranchised blacks under the Republican banner. The result was that Holden had a secure political base for the upcoming gubernatorial election.

The financial problems of the university caused Governor Jonathan Worth to call an urgent trustees' meeting for 22 August 1867. The money invested during the war was lost, and John Jacob Astor III had turned down a request for a loan (by Governor Swain). The trustees had only $10,000 from the sale of land granted the state under the Morrill Act, and they were $110,000 in debt, including $7000 in unpaid faculty salaries.

To relieve the pressure on the trustees, at the 22 August meeting Swain and the entire faculty tendered their resignations, which the trustees accepted effective after the commencement of 1868. In the interim, voters in April 1868 elected Holden governor, chose a Republican-dominated legislature, and ratified a new state constitution which allowed the State Board of Education to select new trustees. As governor, Holden was the ex officio chair-

man of both the Board of Education and the Executive Committee of the trustees, and as a political partisan he appointed only Republicans or men he believed would support his positions.

For the commencement of 1868, Swain had the campus in spic and span condition. "If it were to be its last commencement," Cornelia Spencer declared, "Chapel Hill and the old University resolved at any rate to 'die standing.'" Twenty seniors received diplomas, and Charles Phillips accepted an honorary D.D. In his honors declamation, Chapel Hill senior Charles Fetter may have had trouble convincing his audience that "Thoughts Not Swords Rule the World"; Fabius Haywood Busbee of Raleigh carried on the tradition set by his grandfather and father in delivering the Valedictory Oration. Tuesday, 2 June, through Thursday evenings, the Salem Band provided music for dances in Smith Hall.

After the commencement, the old trustees in an act of desperation reelected Swain and the sitting faculty. It was to no avail. On 24 July the new trustees "accepted" the 1867 resignations. Swain objected, but the new trustees simply ignored the aging former governor and resolved that they would replace him only with a man possessing an "established national reputation as a scholar and educator." Instead they chose UNC alumnus Solomon Pool, a Republican and a "scalawag."

The old faculty quietly dispersed. Dr. Fordyce Hubbard, who had taught Latin for 13 years, went to a Manilius, New York boys school. Dr. Andrew D. Hepburn, who had taught rhetoric and logic since 1860 went to Miami University in Oxford, Ohio. Manuel Fetter went to a Henderson, North Carolina boys school. Professor William J. Martin, who had replaced Elisha Mitchell, went to Tennessee. Hosea H. "Old Tige" Smith went to Lincolnton. Judge Battle moved to a law practice in Raleigh. Dr. Charles Phillips went to Davidson College to teach mathematics. After the death of Swain, Bursar Andrew Mickle was the only "university man" left in the village.

"Chapel Hill is the Deserted Village of the South," wrote Cornelia Spencer on 26 November 1868 as she sat beneath the Davie Poplar observing a Negro girl leaning against the Old Well and a group of Negro soldiers walking into the village. "Nearly twenty of the best families in the place are leaving," she continued, "and their houses are standing untenanted and desolate." Business was "at a stand-still, while I am told that no fewer than six places have been lately established, where liquor is openly sold." To make matters worst for the great majority of those who remained, they had to accept a new president and a new faculty that they found repugnant.

As devastating as wartime inflation had been, life in the "one-industry" village was even worse when that "industry" was crippled, almost mortally. With the student body reduced to a token status, the income of merchants and former university workers dropped below subsistence level, and when they followed the old faculty, area farmers lost their markets for butter, eggs, pork, chickens, and produce. Druggist R.B. Saunders moved to Raleigh; other merchants and professionals either left town or in many cases turned to farming to feed their families.

The price of real estate plummeted, and sheriff's sales became commonplace, creating ill feeling when those few with money bought up family estates and residences. Solomon Pool, who was already hated in the village, had the means to make several advantageous purchases, including a house and four acres on Cameron Avenue. By 1870, Pool was paying more taxes than anyone else in Chapel Hill, $14.80 compared to $7.60 paid by J.W. Carr and $4.60 by Dave McCauley. Local contempt for Pool became outrage in 1869 when he bought Miss Nancy Hilliard's "Crystal Palace" for a paltry $150 in a sheriff's sale, and then allowed Col. Hugh B. Guthrie to live in it rent free to insure that Miss Hilliard would not ask use of it.

Nancy Hilliard, her sister Martha, and her brother-in-law Benton Utley went to Raleigh after the war to operate

the Exchange Hotel. Early in 1872, Cornelia Spencer was in Raleigh helping State Geologist W.C. Kerr prepare a geological map of North Carolina when she visited Nancy and the Utleys. She wrote her brother Charles that the Exchange Hotel was "going down every way." Utley was habitually drunk, the proprietors had no wood for heat, and Utley had borrowed money from every boarder who would trust him. Only Nancy's "table" was still adequate. When the hotel failed later in the year, Nancy and the Utleys returned to Chapel Hill, where Nancy moved into a room in her old Eagle Hotel as the nonpaying guest of Dave McCauley and Thomas Long, who had purchased the building.

Nancy Hilliard died on 8 November 1873, penniless and mourned primarily by Mrs. Spencer and the deaf-mute Lemuel Yancy. For years Nancy had given Lemuel sympathetic treatment and meals. When she died, he followed her casket to the village cemetery, shedding copious tears. Mrs. Spencer appealed to alumni for contributions to help Nancy and to erect a gravestone for the dying old lady who had assisted so many students. Thirteen years later, Mrs. Spencer was able to purchase a stone inscribed in part, "ERECTED 1886, By certain alumni of this University, in grateful rememberance of her unfailing kindness and hospitality."

When Sam Phillips left for Raleigh in the fall of 1867 to become supreme court recorder, Cornelia Spencer moved into his vacant house for a few months and took in boarders, including W.H.S. Burgwyn and the brothers Will and George Maverick. When she moved out in June 1868, friends suggested that she move in with her brother Charles, but she answered defiantly, "No! I stand in mine own place." Stand she did.

In the January 1871 *North Carolina Presbyterian*, she described the concerted community effort to make pincushions, watch cases, sewing baskets, lamp mats, baby socks, emeries, and anything else that could be made "out of nothing" for a Christmas fair to raise money for the Methodist Church: "We all went to the Fair — admission 10 cents — and we all met each other, and nodded, and smiled, and chatted, and laughed, and walked about, and praised everything as if we never had seen it before, and asked the prices which we had set ourselves, and bought everything with the same steady determination to sacrifice ourselves for the good of the church."

W.H.S. Burgwyn, brother of "the boy colonel of the confederacy," kept a team of black horses and a groom, and Lucy Phillips Russell never lost her vivid memories of riding behind the fine animals. But when Governor Swain told Burgwyn he was setting an example that would cause pain to the less fortunate, the considerate young man removed his horses and carriage.

It was during this hard "reconstruction" that the community began to lose one of its architectural distinctions—

While most of the "offices" — popular as student living quarters — disappeared during Reconstruction, this one at the corner of Cameron and Wilson Court survived into this century. Dr. Thomas J. Wilson used it as his office until 1905 when it again became student housing. The three students pictured in this 1911 photograph are Cuban brothers (left to right) Thomas Vicente, Francisco, and Felix Luciano Llorens, engineering students at UNC. Playwright Paul Green also lived there when he was a student. (Photo courtesy of Peter Wilson).

its offices, now preserved only in the Sam Phillips law office. Erected primarily to accomodate the rapidly increasing number of students in the 1850s, almost every substantial residence had one in its yard. After the war, the dormitories were more than sufficient, and large houses were either abandoned and free for the taking or available for nominal rents. The "offices" were, consequently, reduced to serving as storage bins for a citizenry with little to hoard, and most of them perished.

But even with the hardest of times upon them, Chapel Hillians still had a countryside respendent in dogtooth violets, Japan silverworts, phlox, daffodils, jonquils, golden-rod, jasmine, maples, pines, hickory, oaks, rhododendron, and a thousand other flowering plants and trees. Mrs. Spencer never tired of the marvelous scenery in and adjacent to the town, and a spring within a 20-minute walk was "still as wild and secluded as when the Indian stopped to slake his thirst here."

The bitterness between the races in the months immediately following the surrender seemed to be abating by the summer of 1866. Many of the freedmen who had followed the northern armies had returned; in Raleigh attorney Sam Phillips was pleading for the legislature to give blacks a right to testify in the courts; and in Chapel Hill his brother Charles was teaching a black Sunday school class. During the Fourth of July festivities, blacks held a separate celebration, marching beneath a banner on which Mrs. Spencer had sewn their mottoes "Respect for Former Owners" on one side and "Our Hope Is in God" on the other. Col. Hugh B. Guthrie addressed the former slaves, the Declaration of Independence was read and cheered, and members of both races marched in procession for lunch at the new Quaker schoolhouse.

But Solomon Pool's arrival coincided with a marked worsening of racial relations in the area, in the state, and throughout the south. Change was clearly in the saddle, and the Old Guard felt ridden to humiliation. Conservatives believed the Freedman's Bureau, the Union League, and the Republican regime were recklessly encouraging blacks to burn barns, bully and rape whites, and commit other violent outrages. For a while, the Ku Klux Klan and its sister organizations seemed the answer to calm white fears and soothe white indignation, but responsible white leaders soon lost control of the secret organizations and vigilante-like activities became too frequent, too violent, and very often too personal.

Ironically, the village which had grown to symbolize North Carolina enlightenment became a center of organized white resistance to the social revolution being forced upon a defeated people by emissaries from the North and their detested sympathizers in the south. Though definitive proof followed him to the grave, there is little doubt that Col. William L. Saunders was the "emperor of the Invisible Empire" in North Carolina while he was living in Chapel Hill from 1867 to 1870, the period of the most intense KKK activity.

William Lawrence Saunders was a kinsman of Chapel Hill druggist R.B. Saunders and the son of Raleigh minister Joseph Hubbard Saunders, who graduated from UNC with an A.B. in 1821 and an M.A. in 1824, who served as a tutor in 1821-1825, and who died of yellow fever in 1839, leaving a pregnant widow who soon moved to Chapel Hill. William Saunders attended the university, graduated with honors in 1854, studied law under Judge Battle, earned an L.L.B. in 1858, and began practicing law in Salisbury, where he enlisted in the Rowan Rifles.

Serving under Robert E. Lee, Saunders fought in the great battles on the northern front, ending the war as colonel of the 46th NC Regiment. During a lull in the battle of Fredericksburg, he was laughing at a comrade's joke when a minie ball entered his open mouth and penetrated his

William Lawrence Saunders (1835-1891) grew up in Chapel Hill and graduated from UNC in 1854. Wounded two times in the Civil War, during Reconstruction he directed the activities of the Ku Klux Klan in North Carolina from his home in Chapel Hill. He is pictured here in his Confederate uniform. (NCC)

cheek. A witness quipped, "It was said to have been the most abruptly ended laugh heard during the war." On leave in February 1864, he married Florida Cotton of Edgecombe County. Then in the Wilderness campaign of May 1864, Saunders was again shot through the open mouth, this bullet exiting through the back of his neck. During his convalescence he received a more enduring wound when Florida died. The stalwart Saunders returned to action, surrendering at Appomattox along with Ilai Nunn's son Pvt. William Nunn.

On 16 April 1869, Governor Holden proclaimed his intention to break the Klan, and he subsequently employed some 20 detectives to assist him. The centers of Klan activity were in Caswell and Alamance counties, Shelby, Hillsborough, and Chapel Hill. Lucy Phillips Russell never forgot the night her black nurse "Aunt" Ginny pulled her from her bed and held her to the window so she could see a small army of KKK ride silently down Franklin Street on horses with muffled hooves. Chapel Hill lawyer James B. Mason wrote Governor Holden on 22 September 1869, "It has become no uncommon thing to see 40 to 50 ... Ku Klux rowdying up and down through the streets of this village at the late hour of twelve o'clock." In a recent incident, the masked raiders had ridden through the campus, beaten blacks, made a "Negro Republican leader" take an oath of allegiance to the Democratic Party, stoned November Caldwell's house by mistake, and terrorized the inmates at a Negro poorhouse.

One of Holden's detectives was William Huskey who checked into the Union Hotel and began making inquiries, but not discreetly. He publicly displayed his commission, opened private letters, and bragged he would be paid $1000 plus a bonus for each KKK member convicted by his findings, all the time dropping hints that he would like to join the Klan.

Under the guise of accepting him into their order, a group of men escorted Huskey from his hotel one night, tied him to the town pump in front of the present-day Methodist Church, and applied 60 lashes to his bare back, telling him that the whipping was the preliminary portion of an initiation that would be completed the next evening. He later charged Col. Hugh B. Guthrie with being the chief of his tormentors, but he never returned to Chapel Hill. Holden, however, retaliated by sending black troops to occupy the campus.

At noon on 25 September, concerned citizens of Chapel Hill met to draft resolutions protesting Holden's actions. Andrew Mickle nominated John R. Hutchins to be chairman and J.M. Alexander to be secretary of the proceedings. Dr. William P. Mallett explained the purpose of the meeting, and a committee made up of Mickle, Mallett, Col. Saunders, T.M. Argo, Foster Utley, J.F. Freeland, John H. Watson, R.H. Lee, H.J. Stone, W.J. Newton, and Fendall Southerland delivered a report on the issues that

Hamilton Chamberlain Jones, Jr. (1837-1904), lawyer and grandson of Chapel Hill's most prominent villager from 1800 to 1830, Pleasant Henderson, received his BA from UNC in 1858, rose to the rank of Colonel in the Confederate army, and served as a UNC trustee 1889-1897. Jones was the leader of the Ku Klux Klan in Mecklenburg County after the war. (NCC)

William Woods Holden (1818-1892), post-war Republican governor, moved forcefully to bring the Ku Klux Klan to heel in Orange County, the center of its activity. He convinced Dr. Pride Jones (1815-1889) of Hillsborough, a UNC graduate, to help. Jones talked to the Klan leaders in the county, and, whatever he said, it worked: the Klan virtually closed its activities in Orange County and Chapel Hill in the early 1870s. By contrast, Holden found it necessary to place two adjacent counties under martial law. (NCC)

had prompted the meeting.

The committee expressed "surprise and indignation" over Holden's having placed a spy in their midst, declared that citizens "had submitted patiently" to the organization and activities of Negro leagues, and objected to Holden's appointment of Wilson Caldwell as justice of the peace and to the appointment of a Negro constable by a commission headed by Solomon Pool. They charged the state administration with damaging the local economy by refusing to support the university and with appointing "a faculty obnoxious to the people of the State," and they protested the presence of armed Negro soldiers. (Committee member Fendall Southerland hanged himself in January 1878, after a long illness.)

In a set of resolutions sent to newspapers across the state, those in attendance declared that (1) the commission of William M. Huskey was an outrage and a violation of the state constitution, (2) the appointment of blacks tended "to develop an unnecessary antagonism between the two races," (3) any additional armed troops would "put at hazard the peace and quiet of the community," (4) following the disbanding of the Union League "all organizations entered into to ward off such oppression will also be disbanded," (5) "good citizens and true men" could not be condemned when they were forced to provide their own justice, (6) vigilante action was a grave threat "to the peace and harmony of the State," and (7) the majority of the "colored people of this community" had deported themselves with prudence and moderation "in spite of the persistent attempts made to arouse their passions and excite their prejudices against white people, and that from them as a people, if left to themselves, we apprehend no trouble." James B. Mason alone opposed the release of the report.

Clandestine leaders in general tried to halt violence once they realized that vicious men were using the cover of secrecy to express personal prejudices and to settle personal scores. In the summer of 1870, Holden "attacked" the Klan

with an army of approximately 1000 men, commanded by Col. George W. Kirk, who had won the enmity of southerners during the war by leading a Union brigade made up of Confederate deserters and unionists. The governor succeeded in breaking the Klan, but the severity of his measures led directly to his impeachment and expulsion from office once the Democrats regained control of the General Assembly.

In 1871, a joint congressional committee summoned Col. W.L. Saunders to Washington to testify on his knowledge of Klan activity in North Carolina. Friends offered to give him enough money to live on comfortably in Europe, but he chose to submit to arrest and transportation to Washington. To over 100 questions about his involvement in secret organizations, he gave the invariable response, "I decline to answer." The congressmen could not but admire his resolve, and neither their questions nor his monotonous answers appear in the official records. Saunders was secretary of the N.C. Senate in 1870-1871, he founded the Raleigh *Observer* in 1876, and he was the North Carolina secretary of state from 1879 until his death in 1891, during which time he compiled the voluminous *Colonial Records of North Carolina*.

There are two inscriptions on Saunders' tombstone in Tarboro, where he lies by the side of his bride Florida. The first reads, "For Twenty Years He Exerted More Power in North Carolina Than Any Other Man." Below it is his epitath — "I decline to answer." Carrying out a promise he had given the colonel, a Negro servant burned a trunk filled with Saunders' records on the day he died, obscuring perhaps forever his precise role within the "Invisible Empire." In 1906, Prof. Collier Cobb proclaimed Saunders to be the greatest North Carolinian ever to have lived.

However, hostility between the 483 whites and the 454 blacks that W.S. Guthrie counted in Chapel Hill in 1869 was by no means universal. White attitudes toward blacks ranged from hatred to condescension to genuine affection. When Cornelia Spencer could no longer support them,

Jacob Thompson (1810-1885) fled to England in 1865 after Union authorities had named him a co-conspirator in the plot against Lincoln and after President Andrew Johnson had offered a $25,000 reward for his capture. Thompson returned in 1868 when he was no longer under suspicion. Most historians argue that Thompson was innocent, but some revisionists continue to link him with the crime.

Thompson graduated from UNC third-in-class in 1831 and remained as a tutor for two years. He studied law, moved to Mississippi, and built a brilliant career in national politics before the Lincoln assassination ended his public life. Six of his brothers attended UNC. (NCC)

the former Phillips-family house slaves "Aunt" Dilsey and "Uncle" Ben Craig settled with adopted son John Caldwell in a two-room cabin on the Hillsborough Road, but the former ties survived.

Cornelia wrote emotionally of a visit she, her daughter June, and two Phillips nieces paid to Dilsey in August 1869, during the height of the KKK activity in Chapel Hill. The children were fascinated by the simple but functional furnishings in Dilsey's house. Cornelia brought gifts — tea cakes, a pound of freshly ground coffee, a bag of tea, sugar, molasses, and a small bottle of liquid which she passed to Dilsey on the sly. No one escaped the hardships imposed by the deep economic depression, and the shared suffering forged long lasting relationships cutting across all social borders.

Until the Civil War, all the churches in Chapel Hill had served both races, albeit with separate galleries for slaves and free blacks. Toward the end of the war, the first totally black congregation formed when members of what would evolve into St. Paul's African Methodist Episcopal Church began to meet under a fig tree near the intersection of Franklin Street and Merritt Mill Road. About 1870, AME members built a church across Franklin Street from the present St. Paul's, which was built in 1892.

The Baptist Church minutes for 3 September 1865 read, "On motion it was unanimously voted that the colored patrons of this church be allowed to withdraw from this church and organize a church to themselves." The Rev. Eddie H. Cole organized the new church which met in the Quaker School while they were building a frame sanctuary across Franklin Street from the present headquarters of the Chapel Hill *Newspaper*. In 1877, the Rev. Lewis H. Hackney took over ministerial duties and headed the First Baptist Church of Chapel Hill until he died in 1938. During his long tenure, Hackney became something of a moral dictator, strongly opposing secular parties, dancing, drinking, and card playing.

The political tempests of the community seemed always to swirl around Solomon Pool.

Pool was born into an old North Carolina family in Elizabeth City in 1832. He grew into a short, soft-spoken, stout man with curly hair and a pompous manner. He graduated from the university with honors in 1853 and stayed on for seven years as a tutor in mathematics. In 1856 he married Cornelia Kirkland of Chapel Hill, formerly of Hillsborough, and in 1860 he became an adjunct professor of mathematics, a post he held for the duration of the war. In 1866 he left the university for Raleigh and a well publicized salary of $5000 per year as the U.S. Deputy Appraiser for North Carolina. In 1868 his

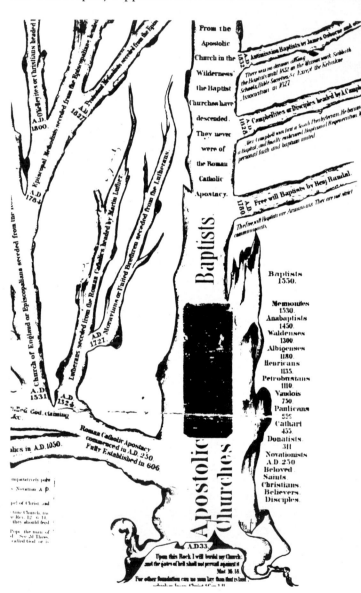

The Baptist preachers around Chapel Hill pressed their version of religious truth on the village during the period of Reconstruction. This 1872 broadside by Rev. G.W. Purefoy purports to prove that all religions except the Baptist are apostasies. During one week of the almost continuous revivals of 1876, nearly 200 people — in a village of less than 150 families — professed religion. One Baptist evangelist, Rev. Thomas Henderson Pritchard, held a 30-day revival and in his last sermon said that immersion was necessary for salvation. Presbyterians were so upset that they imported the "eminent Raleigh minister Rev. Watkins" to refute Pritchard. Watkins' sermon, delivered to over 300 souls, staunchly defended sprinkling. (NCC)

brother John Pool was one of the U.S. Senators elected by the Republican-dominated General Assembly, and when Congress on 20 July recognized the new state constitution and seated the newly-elected congressional delegation, North Carolina was once again a member of the Union.

Like Solomon Pool, all the new faculty were Republicans. Mathematics Professor Alexander McIver came from Davidson College. He was a native of Moore County and had graduated from the university in 1853. Detested at first as a usurper, a Republican, a scalawag, and a minion of Pool's, McIver was eventually accepted by the citizens of Chapel Hill as a dedicated and honorable man; and as State Superintendent of Public Instruction between 1871 and 1873, he worked as hard as anyone to restore the university.

Greek professor and librarian Fisk P. Brewer graduated with distinction from Yale in 1852. A brother of future U.S. Supreme Court Justice David J. Brewer, he had been a tutor at Yale, had taught at Beloit College, and was the principal of a black school in Raleigh when he joined the university faculty. Brewer further offended white Chapel Hillians by boarding with a Negro before moving into The Retreat.

Latin professor and bursar David Settle Patrick, originally from Rockingham County, graduated from the university in 1856 and arrived from the principalship of a school in Arkansas, moving into the Swain house. English professor James A. Martling of Missouri was the brother-in-law of North Carolina Superintendent of Public Instruction Samuel S. Ashley, who had recommended him to the trustees. Professor of Agriculture George Dixon was a Quaker and a native of Yorkshire, England.

Pool's task of rebuilding the university was surely Herculean, and his failure seems to have been inevitable. Parents either could not afford to send their sons to the university or would not give tacit approval of the new administration by so doing. During the spring term of 1869, only three sophomores and seven freshmen attended, and Chapel Hillian Abdel Kader Tenney was the only person to receive an A.B. degree at the 10 June commencement — for work done in 1863-65.

Believing they were acting on the authority of recent state legislation, on 28 February 1870 citizens upset with appointments made by Governor Holden and Solomon Pool's board of commissioners conducted a special election and chose a "rump" board of commissioners made up of John H. Watson, Dave McCauley, J.F. Freeland, J.R. Hutchins, and W.J. Newton. The new commissioners met immediately and named Ruffin Cheek as constable and Andrew Mickle as magistrate of police. On 1 April, Solomon Pool reported to the old board, "The election at which these gentlemen claim to have been elected was held without their having had a copy of any Act of law authorizing it; and ... the proceedings were had under in-

formal notice from Mr. T.M. Argo that such an election should be held." He recommended that "if they give up the books . . . no action against them be begun."

At the sixth meeting of the "rump" commission on 7 April, their counsel advised them that their election was not valid, and the old commission and magistrate of police Col. Hugh Guthrie resumed responsibility for running the town. In reality, it was no great job. Even as late as 1874 total taxable property in the village amounted to only $52,590. With property taxed at $.50 per $100 value, the total taxes due the town that year were only $361.48.

In January 1870, Pool could list only nine students in the university and 15 in the new preparatory department. By November the total number had climbed to 36, but by then the death knell of the university had begun to sound.

Col. Hugh Guthrie was one of the few Chapel Hillians who supported Pool, claiming he was the best president in the history of the university. (On 4 July 1866, Guthrie took as his second wife Jane Cave, the 29-year old daughter of Dr. Hudson and Delia Barbee Cave.) However, the majority of Chapel Hillians detested Pool and fought to have him removed, even if it meant the temporary closure of the university. In April 1869, merchant John W. Carr met Pool on the street and suggested he resign. Pool angrily retorted he would not resign for $50,000. Carr declared he would not hold on under present conditions for $50,000. As a parting shot, Pool promised Carr that he would begin accepting blacks should white students fail to apply.

Students, local farmers, and town residents had cut trees freely during and following the war, but citizens were incensed when the new faculty continued the practice, even

This 1890s photograph shows two Chapel Hill "institutions," Dave McCauley's store on the north side of Franklin Street, and Benjamin Boothe, a former slave reputed to have served James K. Polk when he was a student in 1818, although Boothe's birthdate is listed in the 1870 census as 1830. Boothe moved onto a farm northeast of town near the Tenney home after the Civil War, and lived into the 20th century.

After McCauley died in 1911, Emmett Gooch opened a fruit-and-snack stand in the old wooden building. (NCC)

though they knew the professors were receiving only a small fraction of their salaries and could not afford to buy firewood. McIver cut all but one tree on the Mitchell lot. Brewer cut several large trees around The Retreat on the old Tom Taylor lot. Some faculty members had also appropriated furnishings from the university buildings over the objections of Solomon Pool.

Charles J. Dorland made matters worse early in 1870 when he led two other students in a raid on the library society archive rooms, breaking down the doors and destroying papers. An official investigation exonerated Dorland, but faculty and townfolk were not convinced. Nevertheless, Dorland was one of the student speakers during the commencement of 1870, ceremonies apparently held strictly to satisfy tradition since there is no record of any degree being conferred.

On Thursday, 10 June, Republican U.S. Senator J.C. Abbott delivered the commencement address; Chapel Hill student Walter H. Guthrie spoke on "Mirabeau"; Baptist preacher George W. Purefoy accepted an honorary D.D. degree. The Rev. William Closs of Durham County and trustee A. Haywood Merritt of Chatham declined to accept honorary degrees, so great was their contempt for Pool and his administration. Merritt said he attended the ceremonies to hear Abbott's address, and while there he counted 14 strangers among a total audience of "103 little negroes and big whites and mulottoes all included."

By November 1870, it was evident that the attempt to keep the university going under present conditions was futile, and the trustees voted to cut off faculty salaries effective 1 February 1871. By the end of January only two students remained, and the day the school closed someone left an epitath on a classroom blackboard, "February 1, 1871. This old University has busted and gone to hell to-day."

With the university closed, times became even more difficult for the lawyers of Chapel Hill. J.M. Alexander, Jones Watson, James B. Mason, and Thomas M. Argo were the leading members of the bar, but they had to rely on activities other than the law and outside the village to supplement their incomes. Jones Watson, for example, raised an excellent grade of wheat and competed vigorously with local farmers to grow prized produce.

In 1869, Prof. Fordyce Hubbard's son-in-law Thomas M. Argo was involved in the political dispute that kept Chapel Hill from being linked to the North Carolina Railroad system. The General Assembly chartered the University Railroad Company and authorized $300,000 in state bonds to finance construction. Railroad commissioners chose Henry C. Thompson to be president, but Governor Holden refused to sign the bonds unless Argo were named president, even though Argo had savaged the Republicans under the pen name of "Billy Barlow."

University Railroad Company officers went to court to

Dr. G.W. Purefoy, Jr. (1851-1942), son of the Chapel Hill Baptist preacher, attended UNC in 1869-1870, and, after the university closed, transferred to Wake Forest, returning to Chapel Hill to marry Elizabeth Watson in 1880, and to be part owner of a village drug store, 1882-1884. He moved to Asheville about 1884 and set up a medical practice. Dr. Purefoy was the family doctor of the W.O. and Julia Wolfe family, delivering all of their children, including author Thomas Wolfe. Purefoy appears in Wolfe's novel Look Homeward, Angel is "Dr. Cardiac." (NCC)

force Holden to sign the bonds, but the court declared the act creating the commission unconstitutional, thus ending the proposed line for the time. The General Assembly considered the matter again in 1875, but too many legislators feared that a railroad running near the campus would corrupt the morals of the students, and it was not until 1879 that they chartered a new company and work actually began. (When KKK leader Plato Durham died in Shelby in 1875, T.M. Argo was at his bedside, holding his hand.)

James B. Mason attended the universtiy in 1867-1868, married Solomon Pool's sister-in-law the former Latitia Kirkland, became a practicing lawyer, and supported his brother-in-law in his many contests with villagers and other detractors. In June 1873, Pool charged Cornelia Spencer with having had her young male students break down the door of the Philanthropic Library so she could inspect the condition of the books and the premises. James B. Mason indicted several of the students and tried them in Chapel Hill before a magistrate, who acquitted the boys.

Attorney J.M. Alexander rose to Mrs. Spencer's defense, leading an "indignation" meeting of citizens on 16 August which condemned "the infamous and cowardly conduct of the said Solomon Pool." Three years later, tragedy struck Alexander and his family. A diphtheria epidemic swept through the families living along Morgan Creek, killing four of his children. The immunity to epidemics that Chapel Hill had enjoyed for so long had ended in July 1869 when a mysterious illness invaded the Negro community, killing three children. Cornelia Spencer sympathized deeply for the children who knew they were dying, while unleashing her frustration on the doctors of Chapel Hill who could not diagnose the symptoms.

Conversely, Judge Battle personally found Dr. Johnston B. Jones' prognosis and prescription happily efficacious. The judge was so upset over losing his state supreme court justiceship in 1868 that he could not sleep. Dr. Jones suggested that he try "a wineglass of raw whiskey on going to bed." The hitherto abstemious-minded judge consented to the experiment and discovered a miracle cure. His son Kemp mused, "I have often wondered whether Maecenas, the Prime Minister of Augustus Caesar, who died after three months of insomnia, might not have been cured by Dr. Jones's single glass of whiskey." Already bankrupt, still mourning his wife who had died in 1865, Dr. Jones left in 1868 to set up a practice in Charlotte, where he was joined in 1883 by his son, Dr. Simmons Jones. The aging doctor was disabled by partial paralysis in 1886, but maintained an intense interest in the university until his death in 1889.

Dr. Willis Barbee died in 1869, leaving his Morgan Creek plantation to former slave Harriett Barbee and her children Haywood, David, and Silvy. Harriett's descendants believe that Dr. Barbee was married to Harriett at his death. If so, it must have been in a private ceremony or a common-law union, since the Orange County files contain no entry recording an official marriage.

Throughout the nineteenth century, Chapel Hill remained small enough to mourn collectively for individual deaths, especially those of long-time and revered residents. On the morning of 14 April 1867 just after the bell had signaled the beginning of the school day, Prof. James Phillips entered his classroom much as he had for the last 41 years. One of his favorite students, Eugene Morehead, greeted him, and as he was returning Morehead's salutation, Prof. Phillips fell dead. His granddaughter Lucy Phillips Russell watched from a window as students bore his body home through a spring snow storm. Her aunt Cornelia came to her room later, wrapped her in a large grey shawl, carried her across an orchard separating the Phillips' homes, and held her while she viewed the body of her grandfather, which lay in his study with his cat "Di Vernon" sleeping on his chest.

The children of professors and merchants continued to receive their education mostly from neighbors or at home during Reconstruction. "Education was highly esteemed, carefully provided — but it must be got in the ways the fathers trod," Mrs. George T. Winston later said of the period, otherwise it "was considered 'queer,' revolutionary, archaic."

Soon after the war, the Freedmen's Committee of Yearly Meetings of Friends in Philadelphia sent George Dixon, his wife and daughter to organize a "Quaker School" in Chapel Hill for former slaves. The Craig family donated an acre of land where West Franklin crossed the village limits, and the Quakers built a one-room log-cabin schoolhouse which they operated for a 12-week term each year for about a decade before Orange County began paying teacher salaries.

In Kemp Battle's words, local residents initially resented the teachers as the "creatures" of the "northern abolitionists responsible for the war." But Miss "Quaker" Dixon worked assiduously to make the school a success; and she, if not her parents, was soon accepted into the most prominent homes. Cornelia Spencer, Margaret Mitchell, and Margaret's sister Mrs. Eliza Grant assisted Miss Dixon in the freedmen's school; and Chapel Hill sisters Mrs. Susie Merritt and Mrs. Luther Edwards afterward took over the teaching duties.

John Manning (1830-1899), founder of the UNC law school in 1881, is sitting with his wife and some of his children and grandchildren in this 1880s photograph. Earlier he had been a delegate to the Secession Convention in Raliegh in 1861. In a race for Congress against Joseph Holden in 1870, Manning's campaign broadside declared him to be opposed to the tax on brandy and opposed to a reduction of the national debt. He won the election. (NCC)

In 1871, the village commissioners proposed that a "guard house" be built on the property of Hugh B. Guthrie, Magistrate of Police. The commissioners discussed the price, location, and size of the proposed building for thirteen years and in 1884 authorized its erection.

A three-member team of commissioners supervised the construction of the $150 red building near the intersection of Columbia and Rosemary. Pictured here in the early 20th century, the little shack survived until 1920. (NCC)

George Dixon and his wife also organized a Negro Sunday school in the Presbyterian Church before he joined the new faculty in 1868 as professor of agriculture. In his preparation to lay out a model farm behind the South Building, Dixon cut most of the trees still remaining, thus raising the ire of villagers, especially Mrs. Spencer who in her contempt insisted on spelling the professor's name "Dickson." In the spring of 1869, Dixon obtained a leave of absence to visit his native England to procure educational materials, but he did not return to Chapel Hill.

About 1870 the Chapel Hill School Committee — made up of Morgan Closs, W.H. Bunch, and H.C. Andrews — asked the university for two acres on the Pittsboro Road as the site for a black school. The trustees refused because the land was mortgaged, and the Quaker School, enlarged to three rooms, continued in operation until after World War I. In 1947 the property was sold for $1600, which was loaned to the Lincoln-Norwood PTA to purchase band instruments.

In 1869, ex-slave Wilson Caldwell obtained a license to operate a public school and began offering classes to black children in a frame building at Mallett and Cameron, a block from the campus. He left to become principal of an Elizabeth City school, returned to his old job as university janitor, and went to work in Durham for Julian Shakespeare Carr when the university closed. According to a suspect version of a story Carr loved to tell, when the university reopened Caldwell came to him and said, "I hates to leave here, Mr. Carr, but you knows that Durham ain't no place for a literary man." Wilson Caldwell's father "Doctor" November died in 1872.

For two years after February 1871, the issue of reviving the university languished. Although Mrs. Spencer, former governors Vance and Graham, and others kept the matter alive and before the public, even they realized that a lasting solution was impossible as long as the Board of Trustees was dominated by men the vast majority of North Carolinians considered traitors.

In August 1870, voters returned the Democrats to control of the General Assembly, and in early 1871 the Democrats got their revenge by removing Governor Holden from office after convicting him of six "high crimes and misdemeanors." Republican Lieutenant-Governor Tod R. Caldwell, who graduated with honor from the university in 1840 and who read for the bar under Governor Swain, succeeded Holden and won reelection by a slim majority in 1872. Nevertheless, the Democrats were able to amend the constitution in 1873 to return the selection of trustees to the General Assembly.

That action spurred efforts to reopen the university. Only two of the recent trustees carried over to the new board of 64 members, which included 14 from the board dissolved in 1868, and the new Executive Committee was made up entirely of devoted university men. They were: President, William A. Graham; Secretary, Kemp Plummer Battle; and members W.L. Saunders, John Manning, W.T. Faircloth, John A. Gilmer, and Paul C. Cameron.

In the summer of 1824, the young, red-headed Paul Cameron, dressed in a homemade red suit, was walking from the Alsobrook Hotel to the South Building to enroll in the university when one of the crowd of students shouted, "Red Bird!" The quick-tempered Cameron spun and offered to fight all comers, one at a time. None accepted the invitation, but ever after their challenger was known as "Red Bird" Cameron. In 1874 the very wealthy Cameron headed a committee to inspect the campus before recommending renovation measures. Committee member W.L. Steele wrote of what he felt on a 3 April 1874 inspection: "Never shall I forget the sadness that overpowered me when my eyes fell for the first time upon the ruined spot. It was akin to that which swells within my bosom when I stand before the grave of my mother."

The troops sent by Holden had plundered some of the buildings; a goodly portion of the books, furnishings, and apparatus were in the hands of professors and villagers; Old East was essentially in ruins except for its outer walls; New East was crumbling because of poor workmanship,

Amzi Clarence Dixon (1854-1925) of Shelby, N.C., graduated from Wake Forest College in 1874, then came to Chapel Hill as the $850 per year Baptist minister. His first act on reaching the village was to hold a 21-day revival. He met Susan Mary Faison (1853-1922) in the summer of 1877 when she came to Chapel Hill for the Normal School, and they married soon after.

Dixon was known in the village as the "sportin' parson" because of his expressed love of hunting small game.

Dixon's brother, Thomas Dixon, wrote The Clansman, upon which D.W. Griffith based his epic movie "Birth of a Nation." (NCC)

Charles Force Deems (1820-1893), a Methodist minister who served on the UNC faculty 1842-1847, donated $300 in 1880 to create the Theodore D. Deems Student Loan Fund for indigent students at UNC, a fund named for a son who was born in Chapel Hill and who died at Gettysburg. On 29 December 1880, Deems mentioned the small fund during a sermon at his Church of the Stranger in New York City. W.H. Vanderbuilt was so moved by Deems' statements that the next day he contributed $10,000 to the fund. (NCC)

neglect, and abuse; Old West was "defiled by the ordure of cattle and horses." On the grounds, gates had fallen, walls were broken, plants trampled and eaten by wandering cattle, wells spoiled, trees either cut down or damaged, and the embankments around Old East and Old West eroded by weather, men, and animals. Only Gerrard Hall, which had remained in use as a public hall, was in generally good repair. The committee estimated minimum repairs would cost $6000.

During a 10 February 1875 trustees meeting, William A. Graham recommended that unwise past investments be discounted and that the state grant the trustees use of the interest accruing from the Land Grant Fund, amounting to $7500 annually. State Senator C.M.T. McCauley of Union County, a grandson of Matthew McCauley and a graduate of 1838, was a leader in the General Assembly vote on 17 March which granted Graham's request, by a narrow 51-50 decision in the House but by a comfortable margin in the Senate. When the Senate passed the bill on its third reading on 20 March, perhaps the most famous single event in the history of Chapel Hill followed.

Friends wired the results to Cornelia Spencer, and it came as a happy climax to her fiftieth birthday celebration. With Andrew Mickle, her students, and neighborhood children in her wake, she determinedly marched to the South Building, climbed the attic stairs, and triumphantly rang the university bell, announcing the good news to the countryside.

The trustees met in May to reorganize the university and to announce a September 1875 reopening. Paul Cameron oversaw the renovations personally to insure that the work was done economically and well. He refused reimbursement for his expenses, as did Kemp Battle, who traveled the state at his own expense, eventually raising $18,685. Judge Battle gave $1000, Kemp $500, Paul Cameron $1000, B.F. Moore $1000, and several others amounts in the $250-500 range. In Chapel Hill, S.M. Barbee gave $75, John W. Carr $100, Col. Hugh B. Guthrie $10, merchant Dave McCauley $100, Dr. William P. Mallett $10, Andrew Mickle $30, A.F. Redd $100, and Jones Watson $50. Cameron spent $10,667.76 for repairs

Seaton M. Barbee (1848-1920) prospered after he bought Lucas's drugstore, and he was able to buy several additional properties during Reconstruction. In 1879 he built this house beside his drugstore on the grounds of the present Methodist Church on Franklin Street. In 1921, Seaton's widow, Susan Davis, sold it to the university, and the university traded it to the Methodist Church in 1924. (NCC)

Curtis Hooks Brogden (1816-1901), a lifelong bachelor, served the Republican cause after the Civil War. He remained, nevertheless, a close friend of a number of post-war Democrats and of UNC, serving as a trustee 1869-1872. He was lieutenant-governor under Tod Caldwell, who as Governor refused to support the reopening of UNC because, while he supported public education, he considered the university a haven for the elite. After Caldwell's death in 1874, Brogden succeeded to the governorship and cooperated in reopening the university. He later served in Congress. (NCC)

and $2249.09 for the installation of a gas system and the purchase of scientific apparatus.

On 16 June, trustees named a new faculty, including former professor of agriculture John Kimberly, Ralph Henry Graves, Dr. Charles Phillips, John DeB. Hooper, the Rev. Adolphus W. Magnum, and A.F. Reed. As adjunct professor of Latin and German, George Tayloe Winston began his lengthy tenure at the university. Paul Cameron wanted to nominate former Governor William A. Graham for the presidency, but Graham, who knew he was dying, refused the honor. In lieu of a president, the trustees elected Charles Phillips "Chairman of the Faculty." Andrew Mickle, who had been wrecked financially by the war, consented to serve as bursar at $400 per year; Foster Utley took on the monumental task of university carpenter.

The trustees ordered the faculty to open on the first Monday of September. Accordingly, the faculty met on Saturday, 4 September, the literary societies reorganized, and classes began on the sixth. With the villagers' eager participation, faculty and trustees prepared for elaborate exercises to be held on Wednesday, 15 September.

By that brilliantly sunlit day, workers had transformed the campus into a showplace. The ladies of Chapel Hill had spent two days decorating Gerrard Hall with portraits of the great men responsible for the past success of the university and with a white banner into which Lucy

UNC's living Confederate veterans reassembled almost every year at Commencement time. This photograph shows the group in 1910. There were approximately 1600 1825-1861 graduates living in 1861, and nearly 1100 of them served in the Confederate forces. The war claimed the lives of seven of the 14 UNC faculty members who served in the army. In the class of 1860, 80 of 82 members served in the armed forces, and 23 of them died in battle. (NCC)

Phillips had woven the motto coined by Mrs. Spencer — "Laus Deo" ("Thank God"). As an appropriate natural symbol, the Davie Poplar was once again in full foliage, after having been split from its base to its upper limbs by a bolt of lightning on 7 August 1873.

At 11 a.m. Marshall John R. Hutchins, assisted by several students and marching to "Auld Lang Syne" as rendered by the Salisbury Band, led Governor Curtis H. Brogden, Judge Battle, aging Professor William Hooper, former Governor Vance, the senior sitting professors, trustees, and other dignitaries to Gerrard Hall, overflowing with townspeople and visitors. Prof. A.F. Redd read the opening hymn, composed by student W.A. Betts. In introducing Governor Brogden, Dr. Charles Phillips reminded all that the founders wanted a sound school free from domination by any political party or religious sect.

The governor delivered a carefully prepared speech on educational methods. Zebulon Vance confessed to being overpowered by emotion on this auspicious occasion, but the consummate politician was still able to flatter the ladies present by declaring them to be even more beautiful than their lovely mothers. Judge Battle surveyed the history of the university, pointing repeatedly to the portraits lining the walls and evoking heightened emotion with elegiac praise of former Governor William A. Graham, who had died 35 days previously. Prof. Magnum read the closing hymn, written for the event by Cornelia Spencer, which the audience then sang to the tune "Old Hundred" played by the Salisbury Band.

As a delegate to the Secession Convention in 1861, Kemp Battle signed the Ordinance of Secession, having ceased to be a unionist with Lincoln's call for troops. He spent the war as president of the Chatham Railroad Company, an ill-planned venture to link the North Carolina Railroad to the coal fields of Chatham County. Work on the line was nearing completion in the spring of 1865 when Sherman's troops halted construction, although later tests revealed the deposits were too poor and too limited to have ever mattered in the war effort.

Battle was a trustee from 1862 to 1868, the elected state treasurer in 1865, and later the president of the State Agriculture Society, who directed the North Carolina State Fair. When 25 trustees met in Raleigh on 16 June 1876 to elect a president of the university, one faction wanted a man who had distinguished himself in service to the South, and among others they considered Jefferson Davis, Gen. Joe Johnston, and Gen. Matt W. Ransom. Another faction wanted a native with solid Democratic credentials. In the 17 June vote, Gen. Johnston received five votes, Gen. Ransom one, Montford McGehee (UNC class of 1841) three, and Kemp Plummer Battle 16 — one over the necessary three-fifths majority.

Battle returned to Chapel Hill, purchased his father's house for $2500, repaired it, added the familiar one-story wings and the front porch, and named it Senlac. With the installation of Battle, the university had a president who was determined to see the institution grow in size and excel in quality, and with the university once again firmly established, the village poised to break out of the doldrums of the Reconstruction depression.

Kemp Plummer Battle (1831-1919), known as the "Second Founder of the University," married a distant cousin, Martha Ann "Patty" Battle in 1855 after a one year engagement. They had met at West Point in 1850, to discover that by coincidence they had both attended a Jenny Lind concert earlier in New York City. Kemp was proud of his wife's intellectual accomplishments: she read Gibbon's Decline and Fall of the Roman Empire *in its entirety, and she memorized both the U.S. Constitution and all 176 verses of the 119th Psalm. (NCC)*

The life span of this house, located on the "post office corner" of Franklin and Henderson, roughly corresponds to the time span covered by Chapter 5. Dr. William P. Mallett (1819-1889), son of ante-bellum bookstore owner Charles P. Mallett (1792-1874), built the house in 1881 on the lot he purchased from relatives of Anna Ashe, the mother of Capt. Richard Ashe. Originally the lot held the home of Pleasant Henderson, whose son Dr. Alexander Martin Henderson sold it to Mrs. Ashe in 1839. Mrs. Ashe's brother, Dr. George Moore, lived there until his death in 1857, and his children lived there until the house burned in 1880. The federal government bought the property in 1915 and built a post office on it.

In this 1910 photo, left to right, are Carolina Eliza "Miss Eliza" Mallett (1842-1929), the family cook Alice Neal (1893-1959), and Sophia "Miss Sophie" Mallet MacNider (1846-1929). Miss Eliza loved a young man who gave her a star jasmine bush just before he joined the Confederate army, to be killed in battle. From that time until her death, Miss Eliza picked the first blooms off the star jasmine each spring and wrapped them in a white handkerchief that she always carried. Miss Neal was later manager of the school cafeteria and for a number of years worked in UNC President Frank P. Graham's home. One of her daughters, Pearl, married Edwin Caldwell, the great-great-grandson of "Dr." November Caldwell. Miss Sophie ran one of the most popular boarding houses in town.

(The Malletts were related to Sarah Mumford, the fiancee of Revolutionary War hero Nathan Hale. When Hale was executed, she entered a convent and remained there for the rest of her life.) (NCC)

V
Out of the Shadows
1875 to 1920

When the University of North Carolina reopened in 1875, the campus contained eight principal buildings: Old East, Person Hall, South Building, Gerrard Hall, Old West, Smith Hall (the Playmakers Theatre), New East, and New West. Only one new building, the original Memorial Hall, went up during the presidency of Kemp Plummer Battle, June 1876 to August 1891, but Battle initiated a period of growth that by the end of World War I accounted for 15 additional new buildings—including the Alumni Building, Carr Hall, Bynum Gymnasium, Hill Hall, the Battle-Vance-Pettigrew dormitories, Swain Hall, and Phillips Hall.

Governor David Lowry Swain had placed primary emphasis on expanding the student body. Battle and his successors expanded the curriculum and upgraded the quality of instruction with the goal of attracting more and better prepared students. Battle's first great innovation was the Normal School, a summer school to educate teachers of both sexes and the first college-level summer school in the nation to offer a complete curriculum. During its existence from 1877 to 1884, the Normal School attracted a total enrollment of 2480, a boon both to the university and to the business community of Chapel Hill.

George Tayloe Winston succeeded Battle in August 1891, and during his five years at the helm concentrated on enlarging the student body, improving public education in the state, and increasing endowments to UNC to finance building and scholarships. Winston successfully faced a potentially crippling crisis in 1893. Dr. John B. Shearer was the president of Davidson College and the former pastor of the Chapel Hill Presbyterian Church whose ownership of slaves had incensed Benjamin and Ellen Hedrick in 1858. In 1893 the General Assembly considered a bill drawn up by Shearer which would in effect have abolished the undergraduate school at UNC.

Winston argued his case forcefully before the General Assembly, and the issue dissolved after a joint legislative committee reported "that the University is performing a noble duty to the State. . .and that it merits the care and support of the Legislature, as well as the esteem and patronage of our people." Winston left in 1896 to become president of the University of Texas, returning to Raleigh in 1899 as the president of North Carolina State College.

History and philosophy professor Edwin A. Alderman moved up to replace Winston in August 1896. While a student at UNC (class of 1882), Alderman met his future wife Emma Graves, the daughter of Prof. Ralph Graves I and the aunt of publisher Louis Graves. Alderman had begun teaching at UNC in 1893 after having assisted Dr. Charles D. McIver in founding the State Normal and Industrial School in Greensboro in 1891, which is now UNC-G. He continued his innovative ways by opening the doors of UNC to women before leaving Chapel Hill in 1900 to become president of Tulane University. He was president of the University of Virginia when he died in 1906.

Science professor Francis P. Venable became president in June 1900 and that fall welcomed 512 students, the first time the student body had surpassed the record 461 set in 1858. Venable reorganized the growing administration, oversaw the establishment of several new schools within the university, and got a $55,000 Andrew Carnegie grant in 1905 which provided for the construction of a Carnegie Library on campus, the building that in 1930 was converted by a gift from John Sprunt Hill into the Hill Music Hall. Venable helped organize the Order of the Golden Fleece, saw the

William Mercer Green built this house on East Franklin Street in 1847-48 on the lot he purchased from UNC in 1847 for $64.57. He sold the house to Charles Phillips (1822-1889) in 1849 for $1250, and Phillips lived there until he left Chapel Hill during Reconstruction. Phillips eventually moved back into the house when he returned to the university faculty, but rheumatism and gout forced him to retire and left him a near invalid for the last 11 years of his life. Phillips and his wife, Laura Battle, sister of William Horn Battle, are on the porch in this 1880s photograph. The tree in the left foreground still stands. (NCC)

Edward Kidder Graham (1876-1918) was a member of the family that has been prominently connected to North Carolina education since the Civil War. Dr. Graham, in a Richmond, Va., speech in 1913, two years before he became UNC President, adopted the 1910 equivalent of Women's Lib: "Not until women have every right that men have, equal political power, the same opportunity to make their opinions felt and acted upon in every realm of life, can we hope...to bring one-half of the (human) race into its own." (NCC)

formation of a UNC chapter of the Phi Beta Kappa society, and encouraged the start of publications in law, philosophy, and education. Personally he wrote several textbooks, became a Kenan Professor in 1918, and had served on the faculty for 50 years before he died in 1934.

Edward Kidder Graham, a professor in the English Department and Dean of the College of Liberal Arts, became acting president in June 1913, permanent president in June 1914, suffered the loss of his young wife Susan Moses Graham on 22 December 1916, and saw the student body grow to 1269 in the fall of 1916. He had helped to establish the *Alumni Review*, had encouraged the development of women's programs, was an ardent supporter of the new initiatives in drama and playwriting, and was director of the Southeastern Division of the Student Army Training Corps when he died on 26 October 1918, a victim of the national influenza epidemic. On his death, Marvin Hendrix Stacy became temporary chief administrator with the title "Chairman of the Faculty," but he also perished in the flu epidemic on 21 January 1919.

The sustained growth of the university insured a corresponding growth in numbers and prosperity in the village, with a time lag to recover from the economic devastation left by Reconstruction. However, a one-man constable force remained sufficient to protect Chapel Hill property and to enforce the growing number of local ordinances until 1905, when the force increased to two. The constables spent most of their time casually in the town hall, Algernon S. Barbee's small frame office just east of the current Methodist Church, but the peace was broken in 1877 and 1878 by a "reign of terror" which gripped the town.

Following the attempted rape of a young white woman by a black in April 1877, the first in a long series of nighttime burglaries and cruel attacks on women began when an intruder entered the bedroom of two women attending the Normal School, escaping through a window when one of the women turned out to be unexpectedly robust and ferocious. In the spring of 1878, burglars hit eight homes, including those of J.W. Carr, Cornelia Spencer, and merchant

Tom Kirkland, whose course to bankruptcy was hurried by the robbery.

Then word spread that Mrs. Margaret Hendon was holding $1000 in cash. Near midnight on 15 June 1878, four men approached Mrs. Hendon's East Franklin Street home, in which she, her daughters, and her servants were sleeping. Two of the men broke into the house, using an ax they had found in the yard, burst into Mrs. Hendon's bedroom, and attacked her with the ax and a club as she leaned out the window crying for help. Across the street, Dr. William P. Mallett and his son John heard the screams and rushed to the scene.

The attackers fled, and the Malletts found Mrs. Hendon with several deep scalp wounds. On the way to get his father's medical bag, John encountered Alphonso Davis, who had killed his brother in an August 1875 knife fight and who lived with his father, skilled bootmaker Washington Davis, in the Horace Williams House. Davis asked what was going on and continued calmly on his way after hearing John's hurried report.

The bloody attack threw the village into a panic. The commissioners posted a $300 reward; a Richmond detective came to investigate; a town meeting of black and white men ended with the formation of a vigilante committee. The housebreakers next attacked two more Normal School students, and the reward rose to $1000. Then on 5 August a thwarted burglary at the home of Rev. George W. Purefoy led to the arrest on suspicion of Albert Atwater, a 24-year-old Negro who lived on Smith Level Road.

Under questioning by attorney James M. Alexander and Col. Hugh Guthrie, Atwater agreed to give state's evidence, naming as his accomplices: Lewis Carlton, a black, 35-year-old, enormously strong well digger; Alphonso Davis, a 33-year-old Caucasian and a member of the Chapel Hill String Band, a group that included Isaac Emerson, the inventor of Bromo Seltzer; and Henry Andrews, the 30-year-

This reward notice appeared in the 13 July 1878 issue of the Ledger. *The burglaries prompted Seaton Barbee (1848-1920) to add a line of firearms that would "tickle a burglar prodigiously." (NCC)*

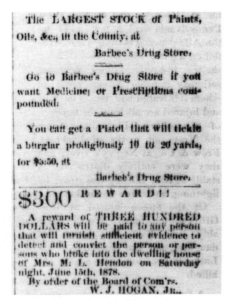

old Caucasian son of an Orange County deputy sheriff. Justices John H. Watson, S.H. Turrentine, and Merritt Cheek bound the accused over in the Hillsborough jail to await an October trial. Jones Watson joined the defense team. The town board called for public donations to help pay James Alexander and James B. Mason $100 each to assist the prosecution.

Alphonso Davis and Henry Andrews claimed they had been in a brothel at the time of the attack, and several prostitutes confirmed their alibi, but four citizens the jury considered more credible contradicted the ladies' testimony. After deliberating 15 minutes, the jury returned a verdict of guilty. The judge sentenced Atwater to prison and the other defendants to be hanged on 22 November 1878. The defense appealed to the state supreme court, which upheld the decision.

Governor Thomas J. Jarvis received petitions from throughout the state protesting the execution of the white men on the contested testimony of a Negro. Scores of Chapel Hillians joined the chorus, but the governor refused to commute the sentence. Consequently, on 16 May 1879, a crowd estimated at 8000 gathered on "old Gallow's Hill" near Hillsborough as the Rev. A.C. Dixon of the Chapel Hill Baptist Church and the Rev. W.H. Wheeler accompanied the men to the scaffold.

Alphonso Davis protested his innocence, forgave everyone, and sat while a deputy read a statement repeating the testimony he had given at the trial. Henry Andrews next proclaimed his innocence. Lewis Carlton then delivered a 15-minute speech, ignoring the Hendon case but pleading innocent to charges that he had killed his wife Isabella. She had died shortly after suspicion fell on her husband, and authorities suspected Carlton had murdered her to keep her from implicating him in the burglaries and the attack on Mrs. Hendon. They exhumed her body, and Prof. A.F. Redd discovered evidence of poison and powdered glass in contents taken from her stomach.

After the protestations of innocence, the preachers prayed, the audience sang "There Is a Fountain Filled with Blood," friends bade the condemned farewell, deputies applied hoods, and the executioner released the traps. A Hillsborough reporter was "happy to state that no white ladies were present."

Later that summer, another sensational case broke in Chapel Hill. In late August postal agent R.B. Long arrested Dr. E.R. Williamson for having mailed obscene post cards to Miss Sallie Davies in Meherrin Station, Virginia. Hillsborough attorney Thomas Ruffin prosecuted; James M. Alexander, Jones Watson, and I.R. Strayhorn defended and succeeded in having the charges dismissed. Dr. Williamson then left for the North, but postal agent Long obtained new warrants, chased the doctor down, and carried him to Greensboro to await a second trial on 11 October. Dr. Williamson pleaded guilty, but the judge let him off with court costs when Sallie's father dropped charges. The

Paul Carrington Cameron (1808-1891), son of Judge Duncan Cameron, entered UNC in 1825, but the university soon expelled him for fighting during prayers. He became the wealthiest man in the state, owning about 1900 slaves before the war. Cameron was extremely generous with financial aid and administrative help in restoring UNC's buildings at the end of Reconstruction. A grateful university invited him to deliver the Commencement Address in 1885. Cameron married Anne Ruffin, daughter of N.C. Chief Justice Thomas Ruffin, in 1832. (NCC)

The first Memorial Hall, beautiful on the outside, was apparently an auditory horror on the inside, and the university condemned it as unusable in 1929. From 1903 to 1911, students used it as a basketball court. The trustees originally intended the building to be a memorial to UNC President David Lowry Swain, but instead dedicated it to the Civil War dead on its completion in 1885. (NCC)

Chapel Hill *Ledger* reported that Dr. Williamson was not responsible for his behavior since he was "an inveterate opium eater."

Opium eating may have been rare in Chapel Hill, but the consumption of unlicensed whiskey never slackened, even in the midst of a renewed temperance crusade in the years following Reconstruction, and Leandrew Graham Sykes made a lifelong effort to keep supplies plentiful. Sykes married Lutinia Andrews in 1869, and the couple soon grew used to the occupational hazard of the moonshiner, arrest and prosecution. Convicted and sentenced to the Hillsborough jail several times, Sykes kept at his occupation even after being sentenced in 1893 to 18 months in the Albany, New York penitentiary, ceasing only with his death on 11 August 1914 from "acute cerebral softening."

In January 1879, following complaints by townspeople the commissioners evicted Jenny Kelly, Mary Nunn, and Beck Mason—"negro . . . women of bad character"—from shanties behind the Presbyterian Church (owned by black preacher Jordan Weaver.) While most students were tolerant of a measure of lewdness, there were those who struggled heroically to keep the purveyors of sin always at a respectable distance. They reached their finest hour one spring night in 1909 when YMCA president and *Tar Heel* editor-in-chief Frank Porter Graham, assisted by constable "Jug" Whitaker, led a small army of righteous-minded students in driving a force of Durham prostitutes and their panderers from their *locus criminis* in the village cemetery.

Jug Whitaker refused to enter the graveyard, and student Henry Johnston had his hat knocked askew by a bullet, but the intrepid crusaders forged onward, capturing two very frightened ladies of the evening. In a preliminary hearing in magistrate A.S. Barbee's office, Law School Dean James C. MacRae bound the women over for later trial and instructed Jug to convey them to the Hillsborough jail, from which they were soon released.

The commissioners fought continuously to eliminate prostitution, and the revised town ordinances of 1879 and 1896 give extended evidence of their determination. Other ordinances attempted to protect trees, bridges, stone walls, pavement, and culverts; to prevent cockfighting, bicycling on the sidewalks of Franklin Street, throwing "Stones or other Missles," building slaughter pens within 100 yards of main streets, setting off fireworks or discharging guns "except in case of absolute necessity," and other unbefitting behavior; and to restrict trade on Sundays and to curb free-roaming livestock.

No issue, not even prostitution, caused a greater stir than the problem of hogs running at large. An 1873 ordinance required owners to remove dead hogs from the streets and prohibited "feeding hogs on sidewalks, or keeping hogs in a pen abutting a sidewalk." In an April 1877 referendum asking "Shall Hogs be allowed to run at large in the town?" citizens voted 43 to 38 in the affirmative. Nevertheless, in

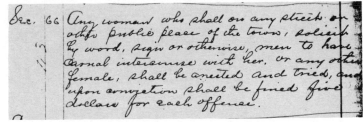

In 1896, three of the 96 ordinances in the Chapel Hill code of laws were devoted to the control of prostitution. Typical of the period, the laws provided punishment for women, but not for the men who patronized them.

Prompted by an outbreak of smallpox, on 31 March 1904 the town fathers attempted to quarantine the village by enacting an ordinance stating that no one from Durham would be allowed to enter Chapel Hill. They lifted the ban after four days.

The handwriting in the illustration is that of A.J. McDade, town clerk and owner of the first brick business building in Chapel Hill. Built in 1880 and razed in 1916 when it became unsafe, it stood on the southwest corner of Columbia and Franklin, near the present-day Baptist Church. (From the Town of Chapel Hill Minutes)

May 1878 the board required that hogs be penned during the upcoming commencement, and in August the board voted to confiscate all hogs running free. The Chapel Hill *Ledger* strongly supported a fencing law, spurring Dr. A.B. Roberson, Oregon B. Tenney, and C.E. King to register their protest by canceling their subscriptions. Agitation on the issue continued, and pigs ran free downtown periodically until 1892.

The General Assembly chartered the Chapel Hill Iron Mountain Railroad Company in 1879, naming Kemp Battle president and forbidding the southern terminus from approaching closer than one mile of the campus. The new line became the State University Railroad Company, and within a few months construction was underway, but not without a serious public controversy over the treatment of the convict labor force, numbering about 100. On 15 February 1880, overseer Charles F. Motz whipped black convict Andrew Fries for "playing lame." Later, after Fries tried to escape, Motz lashed him until he fell. Fries died on 26 March, and Wake County coroner W.W. Richardson concluded that death had resulted from "treatment in prison and the whipping."

The public and several newspaper editors demanded an investigation; a coroner's jury ruled that Fries' death was related to the whipping; and resulting warrants charged Col. John A. Holt, supervisor of the work gang, and Motz with complicity in the death of Fries. Understandably, Kemp Battle grew alarmed and wrote at least one editor, H.A. London of the *Chatham Record*, asking him to exonerate the university on grounds that the coroner's jury had been "misled and prejudiced by their feelings." London refused because he had no substantiating evidence and because Battle did not want his own letter printed. Solicitor Fred N. Strudwick, who had attended UNC in the 1850s investigated and after a thorough review chose not to prosecute.

As work neared completion in the late summer of 1882, over some local objection Cornelia Spencer organized an outdoor luncheon for the convict workers. On 8 October, her daughter June, who was then teaching at Peace Institute

In 1914, passengers wait for the train at O.F. Craig's general store and soda shop at University Station. On 22 November 1889, before there was anything except a track connection at University Station, UNC sophomore B.F. Long of Statesville was killed there by a passing train. (NCC)

"Captain" Fred Smith was the conductor for 48 years, J.P. Nesbitt an engineer for 24 years, Marcus D. Pridgen a brakeman for 20 years, and "Baby Boy" G.M. Ramsey a boilerman for 23 years. Captain Smith's prominence in the public eye gave him a sense of self importance, but beneath his dignified exterior he was a generous-spirited man, especially to children and tipsy students. William Meade Prince recalled that Smith always pronounced University Station "as if he were offering you a trip to New York and a weekend at the Waldorf, all expenses paid."

A major impetus for chartering the railroad was the Iron Mountain Mine Company, incorporated in 1879 to extract ore from a vein of red hematite located west of the Horace Williams Airport. Robert Hoke, William Primrose , William J. Askew, Preston L. and Robert R. Bridges were the stockholders. Mining operations began in 1880 and continued for about a decade, with trains carrying the ore to the Empire Steel and Iron Company in Greensboro for smelting. However, original assessments had overestimated the richness of the vein, and by 1892 the company had ceased operations.

The completion of a paved road to Durham in 1926 signaled the end of the University Railroad, but it kept running until earnings dropped to an average of 21 cents per day a decade later. Bruce Strowd arranged for school children to accompany local dignitaries on the final trip on 24 October 1936, and engineer J.P. Nesbitt treated them to high-speed thrills of over 20 mph, completing the homeward run in a record time of 30 minutes.

With the arrival of the railroad, a motley collection of hackney coaches and daredevil drivers materialized to convey passengers from the depot to town and campus. Archibald Henderson, William Meade Prince, and others have left colorful decriptions of the clamor at the depot to lure customers and of the mad races through the curves of Sunset and down the long Franklin Street straightaway.

People wanting to rent horse-drawn carriages and saddle mounts or desiring to stable animals usually went to one of the Pickards' livery stables. In 1886 brothers George and Walter W. Pickard opened a stable across Henderson Street from the old Methodist Church. On 1 March 1895, George

in Raleigh, drove a bronze spike to complete the line. Several speakers also entertained before the meal. Kemp Battle, as was his wont, used levity to keep the auspicious event from becoming affectedly stately. "Egypt has her pyramids, Athens her Parthenon, Rome her Coliseum," he said, "but neither Egypt, Athens, nor Rome in all their glory had a railroad ten and two-fifths miles long." (In fact, the line measured 10.2 miles.) He defended Governor Swain against charges that he had deliberately kept the railroad out of Chapel Hill, but Jones Watson followed Battle and swore he had personal knowledge of Swain's having delayed construction for a generation.

The rails ran north to University Station, and "The Whooper," as the train came to be known, was always a modest affair. Usually it consisted of an engine, a passenger car, and one boxcar, with extra cars added on football Saturdays and during commencements. The train made two runs daily, six days per week. For over a decade there was nothing at University Station except the track connection, a confusing situation for strangers traveling to Chapel Hill. Finally, Southern Railway placed an old boxcar on a siding, and later a general store—still doing business—offered passengers a chance to relax with refreshments.

The northbound trip, including a fuel stop at Blackwood Station, took 70 minutes, the southbound trip an hour. The tracks were bumpy, and engineers coaxed extra speed out of the small engine at their own and their passengers' peril. In a hurry to return home one 1890s winter, UNC President Winston asked the engineer to speed up. Deferential to the professor's desire, he did so, the train turned over, and Winston ended up with a pot-bellied stove atop him, leaking red-hot coals onto his clothes and hair.

The men who ran "The Whooper" dearly loved the job.

Basil "Bass" Jones (died c. 1914) operated this dray for a number of years, while his wife Carrie ran a private school for blacks about 100 yards south of The Courtyard on Roberson Street. This picture was made about 1910. (NCC)

This ca. 1900 photo looks west on Franklin Street from a point near the Henderson Street junction. The livery stable belonged to George Pickard, the UNC superintendent of buildings and grounds. The building in the left foreground is the Central Hotel, later the site of the Battle-Vance-Pettigrew complex. Louis Graves began the Chapel Hill Weekly in the upstairs of Algernon S. Barbee's office, which sits next to the Central Hotel. (NCC)

bought out "W.W." who agreed not to engage in the livery business for five years. Apparently W.W. had found a way to skirt the contract when his son Marvin opened a competing livery service on 24 June 1897 on the current Lambda Chi Alpha grounds at the corner of Franklin Street and Pickard Lane. The next day George protested in a flyer that W.W. had to have financed the operation since Marvin had "no funds of his own."

E. Vernon Howell, then dean of the School of Pharmacy, introduced a new era of transportation in 1903 when he purchased a one-cylinder Oldsmobile. Howell was popular with students and with townspeople, both young and old. He was a Boy Scouts leader, and he became renowned for the barbecued wild game and hard liquor he served at frolicking parties in the backyard of his home, which is now his nephew Kay Kyser's house. As soon as he brought the car to town, ladies began to complain that its noise dangerously frightened their carriage horses. After two years of incessant pleas, the good-natured professor drove his Oldsmobile to Rocky Mount and left it there.

Dr. Eric A. Abernethy was the second Chapel Hillian to own an automobile, and 15-year-old Bruce Strowd was the third, if his home-made "contrivance" could properly be graced with such formal nomenclature. Using a small marine motor, gears from a corn-cutter, a sewing machine wheel for steering, and wheels from wheelbarrows, young Bruce constructed what he called the "Strowdmobile" and what others called the "Devil Wagon." He had not troubled with a muffler, and his freewheeling through town prompted Mayor A.S. Barbee and the aldermen in 1907 to pass an ordinance specifically banning Strowd's "contrivance from the streets of Chapel Hill."

By 1913 there were 13 cars in Chapel Hill, and Bruce Strowd had attended N.C. State College, worked in the Carr mills, become a Ford salesman, married Mattie Atwater, and completed a mechanics course in the Rambler plant in Wisconsin. He set up a Ford agency in a ramshackle wooden building where the Porthole is today, sold cars in the $440-$975 price range, and on 17 June 1915 announced that new car buyers "will receive from $40-$80 as a share of Ford Motor Co.'s profits"—the first automobile rebate in Chapel Hill. Strowd built a brick garage across the alley from the Carolina Coffee Shop in 1916. By 1924 his business had outgrown those premises, and he built a new and bigger garage on the northwest corner of Franklin and Columbia.

Although ice men, delivery men, and farmers continued to use horse-drawn wagons into the World War II era, the age of motorization quickly changed the way students and townsfolk traveled, and jitney services proliferated, primarily to carry passengers to Durham faster than the train. One of the first operators was J.T. "Bull" Durham. He came to Chapel Hill in 1898, opened a store on the southeast corner of Franklin and Columbia, and in 1912 purchased a fleet of automobiles to carry passengers and to transport university teams to distant events. In his later years, Durham lived above Rose's Department Store, now the Rite-Aid Center, spending his time looking after the Franklin Street property he had accumulated. He died a bachelor at age 81 on Christmas Day 1951.

Durham's chief competition came from Colonel Swain "Kern" Pendergraft, the "Colonel" being a given name. Kern had built a reputation for honesty and natural wit while running a grocery store/news stand out of a corrugated iron shack where The Intimate Bookshop now

C.S. Pendergraft (1871-1924) stands beside one of his three new Studebaker buses a few months before his death. The year before in the Chapel Hill Weekly, Louis Graves had described a prominent feature of the new red vehicles: "Each of the (bench) seats will accommodate five persons of the girth of Dr. Charles S. Mangum, John M. Booker, or Mayor Roberson, or four persons of the proportions of Paul Weaver, C.C. Poindexter or Archie Patterson." (NCC and Frank W. Pendergraft)

stands. He purchased three Cadillacs and two Fords and went up against Bull Durham, who had other rivals in Tank Hunter, Jack Sparrow, and Samuel Jackson "S.J." Brockwell. When Kern cut the $1 fixed passage to Durham in half, he won the gratitude of riders but the wrath of his competitors. Soon afterward, the Rev. W.D. Moss asked how things were going between him and the other jitney operators. Kern answered deliberately, "Well, Parson, I'm a'readin' my Bible and a'tellin' them to go to hell."

The father of 11 children, Pendergraft developed a stomach cancer while Thomas Wolfe was a student, and doctors gave him six months to live. He showed Archibald Henderson a tree with a healthy growth over a deep scar and said he would keep living like the tree. Henderson passed the story on to Wolfe, and 15 years later Wolfe used details from the anecdote in *Of Time and the River*. Kern died in November 1924, two years after his Franklin Street store burned.

S.J. Brockwell also operated a bus line connecting Chapel Hill to Durham. Before that he ran a department store out of the Brockwell Building at the northeast corner of Franklin and Columbia. Brockwell made the bricks for what were originally three stories, but when the weight of the materials threatened to collapse the entire structure, he prudently removed the third level.

Later, S.J. brought the movies to Chapel Hill in the Pickwick Theatre, advertising "High-class Motion Pictures" accompanied by "Instrumental Music." For many years, Mrs. Mabel Hill played the piano, and hers was often no

William James "Tank" Hunter (1868-1950) worked for Pickard's livery stable before opening his own stable on Franklin Street in 1903. In 1910, he bought out W.W. Pickard's livery stable at Franklin and Pickard Lane. A year later he purchased some Hudson automobiles and began a jitney service to Durham, running between the Royal Cafe in what is now Varley's Men's Shop and the companion Royal Cafe in Durham. He is pictured here in 1911, transporting a student. (NCC)

enviable chore. Students collected in crowds for the nightly programs, and they came determined to find entertainment. As soon as the lights went down a hurricane of peanuts, acorns, and other missiles filled the air, and if the films were in any way disappointing, shouts of derision notified the manager. Before his death in 1940, Brockwell financially assisted many university students.

In June 1878, John H. Watson and his wife Nancy took

over the Chapel Hill Hotel, the old Eagle Hotel. John and his brother Jones were the sons of William Watson, who had come to Chapel Hill from Virginia early in the century to work on the South Building. The hotel was in general disrepair, but Watson obtained it while students were pouring in to attend the Normal School, and he was able to fill his rooms with young women who paid $12.50 per month for room, board, and gas lights. The popular "Uncle John" was mayor of Chapel Hill in 1883, 1885-1886, and 1891-1894. By 1891 he had increased his rate to $18 per month, and he had accepted W.W. Pickard as a partner.

In the early 1890s, New York lawyer W.G. Peckham vacationed in Chapel Hill and fell in love with the climate and the village, in part because of low property values. He bought several houses and lots, including the old Dr. Hudson Cave home, and he invested extensively in business properties, including the Chapel Hill Hotel. Using $10,000 provided by Peckham, in 1892 Watson and Pickard tore down the hotel, except for the James Polk apartment, rebuilt it with steeples, painted it a ginger-bread yellow, and added the two-storied, double-piazzaed University Inn Annex to the rear. By then, the relatively affluent faculty were making many of their own purchases by mail order, and local merchants were competing for the faculty dollar by stocking more exquisite items, a competition that made Chapel Hill a popular call for "drummers," who routinely stayed at the Chapel Hill Hotel.

Peckham soon tired of his Chapel Hill ventures and began to sell. In 1907, Horace Williams and George Stephens purchased the hotel, then popularly known as the Pickard Hotel, "subj. to W.W. Pickard's lease." The same year, they sold the property for $19,700 to the university, which operated it as the University Inn and the University Inn Annex, primarily to provide housing and dining facilities

S.J. Brockwell's Pickwick Theatre, first located on the north side of Franklin Street near Columbia Street, opened in the fall of 1909 — his first ad appeared in the Tar Heel 27 November 1909. The movies in this photograph are "Lost Memory," a 1909 British short comedy, and "The Escaped Lunatic," a 1911 production of the Thomas A. Edison Company. Admission was 5–. In 1916 when this photograph was made, Brockwell moved into new, brick quarters on the south side of Franklin.
L.J. Phipps (1898-1969), later a lawyer and a well-known judge in Chapel Hill during the civil rights activities of the 1960s, was the manager of the theatre from 1920 to 1922. (NCC)

In 1893, this ad appeared in area publications. Watson and Pickard charged $18.00 per month for "board and lodging." Garbage and kitchen wastes were simply thrown out back, attracting dogs, cats, hogs and an occasional cow, prompting the University Magazine to lead cries for a village clean-up. Part of the popularity of this hotel was due to the presence of Jesse Jones, a master chef by Chapel Hill standards. (NCC)

for students.

W.W. Pickard and his wife Betty then built a second, 75-room Pickard's Hotel across the street from the University Inn. Pickard managed it until 1916 when a combination of illnesses forced him to sell out to Major William and Mrs. Mary Louisa Cox Uzzell. After the University Inn burned on 30 November 1921, the Pickard Hotel was unquestionably the social center of Chapel Hill. Harry Houdini stayed there, Kay Kyser taught young ladies the Charleston in the "ballroom," Thomas Wolfe roomed there. Phillips Russell called it a "good gathering place to watch the life of the village go by." The second Pickard burned in January 1929, Major Uzzell died soon afterward, and Mrs. Uzzell moved her children to

Archibald Henderson (1877-1963), middle, and "Kern" Pendergraft, right, were close friends when this 1917 photograph was made inside Pendergraft's store located on Franklin Street. The young boy is Pendergraft's son Robert who died in an auto accident at Strowd's bridge in 1925. (Courtesy Frank Pendergraft and NCC)

Durham, where she died at age 99 in 1973.

John Watson's brother Jones purchased the 10-room frame house that stood across McCorkle Place from the Chapel Hill Hotel, the old James Hogg house. Watson remodeled it, named it the Central Hotel, and moved in with his invalid daughter Mary. During the Civil War, Jones Watson lost his son Thomas Love Watson at Chattanooga. He also lost his mercantile business, maintaining ownership of a farm. At age 55 in 1868, he won admission to the bar, about the time he reportedly beat Col. Hugh Guthrie in public. Jones Watson sat in the General Assembly in 1872-74, and he was mayor of Chapel Hill in 1882-1883.

Following Jones Watson's death in 1891, Dr. A.B. Roberson purchased the Central Hotel, moved his drugstore into it, and managed both for a short while. He then leased the hotel for $25 per month to Mr. and Mrs. N.G.L. "Bunn" Patterson, who also operated a drugstore on Franklin Street and managed Patterson's Hotel on Columbia Street in another building owned by Dr. Roberson. "Dr." and Mrs. A.A. Kluttz ran the Central Hotel for a time after Dr. Roberson's death in 1897, before the Patterson's took over once more. Then the university paid the Roberson estate $10,000 for the property, razed the old hotel, and in May 1912 began putting up the Battle-Vance-Pettigrew dormitories. Between 1924 and 1931, the university built Graham Memorial on the old University Inn plot.

Most eating establishments in the post-bellum South were operated by blacks, and it was not until the new century that the first white restaurateur went into business in the village. J.E. Gooch and his wife Amelia came to Chapel Hill from Granville County in 1900 when Gooch was hired to install the first telephones. After he had run lines to the first 40 customers, Gooch filled his spare time by running a cafe

George Trice (1838-1915) and his wife Lucy (1848-1897) owned a shoe repair shop and a restaurant on East Franklin Street near the Presbyterian church. His restaurant, active in the 1890s, specialized in oysters, as did several other Chapel Hill restaurants of the period. One of Trice's sons, Henry, became a physician.

The popularity of oysters resulted, at least in part, from the efforts of Governor Alfred Moore Scales to develop the oyster industry in North Carolina during his term in office, 1885-1889. (NCC)

Lonnie Lee Merritt (1873-1936), great grandson of old Rev. William H. Merritt, is pictured with his new bride Mary Alice Johnson (1875-1930). He ran a livery stable behind what is now the Carolina Coffee Shop for several years, employing Jeter Farrington as his driver, but when the automobile replaced the horse, he moved to Burlington. The Merritt's son, C.L. "Jack," stayed in Chapel Hill to become one of UNC's most famous footballers. His nickname, "The Battering Ram," led to the adoption of the ram as the UNC mascot. (Courtesy Mrs. W.F. Paythress)

at the corner of Columbia and Franklin, in the first of many locations Gooch's Cafe would occupy over the next half century, and it immediately became a favorite hangout for students.

A steak dinner cost a quarter, a country-ham sandwich with fried potatoes or a potato cake was a dime, egg sandwiches were a nickel. In season, strings of quail outside denoted their presence on the menu. The *Tar Heel* staff and the Playmakers made Gooch's their unofficial headquarters, wherever it might be. Gooch's sons also ran a restaurant briefly.

Rooming and boarding houses remained popular and plentiful for several reasons: the student body continued to outpace available dormitory space; several professors were bachelors; and students objected to the food served in the university commons, housed in the gymnasium on the Phillips Hall site from 1896 to 1903 and then in Swain Hall. The most popular boarding houses were run by "Miss

Sophie" McNider, Mrs. Julia Graves, Mrs. A.A. Kluttz, and Mrs. Seaton Barbee.

The McNiders had two sons, George and William. William studied medicine at UNC, the University of Chicago, and Western Reserve University. Having joined the UNC faculty at age 18 in 1899, before he retired in 1950 he was world famous as an authority on kidney diseases and the aging process. He won many prestigious awards for his research, accepted honorary degrees from the University of Virginia and Davidson College, turned down tempting offers from major universities (he said his family had bought milk from Sparrows too long for him to break the tradition), and served as a Kenan Professor and Dean of the Medical School. In 1916 he married Sarah Jane Foard, a member of the first graduating class of nurses at Watts Hospital in Durham.

Julia Hooper came to Chapel Hill in 1875 at 19 when her father John de Berniere Hooper rejoined the faculty. In 1877 she married mathematics professor Ralph Henry Graves II, who lived just west of the Baptist Church on Franklin Street. They had three sons and a daughter. Ralph Henry Graves III was a reporter, an editor and an executive on the New York *Post* and *Times*, the founder of two syndication services, and the biographer of Henry Ford.

Ernest Graves graduated from UNC in 1900, earned an MA in 1901, and graduated from West Point in 1905. He was a star baseball and football player at UNC and West Point and in 1912 the head coach of the Army football team. His exemplary performance of duty during General "Blackjack" Pershing's 1916 expedition into Mexico led to his being chosen to sail with Pershing on the "SS Baltic," the first ship to land contingents of the American Expeditionary Force in Europe, where Graves won the Distinguished Service Medal for supervising wartime construction in France. In May 1953, he received his brigadier's star, a month before his death. The third Graves son, Louis, founded the Chapel Hill *Weekly*.

When Ralph Graves II died in 1889, Mrs. Graves moved to the old Pannill house on the Carolina Inn corner which her husband had purchased in 1885; and, following a long tradition for Chapel Hill widows, she set up a boarding house. One of the area farmers who supplied her was Andrew "Coon" McCauley, a great-grandson of Matthew McCauley. Coon, who got his unenviable nickname in infancy when a relative opined "he grins just like a 'coon," had 16 children, one of them named Ralph after Ralph Graves III.

After running her boarding house profitably for 13 years, Mrs. Graves moved north so her daughter Mary could study art in Baltimore, Philadelphia, and New York. They returned to Chapel Hill, where Mary became a very successful portrait painter, rendering likenesses of Paul Green, Archibald Henderson, Edward Kidder Graham, Horace Williams, Frank Porter Graham, and scores of others. In 1919 Mary wed Arthur Rees.

"There are more baby carriages in Chapel Hill than the combined number of automobiles, carriages, and wheelbarrows.... Everybody pushes the pestiferous perambulators." So wrote Earl Harris about the pre-World War I habit of using baby carriages for every hauling chore. In this 1907 picture, the baby is Walter Warren Wilson (1907-1972), son of Dr. Thomas J. Wilson, Jr. Walter became a textile manufacturer in Graniteville, S.C. (photo courtesy Peter Wilson.)

Druggist Seaton Barbee's wife Sue ran a popular boarding house in her home on the current Methodist Church lot. One dark night in December 1872, young Lucy Phillips and June Spencer were watching a snow storm from their window when they saw a handsome young man dressed in a flowing, scarlet-lined black cape and a wide-brimmed black hat stride briskly past. They learned the next day that they had seen Seaton Barbee on his way to elope with Sue Davis, the pretty 20-year-old daughter of shoemaker Washington Davis.

When the university reopened in 1875, the trustees began to improve sanitary conditions on campus. They had "comfort houses" erected behind the South Building, and later two large water-storage tanks in the attic of the South Building fed a campus water system which became operational early in 1894. Every building had running water, urinals, and toilets; some had showers; and the basement of Smith Hall contained a bath house. Using money from the sale of property bequeathed by Mary Ruffin Smith, in 1895 William Rand Kenan, Jr. built an electric power plant on the current Phillips Hall lot capable of illuminating 800 lights on and off campus. Along with John Motley Morehead and John Sprunt Hill, W.R. Kenan, Jr. made up the Sigma Alpha Epsilon's "Big 3" at UNC.

The Kenans came to North Carolina from Northern Ireland in the 1730s. One married the sister of Royal Governor Gabriel Johnston. Another, W.R. Kenan, Jr.'s great-great grandfather General James Kenan, fought at Moore's Creek Bridge and was an early UNC trustee. William Rand Kenan, Sr. married Mary Hargrave, the daughter of merchant Jesse Hargrave and the great-granddaughter of Old Kit Barbee. William, Sr. left the university to become a Captain in the Duplin Rifles, surrendered with Lee at Appomatox, and prospered as a wholesale grocer in Wilmington after the war. In 1895, while an instructor at UNC conducting research with Dr. Francis P. Venable, W.R. Kenan, Jr. made accidental discoveries that allowed him to figure out the formulas for carbide and acetylene gas.

In 1896, he left UNC to design and oversee the construction of a Carbide Manufacturing Company plant in Niagara Falls, New York, and in 1900 he went to work in Florida supervising massive construction and business operations for Henry Flagler, John D. Rockefeller's partner in founding Standard Oil. In 1901, the 71-year-old Flagler married Kenan's 34-year-old sister Mary Lily Kenan, who inherited the bulk of the Flagler estate when her husband died in 1913. She married Robert W. Bingham in 1916, died a few months later, and left an estate estimated at $128 million to her brother, two sisters, and $2.1 million to set up the Kenan Professorships.

In 1926 Kenan gave $275,000 to construct 24,000-seat Kenan Stadium plus another $28,000 to build a field house, and he was present on Thanksgiving Day 1927 to see the stadium dedicated and UNC defeat Virginia 14 to 13. He later gave $5000 to renovate the stadium in 1944, $75,000 to build a press box in 1949, and $750,000 to add the 20,000-seat upper decks in 1962. Although he lived in Florida and New York, he attended all commencements at his alma mater until prevented by ill health in 1960. When he died in 1965, he left approximately $100 million in educational trusts, including $5 million to endow 25 William R. Kenan, Jr. Professorships at UNC.

Charles Baskerville of Raleigh, another famous chemist, came to UNC in 1892 to star as captain of the football team, to be the founding editor-in-chief of the *Tar Heel*, and to complete his Ph.D. after having studied earlier at Vanderbilt and the universities of Mississippi, Virginia, and Berlin. Baskerville married Mary Snow, also from Raleigh, and remained in Chapel Hill to teach at UNC and to build what is now known as the Kennette House. He left in 1904 for the College of the City of New York, where he did pioneer work in the medical applications of radium, the refining of petroleum, and the composition of plastics. He also prematurely announced the discovery of two new elements, which he named "carolinium" and "berzelium," retracting the announcements when he learned he had erred.

Dr. Baskerville's son Charles II, born in Chapel Hill in 1896, won the Silver Star on duty with Douglas MacArthur's famous Rainbow Division in World War I. As an artist he gained wealth and fame for his portraits of the Duchess of Windsor, Bernard Baruch, Prime Minister Nehru, maharajas, the wealthy, and the famous; and in World War II he received the Legion of Merit for his portraits of 72 commanders and heroes. Charles II remains an active painter in New York City.

Professor of Applied Science Joshua Gore directed an expansion of the primitive campus electrical system in 1901

with the installation of two 25-horsepower, steam-driven generators which ran nightly from dark to 11:30. Naturally, students complained of the frequent breakdowns and heaped ridicule on the operators who manned the generators. But they also turned the plant into an informal social club, especially after the university print shop moved into an annex. Lewis Utley supervised the plant, Joe Sparrow was his chief assistant, and Charles Woollen was the office boy.

Beginning in 1902, Utley and his crew also maintained a pumping station on Bolin Creek and a filtering system just south of the power plant which processed the 25,000 gallons of water pumped daily into a 50,000 gallon, 80'-high tank on the Swain Hall grounds. In 1917, a new power plant 50 yards south of the old one housed a 500-horsepower steam turbine, but it was also soon inadequate, forcing the system to draw from the Southern Power Company until a 570-HP turbine arrived in 1927. The current power plant was built in 1939.

For the town, there were two communal wells—one in front of the Methodist Church became the Susan Graham Memorial Fountain in 1922, the other at the corner of Columbia and Franklin was preferred for the taste and purity of its water. The town installed pumps in both in 1904.

On 1 April 1901, aldermen granted the university permission "to lay pipes for the distribution of water and for a system of sewers along the streets of the town of Chapel Hill; and to operate a water works and sewers." But work progressed slowly, leaving the entire community, business and residential, dependent on privies until sewer lines were installed in 1906. In January 1911, the town took over the system, which simply emptied into Bolin Creek. As early as 1906, aldermen began discussing the extension of sewage lines into the black communities of Potter's Field, Sunset,

This 1892 photograph shows Robert Strange MacRae's drugstore on the northeast corner of Franklin and Henderson. MacRae (1848-1921) left Asheville for Chapel Hill in 1884, bought the drug business from T.W. Harris and the building from Dave McCauley, then in 1893 he sold out the drug business to Dr. R.H. Whitehead and opened a bookstore that he operated for 25 years. He served as village postmaster 1913-1921. His brother, Judge James C. MacRae, was dean of the UNC law school. Two of R.S.'s sons became football stars at UNC. One of them, Cameron, in 1925 built the brick building that today houses Hector's. (NCC)

and Tintop to the west of town, but it was after World War II before the lines extended to the entire western section.

The new sewage system drove at least one man out of business. Fred Sparrow lived in a house on Hillsborough Street near a grist mill, a saw mill, and a cotton gin he operated on Bolin Creek. The raw sewage dumped into the creek ruined Sparrow's operations, and the stench forced him to move to another house farther up Hillsborough Street. He then went into the dairy business, delivering milk at first on foot, then in a buggy, a wagon, and finally a Ford truck.

Merchant H.H. Patterson started the first telephone service in 1901, drawing heavily on advice and assistance from Prof. Joshua Gore. Manager R.R. Best and his assistant J.E. Gooch installed the lines and the equipment; Prof. Eben Alexander received the first telephone—#1. While still in elementary school, Gooch's daughter Mamie, later Mrs. M.J. Dawson, learned to operate the switchboard, located in a dilapidated, clapboard shack on Henderson Street. Patterson's son Fred owned the company after his father and sold it about 1913 to Dr. Charles H. Herty, who in turn sold it to banker M.E. Hogan, cashier Jim Taylor, and Durhamite John Markham. The university acquired the system in 1928. Gooch stayed on for 16 years as operator, lineman, and repairman; Mamie worked for the system for over half a century.

The arrival of electricity and the telephone altered the appearance of the village when trees were cut back or removed to make way for poles and wire, but the sand and gravel sidewalks and the deeply rutted streets were to remain essentially unchanged until the 1920s. By 1900 the population of Chapel Hill had risen to 1623, but subtracting the 524 students left only 1099 villagers, 162 more than W.S. Guthrie had counted in 1869. Full-time residents increased a mere 50 during the first decade of the new century, but the jump was 334 to 1483 by 1920, a whopping 29.1% rise since 1910.

Pre-collegiate education in Chapel Hill remained a private preserve beyond the turn of the century. In the late 1870s, Cornelia and June Spencer, the elder Ralph Graves' daughter Julia, "Miss Sophie" MacNider, and others offered courses for young females; Mrs. V.C. Pell, formerly on the faculty of Davenport Female College, ran a school for young girls; Eugene H. Wilson—the musical director at the Baptist Church, the son-in-law of the Rev. G.W. Purefoy, and the brother of Baptist minister Norvell Wilson—began taking students in vocal training for a fee of $60 per term; and J.W. Carr's son-in-law the Rev. J.F. Heitman, pastor of the Methodist church, opened his Male Academy. The most serious effort to establish a permanent school began in 1896 when new UNC honors graduate John W. Canada opened the Canada School with the backing of concerned villagers and a who's who of the university faculty.

Dr. Thomas Hume had hired Canada, a native of

Pictured here at the Canada School is the 1898 graduating class. In the first row, left to right, are Birdie Pritchard (married R.O.E. Davis and moved to Washington, D.C.), Blanche Pickard (married Fred Patterson, Sr.), Fred Harris (died Christmas day 1899), and Howard Alexander (died his sophomore year at UNC). In the second row are, left to right, Carney Atwater (became a banker in Raleigh), Ralph Riggsbee (a farmer in Chatham County), Charles Maddry (minister in Raleigh), Robert Merritt (on the faculty of Women's College, now UNC-G), Louis Graves (founder of the Chapel Hill Weekly, now the Chapel Hill Newspaper), and Kemp Stephens (moved to Alabama). (NCC)

Summerfield in Guilford County, to tutor his daughter Anne. Soon the youngster was teaching a curriculum including Greek, Latin, Psychology, and English to faculty and village children in the back of the post office. When his enrollment increased sufficiently, Canada engaged Miss Loula Hendon and Mrs. Sallie Wilson as teachers. The Canada School moved to a private house on South Columbia Street, and in January 1897 further growth forced a move into Dr. Roberson's delapidated Patterson Hotel on the current Baptist Church site.

With his number of pupils approaching 200, Canada began building a 10-room schoolhouse on Pittsboro Street. Julian S. Carr and Laurence S. Holt provided financial assistance, but in May 1901, before the building was completed, Canada moved to Denver and later to Texas, and without him the school languished briefly, then folded.

After the Canada School closed, merchant John Edward Clark personally financed the education of a portion of the area youth, particularly those living on the east side of the village. Clark lived at the corner of Elliot Road and Old Oxford Road on a 400-acre farm in what is now Clark Hills. He built a single-room schoolhouse on Old Oxford Road and hired teachers to instruct in grades one to eight. After the schoolhouse burned in 1905, Clark built a new one (still standing) with two classrooms, and classes continued there until buses began carrying students to the elementary school downtown about 1920. Three of Clark's teachers were Bertha Lloyd, Mary Markham, and his daughter-in-law Helena Clark.

William J. Horney opened a private high school on 1 September 1902 with tuition ranging from $1.50 to $3.50 per

In September, 1905, the Chapel Hill School Committee purchased the old Canada School on Pittsboro Street, refurbished it, and opened the first public school in Chapel Hill. UNC student and Orange County native Numa R. Claytor (1879-1949) was the principal; Blanche Pickard and Nellie Roberson were teachers. Claytor became a Presbyterian minister and spent his career in Milton, N.C. (Photo from Lefler and Wager, Orange County: 1753-1953)

month "according to the advancement of the student," but his effort failed utterly, signaling a dire need to establish a public school system.

Four years later, the first school financed by public funds opened in the old Canada School. The Chapel Hill School Committee had purchased and repaired the building; UNC student N.R. Claytor was the first principal; and Canada School alumnae Blanche Pickard and Nellie Roberson were teachers. Then on 26 February 1909, the General Assembly passed "An Act to Establish Graded Schools in the Town of Chapel Hill." The act named Charles H. Herty, W.A. Temple, W.S. Roberson, Robert A. Eubanks, and N.W. Walker as trustees, and on 4 May villagers voted 78 to 30 in favor of school taxes. In the early years three teachers taught approximately 75 students per year, most assigned to the elementary grades. When public funds ran out, usually around 1 January, only those students paying tuition remained in attendance.

Early in 1915 the state legislature enlarged the boundaries of the tax district and approved a bond issue of $35,000 to pay for a lot and a school building. After voters approved the issue 87-42 on 18 May, trustees used local funds to purchase property from Miss Harriett Cole in the first block of West Franklin Street and to build a school on the land now occupied by the University Square complex. On 26 May 1916, the completed and festooned brick building was officially dedicated during the high school commencement ceremonies.

The fitful steps to provide adequately for public education accompanied continuing efforts to provide adequate spiritual sustenance. During the depressed early 1870s, the Baptists either had no pastor or engaged preachers on a half-time basis until the arrival of the Rev. Amzi Clarence Dixon in June 1876. The energetic Dixon baptized 25 new members within weeks, including Issac Emerson, the future Bromo-Seltzer king, and Locke Craig, whose family ran an academy behind the church and who was governor of North Carolina 1913-1917.

In April 1879, Dixon conducted a second successful revival, this time baptizing 20 new converts in Morgan Creek, including Charles B. Aycock, another future governor, J.Y. Joyner, later the state superintendent of education, and Edwin A. Alderman, later the president of three universities, including UNC. Dixon left for Asheville in 1880 to further his distinguished career in the ministry. Later as a world famous evangelist and author, he served in churches in Baltimore, Brooklyn, Boston, Chicago, and London. He returned to Chapel Hill to deliver the Baccalaureate sermon in 1909.

In the 1880s the Baptists turned the Craig Academy building into a parsonage, but the Church itself saw little change. By the World War I era, however, some members complained that the aging and inadequate facilities discouraged the 200 Baptist students at the university from attending. Archibald Henderson led a movement to purchase a new church site on Columbia Street. "One end of the town is rather unsightly," he argued, "the other end is of surpassing loveliness. The Baptist Church is quite near the unsightly section."

The Methodist congregation grew to proportions which demanded a new church to replace their old at the corner of Rosemary and Henderson. On 6 August 1878, church trustees, including J.W. Carr and Solomon Pool, paid $500 for a lot on Franklin Street. In October 1885, pastor R.B. John asked the Methodist Quarterly Conference to help finance the project, the Conference consented, and construction began in 1886. By June 1887, the structure was ready for a roof, but funds ran low and work was not completed until the summer of 1889.

Methodist Bishop W.W. Duncan, who was in town to deliver the Baccalaureate sermon that June, accepted an invitation to dedicate the new church. So moved were the members by his discourse that they contributed some $800 when the plate was passed, enough to pay off all their indebtedness. One portion of the cost was borne entirely by Julian Shakespeare Carr, the son of J.W. Carr. He thought the church should have a steeple and paid for one when the building committee reckoned that such an adornment would be too expensive. The steeple graced the church and Franklin Street until it was knocked off the perpendicular by a bolt of lightning in 1911, and members chose to remove it rather than repair it.

When the congregation moved in 1889, they sold the old church to the Negro Congregational Church for $800, "the Organ, Clock, and Bible alone excepted." Minister William B. North asked the seven remaining Negro members to join the Congregational Church, but when he removed them from the church roll, several white members objected heatedly and had the regional bishop reinstate the black members. Church records of 1923 reveal, "In the death of Augusta Evan Sept. 1, the church lost its oldest member and the last of the colored members of the congregation who had maintained their affiliation with the church since the Civil War."

The Rev. North created another furor on 13 July 1890 when he charged Sunday School superintendent A.S. Barbee and his teachers with maladministration and usurpation. Barbee resigned, church officials suspended North, and the Rev. Lee Whitaker replaced him temporarily. Mediator W.H. Cunningham engineered a reconciliation, North apologized, Barbee accepted, and both returned to their duties.

The old church at Henderson and Rosemary has passed through a remarkable series of incarnations. It has been a black school house, a farmers' market, a cabinet-maker's shop, and more. In 1926, barnstormer Montrose Tull converted it into a repair shop which he named the Club Service Motor Company. He reinforced the floors and added a platform on Henderson Street so he could move cars and his airplanes in and out. In 1934, Macmillan Chevrolet moved from Columbia Street to share the building with Tull until he was killed in an airplane crash in October 1934. Husband and wife Pick and Porter Cowles purchased the property in the 1940s and continued to use it to build and repair airplanes. In the 1950s, Architect Jim Webb moved in and converted the space to offices.

When erect, dignified Wilson "Wiltz" Caldwell returned to UNC as a janitor in 1875, he came as a respected member of the campus community. In the mid-1880s, Wiltz ran on the Republican ticket in the town commissioners race and defeated the Democratic candidate, Prof. Ralph Graves II. When Wiltz died in 1898, Kemp Battle preached his funeral in the Negro Congregational Church with Julian S. Carr and Judge John Manning in attendance. Wilson Caldwell lies in the Chapel Hill cemetery beneath the original Caldwell monument, which also honors his father November and his black co-workers David Barham and Henry Smith.

Sam Morphis perhaps left the most significant legacy of all the 19th century Chapel Hill blacks. His sad life provided

Dr. Edwin Caldwell (1867-1932), son of Wilson Caldwell, studied under Locke Craig in Chapel Hill, took his medical degree at Shaw University, and established a practice in Arkansas. He returned to Chapel Hill and married his brother Bruce's widow, the former Minnie Stroud (1883-1946), in order to help raise her children. Afterwards, he maintained his practice in Durham while living in Chapel Hill. He is credited with many innovative techniques in medicine, including a cure for pellagra. (NCC)

the backdrop for a Pulitizer Prize-winning play by Chapel Hill's most distinguished dramatist. Born on a farm near Chapel Hill, as a child Sam spent the days playing with the master's children, growing ashamed of his black heritage and envious of white culture. When he was 16, Sam ran away to Chapel Hill to take a job as a waiter in a boarding house. Like George Moses Horton, he drank to excess, but he was able to save enough from his earnings and from student gifts to purchase himself for $550. However, by 1858 when he applied to have the state legislature declare him free, southern politics had made his quest hopeless.

Married to a Battle-family "house-girl," after the war the destitute Sam cast his lot with the white race, purchased a cabin about three doors west of the Betty Smith House, and survived on the generosity of white friends and income from driving a hack, which he called the "Chapel Hill Lightning Express." But about 1890, when he could not meet payments for notes long overdue, he lost his house and had to move out, blaming his misery on betrayal rather than on liquor.

Years later Horace Williams recorded Sam's story of his life as an "Uncle Tom." Paul Green read Williams' handwritten narrative and drew on it while writing *In Abraham's Bosom*, which won the Pulitzer Prize for drama in 1928. Like others who have read the manuscript, Green was particularly affected by Sam's final statement: "And there is some gladness that comes to me when I see that my type of Negro will soon be gone from the face of the earth."

Black barber Tom Dunston possessed an entirely different temperament. Once a hack driver, for many years he operated a barber shop between the Presbyterian Church and H.H. Patterson's store. The sign above his shop read "THOMAS DUNSTON, Professor of Tonsorial Art," and photographs of old customers, mostly successful former students, lined the inside walls. True to his trade, Dunston was known for his quaint conversation with those confined to his chair, and his malapropism has become the stuff of legend.

Upon learning that Dr. Francis P. Venable was to succeed Edwin A. Alderman as president of UNC, Dunston supposedly declared, "Dr. Venable is a very fine gentleman, but he can neither orate, norate, nor prevaricate." Once when Alderman was concentrating on an upcoming speech and repeatedly failed to respond to his banter, the barber asked impatiently, "Marse Ed, what's got into you? I believe you are going crazy. As Epaminondas said to Themistecles, 'Much learning doth make thee mad.'" The quote is from Petronius; the characters are original with Tom Dunston.

Cornelia Spencer had taught Dunston's son Kenneth, who took over the tonsorial parlor when Tom retired. In his last years, Dunston spent many pleasant days riding with his friend Prof. M.C.S. Noble in a buggy behind Nellie Bly, Tom's aging mare. It was Noble who drove Dunston to Rex Hospital for what was to be a routine, minor operation. After the surgery, Noble shook his old friend's hand and returned to Chapel Hill, to learn that Dunston was dead.

Among other black businessmen, three cobblers monopolized the shoe-making and repair trade, university janitor Tom McDade also ran a grocery store-catering service used by both races, Vann Nunn owned a grocery store frequented by blacks, Bill Jones operated his "Pressing Club" on West Franklin Street, Henry "Buddy" Guthrie built a movie theater just before World War I in Sunset, the black section between the end of Franklin Street and the

depot. In 1910, Negroes owned 98 lots in Chapel Hill valued at $31,085. A decade later they owned 170 lots valued at $89,140.

On 16 October 1889, Dr. William P. Mallett died, after 32 years in Chapel Hill. In addition to his private practice, he ran the student infirmary in The Retreat, he was a substantial farmer, and he operated a "chemist's shop" out of his home, after 1881 on the post-office corner. From 1885 to 1889, with the assistance of his unmarried daughter Eliza he

Jesse Jones (1858-1912) was the black proprietor of the Coop, a members-only restaurant located near the present-day Porthole restaurant. This picture was taken of Jones and the members, all students, a few months before his death. Earlier, Jones was the chef at W.W. Pickard's hotel. After his death, his assistant Harrison Neville kept the Coop going into the 1930s. (NCC)

Tom Dunston (1855-1916?), seated left in this 1880s photograph, opened his popular barbershop in the early 1870s. His first location was over Seaton Barbee's drugstore, then in 1882 he moved to the location pictured here, on Franklin Street about 100 feet east of the Henderson Street intersection. Earlier, the building was the site of Charles P. Mallett's ante-bellum bookstore. (NCC)

TONSORIAL ART EMPORIUM!!

THOMAS DUNSTON

HAS FITTED UP HIS

BARBER SALOON,

opposite Barbee's drug store, in the most improved style, and will be glad to see his customers any time. He guarantees good work.

Shaving, - - - - - 15cts.
Hair Cutting, - - - - 25cts.
Shampooing, - - - - 25cts.

He has a boot-black always in attendance. Give him a call.
ap 18-tf

The ad shown here appeared in 1878. In an accompanying letter to the editor, Dunston extolled his work: "Professor Tom Dunston, tonsorial artist and shampoo laureate to his majesty, offers his services to the students at reduced rates. Bristles cleaned off, shaggy pilosity made to vanish. Turkish perfumes and India aromas administered, dirt an inch thick scraped off, and in a word, the outer man totally revealed, all for $7.00 from Sept. 1 to June 8." (NCC)

was postmaster of a small wooden office located in his front yard. In the 1890s, postmasters Thomas M. Kirkland and William N. Pritchard distributed the mail from there. By 1908 postmaster William E. Lindsay was operating out of the Lloyd-Webb buildings in the space now occupied by the Little Shop; and in 1921 postmaster Robert L. Strowd moved into a new, small office that had replaced the old one in Dr. Mallett's yard.

From the 1870s to 1897, Dr. A.B. Roberson practiced in and around Chapel Hill, living first on a farm east of town and later on South Columbia Street. Like doctors before and after him, Dr. Roberson was willing to accept produce, pigs, chickens, eggs, and so forth for his fees when his patients were short of cash, a chronic condition for much of the local populace. Dr. Roberson also ran a general store where the Carolina Theatre is today, specializing in drugs and medical supplies and moving his business several hundred feet east in 1891 when he purchased the old Central Hotel.

Dr. Roberson died in 1897; his wife Cornelia lived until 1939, by which time she had seen her children become respected leaders in two towns. One daughter was married to UNC Comptroller Charles T. Woollen. The other, Miss Nellie Roberson, headed the Extension Department of the university library from its foundation in 1921 until she retired in 1955. One son had been mayor of Chapel Hill for 20 years; another was chief of surgery at Watts Hospital in Durham.

William Stone Roberson, the "perpetual mayor" of Chapel Hill, graduated from UNC in 1889 and ran unsuccessfully for mayor in 1899. He ran again in 1903, won, and remained in office for five consecutive terms. Later, the board of aldermen appointed him mayor in every year between 1913 and 1927. Although Mayor Roberson refused to approve any improvements based on borrowed money, he saw the annual town budget rise from $1552 in 1903 to $224,675 in 1927, in part because of some $250,000 in state money received between 1922 and 1927.

"Mayor Will" prospered as a teacher, a dealer in real estate, and a lawyer, but he could have become much wealthier had he not expended so much time and cash on improvements in Chapel Hill, especially in education. He was a driving force in having the new brick schoolhouse built on West Franklin Street, and in the early 1920s he contributed most of the money to build a tin gymnasium behind the school. He died on 7 June 1935, 66 years old and a bachelor.

His brother Foy was captain of the UNC football team in

This ca. 1915 photograph shows the soda fountain counter of the University Athletic Shop, run by James Neville (left) in the store that is now the Carolina Coffee Shop. The customer is Clarence Webb, son of J.D. Webb (1861-1931) who erected the building in 1900 and who ran a general merchandise store next door. The marble countertop stayed with the shop through its transformations into a drugstore and then a restaurant before it was removed for remodeling in 1968. (Photograph taken from Lefler and Wager, Orange County: 1753-1953)

Fred Merritt (1886-1931) was in the cleaning and pressing business in partnership with Willie Morphis, grandson of Sam Morphis. Merritt's business was located on Franklin Street across from present-day Graham Memorial. In the decade before World War I, Merritt charged his customers a monthly fee of $1.00 for all their cleaning and pressing. (NCC)

under the brand name Bromo-Seltzer, and Bromo-Seltzer made Emerson a millionaire. After Mrs. McDade kindly forgave her suddenly wealthy nephew, "Ike" Emerson provided for her and others in his family in Chapel Hill and indulged his love of beautiful women, fashionable clothes, luxurious yachts, and travel to the fun-spots of the world. Among his several contributions to UNC, in 1914 he gave $26,000 for the construction of Emerson Field, which was used for decades as the baseball park, an all-purpose playing field, and until the completion of Kenan Stadium as the football gridiron.

Dr. Thomas W. Harris, the first dean of the Medical School when it was founded in 1879, also ran a drugstore before moving to Durham in 1885. His son Isaac F. Harris attended the Canada School and UNC, earning a B.S. degree in 1900 and an M.S. degree in 1903. While a student, Isaac contributed several articles to respected medical journals, and he also experimented with chemical compounds, eventually developing several vitamin pills that made him wealthy, but long after he left Chapel Hill.

Dr. Thomas James Wilson moved from Hillsborough in 1886 and practiced in Chapel Hill until his death in 1904. His son Thomas James Jr. attended UNC, earning an A.B. in 1894, an M.A. in 1896, and a Ph.D. in 1898. He married W.W. Pickard's daughter Lorena Franklin Pickard and remained at UNC as a professor of Greek and Latin and as an administrator for 46 years. Dr. Wilson's grandson Thomas James III was a Rhodes Scholar who earned his Ph.D. in Romance languages at Oxford in 1928. During World War II he was aboard the fast carrier "Enterprise" while Captain O.B. Hardison, Sr. (UNC class of 1911) was at the helm. After the war, Dr. Wilson directed the UNC Press for a short period before moving on to direct the Harvard Press for 20 years.

Perhaps the last of Chapel Hill's old-time family doctors, Dr. Braxton Lloyd, received his M.D. from the university in 1909. A descendant of Revolutionary War General Thomas Lloyd, he then spent three years at the Eye and Ear Infirmary in Newark, New Jersey, before returning to Carrboro with his bride Mrs. Emma Hanson Lloyd. He was mayor of Carrboro (1917-1921) and a director of the Bank of Chapel Hill, but "Brack" Lloyd was known primarily as an eccentric doctor ready to minister to anyone, anywhere, under any conditions.

According to novelist Robert Ruark, "Dr. Lloyd was picturesquely profane, vastly irreverent, and he never sent out a bill in his life. He would just as leave take a pint of whiskey as a fee for delivering a baby, and often did. He always wore his black hat when he was operating. Said he couldn't see to cut without it." Dr. Lloyd's office was wherever he happened to be, usually in Eubanks' Drugstore, on Franklin Street, or in the Carolina Coffee Shop. When one patient's wife expressed shock over his unsanitary surgical methods, Lloyd told her, "Don't worry. I was born sterilized. I eat

1905 before becoming a surgeon and settling in Durham, where he remained the quintessential UNC sports booster all his life. Dr. Roberson's son Foy, Jr. won the John Sprunt Hill award as the outstanding man in his graduating class at Durham High School before playing basketball at UNC. On 21 December 1941 flying patrol duty off Southern California, Army Lt. Foy Roberson Jr. died in a mid-air collision, at age 23. His father established the Foy Roberson, Jr. Medal awarded to the UNC basketball player contributing most to team morale. Dr. Roberson died on 19 November 1955, exactly 50 years after his last game as captain of the UNC football team. The cemetery east of town, the Roberson Park Development, and the Cedar Terrace Annex now occupy portions of the family farm inherited by Dr. Foy Roberson.

Dr. A.B. Roberson's druggist in the late 1870s was Isaac Edward Emerson, a handsome, well dressed young fellow with a zest for life who also worked for Dr. Mallett. Isaac and his brother John moved in from their home on the Raleigh Road to live with their aunt Mrs. A.J. McDade and her husband on Columbia beside the McDade building at Columbia and Franklin. It was the unbridled zest of others, however, that made Isaac Emerson's fortune.

While teaching chemistry at UNC and working as a druggist, and after listening to customers' complaints of the discomforts attributable to the overconsumption of food and spirits, Emerson began to experiment with concoctions which might provide relief. He married the beautiful but divorced daughter of Colonel W.F. Askew of Raleigh, and when his neighbors' undisguised disapproval of his violation of a southern taboo became overbearing, he left for Baltimore in 1881 and used his wife's capital to open a drug store. Mrs. McDade promptly disowned and disinherited her "wayward" nephew.

Continuing to work on his headache remedy, Emerson eventually produced a pleasing solution which he patented

germs."

In his latter years, the almost toothless Dr. Lloyd ate most of his meals at the Carolina Coffee Shop, never consulting prices, never accepting a check, and always leaving 50 cents on the table no matter what he had consumed. Brusque of manner, salty of speech, he claimed he treated "damn few niggers and none of the faculty," but when the old agnostic died in March 1947 the Carrboro Baptist Church was filled to overflowing by mourners of both races and from all walks of life, come to pay their final respects to the last of an old order.

By the end of Reconstruction, it seemed the old order in the business community had already passed. Only J.W. Carr, McCauley and Long, and two or three other merchants had survived. However, by 1884 the university was growing and economic expansion was in full swing. The village sported no less than five full time blacksmiths and wheelwrights; Foster Utley and Leandrew Graham Sykes operated distilleries, Sykes' supposedly producing turpentine; Massey King was a millwright; and Eugene H. Wilson ran a tannery on West Franklin Street beyond the Baptist Church. There were 14 general stores, four drugstores, five lumber suppliers, and three livery stables.

M.J.W. McCauley was operating Matthew McCauley's old mill on Morgan Creek; G.W. Purefoy ran his grist mill and a saw mill until his death in 1880, after which several men kept them going; William F. Strowd had recently built a saw mill on Bolin Creek to compete with mills owned by Robert Patterson and former professional artist D.J. Ezzell.

In 1873 William Strowd paid W.F. Hargrave $7000 for 905 acres between Franklin Street and Raleigh Road, the lion's share of the 935 acres Jesse Hargrave bought from Lemuel Morgan in 1845. Strowd remained in Chatham County, deeding 1100 acres east of town in 1886 to his son Robert L. Strowd, a farmer and the owner of a store on Franklin Street. In 1917 Robert and his wife Francis built the first house on what is now Davie Circle. They called it Plum Nellie for "plum out of Chapel Hill and nearly to Durham." When Francis and a daughter died the next year, Robert vacated the house.

Encouraged by the commercial building boom, J.W. Carr and Seaton Barbee built large brick kilns. In February 1874, the village commissioners expelled fellow member Carr "in consequence of mental derangement," replacing him with John White. However, Carr led the balloting in May 1874 and returned to his seat again in 1875. He also owned a cotton gin and in 1879 built a second store on Franklin Street, one door west of his first. He died in 1889, long after his son Julian Shakespeare Carr was established in tobacco and textiles in Durham.

When Thomas Long sold his share in the old Jesse Hargrave's store to Dave McCauley in the early 1870s, he

Charles L. Lindsay (1860-1949) ran a hardware store on Franklin Street, pictured here in 1890, as had his father, Matthew, before him. Charles, married to Dave McCauley's daughter, Mary Irene (1876-1959), was the principal owner of the Chapel Hill Insurance and Realty Company, one of the largest firms in the area until it was forced into receivership in 1926. The Lindsays later moved to Tennessee.

Lindsay suffered several losses in Chapel Hill. In the early 1890s his stable was burned by an arsonist, and in the spring of 1926 he and his family turned over in his new Hudson automobile. He repaired it, and on 23 August 1926, thieves in Durham stole it. (Photo of Mr. Lindsay courtesy Mrs. W.G. Polk, Franklin, Tennessee. Photo of store, NCC)

formed a mercantile partnership with Thomas J. Norwood that lasted until both men died within a month of each other in 1879. The purchase left McCauley the sole proprietor of the largest store in Chapel Hill, selling everything from wagons and machinery to groceries to the latest in women's fashions. He had gone into business with less than $125 in 1854, but by 1875 he and his wife Mary were the largest property holders and the largest taxpayers in the village, owning most of the land south of Cameron Avenue and west of the university.

Between 1863 and 1906, McCauley was involved in well over 100 real-estate transactions, including his gifts of McCauley, Vance and Ransom streets to the village, roadways he had cut through his property. He served 10 terms on the board of commissioners, and he was a local leader in Democratic politics. By the mid-1880s, he was able to leave the routine management of the store to his clerks A.P. Birch and W.J. Hogan, freeing himself to concentrate on real estate and to travel twice yearly to Baltimore and New York for stock purchases. In spite of his success, McCauley lived modestly until his death in 1911, the last surviving charter member of the Chapel Hill Baptist Church.

Before McCauley's semi-retirement, other stores had replaced his as the favorite of fashionable shoppers. One of his strongest competitors was a former clerk, Algernon Sydney Barbee, the son of Chapel Hill merchant Sydney Mulholland Barbee. A.S. Barbee graduated from UNC in 1860 and taught a few months in Mississippi before the outbreak of the war. He served in the Confederate army from Shiloh until his surrender near Macon, Georgia in late April 1865. Then, carrying his musket, saddle bags, and a blanket, he walked home to Chapel Hill. After a stint as a railroad agent, he went to work for McCauley and Long while moonlighting as a notary public.

In 1876, Barbee opened his own general store on Franklin Street. He prospered and later purchased Nancy Hilliard's old "Crystal Palace." Barbee and his wife, the former Mary Parker of Enfield, lived childless in the Crystal Palace, using the current Morehead Planetarium plot for a pasture, until Mary died in the early 1930s. Mary served boarders downstairs, and mathematics professor William Cain rented the second floor from 1889 until he was killed by an automobile while crossing Franklin Street in front of the house on 6 December 1930. His nephew Archibald Henderson lived with him from 1894 to 1904. A.S. Barbee was mayor of Chapel Hill twice, 1895-1900 and 1907-1910, and a long-time justice of the peace.

Henry Houston "Hoot" Patterson was born six miles east of Chapel Hill in 1844. At the start of the Civil War, he enlisted as a private in the 1st N.C. Regiment, receiving several wounds, including one at Chancellorsville, before surrendering with Lee as a Lieutenant. He married Mary Hogan, daughter of physician Tom Hogan, with whom they lived until 1881 when Hoot, as he was universally known,

began to sell general merchandise in Chapel Hill. The next year he purchased a storehouse just west of the Presbyterian Church, located between Tom Dunston's barber shop and Dr. Thomas Harris' drugstore at Franklin and Henderson. In the following years, Hoot's emporium became the "high class" shop in the village, particularly attractive to faculty wives, whom Hoot accomodated by billing every three months to coincide with the university pay schedule.

Patterson was a vice president and a director of the Bank of Chapel Hill, a village alderman, and a member of the board of education, chairman when he died in 1917. His brother Wiley lost a leg in the Civil War and afterward was the university bursar for 35 years. Hoot's son James practiced law in Durham, his daughter Jennie married physics professor Dr. James E. Latta, and his son Fred married Blanche Pickard, the daughter of Walter and Betty Pickard. Fred's son Dr. Fred Patterson lived and practiced in Chapel Hill until his death in 1984.

While Patterson was building his business, R.S. MacRae purchased Dr. Harris' drugstore on 1 March 1885, improved the premises, and increased the stock to include confections, stationery, artists supplies, and other sundries. Pharmacist C.E. King stayed with the business, and MacRae was able to succeed where Dr. Harris had essentially failed, having spent the majority of his time attending to his duties as dean of the fledgling Medical School. George W. Purefoy, Jr. and E.S. Merritt established a drugstore in the spring of 1882. Merritt bought out his partner on 1 January 1884, widened his stock, and challenged Harris and later MacRae for the community prescription trade. In August 1904, John Franklin Pickard and Frank Strowd opened a confection and grocery store in what had been MacRae's drugstore.

In 1884 F.P. Boothe, a Chatham County farmer until 1882, was operating a dry goods store out of the only brick building on Franklin Street, very probably the first in the commercial district. A.J. McDade had built the two-story structure in 1880 near the public well at Columbia and Franklin. Several businesses occupied the McDade Building before it became dangerously unsafe and fell to the wrecker in 1915.

The most legendary of Chapel Hill merchants arrived as a student from Rowan County in 1880. Adam Alexander Kluttz studied medicine and left in 1883 to continue his studies at the New York College of Physicians and Surgeons, leaving without a degree and returning to Chapel Hill to assist Dr. A.B. Roberson in his drug- and general-merchandise store. "Dr." Kluttz, realizing he was not suited temperamentally for the medical profession, was happy to take over the store from Roberson, who resurrected his business in the old Cental Hotel in 1891.

"Adam Applejack," as the students labeled Kluttz, made money and in 1890 broke ground for a two-story storehouse across Franklin Street from the Methodist Church. The same year he married Ora Crawford of Goldsboro. In 1894 they purchased the Sam Phillips house for $2800, Mrs.

Kluttz rented rooms and served well appreciated meals, and the couple became favorites of townspeople and students alike. Cornelia Spencer Love lived with the Kluttzes from 1918 to 1929; bachelor Prof. W.S. "Bully" Bernard rented the Sam Phillips law office for several years.

Dr. Kluttz's great weakness in business was also his great strength. He could not resist adding an extra piece of candy to a child's purchase, nor could he turn down requests by students for credit and loans. As a result, he accumulated some $40,000 in bad accounts while building a business and acquiring the property that made him and Mrs. Kluttz the largest taxpayers in the village.

William Meade Prince described the Kluttz store as it was at the turn of the century: "It was a solid, rock-ribbed institution in Chapel Hill, like the stone walls. It was a club a headquarters, a Mecca for everybody." Dr. Kluttz rented the upstairs, and downstairs he sold groceries, candy, stationery, books, shoes, jewelry, clothing, patent medicine, bicycles, delicacies, and hundreds of other items. His black clerk Ernest Thompson was the de facto manager, freeing his boss to engage in an endless series of checkers matches with his crony Oregon Tenney. According to a student ditty, "Ernest runs the business,/Doc chews cig-ar butts,/Everybody works in this old town,/But A.A. Kluttz."

Late in the fall of 1926, Dr. Kluttz suffered his first serious illness. Prof. M.C.S. Noble visited him on 20 December, and the old friends were entertaining each other with jokes and banter when quite suddenly Dr. Kluttz died. Those are the facts. But similar to the legend of the Davie Poplar, it is the romantic version of Dr. Kluttz's demise that has endured. In the myth, Presbyterian minister W.D. Moss was sitting by the bedside when Kluttz asked, "Parson Moss, what do you think heaven is like?" Moss thought a moment and answered, "Dr. Kluttz, I believe heaven must be a lot like Chapel Hill in the spring." "That's good," Dr. Kluttz mused, and quietly expired. William Meade Prince in 1950 drew on that variant for the title to his memoirs *The Southern Part of Heaven*, a description of the village even now repeated from time to time.

Mrs. Kluttz survived her husband by over 20 years; and, according to her next-door neighbor Robert House, who still lives in the Widow Puckett House, she was "a constant joy and delight." She gave the Jackson Training School Dr. Kluttz's stock of books along with cash donations; she consistently championed improvements in the public schools, although tax increases cost her more than anyone in the district; and she was a generous and constant supporter of the Carolina Playmakers. She died childless on 31 May 1947. Her downtown property—including the buildings housing the Varsity Shop, Snipes' Barber Shop, Lacock's, the N.C. Cafeteria, and more—and four houses brought $162,655 at public auction on 1 September 1948.

Dr. Kluttz's checkers crony Oregon B. Tenney was the son of John B. and Jane Tenney. John had come to Chapel Hill from a farm near Boston, probably in the 1830s. He married locally, ran Steward's Hall for a time, and made several property transactions, including the purchase of the homeplace and approximately 20 acres out of the old Benjamin Yeargin plantation. Several of John's sons went off to war. Nathaniel Brooks Tenney died at Gettysburg; William C. Tenney was captured at Gettysburg; Oregon Tenney was shot through both hands on 2 September 1861 at Cedar Mountain, Virginia. A daughter, Sarah Tenney Ballard, pined away and died in 1862 following the death of her husband who had fought in the Yankee army.

After the war Oregon married Mary Ward, the daughter of John and Amanda Partin Ward and a young lady 13 years his junior. They lived and raised 10 children on the "Tenney Plantation," while also caring for John Tenney, who was intermittently insane from the early 1850s until his death in 1892. Oregon continued to farm and to play checkers with Dr. Kluttz and chess with Horace Williams until his death in December 1914. Mary survived until November 1935.

As a 20-year-old in 1890, Robert Allen Eubanks came to Chapel Hill from the White Cross community and opened a grocery store in the building Dr. Kluttz had recently vacated. Renting the upstairs to students, he ran the store for 43 years, closing it in 1933 to become postmaster, a post he held until ill health forced him to retire in 1939. Workmen razed the frame structure in 1934, at which time it was the oldest commercial building in town, dating to about 1860. They discovered fingerless ladies' gloves, high white collars, cuffs, white dress bow ties, and scores of other relics dating back to Dr. Roberson's tenure, including a bottle labeled "Old Nick Corn Whiskey, made in Williamston, North Carolina in 1879, for family use only." A black carpenter broke the gold seal, sampled Old Nick slowly, and finding him agreeable drank the entire contents, attesting that it was "mightly mellow" when he next showed up for work, a week later.

This 1909 scene was a common sight on Franklin Street before it was paved in the 1920s. The sign in the left foreground reads, "NO FISHING ALLOWED." The grocery store of Robert Allen Eubanks (1870-1940) sits on the current Carolina Theatre site. (NCC)

In 1892, R.A. Eubank's cousin Clyde Eubanks came to Chapel Hill from Pittsboro, went to work as Dr. Roberson's assistant, studied pharmacology at the university and in Raleigh, and in 1897 purchased the store and its stock when Dr. Roberson died. The next year he married Stella Pritchard, and in 1901 he moved his business across the street to a new building he had erected on a lot owned by Mrs. Felix Tankersley on the space now occupied by Milton's Clothing Cupboard.

Since Eubanks had put all his capital into materials and supplies, Mrs. Tankersley allowed the rent to accumulate until it equaled the value of the building. Then Eubanks had to make a choice, and he was not one to spend a cent needlessly. Consequently, in 1914 he started his own building on a 25'-wide strip running between Franklin and Rosemary through the area now occupied by the NCNB Plaza.

Eubanks Drug Company became an "institution"—Louis Graves called it the Franklin Street Social Club. Its soda fountain attracted a cross-section of Chapel Hill society, dominated in numbers by businessmen. Eubanks closed the soda fountain during World War II, but so established had it become by then that people still gathered there and at a bench outside to conduct business or exchange gossip. Stella Eubanks died in 1964, and a year later Clyde sold his drugstore to Benjamin and Ellyn Courts, who named it Courts Drugs and moved to University Square when the Eubanks building was removed to make way for NCNB. However, Clyde Eubanks was far more to Chapel Hill than just a druggist.

Active in the Methodist Church until his death in 1965, Eubanks was an alderman for 25 years, a mayor pro-tem, a co-founder with S.E. Lloyd of the Chapel Hill-Carrboro Merchants Association in 1939, president of the N.C. Pharmaceutical Association in 1926-1927, and a storied executive of the Bank of Chapel Hill.

A series of robberies in the vicinity in 1898 was the impetus for merchants Charles Lee Lindsay and his father-in-law Dave McCauley to join with Julian Shakespeare Carr, R.W. Winston, and Crawford Biggs of Durham in putting up $2000 and on 15 February 1899 opening the Bank of Chapel Hill in a small brick building adjacent to A.A. Kluttz's store.

Samuel Thomas Peace, a student from Oxford, was their first cashier, and optometrist/watchmaker W.B. Sorrell made the first deposit—$25. For a while, vice-president C.L. Lindsay took the capital and deposits home at night for safe keeping. He wanted Peace to take half, but the youngster said he would not be able to sleep with $1000 under his pillow. Peace did quietly close the bank one day so he could visit Oxford. Apparently, no one noticed. When Peace left after 18 months, deposits exceeded $25,000 and the Bank of Chapel Hill was firmly a part of the community.,

About 1905, E. Vernon Howell, Horace Williams, and

This 1909 photograph looks east on Franklin Street from about where The Intimate Bookshop is today. In the right background is the Lloyd-Webb building, built by Junius D. Webb and Herbert Lloyd about 1900, and behind the building can be seen, dimly, the Lonnie Merritt livery stable. The Carolina Coffee Shop occupies the first section of the building today.

The young lad is Walter Boger (1900-1965) whose father ran a popular confectionary shop in the basement of the old Central Hotel. Walter was the supervisor of the university laundry for most of his career.

others formed The People's Bank, which competed intensely, and often acrimoniously, with the Bank of Chapel Hill for two decades. In August 1924, however, an assistant cashier for The People's bank committed suicide, and an audit by Prof. Howell revealed that $55,000 was missing. Directors assessed stockholders $66.66 per share to cover losses; no depositor lost a cent; and Prof. Howell won plaudits as the epitome of the honest businessman; but stung by the experience, stockholders voted to merge with the Bank of Chapel Hill.

Clyde Eubanks became a director of the Bank of Chapel Hill in 1907, president in 1942, and built a reputation for never risking a dime of the depositors' money. Reportedly, when Betty Smith requested a loan of $200 to purchase a ticket to New York where she would collect some $25,000 in royalties from *A Tree Grows in Brooklyn*, cashier W.E. Thompson turned her down on the grounds that Eubanks would loan money only to those with tangible collateral. Her response was to promise emphatically that when she returned with some assets she would certainly deposit them with Eubanks, where she could be assured of their safety, and she did.

Two firms still in business were founded in the second decade of this century. In 1911 Robert W. Foister, a native of Chapel Hill, opened Foister's Camera Store where the Rite Aid Center is today. In 1912 he married Nettie Ray, also of Chapel Hill, and they settled into a home on the corner of Henderson and North Streets. In 1913, Foister moved to the store Clyde Eubanks had built on Tankersley property and

remained there until it burned in 1925. He rented the space now occupied by Varley's, using the upstairs for a "Toyland" during Christmas seasons, until 1932, when he moved into the Strowd Building across the street, where the store remained until 1983, by which time it was the oldest business in Chapel Hill.

In the beginning, Foister sold stationery, photographic equipment and supplies, using the town pump in front of the Methodist Church to develop negatives. In 1941 W.F. Kendrick of Mebane joined him to form the Foister-Palm Photo Service, which soon had a score of employees handling orders coming in from far afield. The partnership coincided with a World War II boom spurred by the arrival of the Pre-Flight School students. Demand for film was so great that Foister rationed the precious commodity one roll per week per customer, and each Sunday morning anxious buyers formed a line, often stretching around the post office.

W.O. Lacock began what is now the oldest family-operated business in Chapel Hill in 1918, a shoe shop then in a wooden building next to R.A. Eubank's grocery. In 1928 he moved across Franklin Street, just before the Great Depression almost wiped him out. Like Foister's, his trade rebounded during World War II with the coming of Pre-Flight students. In 1946, Lacock moved to 143 East Franklin, where his son Vernon continues the business.

Once the railroad arrived a mile west of the village in 1882, it was inevitable that an outpost of some sort would develop around the terminus. There was no depot, just a boxcar used for a ticket booth/office and a sign designating it the "Chapel

This photograph of the south side of Franklin Street was made in January 1916 just before the new brick buildings were ready for occupancy. The four businesses that went in were, left to right, Bruce Strowd's Ford garage, the short-lived Tar Heel Theater, Gooch's Cafe, and S.J. Brockwell's second Pickwick Theatre. The automobiles and the white store shack far right are the property of S.J. Brockwell and T.E. Best, who traded as the B&B Auto Station, a Chapel Hill to Durham bus service.

The building with the Coca-Cola sign is the Lloyd-Webb building, presently the home of the Carolina Coffee Shop. (NCC)

Elizabeth Cotten, folk singer and award-winning author of "Freight Train," lived in a house on Church Street beginning in the 1890s. She named her first guitar "Stella" and played it for youngsters in the area for years, although the Rev. L.H. Hackney would never let her perform in church despite repeated pleas by great numbers of his congregation. In 1941, Elizabeth moved to Washington, D.C. to live with a daughter. Many of her songs describe her Chapel Hill childhood. (NCC)

Hill Station." In 1883 Tom Lloyd, a descendant of General Thomas Lloyd, and Isaac W. Pritchard built a grist mill and a cotton gin next to the "depot." Two blacksmiths opened shops. Ruffin Cheek built the first store in the area, and Hiram Stone the second. By 1900, several people had built houses nearby, they had constructed a one-story elementary schoolhouse, and the rail ending had become one of the busiest crosstie collection points in the nation.

By 1885, Tom Lloyd was able to pay attorney James B. Mason $1500 for a Cameron Avenue residence, next door to Wilson Caldwell and now known as the "Wiley House," but after 15 years he had profited little from the grist mill and the cotton gin. Nevertheless, he and his wife Sarah Carolina "Tine" (pronounced Tiny) were determined to succeed, and in 1899 Tom Lloyd turned his existing interests over to his brother Herbert and focused his efforts on building a brick, two-storied, 4000-spindle cotton mill named "Alberta" next to the "depot."

In 1909, Julian Shakespeare Carr gave Lloyd $130,000 for the Alberta Mill, at the same time paying Isaac W. Pritchard $9800 for the adjacent Blanche Hosiery Mills Company. Lloyd used part of the money to build a second mill across Main Street. In 1913, Carr added an east wing to the Alberta Mill, designated No. 4 in his Durham Hosiery chain, and in 1914 he purchased Lloyd's second mill, designated No. 7.

Married to the former Emily Anzanette Atwater, Isaac W. Pritchard also dealt in real estate, he was a state representative in 1907-1908, and he was a director of the Bank of Chapel Hill and a trustee of Elon College. His son Grady, who grew up in the family home on Ransom Street, was the captain of the 1922 Tar Heel football team, a squad that won nine and lost only to Yale while winning the South Atlantic championship. Grady remained in Chapel Hill as an automobile dealer and a clothier.

Isaac's daughter Josephine "Miss Josie" attended Elon, studied art in New York City, taught at Elon, and was teaching at UNC when typhoid fever forced her to curb her activities. Consequently, in 1919 she became the only assistant to UNC Registrar Dr. Thomas J. Wilson, Jr. In 1937 she became Senior Recorder, a year before she relieved Charles Woollen of the job of ordering and preparing UNC's genuine sheepskin diplomas. From 1942 until her retirement in 1952, she edited the annual commencement programs.

Isaac Pritchard's brother William N., a state senator in 1903, ran a store five miles southwest at Pritchard's Mills before joining T.F. Lloyd in 1882 in opening a general store in Chapel Hill. William's daughter Stella married Clyde Eubanks; his son Fred was at one time an assistant postmaster of Chapel Hill and at another the private secretary to Congressman W.W. Kitchin; his son William, Jr. ended a brilliant career as a research chemist on the faculty of the Cooper Union Institute of Technology; his son James Manning graduated from the UNC School of Pharmacy in 1918 and along with Phillip Lloyd later took over Patterson's Drugstore from Glenn Patterson, who had inherited the business from his father Bunn. The good-natured, jovial Manning turned Patterson's into a hangout for students which contrasted sharply with the "social club" next-door in his brother-in-law Clyde Eubanks' drugstore.

Until 1911 the depot area was known simply as West End, an appellation bestowed casually by a mailman. In 1912 residents incorporated under the name Venable in honor of the university president, Francis P. Venable. Few people cared what name the town carried. "But," in the clearly biased opinion of Mrs. Eleanor Alexander Patterson, "Julian Carr, who owned a little department store and who liked to dress up in his Confederate uniform and sit up on the stage at commencement time, didn't like the idea. Anyway, Dr. Venable said he didn't give a damn, so the station was named Carrboro." In fact, the citizens got something in return. Carr agreed to furnish electric lights to the town if it would bear his name.

Chapel Hill continued to be a difficult town for newpaper

Joseph A. Harris (1848-1926) of Raleigh published the Chapel Hill Ledger 1878-1880, operating out of a small frame building just west of the Methodist church on Franklin Street. In 1880, he moved to Hillsborough, established the Orange County Observer and edited it until 1910.

In Chapel Hill, he employed as his first editors Frank D. Winston (1857-1941), later a judge, and Robert P. Pell (1860-1941), later a Presbyterian minister and also the President of Converse College from 1896 to 1929. Winston and Pell immediately announced their political position: "The Ledger will be DEMOCRATIC under all circumstances."

Harris also employed Pell's brother Edward Leigh (1861-1947), later a Methodist minister. (NCC)

THE CHAPEL HILLIAN.

Published semi-monthly at Chapel Hill, N.C.
University of N.C.

Entered at the Post-office at Chapel Hill, N.C., as second-class matter.

S. A. ASHE, Jr., — — — — — — **Manager.**
F. H. ARGO.

William Henry Thompson (1853-1926) first named his newspaper the Chapel Hill News, *but within a year he renamed it* The News of Orange County. *The paper, like others of the period, was given to "boosterism" of its own community and good-natured deprecation of other communities. For example, Durham Globe editor General Al Fairbrother was called to task for his visits to Chapel Hill in 1891. He explained the visits in an editorial: "I expect to buy the University and turn it into a laundry." (NCC)*

publishers. In 1878, J.W. Carr backed 30-year-old Joseph A. Harris in establishing the *Weekly Ledger*, a four-page weekly initially edited by students Robert P. Pell and Frank D. Winston. Cornelia Spencer was editor during the summer of 1879; Charles Aycock followed Mrs. Spencer as editor until his class load forced him to resign; and Robert Pell's brother Edward Leigh contributed articles. Harris then tried his hand at editing and publishing a few months before laying the *Ledger* to rest. In 1913, Edward Leigh Pell's daughter Mary Leigh married Alfred Moore Scales. Her son Junius Irving Scales would become notorious because of his political activity in Chapel Hill in the 1940s and the 1950s.

In 1893, after having edited papers in Reidsville and Yanceyville, William H. Thompson finally succeeded in founding an enduring local newspaper with *The News of Orange County*. The *News* was also four pages, and at first Thompson filled it primarily with moral essays and national news and advertisements. After Thompson died in 1927, his son continued as publisher until 1944 when he sold out to UNC journalism professor J. Roy Parker. Parker moved the *News* to Hillsborough and in 1948 sold it to Edwin J. Hamlin, who returned it to Carrboro. In 1966 Orville Campbell and the Chapel Hill *Newspaper* purchased the *News* and moved the much-traveled publication back to Hillsborough. Then H.G. Coleman bought it on 1 September 1976, and left it in place.

On campus, students published the first issue of the *Tar Heel* on 23 February 1893. From 1891 to 1893, students Samuel A'Court Ashe, Jr. and Fordyce Hubbard Argo published the sports-oriented *Chapel Hillian*, read eagerly by students in a new era of athletics on campus.

Julian M. Baker was a gymnastics enthusiast and a junior in 1876 when he financed a small gym which he and university carpenter Foster Utley built south of Gerrard Hall. Inspired by the new facility, students formed the University Athletic Association, with Julian Baker as president, began playing interclass baseball games, and in the spring of 1884 played Bingham preparatory school, losing 12-11. In February 1884, students held their first field day on the large athletic field southeast of Smith Hall (the Playmakers Theatre). The events included greased pig races, long jumps

with and without dumbbells, a baseball throw, two- and 18-lap races around a one-sixth-mile track, and three-legged, fat-men's, and 100-yard runs.

A growing desire for a substantial gym coincided with a push by some trustees to cease holding the annual commencement ball in Smith Hall because the dance "diverts attention from study, leads to liquor drinking, involves considerable expense, and is a grief to multitudes of our best citizens." The privately directed University Gymnasium Association incorporated on 29 October 1884, raised money by selling shares at $10 each, bought a lot now occupied by Phillips Hall, and raised a tin-roofed, frame structure with a 100' by 45' main arena that served both as a gymnasium and a ballroom.

In 1883, the seniors and freshmen united to defeat the juniors and sophomores in UNC's first organized football game. On 18 October 1888 at the State Fair in Raleigh, UNC began intercollegiate football play, losing to Wake Forest 4-6 with a team captained by Bob Bingham and listing John Motley Morehead and A.H. Patterson as players. In 1889 UNC, Wake Forest, and Trinity College (now Duke University) played spring and fall round robins, each team winning and losing twice. Several serious injuries that year prompted the trustees to ban the sport as a brutal and unwholesome spectacle which encouraged gambling and drinking. Students vigorously protested; professors Horace Williams, Francis Venable, and Eben Alexander urged that the ban be lifted; and the trustees yielded.

Students resumed play in 1891 and fielded a legendary team in 1892, with William P. Graves of Yale as coach, Mike Hoke as captain, and Charles Baskerville and Bill Devin among the players. In October, that team beat Richmond 40-0 and lost to Virginia 18-30. Then during Thanksgiving week they accomplished feats which are, for humanitarian reasons, no longer possible. On Monday, 22 November, they defeated Trinity 24-0 in Chapel Hill. After riding the overnight train to Atlanta, on Tuesday they outscored Auburn 64-0. The next day in Nashville, they beat Vanderbilt 24-0. Returning

The Chapel Hill News.

STAND BY THAT WHICH IS GOOD.

VOL. I.   CHAPEL HILL, N.C., THURSDAY, JAN. 11, 1894.   NO. XI.

Samuel A'Court Ashe, Jr. (1874-1932) and Walter Bonitz (1874-1941), with the editorial assistance of Fordyce Hubbard Argo (1873-1954), produced the first campus newspaper in 1891. Ashe later became clerk of the U.S. District Court in Raleigh, Argo became an Episcopalian minister, and Bonitz made a career as a stockbroker in Goldsboro. (NCC)

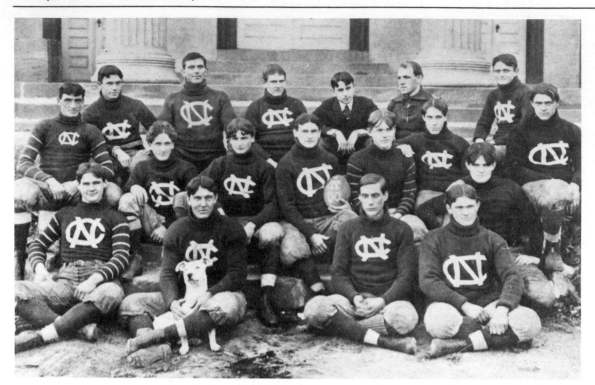

to Atlanta, on Friday, 26 November they revenged their only loss of the season by trouncing Virginia 26-0. In five days, the UNC eleven had traveled approximately 1000 grueling miles and beaten four major teams by a combined score of 138-0 without making a single substitution.

"Oh! What a day of triumph it was when the Varsity team returned from Atlanta," George Tayloe Winston later recalled, "bringing with them the beautiful trophy of victory and the bleeding scalp of our ancient foe, the University of Virginia." Tar Heel fans had to subsist on those memories for a long while. Between the 1892 win and a 7-0 victory in 1916, UNC's record against Virginia was a depressing 3-16-1. One of the victories was in 1898, when UNC's only undefeated football squad went 9-0. Prof. E. Vernon Howell, who had played for Wake Forest as a student in 1888, was a member of the 1898 team in an era when faculty and graduate students were eligible players.

After moving to Knoxville, Tennessee, in 1908, William Meade Prince attended the University of Tennessee practices, copied their plays, and gave them to UNC captain George Thomas. The Tar Heel's first scouting report had little practical value, however, since the team lost 0-12.

In 1905, work was completed on the Bynum Gymnasium, donated by Judge William P. Bynum of Lincoln County as a memorial to his grandson, who died while a student at the university. A decade earlier, trustees had leveled the floor of the old Memorial Hall in an unsuccessful effort to improve acoustics. Students started playing interclass basketball in the unheated building in 1903 and fielded a team in 1911 which began intercollegiate play, accumulating a 7-4 record against teams as diverse as Virginia, Woodberry Forest prep school, and the Durham YMCA. In the 1920s, UNC

This dim 1913 photo has some historic significance. It captures the kickoff of the game in which UNC scored against arch-rival Virginia for the first time since 1907. Walter Fuller (1894-1973) intercepted a pass and ran 70 yards for a touchdown, the only score in UNC's 7-26 loss. Three years later, UNC won 7-0 for its first victory over Virginia in nine games played over an 11 year period.

Fuller edited the Tar Heel and later edited the St. Petersburg, Florida, Times. In 1919 he ventured into real estate and construction, eventually building over 1400 homes in St. Petersburg. (NCC)

would become an established basketball powerhouse, winning the Southern Conference championship, four of five years from 1922 to 1926.

Several turn-of-the-century professors left lasting imprints on Chapel Hill. Kemp Battle devoted himself selflessly to the university while he was president from 1876 to 1891 and a distinguished professor until he died on 4 February 1919. Battle's appearance, with his perpetual black suit, wing-tipped collar, bow tie, and graying whiskers, is perhaps best evoked by citing an exchange he had with a mountain inn-keeper on a trip to Asheville in the 1880s. Looking his

1911 marked the first year that the UNC basketball team played an intercollegiate schedule, although UNC teams had played intramural games since 1903. The 1911 team, pictured here, had a record of 7-4, and it scored 60 points in one game, a figure not reached again for seven years.

Nathaniel J. "Nate" Cartmell (1882-1967), a Kentucky native, former resident of Asheville, and a University of Pennsylvania track star, was head coach. In 1913, he succeeded in getting the trustees to levy a fee of $2.50 per student to support athletics. In late May 1914, Cartmell was caught in a student-townspeople gambling ring. He resigned his post immediately, subsequently coached at several colleges, and from 1951 to his retirement he was track coach at West Point.

In the front row, left to right, are Junius Smith, elected team captain in 1912; G.L. Carrington, later a Durham physician who married Kerr Scott's sister Elizabeth; Marvin Ritch, who founded high school interscholastic athletics in Charlotte in 1914; John W. Hanes, son of the founder of Hanes Hosiery Mills in Winston-Salem; and W.S. Tillett, a Charlotte physician. Back row, left to right, are Cartmell; Cyrus Long, a Charlotte manufacturer; W.E. Wakeley, a New York physician; Roy McKnight, a Charlotte physician; and manager C.S. Cook, a Charlotte banker. (NCC)

guest over, the innkeeper announced, "I never charge preachers." Battle revealed he was not a preacher, "only President of the University." "Well," the determined innkeeper returned, "I never charge them neither."

It was well that Battle possessed a playful sense of humor because his job as president exposed him to complaints from all sides and placed him in positions where he could not avoid offending or even hurting those he knew and respected. A particularly painful episode began in 1885 when he appointed James Lee Love assistant professor of mathematics. That winter Love married June Spencer, Battle's distant relative. Battle had also recommended his cousin William B. Phillips, the eldest son of Dr. Charles Phillips, to be professor of agricultural chemistry and mining. Critics accused him of practicing nepotism, a trustees' committee recommended the abolishment of Love's posi-

tion, and Battle had to call on Governor Alfred M. Scales to convince the board to ignore the recommendation.

Then when mathematics professor Ralph Graves, Jr. died in July 1889, Love wanted to replace him. Battle instead appointed Major William Cain. Cornelia and June Spencer were furious, James Lee Love left for Harvard, where he would teach for 19 years, and in 1894 Mrs. Spencer followed her daughter to Cambridge. She never returned to Chapel Hill, not even for the commencement of 1895 at which the university awarded her an honorary LL.D., the first extended to a woman.

As a historian, Battle's crowning work is his two-volume *History of the University of North Carolina*, published in 1907 and 1912. Indefatigable even in his 82nd year, on 19 December 1912 he began work on his memoirs, edited by his son William James Battle and published by the UNC Press

Kemp Plummer Battle, former UNC president, is watching a fly ball during a baseball game being played on the UNC athletic field in 1914. His young companion is Marvin Pickard Wilson (1905-1958), son of Dr. Thomas J. Wilson, Jr. Behind Marvin stands Dr. Robert B. Lawson (1875-1958), professor of anatomy and physical education director at UNC for half a century. Lawson played professional baseball under the legendary John McGraw and later came to be known as the "father of UNC basketball." He was the father of golfer Estelle Lawson Page, who won the U.S. Women's Amateur title in 1937 prior to a successful professional career. (Courtesy Peter Wilson)

in 1945 as the *Memories of an Old Time Tar Heel.*

In 1893, President Grover Cleveland appointed Greek professor Eben Alexander U.S. Minister to Greece, Romania, and Serbia. The appointment came at a most inopportune time for his daughter Eleanor. She had just met Andrew H. Patterson, and like Ellie Swain earlier she had fallen in love at first sight, fortunately with fewer repercussions. "The first time I saw him," she said, "I thought he was the most beautiful man I had ever seen." After her family returned in 1897, Eleanor made her own white organdy wedding dress, and Louis Graves played the organ in the Chapel of the Cross when she married Patterson, later Dean of Applied Science at UNC. In 1918 the Pattersons built a home on East Franklin Street that is now part of the Chi Omega sorority house.

A.H. Patterson was a founding member of the most intriguing UNC fraternity, the Order of the Gimghouls. When Edward Wray Martin of Little Rock, Arkansas, was a

student in the late 1880s, he loved to sit at Piney Prospect, look out over the plain below, and let an imagination fed by Malory's *Morte d'Arthur* run wild, envisioning knights in armor, a sparkling inland sea, and a "Hippol Castle" rising out of the forest of Battle Park. In 1889 Martin, Patterson, W.W. Davies, Bob Bingham, and Stephen Bryan organized a fraternity based on the ideals of chivalry. Seven years later, members built a plain wooden lodge at the corner of Rosemary and Boundary.

Martin died at Pine Bluff, Arkansas, on 29 December 1896, but his concepts lived on with the Order—which grew to include Governor J.C.B. Ehringhaus, W.R. Kenan, Jr., Frank Porter Graham, William Carmichael, George Watts Hill, and other renowned UNC alumni. In 1915 members purchased 95 acres out of Battle Park as the site for a new lodge. They traded a third to UNC for a small adjacent tract, sold 35 acres, and developed the remainder into the Glandon Forest subdivision, now called Gimghoul, to raise more cash. A.H. Patterson and T. Felix Hickerson headed a building committee which recommended a castle "of unique design, medieval and mysterious looking, containing a dance hall, bedrooms, kitchen, dressing rooms, club room, observation tower, terrace, and unusual and attractive 'mystic' features." World War I scattered the Gimghouls, delaying construction, and financial reality forced cancellation of the grand plans.

Doing much of the work themselves, in 1923 the Gimghouls hauled in 1300 tons of stone and imported Waldensian master masons from Valdese, North Carolina, to build a towered castle containing a 55' x 35' meeting hall, decorated with a mural done by Charles Baskerville II showing St. George killing the dragon. Completed in 1927, the Gimghoul Castle has since enjoyed the distinction of being the most mysterious structure in Chapel Hill.

Prof. Collier Cobb married William Horn Battle's daughter Mary Lindsey Battle in 1891 and in 1893 he bought a lot just east of the Charles Phillips house from Charles' widow, Mrs. Laura Battle Phillips. He built a small home which he and Mary called the Pigeon Box and which he enlarged after the birth of their children William, Collier, Jr., and Louisa. When Mary died in November 1900, her sister Nell moved in to help care for the children. Cobb soon tired of bachelorhood and in the summer of 1903 embarked on an intense courtship of Lucy Plummer Battle, Mary's 40-year-old cousin.

In letters to Lucy in Raleigh, Cobb relayed family news and campus gossip, but most ardently he pleaded for her hand. On 8 September 1903, he was concerned that "William's best friend, Willie Meade Prince is a perfect infant; and is constantly wasting his time and William's as well." In January he criticized Mr. Prince for his extravagance at Christmas in giving Willie a bicycle and several books and for giving Mrs. Prince "a complete toilet set of sterling silver." "Champagne appetites on beer

Mary Morgan Mason (1825-1894), far left, wife of Baptist minister James Pleasant Mason (1827-1893), near left, willed Mason Farm to the university with the stipulation that portraits of her two daughters be painted and hung on campus. The original portraits were considered poor likenesses, and in 1941 William D. Carmichael, Jr. arranged for Mary Graves Rees (1886-1950) to paint new portraits, using Lena May Williams, a Morgan descendant, as the model. The old "Varina Mason" is above left, the new is above right. The 1895 portraits hang in Parker dormitory; the 1941 pair in the UNC News Bureau. ("New Varina" photo courtesy Lena May Williams; the other three NCC)

incomes," the frugal Cobb conjectured, "explain a great many of the failures of the world."

After Lucy consented to marry him, Cobb missed a lecture by Dr. Wisconsin Illinois Royster on 17 March 1904 to implore her to conserve her strength, even to the extent of skipping church. He had a convincing negative example: "Miss Frances MacRae, now Mrs. John Lamb, came home from her wedding journey looking worse than she ever did before in her life, and everybody in Chapel Hill remarks upon it. It just must not be that way with you, my darling." The couple married on 6 April 1904. On 22 April 1905, Lucy gave birth to a son, Richard. Five days later mother and infant died in Watts Hospital in Durham.

In 1910, Collier Cobb married Mary Know Gatlin of Arkansas, and he used a portion of Mary's dowry to purchase the land to build 11 houses on what in 1915 became Cobb Terrace. His son William's daughter Carol and her husband, Texaco geologist Dan Hamilton, purchased the Pigeon Box in 1977. Their son Kirk designed an extensive remodeling to modernize the house, whose strange sounds, illusions, and movements make it one of the several

"haunted" houses in Chapel Hill, a list that includes the Kay Kyser House and the Horace Williams House.

A double tragedy in the family of one of the original donors of land to the university led to the largest single gift to UNC in the post-bellum era. Mark Morgan left his estate on Morgan Creek to his son John, who passed it on to his son Solomon P. Morgan. Solomon had several children, two of whom remained in Orange County. His son Jones married Amy Barbee, the daughter of Gray Barbee and a distant relative of Old Kit Barbee. In 1854, his daughter Mary E., who inherited the homestead tract of the plantation, married James Pleasant Mason, a Baptist minister educated at Wake Forest and the pastor of several churches in Orange and Chatham counties.

Born in 1825, as a youngster Mary had to care for her sickly mother, her deranged father, and the plantation slaves. Consequently, she missed an early formal education, but developed an independence of mind that she vigorously sustained after a marriage which Mrs. Spencer capsuled bluntly, "He asked and deferred to her judgement, continually."

The Masons had four daughters. Two died in infancy.

In this 1917 "Liberty Bond" parade on Franklin Street, the two boys carrying the stretcher are, left to right, William Uzzell, son of Chapel Hill's hotel owner, and John "Jack" Latta, who later moved to Raleigh. The two young "nurses" are Jack's sister Louise Latta, left, and Lena May Williams, right. Carrying the flag behind "Kern" Pendergraft's Reo pickup truck is Lorena Pickard Wilson, daughter of W.W. Pickard and wife of Dr. Thomas J. Wilson. (NCC)

Martha James, born in 1857, and Carolina Varina, born in 1861, lived into young adulthood. Both studied under Mrs. Spencer from 1869 to 1875 before completing their education at the Baptist Female Institute in Raleigh. They were intelligent, energetic, and accomplished young ladies, and the proud parents looked forward to passing Mason Farm on to them. Those plans, and the happiness of the family, terminated in the fall of 1881.

Varina came down with typhoid fever in August and died at dawn on 6 September. By then Mr. Mason and Martha had also contracted the fever. He survived after a long struggle, but "Mattie" died at 1 a.m. on 22 November after two months of relentless deterioration and after 18 successive nightly visits from Dr. Thomas Harris, dean of the Medical School. The Rev. Needham B. Cobb preached both funerals.

The Rev. Mason died after a long illness in June 1893; Mary succumbed to pulmonary consumption on 17 July 1894. Public concern over what would happen to Mason Farm was laid to rest with Mrs. Mason. At her gravesite, Kemp Battle read the will he had written a decade earlier. It left the 800-acre plantation and $1000 to the university with the stipulation that the money be used to purchase portraits of the daughters and their father to hang on campus and that the university expend $15 per year for upkeep of the Morgan-Mason cemetery, now a few steps from the Finley Golf Course parking lot.

A woman also made the other major contribution to UNC in the post-bellum era. Mary Ruffin Smith was the daughter of U.S. Congressman Dr. James Smith of Hillsborough and the former Delia Jones, daughter of Francis Jones, a veteran of the Revolution and owner of thousands of acres in Chatham County. Mary studied in Hillsborough under the Rev. William Mercer Green and his assistant Maria L. Spear, who later lived with Miss Smith.

In the 1840s, Dr. Smith built an imposing manor house on a 1300-acre plantation on what is now Smith Level Road, from where he also managed the 1440-acre Jones' Grove plantation five miles to the south. He and Delia died in the manor house, as did their two bachelor sons, both of whom had indulged their affinity for alcohol and slave women. When she died in 1885, Miss Smith left the homestead plantation and capital to her Episcopalian diocese, some Chapel Hill property to the Chapel of the Cross, and the Jones' Grove plantation to UNC. Trustees sold the land and used the money to install the first electric lights on campus and to establish scholarships.

UNC's most famous literary figure came to Chapel Hill not because of desire but because his father made him. In the summer of 1916, 15-year-old Thomas Wolfe stood 6' 3" and weighed 130 pounds. His hands dangled to knee level, he was ungainly, and although his family was one of the richest in Asheville the parsimony of his mother forced the youth to dress in ill-fitting, hand-me-down clothes and in shoes that invariably cramped his rapidly growing feet. He had wanted to attend either Princeton or the University of Virginia to prepare for a career as a writer. His father W.O. Wolfe wanted his youngest son and last hope to become a lawyer and a politician, and W.O. insisted on UNC.

The green freshman fell into all the traps: he took a bogus examination on the school catalolgue; he had a sophomore lead him in prayer at noon Saturday in the campus chapel; to the great delight of Di members he made a formal acceptance speech ending with his declaration that he hoped his portrait would one day hang alongside Zeb Vance's in Di

Hall. He initially roomed and boarded with Mrs. Mattie Eva Hardee, an Asheville widow living on Cameron Avenue, but dislike of her son Charles and her high prices induced Wolfe to leave after two months to begin a four-year odyssey that would find him rooming over Eubank's Drug Store, in a fraternity house, in Kemp Battle's cottage, on the first floor of Battle Hall, at the University Inn, and elsewhere.

Along with several hundred others, in November 1916 Wolfe paid $3 for a roundtrip train ticket to Richmond to attend the annual Thanksgiving Day football game between UNC and Virginia. Carolina had not beaten Virginia since 1905, but that year the Tar Heels eked out a 7-0 victory on a thrilling third-quarter touchdown run by Bill Folger. Wolfe recounted the glorious triumph and the gala homecoming victory celebration in a 1919 *Daily Tar Heel* article, "Ye Who

Thomas Wolfe's play "The Third Night" was produced by the Playmakers in the fall of 1919. The actors shown in this scene are, left to right, Jonathan Daniels (1902-1981), Frederick J. Cohn (1897-1982), and Tom Wolfe. Daniels edited the Daily Tar Heel *and later took over his family's newspaper, the* Raleigh News and Observer. *Cohn, a New Bern native, was a judge at the Nuremburg war-criminal trials. (NCC)*

The Carolina Playmakers
The University of North Caroli:

ANNOUNCE THEIR OPENING PERFORMANCE
IN
THE PLAY-HOUSE
CHAPEL HILL
A PROGRAM CONSISTING OF THE

Original Folk Plays

WHEN WITCHES RIDE
A Play of Carolina Folk Superstition, by Elizbeth Lay

THE RETURN OF BUCK GAVIN
A Tragedy of the Mountain People, by Thomas Wolfe

Together With

WHAT WILL BARBARA SAY!
A Romance of Chapel Hill, by Minnie Shepherd Sparrow

Friday and Saturday, March 14th and 15th, 1919
All Seats Reserved at Eubanks' Drug Store, Chapel Hill
Curtain Promptly at Eight O'clock

The first Playmakers' playbill, shown here, was a 2' by 3' poster. Elizbeth Lay married dramatist Paul Green (1894-1981). Minnie Shepherd Sparrow (1887-1971), from Washington, N.C., graduated from UNC and taught at Chapel Hill High School for several years before she married Clinton Walker Keyes and moved to New York City. Thomas Wolfe is the famous North Carolina author. (NCC)

Have Been There Only Know"; still later he drew on those events for a lengthy fictional account incorporated into his posthumous novel, *The Web and the Rock*.

A week or so after the game, he received his sexual initiation. Friends took him to Durham where he enjoyed a prostitute working under the nom de tart "Mamie Smith." Thereafter, weekly trips to Durham and late-night gabfests at the YMCA and Gooch's Cafe were the heart of his regimen, but he also came to appreciate Horace Williams, Edwin Greenlaw, and W.S. "Bully" Bernard, three professors who would inspire him academically and who would leave a lasting impression on his values and his work.

During Wolfe's sophomore year, the campus grew to resemble an army camp as administrators endeavored to do their part to aid the war effort. Wolfe wrote his brother Ben on 18 February 1918: "They're giving us blazes in this military stuff. Military engineering, bomb throwing, trench warfare, bayonet fighting are a few of the things we are doing."

In the fall of his junior year, Wolfe hurried to Asheville to see his dying brother Ben. He returned with the experience that would form the basis of his great death scene in *Look Homeward Angel*, but he resumed his campus life with his customary vigor and humor. He had already published his first creative efforts in the *University Magazine*, and he had excitedly joined the Pi Kappa Phi fraternity. That fall he was the only male member of Frederick H. "Proff" Koch's playmaking class.

Born in Covington, Kentucky, in 1877, Koch taught drama at the University of North Dakota after receiving an A.B. at Ohio Wesleyan. In 1909 he earned an M.A. at Harvard, where he attended Prof. George Pierce Baker's famous

When the United States entered World War I, UNC created a mock battlefield, complete with trenches. In this 1918 photograph, students are practicing a charge out of the trenches. In the beginning, the U.S. government offered no help in getting the training program underway, but Julius Cone of Greensboro sent the students 180 Civil War carbines, and in 1918 the Canadian government sent Captain J. Stuart Allen to train UNC's eager troops.

Barbara Bynum Henderson (1882-1955), left, wife of UNC professor Archibald Henderson, devoted part of her energies to woman's suffrage efforts before World War I. On 4 December 1913 she became President of the Equal Suffrage League of North Carolina and within a year had developed chapters in 20 North Carolina towns. Her Chapel Hill chapter had 29 members, of whom 14 were male.

Mrs. Henderson was a 1902 UNC graduate and through much of her life translated German and French poetry. (NCC)

When the 1966 senior class officers decided that their gift to the university would be a sculpture thematically based on Thomas Wolfe's Look Homeward, Angel, *author Armistead Maupin headed the committee to select a sculptor. After several interviews, Maupin chose to commission UNC Art professor Richard Kinnaird. Kinnaird's muscular / ethereal angel captures the Hegelian themes so prominent in all of Wolfe's work, concepts Wolfe picked up from Horace Williams.*

Richard Kinnaird's paintings hang in public galleries from coast to coast: the Aldrich Museum of Contemporary Art in Ridgefield, CT; the Seattle, Washington Museum of Fine Art; the North Carolina Museum of Art in Raleigh, where two Kinnairds are in the company of masterpieces by Rembrandt, Rubens, Van Dyck, and other artists old and new. Kinnairds also complement corporate and private collections: Hanes, R.J. Reynolds, The Freeman Collection, and more. (UNC Photo Lab)

Workshop 42, and he quickly gained renown as the mentor of the Dakota Playmakers and as an advocate of "folk drama," a genre which asked actor-writers to draw from the locale they understood best for their themes and their plots.

Edwin Greenlaw, with President Edward Kidder Graham's support, brought Koch to Chapel Hill, where Proff evolved into a statewide cultural resource, conducting readings widely and assisting continuously with the development of community dramatic groups. On campus he instantly became a landmark figure, identified by his belted Norfolk jacket, Windsor tie, pince-nez, briar pipe, and his faithful dog Dixie.

Koch's first playwriting class attracted seven co-eds and Thomas Wolfe, who assured Proff that plenty of "he-men" would soon join the "Ladies Aid Society." One of the first was Paul Green of Harnett County, who had first enrolled in 1916. Koch had influenced one Pulitzer Prize winner at North Dakota, Maxwell Anderson; he would influence another at UNC in Paul Green. Koch and his successors on the Playmaker's faculty helped train many distinguished actors—including, but certainly not limited to, Sidney Blackmer, Shepherd Strudwick, Earl Wynn, Eugenia Rawls, Douglas Watson, Andy Griffith, Robert Carroll, Whit Bissell, Robert Armstrong, William Hardy, James Pritchett, and Academy Award winner Louise Fletcher.

During his last two years, Wolfe headed the editorial staff of the *Tar Heel*, wrote the column "With Apologies to Pepys," and contributed special features. He turned in his assignments late. He got to class late. He often completed his editing on the *Tar Heel* on his way to Durham or in Seeman's Printing Shop itself. But his unassuming good humor and his obvious talents made others, especially professors, tolerant of his habitual tardiness.

Upon his graduation in 1920 Wolfe, like Proff before him, enrolled in George Pierce Baker's Workshop 42 at Harvard, where he roomed for a while with Albert Coates. It would take years of anguished trials before he learned that his great talent was for prose fiction, not drama. He returned to Chapel Hill only once, in January 1937 when he was working on "I Have a Thing to Tell You," the novella on the rise of Nazism in his beloved Germany which was used in his second posthumous novel, *You Can't Go Home Again*. "I have been unable to do much to this first installment since coming here," he wrote his editor and his first biographer Elizabeth Nowell. "People have swarmed around me—old friends I have not seen in seventeen years or so—and there has been no time for anything." He stayed with Economics professor Corydon P. "Shorty" Spruill, and he saw Paul Green, Phillips Russell, Jonathan Daniels, Albert Coates, and others.

Although he could still distinguish flashes of wit and intellect in his aging mentor Horace Williams, Wolfe was saddened by the lonely old man who he supposed had lived beyond his productive years to become "more or less of a legend" to the present generation of students. On 15 December 1938 in Baltimore, Wolfe died in the Johns Hopkins Hospital, 18 days before his 38th birthday.

In the years immediately following his death, it appeared that Wolfe had left Chapel Hill a far greater legacy than the honor of once having been home to a recognized literary artist. Under the vigorous leadership of Frank Porter Graham, UNC had become the emblem of southern progressivism. On a per capita basis, Chapel Hill had become the best educated town in the nation, while maintaining its "village" atmosphere. Lured by the "ghost" of Thomas Wolfe and the very living presence of Paul Green and Proff Koch, young writers and liberal activists were arriving from all points of the compass to infuse Chapel Hill with a new kind of vitality and to inspire interested observers to dream it would become the "fountainhead of the South."

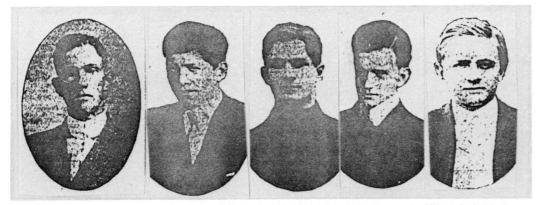

On 12 September 1912, freshman Isaac William Rand of Smithfield, far left, died in a hazing accident on the athletic field. The resulting arrests of, left to right, R.W. Oldham of Raleigh, A.H. Styron and W.L. Merriman of Wilmington, and A.C. Hatch of Mount Olive for manslaughter created a sensation. Oldham's family was well known in Chapel Hill, having moved from the village area to Raleigh a few years earlier, and when $5000 bonds were required for each of the boys, who were being held in W.W. Pickard's hotel, R.A. Eubanks, S.J. Brockwell, W.W. Pickard, and W.S. Roberson posted Oldham's bail. J.S. Carr put up the other three bonds.

Following a three-day trial in May 1913, in which some two dozen lawyers took active parts, Styron was absolved, the other three received suspended four-month sentences, and UNC President Francis P. Venable expelled the four plus 12 others. Oldham and Merriman never again communicated with the university; Hatch (1893-1973) became a successful merchant in his hometown; Styron (1891-1958) became an Episcopal minister in the New York area and the author of some widely read religious monographs.

The pictures seen here are the only available likenesses of the men. (NCC)

William Rand Kenan, Jr. (1872-1965) was the great-great-grandson of Old Kit Barbee, who gave over 200 acres of land to UNC in 1792. Kenan himself made contributions to UNC that matched his ancestor's largesse. His most famous gift was Kenan Stadium.

Kenan raised 500 milk cows on a Lockport, New York, dairy farm after World War II. He did not believe in pasteurization, so the milk went directly from the cow into bottles which were then capped before the milk cooled. (NCC)

The Kenan Stadium site is pictured, above left, in the fall of 1926 after Nello Teer had cleared the area and filled in the ravine to make the football playing field. The white building, right background, is the construction company's headquarters.

By the spring of 1927, Kenan Stadium was half completed; the east stand is pictured, above right, ready to seat 12,000. T.C. Thompson was the major contractor on the stands and the fieldhouse.

The stadium was dedicated in 1927 at the annual UNC-UVa Thanksgiving football game, above, won by UNC 14-13 (NCC)

VI
The Problems of Maturity
1920 to 1945

When UNC President Harry Woodburn Chase, a Massachusetts native, announced on 20 February 1930 that he intended to leave UNC to assume the presidency of the University of Illinois, the majority of trustees wanted to replace him with a native Tar Heel already on the UNC faculty. Three members caught their interest: Kenan Professor of History R.W.D. Connor, Kenan Professor of Mathematics Archibald Henderson, and history professor Frank Porter Graham.

On 24 February, Dr. William deB. MacNider casually assured Graham of his support, only to learn that Graham was supremely uninterested. MacNider protested pointedly, to no effect; in a 28 February *Weekly* editorial, Louis Graves urged the trustees to select Graham in spite of his position; friends from throughout the state tried to change his mind; his mother even wrote, pleading for him to seek the post. With Graham adamantly trying to halt efforts on his behalf, Dr. Connor, who coveted the job, seemed to have a clear path.

Kemp D. Battle reluctantly agreed to withdraw Graham's name should it be placed in nomination when the trustees met in Chapel Hill to vote on 9 June, but the trustees flanked that maneuver with

Frank Porter Graham (1886-1972) graduated from UNC in 1909, and in June 1930, became President of the university. "Dr. Frank" and his wife Marian Drane (1899-1967) were as famous in Chapel Hill for their Sunday evening open houses as they were for academic activities.

Mrs. Graham, whom Dr. Frank married in 1932, was a St. Mary's graduate and the daughter of an Edenton minister. (NCC)

a simple stratagem—they voted without nominations. Connor led after the first ballot, followed in order by Graham and Henderson. Graham's forces picked up strength, and elected their man on the fourth ballot.

Outwardly at least, it seemed the trustees had made a curious choice. Graham stood only 5' 3" tall, weighed a slight 125 pounds, and wore children's shoes; he had no Ph.D. in an environment rich with advanced degrees; among public figures in North Carolina, he was the leading advocate of workers' rights, collective bargaining, labor reform, and liberal principles in general—in a conservative state with a decidedly anti-labor bias; but the trustees wanted a leader who would continue President Chase's success in building a quality university and in guaranteeing the faculty freedom of expression, and they knew Frank Porter Graham was a "fighting half-pint" who would not be intimidated by disgruntled interest groups, no matter how powerful.

In Chase's 11 years at the helm, UNC and its personnel boosted state pride by adding eight major departments or schools, organizing the UNC Press, founding the Institute of Government and the Southern Historical Collection and turning UNC into a *genuine* university which in 1922 became the 25th member of the Association of American Universities.

Chase had instilled further pride by quietly but unwaveringly defending the university and its faculty against attacks from KKK extremists, from those upset with the findings and publications emanating out of Dr. Howard W. Odum's Institute for Research in the Social Science, and from fundamentalists opposed to the teaching of evolutionary theory. Frank Porter Graham was to continue Chase's policies, but he would do so from the spotlight, often as the personification of what many believed to be an *un-American* university. He would prevail, and he would do more than any other resident to lend Chapel Hill its distinguishing spirit.

The size, appearance, and ambience of Chapel Hill changed conspicuously in the 1920s as a village became a

town. Paved roadways replaced dirt, brick replaced wood in the business district, and sophistication displaced the lingering remnants of the rustic in the community.

From the 1890s to the 1920s, the village relied on crushed gravel to keep the streets and sidewalks passable in all weather, and they were often passable only through mud ankle deep or deeper. In 1919 the state agreed to pave an 18'-wide strip down the middle of Franklin Street from Columbia Street to the Durham County line. Businessmen refused to pay the additional costs to pave the entire 45' width of Franklin Street between Columbia and Henderson; consequently, until it was covered in 1925, the spaces between the central strip and the sidewalks continued to be a quagmire in bad weather.

In February 1920, the aldermen voted to pave the first block of South Columbia and, contingent upon the willingness of property owners to help defray costs, to pave, curb, and run sidewalks along Franklin west to the town limits. After six years of fruitless debate, in 1926 the aldermen assessed property owners $7.70 per front foot and began work, but the owners protested and initiated legal actions that dragged on for 15 years. Some of them, such as Mayors W.S. Roberson and Zeb Council, sold property to avoid the charges. The owners' attorney, John Manning, suggested the assessments should have been no more than $2.50 per foot between Columbia and Church Streets and $1.50 on to the town limits. After a committee headed by Mayor John Foushee and Town Manager John L. Caldwell decided that $5.267 per foot would have been a fair assessment, the town issued $8500 in bonds to repay the overcharges.

Federal funds issued under the CWA, PWA, and WPA programs allowed an acceleration of paving, and by World War II all the main streets in the village were paved.

Most of the residential development of the 1920s occurred around Tenney Circle, in the area south of Cameron Avenue, and in Isaac W. Pritchard's Westwood subdivision. In 1920-1921, UNC built 10 two-room bungalows in an area bordered by Hooper Lane, Battle Lane, and Battle Park. Officially designated Park Place, the development was popularly known as "Baby Hollow" because the young professors who lived there, including Proff Koch and Dr. William F. Prouty, averaged three children each. For a while in 1925, there was a possibility that growth would be spurred by a second college in Chapel Hill. Atlantic Christian College President H.S. Hilley visited twice, and on 17 July Mayor W.S. Roberson offered him a choice of three prospective campus sites: one on the Strowd Plantation; another near Gimghoul Castle; and a third south of town. Hilley was interested, but declined the offer.

The Chapel Hill Insurance and Realty Company handled much of the property sold for residential use during the early 1920s, including the 1200-acre Robert Strowd Plantation out of which Davie Woods was cut in 1924. After the company went bankrupt in 1927, Collier Cobb, Jr. and Bill

These three scenes reveal different views of Columbia Street in 1925. In the top scene, looking south from about North Street, the Pentecostal Church occupies the left background, the new firehouse sits in the middle of Columbia, and William N. Pritchard's barn stands on part of his 15-acre farm to the right.

The middle photo shows construction and paving work underway on Pittsboro Road (South Columbia) looking north from about the McCauley Street intersection. The pavement ran from the Carolina Inn to Morgan Creek, where in 1922 the state had built a new concrete bridge, using gravel from Collier Cobb, Jr.'s new stone-crushing business.

The bottom photo looks north on Columbia from the Franklin Street intersection. The firehouse and jail occupied the middle of Columbia until it was razed in 1939. The building in the left foreground is Bruce Strowd's new Ford agency. The cars on the right are Strowd's, parked there for the shade. Car theft became a serious problem during the 1920s. In one week of April 1928, the Weekly reported four cars stolen, including one owned by Jeff Thomas, the founder of Jeff's Confectionary, the magazine shop now beside the Varsity Theatre. (NCC)

Scott of Graham gave $7250 for the insurance end of the business and founded what is now Collier Cobb Associates with headquarters at the corner of East Franklin Street and Estes Drive. When Scott died in 1944, Cobb purchased his former partner's interest and expanded the business by gradually opening offices in Charlotte, Houston, Detroit, Boston, Washington, D.C. and other major cities.

Building in the late 1920s radically altered the appearance of Franklin Street. Between 1923 and 1925, the north side of the business block was almost entirely rebuilt with brick. W.L. Tankersley put up the Tankersley Building beside the post office; Robert Strowd erected the Strowd Building and soon had Sutton's Drug Store as a tenant; Cameron MacRae constructed the building at Henderson and Franklin that now houses Hector's; Bruce Strowd opened his new Ford agency at the northwest corner of Franklin and Columbia.

A few years earlier, John W. Umstead, Jr. and others had considered forming a joint-stock company to build a luxury hotel. When their plans fell through, John Sprunt Hill carried the idea to fruition. Arthur C. Nash had graduated cum laude from Harvard in 1897 and had continued his architectural studies for five years at L'Ecole des Beaux Arts in Paris. After having designed several campus buildings, including Graham Memorial and Wilson Library, Nash executed a hotel design for Hill, and the result was the

This 1927 photo, looking east, shows McCauley Street as seen from the Pittsboro Street intersection. When Dave McCauley donated the street to the village in 1903, the commissioners gave it his name. It was paved in 1934.

In the 19th century, McCauley had cut two other streets through his property, and, in keeping with his strong political affiliations, named them after North Carolina's two Democratic U.S. Senators, Vance and Ransom.

The workmen shown here are hourly wage earners, but from the end of the Civil War into the 20th century, streets were maintained through a system that allowed townspeople to work out their property taxes by doing street work. A laborer received a credit of 75¢ per day, and a two-horse wagon with a driver received $3.00. (NCC)

Carolina Inn, opened for business in 1924 and given to the University along with the Webb-Lloyd Building by John Sprunt Hill in 1935.

Each of the major religious denominations built a new house of worship between 1920 and 1926. The Presbyterians were able to rebuild their church from its foundation up thanks to the generosity of James Sprunt of Wilmington—Civil War blockade runner, wealthy cotton merchant, owner of Orton Plantation, noted North Carolina historian and author, and a liberal supporter of Presbyterian churches, missions, and schools. Sprunt donated the church as a memorial to his wife Luola Murchison Sprunt, and the Rev. W.D. Moss preached the dedication sermon on 21 November 1920.

By then, the Baptists were well along with plans for a grand new church. In 1921, the deacons paid $1000 for a site on South Columbia near Franklin and within a year committees had raised some $125,000—aided by large donations from W.C. Coker of Chapel Hill and Mrs. W.O. Allen of Windsor. On 7 October 1923, the Rev. Dr. Charles E. Maddry preached the inaugural sermon in the new church, described by a reporter as having been built in "a style-defying example of architecture."

The Episcopal congregation had outgrown its exquisitely diminutive Chapel of the Cross. Durham cotton manufacturer W.A. Erwin contributed $150,000 toward the construction of a perpendicular gothic church east of the chapel as a memorial to Dr. William Rainey Holt, a UNC graduate of 1847 and a distinguished physician. On 2 February 1924, the cornerstone was laid for the pink granite edifice which was dedicated on 12 May 1925 during the 190th annual convention of the diocese, then meeting in Chapel Hill.

When the Methodists decided to build a new church just west of their existing church on Franklin Street, inspirational considerations and human vanity outweighed economic concerns in the decision regarding its most imme-

diately striking feature—the steeple. The Rev. Walter Patten, Clyde Eubanks, and Louis Round Wilson were on the "steeple committee." Patten argued that a steeple would be both an aesthetic and a religious inspiration to the community; Eubanks pointed out that the nonessential adornment would cost $10,000 to build and $500 every five years to paint; Wilson noted that the proposed steeple would be taller and more magnificent than any other in Chapel Hill—and cast the deciding vote.

The Methodists traded the old A.S. Barbee office/store property to the university for the Seaton Barbee home place and a strip to the rear of the existing church property; James Gamble Rogers of New York City drew the plans; and contractors delivered the new church in April 1926 for a cost of $225,000—including the steeple.

One of the most enduring and charming "building jobs" ever in Chapel Hill had its start in 1923. Louis Graves was

In 1920, Chapel Hill Presbyterians built a new church (top) directly onto the foundations of the old one (bottom), using money donated by Dr. James Sprunt of Wilmington. The new church is pictured here a few days after it was opened. (NCC)

In 1923, Chapel Hill Baptists moved into their new church at
Columbia and Franklin, pictured here a few months after it was
dedicated. In 1930, the Baptists sold their old church building on
West Franklin to Masonic Lodge #80.
Louis Graves, noting that every church in Chapel Hill was
building or trying to build in the early 1920s, wrote in the Weekly,
"About the only thing the Fundamentalists and the Modernists agree
on as essential to Religion is the regular collection." (NCC)

The Chapel of the Cross, pictured here in 1913, was designed by
Thomas U. Walter, on commission by William Mercer Green.
Walter submitted the design without a visit to the site, and received
$25 for his work. He had designed St. James Church in Wilmington,
N.C., in 1840. (NCC)

born in 1885, grew up in his mother Julia's boarding house,
attended the Canada School in Chapel Hill and the
Bingham School in Asheville, and graduated from UNC in
1902. With the help of his older brother Ralph, Louis got a
job as a reporter on the New York *Times* in 1903. In 1906 he
struck out as a free-lance writer, later worked for a public-
relations firm and for the City of New York, and served
with the 81st Division in France. Returning to Chapel Hill
in 1921 as a professor of journalism and head of the UNC
news bureau, he married Edward Kidder Graham's sister-
in-law Mildred Moses, who had declined to marry Frank
Porter Graham.

Early in 1923, Graves decided to establish a newspaper
which would concentrate on local news. He rented editorial
offices in the upstairs of A.S. Barbee's office/store, and he
wrote all the copy for the first four-page edition of the
Chapel Hill *Weekly*, issued on 1 March 1923. The lead story
concerned a decision by the 94 members of the new country
club involving priorities in developing the land to the south
of Raleigh Road given them by Dr. W.C. Coker. The
recently cut Country Club Road provided access, and the
members were divided over whether to continue by
building a clubhouse or by laying out a golf course. In
Graves' parlance, the "Pink Tea-ers" were better organized
and outvoted the "Golf Grouches." (The Golf Grouches
eventually prevailed.)

For a few weeks, Graves hauled his papers from Durham;
then in April he bought some second-hand printing equipment and set up his own Orange Printshop in a cramped,
damp basement under Sutton's Drug Store. Later he
bought Miss Belle Hutchins' back yard on Rosemary Street
behind the Bank of Chapel Hill, built a one-story brick
building, and moved in "after a year and four months of

The Methodist Church was
dedicated during 1 May 1926
services, a few days before this
photograph was taken. Four
years later, Louis Graves ran
as a headline on page one of
the Weekly: "METHODIST
CHURCH PLATE-PASSERS
END THE YEAR
WITHOUT STEALING A
CENT; CONGREGATION
IS JUBILANT. Plate passers
who came through the year
with their honesty absolutely
unimpeached are J.S. Bennett,
Allen Koontz, F.P. Brooks,
H.M. Wagstaff, L.R. Wilson,
E.W. Knight, and Harry
Comer." (NCC)

amphibian life in the basement." Within five years, the
Baltimore *Evening Sun*, the New York *Herald-Tribune*, and
other major papers had praised the consistent quality of
Graves' reporting of village and campus news, activities,
and personalities. In his fifteenth-anniversary issue of 1938,
Graves wrote, "This newspaper is 15 years old today, and I
am very tired of it." He was not tired enough to quit.

John Bennett, who had been the city manager of
Morehead City, arrived as superintendent of the University
Consolidated Service Plant in 1921, just in time to take
charge of a general upgrading of the university/town
utilities. UNC purchased the 300-unit telephone system in
1925, and Bennett oversaw the start in 1927 of a new exchange on Rosemary Street, which would house a dial
switchboard capable of handling 500 lines.

By 1932, Bennett believed he had rendered a lasting solution to one recurring problem when he supervised the construction of a 30' dam on Morgan Creek which created the 600-million-gallon University Lake. Engineers complained that the reservoir greatly exceeded the need, and Bennett believed it would be sufficient for the century to come. However, the growing prestige of UNC generated a subsequent growth that few then would have dared to predict. Soon the million gallons of water processed daily in the filtration plant behind Phillips Hall was hardly more than adequate, but it was not until February 1950 that a facility on Jones Ferry Road west of Carrboro was in operation, processing 3 million gallons per day. By the 1960s, summer water shortages were once again chronic, and stopgap measures had to suffice while plans were being hammered out for a new reservoir on Cane Creek.

But while the town sustained growth and *relative* prosperity, it did not escape the social and economic buffeting of the Great Depression. The Carrboro cotton mills closed, and a number of Franklin Street businesses closed. Even as firmly established a business as Berman's Department Store, founded in 1914 and located after 1926 where The Intimate Bookshop now resides, had to go into receivership in 1930 in order to stave off creditors. The tactic worked, and Berman's stayed in business into the 1950s.

Edwin "Ed" Lanier directed a National Youth Administration Program, boosted by contributions from alumni, that provided jobs for students at 25 cents per hour. Students also took over many of the menial jobs formerly held by blacks. Particularly strapped during the Depression, the black community found relief only after the beginning of World War II when jobs opened in the defense plant in

The Chapel Hill Weekly

Louis Graves (1883-1965), pictured here in 1931, graduated from UNC and went to work as a New York Times reporter. He returned to Chapel Hill as a professor of journalism in 1921, then on 1 March 1923 he founded the Chapel Hill Weekly. It prospered, thanks mostly to the gentle wit and humor with which Graves reported the news of Chapel Hill. In 1932, the New York Times, in a long editorial in praise of the Weekly, concluded, "It has made a distinct contribution to American journalism." (NCC)

Carrboro and in the expanded UNC medical facilities, at which time relatively prosperous whites lost access to inexpensive black servants.

In the winter of 1932-1933, with the Depression intensifying, 308 white and 518 black citizens in Chapel Hill township received public assistance. The King's Daughters, a charity organization created by the women of Chapel Hill in 1886, gave cash, loans, food and clothing to 36 whites and 241 blacks that winter. By 1937, 915 whites and 1661 blacks were receiving public assistance in the township.

Of historical interest, in August 1937, 77-year-old Wiley P. Morgan, a descendant of Mark and Solomon Morgan, accepted the first old-age pension check issued in Orange County. Illiterate and living in a three-room hut three miles east of Chapel Hill, Morgan used his initial $10 to buy groceries. Unfortunately, Morgan's economic predicament was commonplace, but taken on the whole the cultural climate in the Chapel Hill region was hardly as backward as some have suggested.

In 1920, the population consisted of 1483 Caucasians and 735 Negroes, a total of 2218. By 1940, 3654 people lived in Chapel Hill. The newcomers had little in common with their native farmer and merchant neighbors, and only a few of the established families could trace their ancestry back more than a generation in the village. Nonetheless, while the recent arrivals may have disturbed the town's air of tranquility, they gave it a proud eminence: the highest per capita standard of education in the United States. In 1940, the 2155 Chapel Hillians over 25 possessed an average of 13.7 years of schooling, compared to 12.5 at Palo Alto and 12.3 at Berkeley, California, the next ranking statistical areas.

After he purchased Tom Lloyd's Alberta Mill in 1909, J.S. Carr operated it as part of his Durham Hosiery Mill chain. The only drinking water was a bucket and dipper shared by all, hence the rapid spread of influenza through the mill at the end of World War I. It was not until the early 1920s that the first indoor toilet was installed. Earlier, workers used the outhouse at the depot. The mill closed in 1930, but was reopened as a munitions plant in World War II. It is now the site of the Carr Mill shopping mall.

The adult men's Sunday school class of the Carrboro Baptist Church posed for their picture in front of the mill in 1921. (Courtesy of Tom Goodrich, first row, far right)

The university families and the more sophisticated merchant and professional families had long considered their village elite among its sister communities. Elisha Mitchell's granddaughter Hope Chamberlain reflected that outook in a 1926 evaluation of her former and future hometown, "Now and today, and from the first, it has always been the most worth-while, and the least 'Main-streety' of all North Carolina communities." Newcomers saw that self satisfaction from a different perspective, and were apt to be less generous.

"Those who have lived here a number of years have a certain air of smugness," James Boni wrote a friend in October 1933. "There is a caste system, with the oldest residents comprising the top layer and they're none too anxious to take the stranger into their homes unless he is a paying guest; and they make him pay well for Ancestors and Antiques. They will ignore him until they want him to do something for them or vote their way; then they will wear an ingratiating smile." Still, Boni believed, "The most delightful people I've ever known live in Chapel Hill . . . . And there are a few people here, people who stroll beneath the hallowed oaks of this village, who are so fine and good that just to see them, pass them on a gravel walk, or answer their cheery 'Hello' makes one want to quote Browning."

When Weston LaBarre was researching southern religious practices for his doctoral dissertation at Duke, published as *They Shall Take Up Serpents* in 1962, "an experienced and compassionate social worker" told him of the time she "met a bedraggled mountain woman, near heat-exhaustion, on a street in the village of Chapel Hill." The social worker suggested refreshments in an ice-cream parlor, but the weary woman would not enter a public spot that sold Coca Cola and other sinful delights her preacher had declared taboo. She did accept an ice-cream cone, but only when the social

worker delivered it to her off the forbidden premises. LaBarre may have suspected the social worker's story had he been familiar with "Hills of Zion," in which H.L. Mencken in 1925 described a strikingly similar incident set in Dayton, Tennessee, which he had picked up from "an amiable newspaper woman of Chattanooga."

The town remained only a short stroll in most directions from dense wilderness. It was common for hikers to lose their way and wander in the woods until lights guided them home after nightfall. Young Morgan P. Mooser became lost south of town in 1930, and his body lay undiscovered within two miles of the campus for over a year, even though search parties had repeatedly scoured the wooded terrain. Even as late as 1941, a black family, the Caldwells, ran a bona fide farm on Davie Circle, still a dirt road.

Residental expansion continued into the 1930s in Paul Green's Greenwood development, around the Country Club area, around Davie Circle, and in H.M. Burlage's Hidden Hills subdivision between Estes Drive and East Franklin Street. But with the exception of the 30-unit Village Apartments, construction in the Chapel Hill business district almost ceased before the New Deal programs went into effect.

Capital spent on construction in town and on campus declined from $750,000 in 1929 to $297,000 in 1931 to $50,000 in 1934. After the completion of Graham Memorial in 1931, the next university building was Alderman Hall, built in 1937. Thereafter, assisted by WPA funds, construction increased dramatically with the completion of Woollen Gym, the Bowman Gray Pool, the new power plant, additions to the Carolina Inn, and eight other new halls by the end of 1939, when total expeditures for construction in the town limits amounted to $1,368,000, but even then only $31,000 was spent on new business properties, a figure that dropped to $21,000 in 1940.

Although the General Assembly reduced professors' salaries several times while cutting UNC appropriations early in the Depression—25% in 1929, 20% in 1930, 22% in 1932—Chapel Hillians remained staunchly Democratic, voting overwhelmingly for Al Smith in 1928 and for Franklin D. Roosevelt in 1932. With the tax base and state funds diminishing, in 1932-1933 Mayor John Foushee and Town Manager John L. Caldwell had to manage with a total budget of $27,918—approximately 12% of what Mayor W.S. Roberson and Edward M. Knox, who became the first town manager in 1922, had to work with in 1927.

The state was able to restore professors' salaries to their 1929 level in 1935, and the next year the New Deal program of building new post offices to provide jobs and to assist local economies reached Chapel Hill. The U.S. Government had purchased the old Mallett property in 1915, and on 6 October 1936 it bought an adjacent strip of the Tankersley property and began building behind the old post office, the front portion of which remained open during

In this c. 1895 photograph, Mrs. Dave McCauley, left, and her daughter Mary, the future Mrs. C.L. Lindsay, stand in front of their Cameron Avenue home, built before the Civil War by Dr. Johnston Blakeley Jones. In 1928 Mary sold the house to W.C. Coker, who purchased it for his Chi Psi fraternity because he loved the huge boxwoods on the property. According to her daughter, Mrs. W.G. Polk, Mary was willing to sell because UNC had run the campus railroad spur across what had been her garden plot. When the old home burned at Christmas 1929, the boxwoods survived and now grace the grounds of a brick Chi Psi house. (NCC)

The new post office at the corner of Franklin and Henderson was nearing completion when this picture was made 28 April 1938. Principal brick masons on the job were Johnny Johnston, who was the only black volunteer fireman in the village, and Will Strayhorn.

The first RFD routes to operate in Chapel Hill opened in 1903. RFD #1 ran south with James E. Merritt as carrier, and #2 ran north with Samuel C. Johnston as carrier.

On 21 December 1928, the town assigned new street numbers to meet Federal postal requirements, assigning numbers for each 25 feet in the business district and each 50 feet in residential areas. (DAH)

construction. Completed at a cost of $94,500, the new post office opened on 5 July 1938 with 825 individual boxes and space to accomodate a staff of 18.

The building was, however, incomplete without an appropriate decoration for the lobby, and the Treasury Department selected artist Dean Cornwell, an old friend of William Meade Prince, to render a depiction of William R. Davie laying the cornerstone of Old East. The Sons of the American Revolution sponsored the dedication of Cornwell's 6' x 17' painting, with Davie wearing George Washington's Mason's apron, on 10 April 1941. During the ceremony, Archibald Henderson exhibited and spoke on the original Old East commemorative plaque, which had been discovered on a junk pile at a smelting-factory in Clarksville, Tennessee.

New Deal funds also assisted in providing a much-needed municipal building to consolidate town offices. In the mid-1930s, the recorder's court was convening in the old Pickwick Theatre, the police had a substation on Franklin Street, the fire station was *on* Columbia Street, and town officers were scattered here and there. In August 1938, voters approved a bond issue of $22,450 which secured a federal building grant of $17,550, and on 28 March 1939 Judge L.J. Phipps held court for the first time in his new chambers in the Town Hall on the northwest corner of Columbia and Rosemary.

Chapel Hill greatly increased its influence within the Roosevelt administration when druggist Carl Durham won a seat in the U.S. House of Representatives on the night of Wednesday, 2 November 1938—six days *before* the general election. Durham was born six miles west of Chapel Hill at White Cross on 28 August 1892, the eldest child of Claude and Delia Ann Lloyd Durham. As a youngster, he lived with his uncle Tom Lloyd and worked as a water boy on the crew building Lloyd's cotton mill.

Durham moved to Chapel Hill permanently in 1913 when he took a job in Clyde Eubanks' drugstore. In 1915, he borrowed $50 and entered UNC, continuing to work as a clerk for Eubanks and as a waiter in the University Inn. He left school to serve in the Navy from New Year's Day until Christmas Eve 1918 and married Margaret Joe Whitsell of Guilford County six days after his discharge.

While Margaret was bearing five children, her husband was using his very public position at the drugstore as a base for a constantly expanding public career. He was an active deacon in the Baptist Church and a member of the Chapel Hill board of aldermen 1924-1932, the Chapel Hill School Board 1924-1938, and the Orange County Board of Commissioners 1932-1938. In 1937 Louis Graves praised Durham as a man characterized by "absolute integrity, an ever lively public spirit, sound judgement, kindliness to all comers, no matter what their station." It was also in 1937 that Durham was selected to be a UNC trustee, a rare honor for a nongraduating alumnus.

Although Durham had run for no office outside Orange County, he had worked vigorously on state and national campaigns, and he had won a $22,000 federal grant that financed the extension of power lines into the Calvander area—the first rural electrification project in the nation. After William B. Umstead announced in 1938 that he would not seek a fourth term in Congress, Judge Lewis E. Teague of High Point narrowly defeated Oscar G. Barker of Durham in a primary election to choose Umstead's successor—there would be no Republican challenger in the fall. Judge Teague died on 27 October, 12 days before the election, and the four-member Sixth District Democratic Committee met in Greensboro on Tuesday, 1 November to name his replacement.

Dr. E.J. Woodhouse of the UNC Political Science Department strongly supported Oscar Barker, who had collected 47% of the primary vote, and Woodhouse objected vehemently on 2 November when the Committee, under the prodding of Orange and Alamance County politicos, selected Carl Durham as the nominee. Woodhouse organized a write-in effort for Barker, but Durham won without campaigning, and he would win 10 subsequent elections, always the "champion non-campaigner."

In Washington, Durham supported most New Deal programs, and he became a drinking companion of President Roosevelt's, who, he said, "could drink everyone else under the table [because] he was confined to a wheel chair." As a member of the Military Affairs Committee, Durham worked to reform military justice even in the midst of war. After the war until his retirement in January 1961, he played

Sidney Fremont Long (1862-1928) was chief of police in Chapel Hill during World War I. On 5 February 1920, the town commissioners raised his salary to $100 per month and gave him a $50 suit of clothes. He is pictured here a few months later. On 21 January 1922, the commissioners released him, and from 1923 until his death he served as the police officer for UNC. Long raised cows and sold buttermilk to supplement his income. (NCC)

a leading role in determining nuclear policy, in fact drafting the act that kept the Atomic Energy Commission securely under civilian control. Mrs. Margaret Durham had died in 1953. In June 1961, Durham married Mrs. Louise Ashworth Jefferson and spent the remaining 13 years of his life in contented retirement in Chapel Hill.

Had it not been for the Eighteenth Amendment, crime in Chapel Hill between the wars would have amounted to little more than a minor public irritant. As it was, with the thrill heightened by illegality, students consumed alcoholic beverages with an abandoned passion, and those with cash were never in short supply. The livery stables had earlier done a brisk business renting horses and carriages to thirsty students. By the 1920s, the jitney and bus operators were the benefactors. During Prohibition, students usually bought their beer at a place near Brady's Restaurant or at a house near the Blue Cross - Blue Shield headquarters. Blacks operated a perfunctorily clandestine saloon, then known as "a blind tiger," beside the Presbyterian church, where the Village Apartments are now.

While John Foushee was mayor from 1933 to 1942, he evolved a simple but effective way to keep tipsy students off the streets—each fall he ordered the constables to arrest the first wobbly student, thereby setting an example early in the term. But even a minimal enforcement of the liquor laws compelled the town to enlarge the constable force and inconvenienced officials and defendants who had to travel to Hillsborough for trial. In 1925, for example, 100 of the 347 cases originating in Chapel Hill dealt directly with liquor and drunkenness. In April 1929, aldermen proposed that a recorder's court be located in Chapel Hill. Justice of the Peace June Harris objected, the aldermen put the issue to the

voters, and the referendum carried overwhelmingly 93-8.

On 13 April the aldermen chose C.P. Hinshaw to be the first judge of the recorder's court, turning down an application from L.J. Phipps for the $600 yearly post. By the end of the year, Judge Hinshaw had heard 240 cases, finding 210 defendants guilty, 25 not guilty, sending three cases up to superior court, and having two cases appealed. About half involved liquor; there were single cases dealing with assault on a female, seduction, manslaughter, and robbery. Luther "L.J." Phipps became judge of the recorder's court in 1933 and remained on the bench until 1968, with time off to teach mathematics at UNC during World War II and to complete the term of State Representative John W. Umstead, Jr. in 1963-1964.

Many Chapel Hillians saw the beginning of a sensational, bloody crime on the night of Thursday, 31 March 1932. A little after 9 p.m., three men entered George Coleman's University Hot Dog Stand on Franklin Street near the Carolina Theatre. The men lured Coleman out the back door and slugged him with a blunt object, apparently with the intent to rob him. They ran to Columbia Street, jumped into a getaway Hudson sedan, and roared off on the road to Graham. UNC junior Ashby Penn and his date Anne Gordon Edmunds had just left the Carolina Theatre and were getting into Penn's Cadillac when police officer U.M. Rackley asked Penn to give chase. Robert Stone, a local youth, jumped in with Miss Edmunds, Rackley climbed onto the running board, and Penn sped off after the Hudson.

A tire on Penn's car went flat about five miles west of town, but he was able to overtake the Hudson and come to a stop in front of it. Penn got out, took Rackley's gun, opened the door of the sedan, and fired a shot, hitting one of the occupants. One of them shot back, sending a bullet through one of Penn's lungs. The hoodlums drove on, and Miss Edmunds drove Penn back to the student infirmary. UNC doctors sent him to Duke Hospital, where he received an emergency transfusion from his Beta Theta Pi fraternity brother James Cordon.

Orange County sheriff W.T. Sloan learned the next day that the Hudson had been abandoned in Chatham County and that one of the men in it had been wounded. Sloan followed the wounded man's trail to Spencer, from where he called authorities in Charlotte, who arrested Edward Johnson of Siler City. Johnson named his three accomplices, who turned out to be Robert G. Thompson, a former police chief of Mount Holly, Thompson's cousin Jack Thomas, who had shot Penn, and Laurence Armstrong, also of Mount Holly.

After a difficult struggle, Ashby Penn recovered. A native of Reidsville and the son of an American Tobacco Company vice president, Penn later married Anne Edmunds, commanded a patrol craft in the Pacific during World War II, settled in Syracuse, New York as an executive with a coal-sales firm, and died at the age of 39 in January 1950.

Franklin Street in the summer of 1925 (top), looking west from Columbia Street, was not yet paved, although the number of automobiles owned in Chapel Hill had increased from 95 in 1921 to 500 at this time. Another impetus to pave was a Federal Bureau of Standards report stating that a motor vehicle's gas mileage on gravel roads was 50% more and on paved roads was 100% more than on a dirt road.

The bottom photo shows the main block of Franklin Street on 12 October 1925 while it was being prepared for paving. Visible just right of center is the clock on the People's Bank, a venture that had been forced to sell out to the Bank of Chapel Hill, two doors east, about one month before this picture was taken.

Berman's Department Store moved into the Pope Mattress building in 1926 (presently the home of The Intimate Bookshop), and in 1927 the Carolina Theatre building (now the Varsity) filled up the vacant lot beside that building.

Property prices on the north side of Franklin Street were "skyrocketing" in this period when a 24-foot wide store rented for $200 per month. (NCC)

Anticipating the end of Prohibition, the General Assembly passed a new beer law that went into effect on Monday, 1 May 1933. When the long-awaited day arrived, restaurateur J.E. Gooch and Model Market manager Robert Fowler were ready. They had purchased an entire truck load of Esslinger's Beer, 170 cases and six kegs. By early evening, they had sold out. Soon, every proprietor in town with appropriate facilities was selling beer, with the exception of Clyde Eubanks, a staunch prohibitionist in all seasons. Located where the Porthole now stands, the Bloody Bucket was well situated to be the first stop for students strolling off campus.

University maintenance supervisor Joe Sparrow thought he had supplied a respectable alternative to drink-related entertainment in the summer of 1922 when he opened Sparrow's Pool off the Old Pittsboro Road in Carrboro. He

had unintentionally broken open a hornets' nest. In September, Carrboro Baptist Church preacher J.B. Davis condemned mixed bathing at the pool as sinful and turned Dr. Brack Lloyd's wife Emma, Mrs. Ralph Merritt, and Miss Grace Womble out of his church for frequenting the pool in defiance of his dictum. Defenders of the women revealed that the Rev. Davis had been swimming with a mixed group at Lakewood Pool in Durham. Davis admitted he had, but stood by his ban.

In the end, Davis' wrath may have been a boon to Sparrow. One observer noted, "Chapel Hill people would not have patronized the pool had the Carrboro mill people gone there to wash the dirt off." Any washing would have certainly been done in cold comfort, since the pool was fed in large measure by natural springs and shaded by tall trees.

Mayor W.S. Roberson had rented the Pickwick Theatre from S.J. Brockwell and was managing it when it burned in 1923. While a new theatre was being constructed, Roberson showed films in Gerrard Hall, taking advantage of the situation to outlaw the hurling of peanuts, acorns, and other missiles. In 1927, a Raleigh firm built a second theatre, what is now the Varsity, named it the Carolina, and opened it on 26 September 1926 with E. Carrington Smith as manager and prices set at 30 cents for adults and 10 cents for children. In September 1928, they purchased the Pickwick, thereafter also managed by Smith.

Early in September 1929, Smith installed a Vitaphone system in the Carolina in preparation for the arrival of the entertainment phenomenon of the century—the talkies. During the week of 16-21 September, every bill included a feature film accompanied by sound from a synchronized disc: on Monday, William Powell in "Charming Sinners"; on Tuesday, Warner Oland in "The Mysterious Dr. Fu Manchu"; on Wednesday and Thursday, the Marx Brothers in their first feature, "The Cocoanuts"; on Friday, Douglas Fairbanks, Jr. in "Fast Life"; and on Saturday, William Powell again in "The Greene Murder Case."

During the Depression, the Pickwick closed and the Carolina became on of the first theaters in the state to show movies on Sundays, a portion of the proceeds going to assist the poor. It was reputed to be the first in the South to show foreign films regularly. Smith ran the "art" films at 1:30 p.m. on weekdays, and students could receive credit for attending. When the Pickwick reopened in 1939 as The Pick, Smith again managed it until it closed after World War II.

Smith's employers, N.C. Theatres, Inc., purchased the current Carolina site from the heirs of Dr. A.B. Roberson in May 1941. Fortunately, Smith had building materials on hand at the outbreak of World War II, when federal restrictions in effect halted nonessential construction. When the new Carolina opened in the fall of 1942, the old became the Village Theatre, used during the war by the Naval Pre-Flight students in their training and now operated as the Varsity.

E. Carrington Smith was a dedicated Rams Club booster

until his death in 1977. He attended every home football game and most road games for 40 years, he handed out the most-valuable-player trophy at the annual football banquets, and he traditionally joined the reigning football coach and his family for Thanksgiving dinner.

By the mid-1930s, when the Chapel Hill school district had grown to contain approximately 1000 students, administrators realized that the time had come to build a separate high school and to expand the high-school curriculum. Following Frank Porter Graham's recommendation, the trustees donated a university-owned plot on Pittsboro Street that enabled the district to qualify for a federal building grant. H. Raymond Weeks of Durham drew the plans, educational leaders laid the corner stone on 11 May 1936, and contractor George W. Kane delivered the new high school that fall at a cost of $106,178.

While making his 2 a.m. round on 8 August 1942, UNC night watchman John Hines noticed a fire in the home-economics classroom on the southeast corner of the second floor of the high school. He called Jack Merritt at the police station, Merritt called the fire station, and J.S. Boone and Frank Partin sounded the alarm signaling volunteer firefighters and drove the American-La France to the school. When firemen broke windows to hose in water, oxygen fed the flames, and soon the entire building was aflame. A Durham truck and crew arrived to assist, but the cause was lost. Only some office equipment, the band instruments, and a few other items had been saved.

With their school gone, students attended classes at the elementary school and in two houses adjacent to the elementary school. But even though the school board shortly decided to build a new high school on the former Thomas Hume site behind the Baptist Church, then owned by Ceasar Cone, nothing could be done until the war ended, and in fact it was not until December 1951 that the first wing of a new high school was ready.

Higher education in Chapel Hill had a powerful friend in John Sprunt Hill. Born in Faison, North Carolina, in 1869, Hill graduated from high school at age 12, entered UNC at 16, and graduated at 20. After earning a degree from the Columbia University Law School in 1894, he set up a law firm in New York City. Following duty in Puerto Rico during the Spanish-American War, in November 1899 he married Annie Louise Watts, the daughter of George Watts of Durham, and in 1903 he moved to Durham. He founded the Durham Bank and Trust Company and the Home Savings Bank, he helped to establish Erwin Mills and the Home Security Life Insurance Company, and from 1933 to 1939 he was a very influential state senator. A UNC trustee from 1905 until his death in 1961, Hill made many generous contributions to the university.

From on-the-scene observations, Hill became an expert on European insurance plans, and he passed his insights on to his son George Watts Hill and Dr. W.C. Davison of the

John Sprunt Hill (1869-1961) entered UNC at age 16 and graduated with highest honors. The Yackety Yack noted that while he was a student, Hill was known for his "boarding house reach." His gifts to UNC are legendary, among them the Carolina Inn and the Lloyd-Webb building, the building that today houses Varley's, the Little Shop, Julian's, and the Carolina Coffee Shop. Hill stipulated that the income from the latter building be used to finance the North Carolina Collection, housed now on the fifth floor of Wilson Library. (NCC)

Duke University School of Medicine, who were in the late stages of planning the Durham Hospital Association when the stock market crashed in 1929, delaying but not halting their endeavor.

With the encouragement of Watts Hill, on 7 August 1933 Raleigh businessman Dwight Snyder incorporated the Hospital Care Association in his hometown. Snyder's only assets were $1000 credit extensions granted by Duke and Watts Hospitals, and a $250 loan from Durham Bank and Trust underwritten by Watts Hill. After three months, the Association moved its offices and its single employee, Elisha M. Herndon, to Durham. Marvin E. Woodard, a UNC employee living in Chapel Hill, bought one of the first policies, and his daughter Ann, born 27 December 1933, was the first baby in the United States whose birth costs were paid for by maternity benefits included in a family health insurance policy. The Hospital Care Association paid $60 for 10 days care.

In 1935, using a $25,000 grant from the Duke Endowment, Dr. Isaac Hall Manning of the UNC School of Medicine and Graham L. Davis of the Duke Endowment founded the Hospital Saving Association of Chapel Hill and set up offices in the old Delta Kappa Epsilon fraternity house, located behind the Carolina Coffee Shop. Hospital Saving moved in quick succession to the building across the walkway that now houses the Porthole Restaurant, to the new DKE house on Columbia Street, and into the Tankersley Building on East Franklin, where it remained from 1938 until a new home office was completed on West Franklin in 1951.

Dr. Isaac Manning was the son of John Manning, the Pittsboro lawyer who founded the UNC Law School. John Manning won a special election on 7 December 1870 to complete the remaining four months of deceased Congressman Robert B. Gilliam's term. Manning never ran for

Mr. Blackwood's Shoe Shop, located on the corner of Greensboro and Main Streets in Carrboro, boasted the first electric shoe repair equipment in the area. In this picture from 1925 are, left to right, Willie Mae Taylor, Dora Clark, Laura Sparrow, and Carrboro mayor Armand West. Mr. West was a supervisor in the Durham Hosiery Mills, located where Carr Mill Mall is today.

Visible in the background at the far right is Carrboro's only hotel, run by Mr. and Mrs. Ralph Merritt, descendants of Rev. William H. Merritt. The hotel catered almost exclusively to young single people who worked in the mill. The Merritts set a lunch table that was frequented by working people, including as regulars the train crew and any passengers who were around. (Courtesy of Tom Goodrich)

In 1921, the village, with financial assistance from UNC, purchased for $12,000 an American-La France fire truck to replace the old 1914 Ford T Model. The new truck was housed in a firehouse built in the middle of Columbia Street at the Rosemary Street intersection. Firemen shared their upstairs quarters with prisoners housed in cells built in the rear. The range of the La France's hoses was a factor in the aldermen's decision in 1928 to restrict downtown buildings to three stories or a maximum height of 45 feet, a safety ordinance that has been retained in modern times for aesthetic reasons. (NCC)

a full term in Congress, and he turned down offers to become a superior court judge, N.C. Secretary of State, and Chief Justice of the N.C. Supreme court. It was at UNC that he earned a prominent niche in the history of his state. Serving without pay, he established the UNC Law School in 1881, teaching seven students the first year and seeing the school become firmly established before his death in 1899. He and his wife Louisa Hall Manning, had six daughters and two sons, one of whom was Isaac Hall Manning, who became Dean of the School of Medicine in 1905.

As dean, Manning limited Jewish students to 10% of each entering class, on the grounds that they were difficult to place in leading medical schools and that it was unfair to provide initial training to those who could not continue their medical education. When he accepted only four Jewish enrollees in the class of 40 in 1933, President Frank Porter Graham overruled him in the case of a fifth student who appealed the exclusion. Manning resigned as dean, remaining on the faculty to become Kenan Professor Emeritus of Physiology in 1939.

Dr. Manning guided the Hospital Saving Association as president until 1941, by which time 166,201 policies were in force, and as chairman of the board and medical director until his death in 1946. He and Mary Best Jones Manning had three sons. Isaac, Jr. studied medicine at UNC and Harvard, rose to the rank of Lt. Col. in the Army Medical Corps as head of a hospital in Europe, and has served on the medical faculties at UNC and Duke while practicing privately as one of Durham's most prominent physicians. John T. received his LL.B. from UNC in 1936, served with U.S. Navy Intelligence during World War II, and spent his career as a lawyer and as a judge in the recorder's court in Chapel Hill. Howard E. graduated from the Harvard Law School in 1938 and became a leading lawyer in Raleigh, serving as head of the State Board of Public Welfare under Governor Hodges.

On 1 January 1968, the Hospital Care Association and the Hospital Saving Association merged to form Blue Cross and Blue Shield of North Carolina, which located its home office on the Chapel Hill-Durham Boulevard a mile east of Eastgate. Odell Associates, Inc. of Charlotte designed and the Nello L. Teer Company of Durham constructed the avant-garde headquarters, a three-dimensional, glass and steel, 100' X 500' rhomboid tilting 45 degrees east and south. In 1983, over 1.4 million North Carolinians held Blue Cross/Blue Shield policies.

The 1930s were years of political turmoil in Chapel Hill, which came to be recognized as the center of leftwing activity in North Carolina. Memories of the turbulent 1930s were vividly revived on 20 September 1953 when Indiana Senator William E. Jenner released the transcripts of testimony previously heard by the Senate Internal Security Subcommittee. Most of the testimony regarding earlier communist activities in Chapel Hill came from Paul

Crouch. Crouch described himself as a former communist who had in the 1930s been a representative to a meeting of the executive committee of the Communist Internationale in Moscow, a colonel in the Russian Army, a lecturer at a Soviet military academy, and an editor of the *Daily Worker* and other communist publications. He said he had broken with the communists in 1942 and had revealed his inside information to the FBI in 1947.

Crouch testified that UNC English professor Dr. Eston Everett Ericson, under the party name "Spartacus" and with the assistance of English instructor Arnold Williams, had led a large communist group at UNC between 1934 and 1937. Among other local and regional organizers, Crouch named Lester Wilson, Clarence Walter, Bill Levitt, and Don West, alias "Jim Weaver." He surprised no one in Chapel Hill when he named Milton "Ab" and Minna Abernethy.

In 1929 Ab Abernethy left N.C. State College at the request of the student council, whose members were upset over an article Abernethy had written for the *News and Observer* reviewing a professor's dissertation on cheating in colleges. He came to Chapel Hill in 1930, enrolled in UNC, and founded The Intimate Bookshop in his dormitory room in Steele Hall. At the time Elizabeth Lay Green was reviewing books for the *News and Observer* and several other North Carolina newspapers. To help Ab get started, she and her husband gave him several hundred books, plus additional review volumes as she received them. According to Paul Crouch, Abernethy was never a card-carrying communist, but he had "accepted party discipline."

In May 1931, Abernethy joined Anthony Butitta of Durham in publishing *Contempo*, a literary review printed in Louis Graves' Orange Printshop. Before *Contempo* ceased publication in February 1934, Paul Green, Ezra Pound, Langston Hughes, Lewis Mumford, and William Faulkner were a few of the notables who had been on its editorial board. Some observers, noting Abernethy's tireless efforts to make The Intimate a success, suspected that his primary goal was more free review copies of new books. In June 1931, he poked fun at his radical reputation and his male-dorm beginning in announcing the move of The Intimate to a new "attractive and central location, over the Carolina Cafeteria and next to the United States Post Office where any cautious co-ed may now join the booklovers on their daily pilgrimage."

Later that year, Dr. Guy B. Johnson and Paul Green invited the black poet Langston Hughes to speak at UNC. Hughes stayed with Abernethy and Butitta; and, on the day he gave four lecture/readings on campus, the *Contempo* carried two of his pieces: a satirical article on the Scottsboro case entitled "Southern Gentlemen, White Prostitutes, Millowners, and Negroes" and the poem "Christ in Alabama," which concluded with the quartrain "Most holy bastard/ Of the bloody mouth/*Nigger Christ/On the Cross of the South*." Hughes' addresses and his dinner that evening with

William Faulkner, left in the photo above, was photographed with Milton "Ab" Abernethy in 1931 when Faulkner visited Chapel Hill. Abernethy's magazine, Contempo, devoted one whole issue to Faulkner's work. At the time, the issue sold for 10¢. Today, copies of that issue sell for several hundred dollars each. (Courtesy of Wallace Kuralt) Minna Abernethy, right, stands with her husband "Ab" in front of their bookstore in 1933. By this time, The Intimate Bookshop was located on Franklin Street west of the Presbyterian Church (Courtesy of Mrs. Amy Menache)

his hosts in the Carolina Cafeteria went off without incident, but the North Carolina press assumed that the strongly worded material in the *Contempo* was representative of Hughes' lecture statements. In the ensuing furor, with his typical fortitude Frank Porter Graham assumed all the responsibility and rode out the buffeting.

In 1932 Ab married Minna Krupskaya, a native of New York City who shared his political instincts, and in 1933 he moved The Intimate into "Hoot" Patterson's former store at 205 East Franklin. According to Paul Crouch, in the mid-1930s a Comintern agent operating under the name "J. Peters" gave Abernethy a small printing press which he installed in the back of The Intimate and which Alton Lawrence and T. Owen Matthews used to publish propaganda, including "Carolina Youth," edited by Crouch's wife Sylvia, head of the local Young Communist League. At the time, there was nothing "underground" about the press; however, while Ab privately acknowledged that Matthews ran

Thomas Joseph O'Flaherty (1915-1938) was on the UNC boxing team in 1934-1935. O'Flaherty, from Connecticut, listed Charlotte as his home town in order to get in-state tuition rates ($75 versus $175), and when the administration learned the truth in February, 1935, they ruled him ineligible for athletics.

While at UNC, O'Flaherty became intensely interested in politics, becoming a close friend of Milton Abernethy who ran The Intimate Bookshop. After graduating in 1937, O'Flaherty joined the Loyalist side in the Spanish Civil War, and died in battle on 12 September 1938. (NCC)

the press in rented space behind The Intimate Bookshop, in their testimony before the Internal Security Subcommittee, both he and Minna consistently pleaded the Fifth Amendment in response to questions about their knowledge of communist activities, the press, and Crouch.

Once the leftists had established a base on campus, Chapel Hill became the focal point in North Carolina for further recruitment. Mark Johnson, a black graduate of the Lenin School in Moscow, worked full time in the mid-1930s organizing the Chapel Hill-Durham-Raleigh area. *Daily Worker* editor Clarence Hathaway spoke to the student body. Encouraged by earlier successes, national Communist party officer V.J. Jerome spent several weeks helping to recruit in Chapel Hill during the winter of 1935-1936. Paul Crouch was the Communist party's candidate for governor in 1936, and in the fall party members held a dinner in Durham honoring Crouch and James Ford, the Negro vice-presidential candidate of the Communist party. Professor Eston Everett Ericson attended the dinner, and his presence there became an issue that intimately involved the university and Chapel Hill.

In the 25 October edition of the *News and Observer*, columnist Frank Smethurst attacked Dr. Ericson for having been a guest of the communists. Ericson admitted to being a socialist, but denied ever having taught any ideology, and insisted he had attended the dinner only to observe the inner workings of the Communist party. UNC alumni, most notably Charlotte physicians Dr. Roy McKnight (class of 1914) and Dr. Henry Sloan (class of 1909), led the chorus demanding that the university rid the faculty of leftists.

The Southern Committee for People's Rights, headquartered in Chapel Hill, rushed to Ericson's defense in a letter addressed "To All Southern Liberals" which repudiated "utterly the doctrine that no white person may eat with a negro without lowering himself in some way." The committee published the *People's Rights Bulletin* in 1936-1937 and numbered among its members Paul Green, Phillips Russell, Minna K. Abernethy, UNC Press director

William T. Couch, and Jonathan Daniels. Daniels was caught in the middle as a member of the committee and as editor of the *News and Observer*. In an editorial, he conceded that Ericson had acted within his rights, but accused him of being careless and indulgent in "delicate matters of race relationships in the South."

Critics have always seen the university as the "hotbed" of something—Jeffersonian-Republican radicalism, Federalist conservatism, Presbyterianism, secessionism, unionism, elitism, socialism, communism, pacifism. As a vocal opponent of commercialized collegiate football and an equally open proponent of collective bargaining and liberal Democratic policies, Frank Porter Graham placed himself at storm center, and he became nationally known because of his adversaries' repeated charges that he was trying to indoctrinate the youth of North Carolina with dangerous doctrines and ideas.

Writing in the *Atlantic Monthly* in March 1941, David L. Cohn focused on Graham's predicament: "No one in North Carolina (or elsewhere) denies that it is the business of a university to uphold the standard of freedom, truth, and justice. But the university president who actually does it not infrequently finds himself in trouble." Cohn ridiculed the "communist faculty" theme: "A tiny minority are leftist, and they serve, or ought to serve, the valuable function of gadflies to sting the many out of their smugness. The U., on the whole, however, is about as communist as the First Baptist Church of Chalk Level [Tennessee?]."

In December 1942, the War Department notified Professor Ericson that his son Ervid Eric Ericson was a prisoner of the Japanese. Eric wrote home in September 1943, revealing that he had beriberi. He wrote one more letter before he boarded a transport in December 1944 which was to carry 1600 prisoners to Japan. The transport sank during action off Luzon, but it was not until 2 September 1945 that Professor Ericson learned that Eric was one of the 942 men who died when the ship went down. Dr. Ericson left UNC in 1946 to join the Massachusetts State College system, later moving to Gustavus Adolphus College in St. Peter, Minnesota, and retiring to Iowa City in 1961, where he died in 1964 at age 73.

While Ab Abernethy may have supported communist theory, as the proprietor of The Intimate Bookshop he was a thoroughgoing capitalist, and he built it into a thriving enterprise before selling out in 1950, later to become a partner in a very successful stockbroker firm in New York City, where he and Minna established a residence on fashionable Riverside Drive.

When the subcommittee transcripts were released in September 1952, the *News and Observer* discarded Paul Crouch's testimony as outdated and "badly shopworn," and Ab Abernethy wrote Louis Graves, "We were confronted with a paid, professional informer who made wild and lurid statements, and imputed to us the most fantastic associations of which we had never heard before." In a press release Abernethy proclaimed that he and Minna had "never done anything disloyal in our lives" and that their activities in Chapel Hill were public and well known.

Paul and Isabel "Bunny" Smith purchased The Intimate. The Smiths had opened the Provincetown Book Shop on Cape Cod in 1932. They retained the Cape Cod property but moved their stock to Key West and a new bookshop in mid-November 1941, just in time for Pearl Harbor to destroy the tourist trade. Nevertheless, they stayed in Key West until 1947, when they opened their third book store in New Orleans, an undertaking Isabel described later as "a complete, total, unmitigated flop," prompting them to move to Chapel Hill and take over The Intimate in September 1950.

Paul Smith soon left his own imprint on the business. He drew original, intentionally corny signs and ads. He kept a wide selection of prints. Tall bookshelves filled with cheap used hardbacks and paperbacks kept booklovers on the premises for hours. Each April selected books went for 29 cents the first day, 19 cents the second, 9 cents the third, and for free on the fourth. Smith had a lasting love for old books, which he collected, repaired, and sold; and he shared an interest with Isabel in Mexican and Central American archaeology.

The Smiths moved The Intimate to its present location in 1958, sold the Provincetown bookshop in 1965, and in December 1965 sold The Intimate to Wallace and Brenda Kuralt, retaining the old- and rare-book trade within The Intimate until they opened the Old Book Corner in 1969 at 137-A East Rosemary. After Paul Smith died in 1977, Isabel kept the Old Book Corner going until her lease expired. In January 1981, the farewell issue of the shop's newsletter, "Old Book News," was signed with a poignant farewell—"Your Crochety Old Bookseller (In Absentia) and Your Crochety Old Bookseller's Rickety wife, Isabel Smith."

Between the world wars, UNC developed a nationally recognized athletic program with multichampionship teams in football, basketball, and track and field. When William "Bill" and Robert "Bob" Fetzer came to UNC in 1921, the sports facilities were still in the "first generation" stage of development. Bynum gym was available for basketball, gymnastics, and boxing, but its pool had been declared unsanitary and closed. There were a dozen or so tennis courts. Emerson Field hosted organized baseball, football, and track and field events.

In 1922, Bob Fetzer became athletic director and the brothers assumed the shared responsibility of coaching the basketball team. Since neither knew very much about the game, their "coaching" consisted primarily of being present at games. They could hardly have devised a better strategy. Their 1922 team went 9-3 during the regular season, then won the Southern Conference Tournament with victories over Harvard, Newberry, Alabama, Georgia, and Mercer. The 1923 squad was undefeated in 14 scheduled

games—including a 39-9 rout of N.C. State—and beat Mississippi College in the opening round of the tournament, then fell to the University of Mississippi 32-34. Norman Shepherd took over as coach in 1924 and guided the Tar Heels to a perfect 23-0 season, including four lopsided tournament triumphs.

When the students learned that their Tar Heels had defeated Alabama in the title game that year, head cheerleader Vic Huggins led 500 of his classmates to the Durham train station to welcome Cartwright "Cart" Carmichael, Jack "Spratt" Cobb, and their teammates. The loud, well oiled trek back to Chapel Hill ended at 4 a.m., no doubt to the relief of the solemn element of the community. Among the innovations that have alloted him a permanent slot in UNC sports history, Huggins invited co-eds to join the cheerleader corps, he wrote "Here Comes Carolina," and he convinced Charles Thomas Woollen to shell out $25 to order a mascot from Texas—Rameses I.

Carolina fever became chronic during the 1922 football season. Bill and Bob Fetzer were the coaches and Grady Pritchard the captain of a team that won nine and lost only to powerhouse Yale, 0-18, in a game in which UNC had three touchdown plays called back because of penalties. Chapel Hill the village was well represented on the 1922 team. Besides guard Pritchard, there were halfbacks Edwin Tenny and Ralph Pendergraft, tackle Herman McIver, quarterback George Sparrow, and the great running back Chancie Lee "Jack" Merritt, the great-great-great-grandson of Old Kit Barbee, the great-great-grandson of the Rev. William H. and Susanna Barbee Merritt, and the son of Lonnie Lee Merritt.

During 1918-1921 when Jack Merritt played for the Chapel

These six boys were members of the Chapel Hill High School team that beat Greensboro 70-0 for the state football title in 1919. While they were at CHHS, they also won championships in track and basketball. In 1922, all six were on the UNC football team that lost only to Yale, at Yale.

The six are, left to right, Ed Tenny, Ralph Pendergraft, Grady Pritchard, Herman McIver, Jack Merritt, and George Sparrow. Pendergraft operated a Chevrolet sub-dealership in Chapel Hill for several years, but he lost his business on 14 May 1928 when a fire destroyed his uninsured West Franklin Street Building and 34 cars, including four customers' cars. (NCC)

Hill High School, his teams lost only once to a high school and beat several college teams. The "Hillians" defeated Greensboro 70-0 to win the state high school championship in 1919 and repeated in 1920, losing only to Elon College while beating freshman teams at State, Wake Forest, and UNC. Merritt carried his nickname, The Battering Ram, with him to UNC, and by 1924 when Vic Huggins decided it was time to select a team mascot, a "battering ram" was the immediately obvious choice.

Huggins and some tuxedo-clad classmates introduced Rameses I to the student body by escorting him to mid court in the Tin Can, the all-purpose, tin, perpetually leaky gymnasium built in 1923 on the site now occupied by Fetzer Gymnasium. While the audience and his dignified attendants sang "Hark the Sound," Rameses broke the ice by relieving himself on the polished floor. Huggins led the mascot onto the football field for the first time on 8 November 1924 while Carolina was warming up to face favored VMI. But the ram came through. Late in the fourth quarter of a scoreless game, Jack Merritt broke free for a 37-yard run which set up a Bunn Hackney drop-kick field goal for a 3-0 UNC win.

After graduating in 1925, Vic Huggins married Rebecca Ray of Carthage and worked as a salesman for the Haas Tailoring Company until he purchased University Hardware from L.E. Jones in 1949, changing its name to Huggins Hardware. Jack Merritt remained in Chapel Hill, joined the police department in 1939, rose to the rank of lieutenant, and since 1965 has enjoyed his retirement years as one of the most popular figures in town.

Bob Fetzer also coached track, winning 14 of 26 Southern Conference outdoor championship meets between 1923 and his retirement as athletic director in 1952 to become execu-tive director of the Morehead Foundation. He founded the Southern Conference Indoor Championships in 1930 and coached teams to nine victories before the events were temporarily suspended during World War II.

In 1926, Bob Fetzer hired a full time football coach, Charles C. Collins, one of the "Seven Mules" who had blocked for Notre Dame's famed "Four Horsemen." Collins introduced specialty players with kicker Ezra Rowe, and Johnny Branch was a star punt returner and running back on Collins' 1929 "team of a hundred backs," a squad that contained a dozen talented ball carriers including Branch, Chuck Erickson, Henry House, and Yank Spaulding. It was also in 1927 that head cheerleader Kay Kyser formed the Cheerios, and gave them his antic stamp,

James Kern "Kay" Kyser arrived from Rocky Mount as a student in 1924. His mother, Emily Howell Kyser, was the sister of Professor E. Vernon Howell and the first licensed female pharmacist in the state. Hal Kemp had led a popular dance band while a student at UNC, and when he left to play professionally, Kyser filled the vacuum with a collection of music-makers who drew attention away from their pedestrian musical abilities with on-stage stunts and comical costumes. Kyser took the band on the road the summer of his junior year and returned in the fall hungry, bedraggled, and dejected, but accompanied by four professional musicians and still possessed of a spirited sense of humor. The group practiced their music and comic acts during the winter of 1927-1928, and when Kyser graduated in the spring they returned to the road.

Through the ups and downs of the next nine years, the group became one of the most popular one-night-stand dance bands in the nation, while refining their act into what Kyser labeled "nine-tenths Stardust and Rosalie, and

James K. "Kay" Kyser sits with his chauffeur Mack Riggsbee in the Model T that Kyser bought for $30 in 1928 and named "Passion" ("I named it that because it got hot so fast"). Riggsbee used the name "Ulford Madison Maxwell Clementine Cordell Riggsbee" while he worked for Kyser as a jack-of-all-trades. About 1930, Riggsbee drove "Passion" to California and back, noting that it burned 33 quarts of oil going there and 34 coming back. Whenever the car stopped, Kyser and Riggsbee would "drop anchor" to prevent the car from running off. Mack stayed in California after Kay retired. (Courtesy of Kay Kyser)

George Barclay (b. 1912), from Natrona, Pa., was a UNC first-team All-American in 1934, under new head coach Carl Snavely. UNC's record went from 4-5 in 1933 to 7-1-1 in 1934, marking, according to contemporary observers, UNC's entrance into big time athletics.

Barclay played only four games as a professional due to a knee injury, then spent most of his career coaching, including 3 years as head coach at UNC 1953-1955. After he left coaching in 1955, he and his family chose to stay in Chapel Hill, and they still live here. (NCC)

one-tenth clowning." Then in the fall of 1937, exploiting the current popularity of radio quiz shows, Kyser and a booking-agency executive worked out the format for "Kay Kyser's Kollege of Musical Knowledge," which offered "diplomas" to contestants who gave correct answers to questions, some serious, some frivolous. The show was a hit, gaining a weekly audience of 20 million listeners, and after years of frantic travel Kyser could enjoy the pleasure of a backlog of recording contracts, movie contracts, and sleeping until 1 p.m. in his Waldorf-Astoria suite, before beginning his typical 18-hour day.

In 1943, Kyser married his lead singer, Georgia Carroll, who as a John Powers model had appeared on the covers of *Vogue*, *Redbook*, and other fashion magazines. Kyser and his band toured extensively for the USO during World War II, at times following the island-hopping deep into the South Pacific to entertain men only a few hours from combat. Kyser appeared in several movies, retired from his radio show in 1948, and spent a year on television. His comical bearded "judges," his and Ish Kabbible's (Merwyn Bogue) antics, and the band's vocalists (including Mike Douglas) made the show a hit, but a dispute between the sponsor and NBC led to cancellation.

In 1951, Kyser retired and with Georgia and their two daughters moved into the William Hooper/Vernon Howell house in Chapel Hill. Since the birth of their third daughter in 1953, Kay Kyser has turned his unflagging energy into promoting Christian Science, and Georgia Carroll Kyser has become a leading activist in preserving historic Chapel Hill.

Kay Kyser was the last of the great cheerleaders of the pre-World War II era, but the Carolina sports teams maintained their winning tradition, and spawned their first nationally recognized stars. Carl Snavely replaced Charles Collins as head football coach in 1934 after having accumulated a 42-16-8 record at Bucknell. Snavely coached UNC's first All-American in 1934, captain George Barclay, who joined

Jim Tatum, Charlie Shaffer, Harry Montgomery, and Dick Buck in leading the team through a 7-1-1 season. The 1935 team, which included Crowell Little, lost only to Duke, a defeat that may have kept UNC out of the Rose Bowl.

Snavely also recruited Andy Bershak, one of several outstanding UNC players from the coal fields of Pennsylvania. Playing under coach Raymond Wolf, Bershak's teams accumulated records of 8-2 in 1936 and 7-1-1 in 1937, the year he won All-American honors. Snavely left UNC to coach at Cornell for nine years. Returning to UNC in 1945, he took over a team rebuilding after the war and a funereal 1-7-1 1944 season, won five and lost five in 1945, but more importantly recruited a 22-year-old from Asheville who had won some recognition playing on U.S. Navy teams, a fellow by the name of Charlie Justice.

During the 1930s, the UNC basketball team had winning records every year except 1939, winning the Southern Conference Tournament in 1935 and 1936. The team vaulted back from their losing season to win 23 games and the S.C. Tournament in 1940 while losing only three times. The 1941 team won 19 games during the regular season, but lost 37-38 to Duke in the opening round of the Southern Conference tournament, and lost to Pittsburgh and Dartmouth in the NCAA tournament. Nevertheless, George Glamack (known as the "Blind Bomber" because of his poor eyesight) repeated as an All-American, after having been the first Tar Heel cager to win those honors in 1940.

The days of glory for Tar Heel athletes were soon to have a hiatus, imposed not by superior opponents but by the wars enshrouding Europe and Asia. Long before Pearl Harbor, Chapel Hillians had become personally involved in World War II, tragically in one instance.

The racial policies of the Third Reich forced Edward Gustav Danziger, who had a Jewish grandfather, to leave his wife Emily and his two sons Theodor and Erwin in his native Austria and emigrate to the United States in March 1939 with $4 in his possession. Although Danziger had been a wealthy confectionary-cafe owner in Vienna, he was happy to take a job as a janitor in the International House of Columbia University, a job arranged for him by the Friend's Service Committee of Philadelphia. He was making candies for a fellow Austrian immigrant, Emil Altman, a few weeks later when he learned that Dr. D.D. Carroll, dean of the UNC School of Commerce and chairman of the Chapel Hill Quaker committee, was prepared to assist him in setting up a small candy shop. Danziger came to Chapel Hill in April and, after looking over Durham, decided he preferred Franklin Street.

He rented space once used for Gooch's Restaurant across the street from the Methodist Church, borrowed $1500 from the Quakers and friends in Chapel Hill, returned to New York to buy supplies, and spent the summer working day and night to fashion a modernistic, Viennese-styled candy store-coffee house. On 12 September 1939 he began serving his staple fare of American and "Viennese" coffee, cider, sandwiches, pastries, ice cream, and candies galore. Very shortly Danziger's Viennese Candy Kitchen was a regular stop for students and visitors, and "Papa D" was something of a celebrity.

His family joined him, and his son Theodor "Ted" enrolled in UNC and graduated Phi Beta Kappa before entering the U.S. Army. After his discharge, Ted married Mrs. Mary Alice "Bibi" Hoover Ashley, who was working at Danziger's while attending UNC. When Ted decided that he too would go into the restaurant business, neither he nor his father had a reserve of cash, but both had limitless energy, and they used it to dig out the area beneath the Candy Kitchen, carrying the dirt away in the trunk of Ted's car, and to create the "underground" Rathskeller, which immediately appealed to returning veterans who had grown to love German beer and the lively atmosphere of the beer hall. Both Ted and his father did well in the post-war prosperity, by which time Papa D had begun selling imported items and had added Old World Gift Shop to his cafe's title.

Emily Danziger, near death from a decade-old cancer and wanting to see the bright lights and the Metropolitan Opera, convinced her husband to spend the Christmas season of 1952 in New York. They arrived on 23 December and were attending a performance of *The King and I* on Christmas Day when she had a fatal heart attack. Papa D later married Trude Flack, the sister-in-law of his former employer Emil Altman.

Ted Danziger expanded by converting The Buccaneer, a beer bar on Airport Road, into a steak house. He named it the Ranch House, and when customers began to overflow the confining premises he enlarged it haphazardly until it spread over several thousand square feet. Ted later opened the Zoom Zoom where Mr. Gatti's is today, before his death in 1964.

World War II touched Chapel Hill painfully on 4 February 1941 when John Yates Varley died in a hopsital in Inverness, Scotland. The Englishman Fred Varley had settled in Haw River in 1930 before moving on to a house on Davie Circle in Chapel Hill. His son Robert "Bob" graduated from UNC in 1937 and opened Varley's Men's Shop in 1938. Robert's brother John Yates joined the Royal Air Force as an aircraftsman and was probably injured during a German air raid.

Using $1160 raised from a bazaar, in April 1941 the Chapel Hill British War Relief Committee purchased a mobile tea kitchen and a large supply of food intended to provide meals in the field for English soldiers or firefighters or families bombed out of their homes. By the time the kitchen and food arrived in England in July 1941, the island was filling with refugees, and U.S. Ambassador Anthony J. Drexel Biddle presented the gifts to Crown Prince Olaf and General Carl Fleischer for use by the Norwegian government in exile.

On a more personal scale, that fall historian Hope Chamberlain received a note of thanks from a British sailor who had received a pair of socks she had knitted. Brandishing the archetypal British confidence of those days when England stood alone, the sailor looked forward to America's joining England to "rid the world, once and for all, of that dope Hitler."

Immediately following Pearl Harbor, Mayor John Foushee directed the formation of a joint town-university defense program, assisted by Dean Francis F. Bradshaw, Town Manager J.L. Caldwell, and L.B. Rogerson. W.E. Thompson and Mrs. S.E. Leavitt headed a series of E-Bond rallies that continued for the duration of the war. Working out of headquarters across the alley from the Carolina Coffee Shop, Red Cross workers collected donations for their War Fund and in conjunction with the Chapel Hill Ladies Community Workshop spent thousands of hours knitting clothing, making bandages, running the rationing program, and assisting with civil-defense measures. By the end of February 1945, volunteers had turned out over 670,000 bandages and over 8700 garments. Red Cross volunteers also operated the Community Recreation Center in the old Methodist Church, with USO programs on weekends.

In May 1940, Frank Porter Graham had offered UNC *in toto* to the defense effort. That September, the War Department approved a WPA grant of $154,835 to improve airport facilities to accommodate a UNC-Duke CAA training program. On 26 December, Prof. Horace Williams died, leaving UNC approximately 1000 acres, including 400 to enlarge the airport.

No one was more spellbinding in the classroom; outside the classroom, few were more unpleasantly eccentric than Williams, who refused to use either electricity or running water, leaving his wife Behta Colton Williams to carry water from a spring 250 yards down Strowd's Hill. He built a barn closer to the front doors of Drs. Louis Round Wilson and Henry McGilbert Wagstaff than to his own back door,

ALL CITIZENS
interested in
THE DEFENSE OF AMERICA
are invited to a
Public Meeting
8 p. m. THURSDAY, June 6
Gerrard Hall

Speech by
KEMP BATTLE

Short talks by local members

Dr. W. W. Pierson, Jr.
Mayor John M. Foushee
Reverend A. S. Lawrence
Colonel Joseph Hyde Pratt
Louis Graves
Admiral Percy Foote

Auspices of Chapel Hill Branch of Committee to Defend America by Aid to the Allies

In the spring of 1940, anti-Nazi feeling was running high in Chapel Hill. William Allen White, a newspaperman in Emporia, Kansas, called for the creation of a national organization to promote England's defense, and Chapel Hill immediately organized its chapter, naming Archibald Henderson chairperson. The group distributed the handbill shown here to advertise its organizational meeting.

Two weeks later, a sizable group of villagers signed a petition asking for an immediate declaration of war on Germany, and other villagers made extensive plans to house the expected influx of British children who would flee from the imminent German invasion. (NCC)

John Foushee, former mayor, took out this ad in the Chapel Hill Weekly *in June 1942. (NCC)*

forcing them to find relief from flies and the stench by convincing the aldermen to ban barns after Williams refused to respond to their complaints.

UNC Comptroller William D. Carmichael obtained more WPA funds, purchased the C.L. Martindale Airport north of town, and built the Horace Williams Airport into the largest college-owned airport in the nation, covering 607 acres and capable of handling all existing military aircraft.

In February 1942, the U.S. Navy chose UNC to house a Naval Pre-Flight Pilot Training School, which trained 18,700 men in Pre-Flight and reserve-officers programs during the war, including future President Gerald Ford. By the summer of 1942, 1875 cadets were on campus, creating hardly a ripple in the village. Their daily schedule was full from 5 a.m. reveille until 9 p.m. taps, except for free periods from 1:15-1:45 p.m. daily and from 7:30-8:50 p.m. on alternate nights. Few left the campus during the permissible periods on Wednesdays and weekends.

UNC benefited physically and financially from the relationship. The Navy built a 53-bed hospital, Women's Gym, the Naval Armory, Kessing Pool (named after commanding officer Commander Oliver Owen Kessing), an officers' club that became the Monogram Club, athletic fields, a canteen, shops, storage areas, a laundry, an airport hanger, and dressing rooms in Emerson Stadium. The Navy also paid to complete the Negro Community Center in Carrboro, used as living quarters by the all-black Navy Pre-Flight School Band, which played for drills, ceremonies, and entertainment.

From September 1941 until October 1945, the Pre-Flight School put out a newspaper, the *Cloud Buster*, with Lt. P.O. "Kidd" Brewer as public relations officer and Yeoman 1st Class (designated) Orville Campbell as associate editor

for part of the run. But it was on the playing fields that the Pre-Flight School had its greatest immediate impact locally. The "Cloudbusters" played full schedules in football, baseball, and basketball and participated in boxing, wrestling, and soccer matches.

The Cloudbusters baseball team lost three games in July 1943 to a team from the Norfolk Naval Training Center, but a team that included major leaguers Ted Williams, Phil Rizzuto, Dom DiMaggio, John Pesky, and John Hassett. Then on 28 July 1943, the Cloudbusters played before 27,281 fans in Yankee Stadium, winning 11-5 over a team made up of New York Yankees and Cleveland Indians. In addition to dozens of college players over the seasons, the Cloudbusters had some major leaguers of their own: second-baseman Lt. Charlie Gehringer of the Detroit Tigers; pitcher Hal Schumacher of the New York Giants; and manager Lt. George Killinger, an ex-Yankee.

In the fall of 1944, Lt. Killinger took over as football coach, assisted by Paul "Bear" Bryant, who in the post-war era would make it on his own. Otto Graham, then an All-American from Northwestern and now a member of the Pro Football Hall of Fame, quarterbacked the Cloudbusters in 1944 when they accumulated a record of 5-2-1, including victories over Duke and the U.S. Naval Academy.

The most demanding contributions to the war effort by Chapel Hillians were made by the men who fought and died in Africa, Europe, and the Pacific—and by their relatives and friends who waited apprehensively in Chapel Hill. The restrictions of space prevent anything more than a cursory treatment of the hundreds of Chapel Hillians who served with honor in the great world conflict.

Dr. Howard Patterson, the son of Eleanor and A.H. Patterson, participated in invasions in Africa, in Italy, and in Southern France. He received the Bronze Star for his conduct under fire at Anzio, where he was a member of the first medical unit ever to go ashore with the first waves of an invasion. Lt. Col. Patterson graduated from UNC in 1921 and from Harvard Medical School in 1925. After the war he drew the international spotlight when he treated Mrs. Okasana Stepanova Kosenkina for the massive injuries she received when she defected to the West by jumping from the third floor of the Russian consulate in New York City. Later,

From 1942 to 1945, the Navy Pre-Flight program at UNC published a four-page newspaper that concentrated on sports, pinups, and a daily comic strip drawn by Milton Caniff.

The logo shown here was drawn by James T. Berryman of the Washington Evening Star. *Berryman was the cartoonist who, using verbal descriptions, sketched a likeness of the Lindbergh baby kidnapper, a sketch that helped lead to the arrest of Bruno Hauptmann. (NCC)*

Dr. Patterson was president of the American College of Surgeons; he is now the arthroscopic surgeon for the New York Yankees.

Hoot Patterson's grandson Dr. Fred Patterson followed the initial waves onto the Normandy beachhead and stayed with forward fighting units through France and Belgium into Germany, collecting five battle stars. After the war, he opened a private office at 227 East Franklin Street in the former home of his grandparents, Mr. and Mrs. Walter W. Pickard. Dr. Patterson ended his 40-year career in Chapel Hill in a partnership with Drs. William Joyner, J. Kempton Jones, and W. Julio Angelis.

At least 14 Chapel Hillians died in the European theater of operations. In addition to John Yates Varley, Alexander King died in Italy; Grady Pope King died in Luxemburg; Bynum Griffin Crabtree went down over the English Channel; James Finley Spear, Jr. crashed into the North Sea after his plane was damaged over Germany; Clarence Roland Jones died in England from wounds received in France; Harold Green Bowden, Clyde W. Brewer, and Carl Craig Hogan died in France; Joseph Riddick Blackwood, Lawrence Flinn, and Whitney Fulton Poythress died in action in Germany; Winslow Philip Cole died from an accidental gunshot in Germany on 19 June 1945—40 days after the German surrender. Alexander Patterson "Byng" Farrar was master of an Army tanker ferrying high-octane fuel from Southhampton to the Continent when it exploded on 9 April 1945, killing Farrar and his entire 17-member crew.

"Byng's" father, Preston C. Farrar, began teaching English at UNC in 1927. After graduating from Amherst in 1932, Byng returned to Chapel Hill, where he continued his interest in boats. Early in the war, he worked in the North Carolina Shipbuilding Company yards near Wilmington while the firm was building several Liberty Ships that would carry names familiar to Chapel Hillians—the SS *Cornelia P. Spencer*, the SS *Horace Williams*, the SS *David L. Swain*, the SS *Elisha Mitchell*, the SS *Kemp P. Battle*, and the SS *James Sprunt*. After a stint as a shipbuilder in Newport News, Byng took a merchant marine exam, qualified as a master, and began ferrying gasoline through the dangerous waters of the English Channel. A few weeks after his death, the Maritime Commission honored his memory by naming a Liberty Ship the SS *Byng Farrar*.

Scores of other Chapel Hillians served in Europe and returned. Archibald Henderson, Jr. flew 30 missions over Europe in Liberator bombers, between flights playing for the Army tennis team at Wimbledon. Lt. Lindsay C. Neville won the Bronze Star in North Africa and was preparing for the Normandy invasion when he came down with typhus fever. Capt. A.L. Cheek, Jr. also fought in North Africa and later won the Croix de Guerre for meritorious service during the liberation of France. Navy Lt. Sheldon White was an engineering officer in landing craft at Sicily, Salerno, Anzio, and Normandy, then transferred to the Pacific after V-E Day.

Staff Sgt. Melville Jordan landed at Omaha Beach on D-Day, surviving a murderous struggle that left half his battalion dead. Navy Lt. Coit M. Coker, the son of Dr. R.E. Coker, spent a terrifying D-Day. On his way to the beach, his landing craft ran atop German underwater barriers, forcing him to swim ashore carrying 65 pounds of radio equipment through withering gunfire and a sea filled with wounded, drowning, and dead soldiers. There was no respite on the beach, defended by prime German detachments from atop the Atlantic Wall. Wounded in the legs by shrapnel, Coker stayed at his radio, directing incoming cover fire from ships offshore and earning the Silver Star for displaying "marked bravery and great knowledge of his profession." Coker remained in the action to enlarge the beachhead, and it was well into July before he first removed the bloodied shoes and trousers he had worn ashore.

Roland "Sandy" McClamroch spent 20 days in the front lines during the Battle of the Bulge, then accompanied his command across the Rhine at Wesel. Sgt. Claude E. Teague, Jr. also fought in the Battle of the Bulge, continued through Germany, and was engaged in mopping up operations in the Austrian Alps when Germany surrendered on 7 May 1945. Roland Giduz received shrapnel wounds in France and discovered during his treatment that he was also suffering from "trenchfoot," a malady caused by frozen tissue.

In addition to Arnold Breckenridge, Thomas Benjamin Pritchard, Jr., and Foy Roberson, Jr., all of whom died in airborne accidents on the West Coast, at least five Chapel Hillians died in the Pacific theater of operations: Marshall Reid Cheek, Ervid Eric Ericson, Vernon Strowd Hogan, John Wesley Umstead III, and Henry McGilbert Wagstaff.

Roy Armstrong, who graduated from UNC in 1926 and returned to study law in 1939, left as director of the UNC College Guidance Program to serve first as an armed guard on a merchant marine ship and later on duty with the Army in the Pacific. After the war he returned to UNC as director of admissions before becoming director of the Morehead Foundation. Three sons of Charles T. Woollen served in the Navy air forces in the Pacific. Lt. Charles C. Phillips, son of Mr. and Mrs. Guy B. Phillips, flew 51 missions aboard B-25s during the last 13 months of the war on low-level strafing runs on New Guinea, the Philippines, the China mainland, and the Formosa area. His brothers, Guy, Jr. and Craig also served in the Pacific.

Coast Guard Seaman 1st Class George Pickard, the son of UNC Superintendent of Buildings and Grounds Alfred Pickard, crossed the equator 14 times on troop ships and lowered the ramps of landing craft in the invasions of the Marshalls, Saipan, Anguar, Leyte, and Luzon. His cousins Thomas James Wilson III and Peter Wilson, the sons of Dean of Admissions Thomas James Wilson II, both served

Sunday morning on McCorkle Place.

Above: The early morning summer sunlight casts haunting shadows across the lawn of the Horace Williams House, sitting in seeming isolation on the eastern rim of the village plateau.

Left: The "Horace Williams House Quilt," which also depicts 20 other buildings of historical interest in Chapel Hill, hangs in the Horace Williams House. Some thirty women from the Chapel Hill Preservation Society spent the summer of 1977 designing and sewing the quilt.

In the village cemetery off South Road, an iron fence encloses the graves of five Dialectic Society members. The first of them to die was Zenas Johnston, who was one of three students who succumbed to what was probably typhoid fever in August and September 1825.

The Philanthropic Society burial plot contains the bodies of five members who died between 1845 and 1882. The pillar to the left marks the grave of sophomore John A. Burton, son of North Carolina Governor Hutchins G. Burton.

A maple grows at an oblique angle out of the grave of Charles A. Brewster of New York City, who died in Chapel Hill on 1 March 1815 while he was a guest of UNC President Robert H. Chapman. Chapman's daughter Margaretta Blanche, who died in November 1815 at age 15, lies to the left of Brewster beneath a cedar that was removed in 1984.

An autumn sky and late blooming crepe myrtle complement the Archibald Henderson House on East Franklin Street, former home of the renowned mathematics professor and biographer of George Bernard Shaw.

Two young girls stroll beneath the fall foliage of East Franklin Street, heading downtown.

Boxwoods and the crepe myrtles of August lend grandeur to the Lloyd-Wiley House on West Cameron Avenue. In 1934, when Dorothy and William Leon Wiley moved into the house once owned by cotton manufacturer Tom Lloyd, it had no electricity, water, nor furnace, 125 windows were broken, and the roof was more picturesque than functional. Now sound and ensured of survival, the Wiley home is one of the most treasured historical houses in Chapel Hill.

Future Episcopalian Bishop William Mercer Green built this house at 513 East Franklin Street for Professor Charles Phillips. The Presbyterian Church purchased the home in 1889, used it as a manse, and sold it in 1966. It is now the home of Duke Law School Professor Walter E. Dellinger and his wife Annie, a UNC professor with the Institute of Government.

Autumn leaves litter the lawn of the Widow Puckett House on East Franklin Street. Purchased by the university from Professor Denison Olmstead in 1825, what is probably the second oldest home in Chapel Hill has been the residence of former Chancellor Robert House since 1934.

Mrs. Lula Foushee Gattis, the widow of physician Dr. Robert Lee Gattis, ran a boarding house out of her home on Cameron Avenue early in this century. One of her boarders was the young Frank Porter Graham.

The azaleas and wisteria of April festoon the "Pigeon Box" beside the public library on East Franklin Street. Professor Collier Cobb built the original living quarters in 1895 and enlarged the house as his family grew.

In 1887, James Lee Love, who married Cornelia Spencer's daughter June, built this residence, which now stands next to the President's House on East Franklin Street. Ferris W. Womack, UNC Vice Chancellor of Business and Finance, now lives in the so-called "House of Seven Gables," across the street from his harmonica teacher, Chancellor Robert House.

When Kemp Plummer Battle returned to Chapel Hill in 1876 as President of UNC, he purchased the family home from his father, Judge William Horn Battle. An inveterate punner, Kemp Battle gave the language a novel twist in naming his house "Senlac." Senlac was the name of the hill on which the Battle of Hastings was fought in 1099. Later, Senlac became known as "Battle," a transformation that induced the playful president to replace "Battle House" with "Senlac."

Betty Smith purchased the old Andrew Mickle home on East Rosemary Street with the early royalties from A Tree Grows in Brooklyn. She later wrote of her home, "There is a kind of immortality about it. I shall never be forgotten as long as people pass by and say, 'That was Betty Smith's house.'"

J. Mayron "Spike" Saunders edited the Daily Tar Heel as an undergraduate. He returned to Chapel Hill in 1927 on the staff of the General Alumni Association, serving as editor of the Alumni Review and as a long-term executive secretary until his retirement in 1970. In the mid-1930s, Spike planted a wisteria sprout beside an oak in the yard of his home in Westwood. The two growths have now enjoyed a close, if not precisely symbiotic, relationship for half a century.

Merchant H.H. "Hoot" Patterson bought this house at 403 West Cameron Avenue from Dr. Thomas W. Harris in 1888. The grandfather of recently deceased Dr. Fred Patterson, H.H. Patterson was the first Chapel Hillian to install indoor plumbing.

The Sam Phillips house at the northeast corner of Hillsborough and Franklin streets now serves as the Delta Delta Delta sorority house.

Professor William Hooper III built this house at 504 East Franklin Street in 1814 for his bride Fanny Jones. It is now the home of Kay and Georgia Carroll Kyser.

Stephanie and Philip Ben purchased the "Sam Phillips Law Office" in 1982 and spent most of 1983 and 1984 turning it into a family residence. Workers were careful to preserve the original features during the restoration and equally careful in matching an addition to the rear that has doubled the floor space. The Bens are house parents to the Delta Delta Delta sorority women next door in the Sam Phillips House.

In a 1923 letter to Chapel Hill artist Mary Graves Rees, former UNC President Edwin A. Alderman referred to an inspiration he had in the fall of 1897, "Looking out of my window on the first floor of South Building, I beheld the old well squalid and ramshackled. I determined to tear it down and put something there having beauty." That "something" is now the emblem of UNC, a shelter "derived largely from the Temple of Love in the Garden at Versailles." Old East stands in the background, the oldest state-university building in the United States.

The corn-and-wheat capitals on the columns of the Playmakers Theatre represented more than architectural bric-a-brac when they were installed in 1851. They symbolized the Southern belief that the agrarian life, even with the stigma of slavery, was superior in quality to the industrialism of the North.

Master ballet instructor Barbara Bounds Malone, who has sent almost 90 students to the North Carolina School of the Arts, positions members from the cast of "A Tribute to Degas" on the steps of the Playmakers Theatre, originally named Smith Hall in honor of Benjamin Smith, a colonel in the Revolution, a governor of North Carolina, and "the first benefactor of the University."

John Sprunt Hill built the Carolina Inn and donated it to UNC. Reporter J.A.C. "Jim" Dunn has observed that "desk clerks, porters, etc., give the impression that they work there not to run a hotel but simply to be part of the Inn. The result is a slightly unhinged atmosphere of charming chaos." The Inn remains the favorite gathering place for returning alumni.

William Lanier Hunt donated the Hunt Arboretum to the N.C. Botanical Garden, which he helped to found. He is a member of the Royal Historical Society, and he has gained international recognition as an expert in designing and restoring botanical gardens. Mr. Hunt is a familiar sight each Sunday morning in the lobby of the Carolina Inn, usually reading his newspaper, but this day perusing Archibald Henderson's The Campus of the First State University.

A pretty young mother and her daughters relax during a tour of the Ackland Art Museum.

Built at a cost of $15,000 in 1907 and extensively remodeled in 1929, the official President's House is now the home of William Clyde Friday, who will retire on 1 July 1986 after a tenure of 30 years as president of The University of North Carolina.

Professor Elisha Mitchell called on memories from his native Connecticut when building the first of Chapel Hill's famed stone walls. This wall borders the grounds of the president's house, running along Raleigh Street.

The early morning sunlight breaks across the former "John Huskey House," now the residence of architect Jon Condoret and his family. In 1977 the Chapel Hill Preservation Society moved the then delapidated structure from 215 East Rosemary Street to its present location on Henderson Street. Condoret designed a spacious addition to the rear which has transformed a building once valued solely for its longevity into a beautiful and comfortable home and an asset to its neighborhood.

A couple takes a familiar shortcut across the Coker Arboretum, named for Dr. W.C. Coker, the erstwhile banker turned botanist who converted a swampy cow pasture into a laboratory-garden stocked with approximately five-hundred species of domestic and exotic plantlife.

The sundial/rose garden in the Morehead Planetarium parking lot has joined the Old Well and the Carolina Inn as a "must" point of call for visiting alumni. Many remember Nancy Hilliard's old "Crystal Palace," which occupied the small knoll leveled in preparation for the parking lot.

The John Motley Morehead Foundation built the Morehead Planetarium, which also houses the foundation offices, the Genevieve B. Morehead Art Gallery, the Copernican Orrery, and a luxurious executive suite used for meetings and by very special visitors. All the American astronauts have trained at the Morehead Planetarium, and visits there have given hundreds of thousands of North Carolina school children their first look at Chapel Hill.

Crepe myrtles in full foliage highlight the steeple of the Presbyterian Church on East Franklin Street. Every president of the University of North Carolina until 1868 was a Presbyterian, as were most of the early faculty. Consequently, Presbyterian influence has always been lively in the village.

Fall crocuses from a long-ago planting bloom between the sidewalk and curb of East Franklin Street.

For many decades church historians believed that Richard Upjohn, famed for his design of Trinity Church in New York City, drew the plans for the original Chapel of the Cross. After an exhaustive search of church records, Archibald Henderson concluded that the chapel was "undoubtedly" modeled after a design in a book on architecture published in 1836 by Henry Hopkins, D.D., Bishop of Vermont. More recent research by Philip A. Rees has revealed that in fact Thomas U. Walter of Philadelphia provided the plans, for a fee of $25.

Left: The bodies of Joseph Caldwell, the first president of UNC, his wife Helen Hogg Hooper Caldwell, and her son William Hooper III lie east of the Caldwell Monument in McCorkle Place. In another view of McCorkle Place (right) as seen from Graham Memorial, Silent Sam gazes over a spot favored by lovers, picnickers, and the indolent.

The "flower ladies," once a sidewalk fixture on Franklin Street, now sell their home-grown flowers in the passageway through the NCNB Plaza and the alleyway beside The Intimate Bookshop.

Proprietor Byron Freeman entertains a regular in the Carolina Coffee Shop.

Only the Danziger sign remains to mark the location of Edward "Papa D" Danziger's once popular Old World Gift Shop on Franklin Street.

As the university spreads, the bicycle becomes an increasingly popular mode of transportation.

Clothed against the weather, shoppers pace determinedly up and down Franklin Street.

A typical Saturday after-the-football-game crowd enjoys a party at the Kappa Alpha house.

Right: Two young Tar Heels inspect progress on the new Student Activities Center off Manning Drive. When completed in time for the 1985-1986 basketball season, the facility will include a 21,000-seat arena, an Olympic-size pool, and offices for the athletic department staff. Hargrove "Skipper" Bowles has headed a construction-fund drive that has gone well over its goal of $34 million.

Below: The Tar Heels come on the field for the homecoming game of 1983 against William and Mary, won by Carolina 51-20.

Bruce Stroud (1891-1955), Chapel Hill's long time Ford dealer, is pictured here in 1938 at the corner of Franklin and Columbia with a 1914 Ford, the first one he ever sold. It had been bought by Ralph Ward, manager of the Durham Hosiery Mill, on Thanksgiving Day 1914. Ward sold it to barber Moody Lloyd, who sold it to pressing club operator Will Morphis, who, in turn, traded in the vehicle on a new Ford.

In 1928, Stroud received his first new Ford of the year, and Louis Graves wrote in the Weekly that the auto was "...a common possession of the village, because Mr. Stroud is taking to ride everybody who wants to go." The New York Sun picked up on the remark and headlined the event seriously, "COMMUNISM IN NORTH CAROLINA."

On another occasion, when Sears and Roebuck began selling tires and batteries, Stroud hung a sign on his entry door that read, "If you get your tires and batteries at Sears, get your free air and water at the post office." (NCC)

on fast carriers. As hanger-deck officer on the *Enterprise*, Thomas Wilson guided his fleet into New Caledonia for the 10 March 1942 landing. Lt. Commander Peter Wilson was aboard the *Yorktown* from the summer of 1944 until the end of the war, a period that encompassed the battles of Leyte Gulf, Luzon, Iwo Jima, Okinawa, and more. He was knocked off his feet by the impact of kamikazes three times on Palm Sunday 1945, christened "Bomb Sunday" by the men aboard the *Yorktown*.

When the war ended on 14 August 1945, Lt. J.G. Dick Jamerson was among the first Americans to enter Tokyo Bay, aboard the super-destroyer *SS Frank Knox*. As the UNC swimming coach beginning in 1938, Jamerson guided teams that captured 12 Southern Conference championships and produced 30 All-Americans.

When the news of the Japanese surrender reached Chapel Hill at 7 p.m. on Tuesday, 14 August, "Suddenly all the village was in a frenzy," reported Louis Graves. "From houses, from the University campus, from business buildings, people came flocking to the central block on Franklin street. Shouting and laughter, added to the pealing of the bell and the blasts from the siren, raised such a din as had never before been heard in Chapel Hill." Pre-Flight and V-12 students, co-eds, and other youths danced joyously in the street. For a while the more sedate were content to stand on the sidewalks and applaud the boisterous merry-makers, but the exhilaration was infectious, and all merged into a happy mass of revelry.

Rolls of toilet paper left trails of tissue to snag on the elms and utility lines. When firemen Jake Leigh and Frank Partin

answered a false alarm downtown, their trucks became chariots of triumph as the celebrants clambered aboard to arouse onlookers to greater frenzy. The crowd started a bonfire at Franklin and Henderson, and "brushed aside" a policeman who attempted to put it out. "This was a once-in-a-lifetime occasion," Louis Graves pronounced, "when police control. . .had to be canceled." When the celebration ended about 1 a.m., the only malicious damage had occurred at Fowler's food store two doors east of the Carolina Theatre, where unknown parties had broken a window to steal a couple of bottles of wine.

It was only after the war was over that Chapel Hillians learned that their neighbor Dr. William deB. MacNider had taken part in the Manhattan Project, providing advice on methods to avoid radiation poisoning, a specialty of his since he had published his first article on uranium toxicity in 1916.

By the conclusion of World War II, Chapel Hill had become a mecca for writers of widely diverse purpose and style, and "cultural boosters" were predicting that the village would become an important and a permanent "literary colony."

Born in Salisbury in 1877 to John Steele and Elizabeth Brownrigg Cain Henderson, Archibald Henderson enrolled in UNC in 1894, lived with his uncle Major William Cain on the second floor of Nancy Hilliard's old "Crystal Palace," and graduated first in his class in 1898. He stayed on as an instructor in mathematics, earned his M.A. and Ph.D., and married Minna Curtis Bynum in 1903. Henderson later studied at Cambridge, the Sorbonne, and with Albert Einstein in Berlin. He replaced his uncle as chairman of the Mathematics Department in 1920 and became a Kenan Professor in 1925, but Henderson was to leave his mark primarily as a man of letters.

An early admirer of George Bernard Shaw, Henderson began a correspondence with the Irish playwright in 1903. The men became friends, and Henderson became Shaw's "official" biographer, eventually writing hundreds of articles and five book-length biographical and critical studies. Henderson also produced other critical studies of modern drama, a history of the settling of the American West, a history of the physical development of UNC, plus books and hundreds of articles dealing with North Carolina history.

A substantial contribution to the study of North Carolina history came from a transplanted Texan in 1937. Guion Griffis and Guy Johnson met while they were undergraduates at Baylor. He earned an M.A. at the University of Chicago in 1923, and that fall they married while both had positions at Baylor, she as head of the Department of Journalism at the College for Women and he as a research assistant. They came to UNC in 1924 as research assistants in Dr. Howard W. Odum's newly formed Institute for Research in Social Science. Both earned their Ph.D.'s in 1927 and remained with the Institute, she for 10

Frederick Henry Koch (1877-1944), left, and Paul Green (1894-1981), right, are pictured here in the 1920s. Koch came to UNC in 1918 from the University of North Dakota and created the Playmakers. Green was one of Koch's prize students, graduating in 1921. Green joined the faculty in 1923 and became famous as a Pulitzer Prize winning dramatist. He married Elizabeth Lay, a fellow Playmaker and playwright. (NCC)

years, he until he retired as Kenan Professor of Sociology and Anthropology in 1969.

For over a decade, Guion Griffis Johnson perused old newspapers, exhausted the published material on North Carolina history, and plowed through a prodigious number and range of documents. She organized the monumental store of information into *Ante-Bellum North Carolina: A Social History* (1937). Instantly recognized for its quality, it remains the finest volume on North Carolina. Along with Dr. Odum, the Johnsons were pioneers in the study of Negro culture, and they have spent six decades working on the national and international levels for improvements in race relations.

The most important literary artist to reside in Chapel Hill between the wars was, of course, Paul Green. Born on 17 March 1894 to Harnett County farmer William Green and his second wife Betty Byrd Green, Paul Green had graduated from Buie's Creek Academy, spent two years as a high school principal, and played professional baseball in Lillington before entering UNC in 1916. As a freshman he wrote the play *Surrender to the Enemy*, based on the Ellie Swain romance and performed in the Forest Theatre by the senior class. Green left during World War I for combat duty in Belgium, returned to his classes, and began to write plays for production by Proff Koch's Playmakers. On one play, "Blackbeard, Pirate of the Carolina Coast," he collaborated with fellow Playmaker Elizabeth Lay, a native of Concord, New Hampshire, and a graduate of St. Mary's in Raleigh, where her father was rector.

Paul Green and Elizabeth Lay married in July 1922, and in 1923 they built a house on East Franklin which they shared periodically with his two and her four sisters. After the birth of Paul Green, Jr., the Greens built a house in The Glen off East Franklin, where a daughter, Nancy Byrd, was born. Their home soon became a haven for visiting artists and liberal thinkers and the editorial headquarters for *The*

Literary Lantern, a review begun by UNC English professors Raymond Adams and Addison Hibbard.

Green was a lifelong opponent of capital punishment and a lifelong proponent of expanded civil rights for Negroes and for political liberalism in general, themes he included in his constant outpouring of folk plays. Drawing on the Sam Morphis story and other sources, he wrote *In Abraham's Bosom*, which played on Broadway and earned Green the Pulitzer Prize for drama in 1927. He followed that success with *The Field God* and a year studying the German theater on a Guggenheim fellowship.

The Greens returned to the Glen, renting their Franklin Street house to short-story writer Wilbur Daniel Steele, a four-time winner of the O. Henry Prize. A native of Greensboro, Steele had published five volumes of stories previously and maintained his prolific output in Chapel Hill until the death of his wife Margaret in 1931. He moved to Connecticut and later wrote *The Man without a God*, a novella partially set in Chapel Hill.

After the birth of daughters in 1930 and 1931, Green worked on movie scripts in Hollywood for Warner Brothers. His own play *The House of Connelly* was the basis for the film "Carolina," starring Lionel Barrymore and Janet Gaynor. Green did not approve of the adaptation, and he did not like the movie. After another stint in Hollywood during World War II, he commented bitterly, "The men who control the movies are menaces to civilization."

In 1933, Green bought 200 acres off Raleigh Road out of the Hargrave/Strowd plantation, a tract extending from

Morehead Planetarium donor John Motley Morehead (1870-1965), left, and President of American Machine and Foundry Rufus Lenoir Patterson (1872-1943), right, are pictured here near the time of the Thanksgiving Day, 1931, dedication of their gift to the university, the Bell Tower. Chester Meneely, head of the company that cast the twelve bells (78% copper and 22% tin) played, first, The Bells of St. Mary's, followed by one of Morehead's favorite hymns, How Tedious and Tasteless the Hours When Jesus No Longer I See.

On 20 October 1956, UNC beat Maryland 34-6 for its first football victory after five losses, and Byron Freeman, now proprietor of the Carolina Coffee Shop, played Praise God From Whom All Blessings Flow on the bells, in spirited celebration. (NCC)

Joe Jones, left, lived with Mrs. Julia Graves and her daughter Mary Rees while he was a student and afterwards while he was a reporter and the advertising manager of the Chapel Hill Weekly.

Betty Smith (1896-1972), below, author of A Tree Grows in Brooklyn *and the wife of Joe Jones, held a number of jobs before her novels made her financially independent. One job was as a "complaint answerer" for a mail order house. (NCC)*

Greenwood Road across the By-Pass. He built a home on Greenwood Road, began developing the area, wrote two novels, and continued to experiment with what he called the "symphonic drama," a dramatic form incorporating "folk song, poetry, dance, pantomime, and even the metal speech of the grisly microphone and echo chamber." One of his early efforts, *Johnny Johnson*, incorporated music by Kurt Weill, who had come to Chapel Hill to work with him. Then in 1936, Green began work on a play he had been considering since 1929, *The Lost Colony*. Lamar Stringfield and Adeline McCaull composed the score, and the success of *The Lost Colony* confirmed Green's opinion that he had discovered a valuable and lucrative new genre.

The combination of Paul Green and Proff Koch attracted scores of aspiring and working writers to Chapel Hill in the 1930s and the early 1940s. Several of them were to enjoy successful careers, perhaps more successful in terms of lucre than in artistic creativity.

Noel Houston arrived from Oklahoma in 1937 after work-

ing as a reporter and after being turned down by the Yale Drama School because he did not want to earn a degree. Paul Green invited him to come "and take as many or as few courses as you like. Writing's the main thing." Houston came, and like Green incorporated liberal political themes in his early dramatic efforts. His *According to Law* won an American Civil Liberties Union prize in 1939, went on to Broadway, and established Houston as a writer. He turned to writing short stories for the *New Yorker, Holiday*, and other slick magazines, and his 1946 novel *The Great Promise* enjoyed large sales.

Houston and his wife, the former Kay Replogel, built a house on Greenwood Road, where Houston continued to work until his death in 1958, always a believer that Chapel Hill was "the last real stronghold of liberalism in the South." His son Paul Green Houston was an award-winning reporter for the Los Angeles *Times* during the Watergate troubles.

Proff Koch's emphasis on folk drama brought Josephina Niggli to Chapel Hill. Born in Monterrey, Mexico, and educated in San Antonio, Niggli enrolled as a Playmaker in 1935, published *Mexican Folk Plays* in 1938, and organized a set of interwoven short stories into the novel-like *Mexican Village* in 1945. Her play *The Red Velvet Goat* was immensely popular in England during World War II; her novel *Step Down, Elder Brother* was a Book-of-the-Month-Club selection in 1948. She later wrote screen plays and helped with the adaptation of *Mexican Village*, which was filmed as "Sombrero" in 1953. After teaching in England briefly in the mid-1950s, Niggli joined the faculty at Western Carolina University, where she remained until her death in 1983.

Niggli said the thing that kept people in Chapel Hill was "chapelhillitis," explaining that "the curious thing about this disease is that you either get it within 24 hours after you enter the town, or you never do get it at all."

The writer who has sold more books than any other Chapel Hill author developed "chapelhillitis" on contact.

Betty Smith was born Elizabeth Wehner in 1896 in Brooklyn, the daughter of poor Austrian immigrants. When she was 12, her father died, forcing her to drop out of school. Nevertheless, determined to study writing and acting, at 17 she enrolled in special classes at the University of Michigan. While in Ann Arbor, she married H.E. Smith. In the early 1930s, after the marriage had dissolved, Mrs. Smith took her two daughters to New Haven and studied for three years under George Pierce Baker in the Yale Drama School. She then acted in summer stock in Detroit, wrote feature newspaper articles, and signed on with the WPA Federal Theatre Project, which awarded her a scholarship in 1938 to study playwrighting at UNC. Five minutes after arriving at the bus station downtown, she told her daughters, "I am going to live here till I die."

During the next five years, she lived in a cottage on North Street rented from Miss Alice Jones and wrote over 70 plays, most of them one act in length and many of them written jointly with Robert Voris Finch, with whom she had studied at Yale. When her scholarship ended, a Rockefeller Foundation grant of $1000 per year for two years allowed her to remain in Chapel Hill, where she spent the better part of the two years working on an autobiographical novel based on her impoverished childhood in Brooklyn.

A dozen publishers rejected the 1000-page manuscript before Harper and Row accepted it, cut it in half, and set the publication date for 18 Agusut 1943. While the book was being edited, Smith struck up a correspondence with Joe Jones, the author of a Chapel Hill *Weekly* column on Army life she had come to admire. Ironically, she and Jones were writers who had both lived in Chapel Hill for almost six years without meeting. Jones came to UNC from Berryville, Virginia, in 1927, was an associate editor of the *Tar Heel*, and worked part-time for Louis Graves on the *Weekly*. In August 1937, he was passing through town when he stopped by to see Graves. Within half an hour, Graves had him on a reporting assignment, and Jones stayed on to relieve Graves of many of his publishing duties—writing, editing, selling ads, and dealing with circulation business.

Inducted into the Army in December 1942, Jones began sending Graves articles about his life as a buck private in boot camp and in coastal artillery units in Virginia, articles published by Harper and Brothers in 1944 as *1-B Soldier*—Jones was classified 1-B because of a childhood accident that left him blind in one eye. In one of his letters, Jones invited Betty Smith to visit him in Norfolk, Virginia. She arrived on Thursday, 7 August 1943, he proposed on Friday, and they were married on Saturday, nine days before the publication of *A Tree Grows in Brooklyn*.

Within weeks the novel sold 300,000 copies. Twentieth-Century Fox paid $55,000 for the film rights and turned

what Smith considered an excellent adaptation over to first-time director Elia Kazan. Kazan coaxed superb performances from lead actors Dorothy McGuire, Joan Blondell, Lloyd Nolan, Peggy Ann Garner, and James Dunn, whose portrayal of the drunken father won him the Academy Award for Best Supporting Actor in 1945.

After the war, Joe Jones returned to the *Weekly*, and Betty Smith returned to writing, working under more comfortable conditions in the renovated "Andrew Mickle" home on Rosemary Street, which she had purchased. Her play *The First in Heart* was produced at Yale in November 1947, and a musical version of *Tree* enjoyed a resounding success on Broadway in 1951. However, Smith would never again

Robert Watson Winston (1860-1944), the brother of one-time UNC President George Tayloe Winston, was the first student to enter UNC when it re-opened in 1877. After a notable career in the law, Robert retired to Chapel Hill in 1923 to live in the Carolina Inn, to study at UNC, and to fulfill a lifelong desire to write. At age 68 he began a biography of Andrew Johnson, followed by biographies of Jefferson Davis, Robert E. Lee, Horace Williams, and an autobiography, It's a Far Cry. Always gracious, Winston spent most of his evenings in the Carolina Inn lobby, or weather permitting on the porch or lawn, at the center of an admiring entourage. In apparently good health, he exercised on the Inn lawn on the morning of 13 November 1944, then died quietly that night.

The Carolina Inn opened in 1924 with 75 rooms, each with its own bath. Guests were extended the privileges of the Hope Valley County Club. Daily rates were $3.00 for a single, $5.00 for a double.

After the university took over the Inn, it achieved another distinction, according to the Chapel Hill Weekly. *It became the only place in town that charged—5¢—for using the telephone. (NCC)*

achieve either the artistic or financial success of her first novel. After having written *Tomorrow Will Be Better* in 1948, *Maggie Now* in 1958, and *Joy in the Morning* in 1963, she told her publisher, "I wish I had written my books in reverse."

Betty Smith divorced Joe Jones in 1951 and married old acquaintance Robert V. Finch in 1956. Following Finch's death from a heart attack on 4 February 1959, Smith remained in Chapel Hill until she entered a convalescent home in Shelton, Connecticut in late 1971. She died there on 17 January 1972. Joe Jones left the *Weekly* in 1964 to edit the *Alumni Review* until he retired in 1966. After living with a sister in Albany, Georgia, for a few years, Jones retired permanently to Berryville, Virginia.

When World War II ended, "cultural boosters" were more convinced than ever that Chapel Hill was destined to become famous as a quiet, homey "writers' colony." The great influx of veterans after the war, the expansion of the UNC Medical School and the creation of Memorial Hospital, and the phenomenal growth of the Research Triangle Park collectively have given Chapel Hill an urbanity that embraces the arts, but which dictates a future more soundly than ever entrenched in education, science, and an expanding economy.

ATTENTION!
Students and Townspeople

The Forest Theatre Shots in the Movie about the Life of Tom Wolfe, Famous Carolina Alumnus, Will Be Taken at Noon Thursday

THE PUBLIC IS INVITED

The Movie "Takes" Will Be Followed by a Talk on Pictures by
Mr. Arthur Ripley, Prominent Director

Thursday, October 26
12 O'clock Noon
FOREST THEATRE
CHAPEL HILL

If You Want to See and Take Part in a Movie in the Making,
YOU ARE CORDIALLY INVITED TO BE PRESENT

Arthur D. Ripley (1895-1961), film director and producer, came to Chapel Hill in October 1944 to film background material for a movie based on Thomas Wolfe's novel Look Homeward Angel, *sponsored by David O. Selznick.*

One scene was shot in the Forest Theatre: 400 students and townspeople gathered, and, to the baton of UNC music department legend Glen Haydon, sang "Hark the Sound." The handbill shown above advertised the scene.

The next week, Ripley set up his camera on the quadrangle behind South Building, and students dressed in 1910s costumes walked past to recreate the Tom Wolfe time period.

Ripley wrote a screenplay in 1947 and picked Don Taylor to portray "Eugene Gant," but a disagreement with Selznick ended plans for the movie.

Ripley's son, A.D., Jr., was so enchanted with Chapel Hill that he entered graduate school here in the autumn of 1945 and received his M.A. in 1947.

In the picture to the right, A.D., Jr. is far left beside his father, who has one foot resting on the camera dolly. (NCC)

The "Flower Ladies" have been a tradition in Chapel Hill since the 1920s. When this photo was taken on 5 March 1955, diagonal parking was still in force on two-laned Franklin Street, and flowers were 25 cents per bunch. In 1971, when the town banned all steet vending to clear the sidewalks in the business district, NCNB made the NCNB Plaza passageway and Watts Hill made the alleyway beside The Intimate Bookshop available to the ladies, who still remain in both locations. (Courtesy of Roland Giduz)

VII
A Village No More
1945 to Present

The population of Chapel Hill grew by 251% from 3654 in 1940 to 9177 in 1950. Measured by percentage, only Jacksonville with its nearby Marine base grew faster in North Carolina, from 873 to 3960. Civilian enrollment in UNC dropped from approximately 4100 in 1941 to 1681 in the fall of 1944, but rebounded to approximately 6800 in the fall of 1946, including about 4500 veterans, most of whom were taking advantage of the $90-per-month educational allowance provided by the G.I. Bill. UNC eased the massive housing problem somewhat by purchasing pre-fabricated housing put up during wartime at nearby Camp Butner and elsewhere. Workmen dismantled the units and ultimately reassembled 356 of them in Victory Village, across Manning Drive from Memorial Hospital. Veterans with families rented the two-bedroom units for $28 per month.

In January 1947, UNC President Frank Porter Graham drove the first nail to start work on a Federal Housing Administration project to build 30 $6000-$6500 homes on Rogerson Drive beyond

Betsy Anne Bowman, the daughter of Judge and Mrs. Frederick O. Bowman of Chapel Hill, christened the Liberty ship SS Chapel Hill Victory in Baltimore on 4 January 1944. The Chapel Hill Victory carried its capacity of 1600 troops across the Atlantic on several runs, including those bringing troops home after the war. A Rotterdam line bought the ship in 1947 and renamed it the Alwaki. The China Union Lines of Taiwan purchased it in 1964 and sailed it as the Kaohsiung Victory before scrapping it in 1974. (NCC)

Glen Lennox and the Oakwood development, with veterans being given preference as purchasers. In the spring of 1946, Collier Cobb, Jr. and C.E. Hornaday bought 13 acres north of town and began developing Noble Heights. In addition, John Umstead was developing Elkin Hills, Kemp Cole was building Dogwood Acres, and new homes were beginning to dot Mount Bolus. Well over 100 student families found cheap housing in a trailer park on the Pittsboro highway beyond the Chatham County line. The park had only one telephone, but within a year it had its own "baby boom," with 30 new infants and more on the way.

UNC enrollment began to decline in the late 1940s as the wave of GI's passed, and developer William Muirhead provided further relief from the housing crisis in December 1949 when he began taking applications for the 314 apartments he had built in the Glen Lennox development bordering Raleigh Road. Muirhead began the Glen Lennox Shopping Center in the winter of 1950-1951 and also continued to add apartments until they totaled 440 in the fall of 1953, by which time the growing number of children in the neighborhood had induced the school board to build Glenwood Elementary School.

In *Inside USA*, author John Gunther heaped praise on the university, while observing that the town of 1947 "looks informal, comfortable, and a bit down at the heels." Earlier concern over downtown deterioration and fear of haphazard development had led to the creation of a town planning board in 1941. Col. Joseph Hyde Pratt was the first chairman, followed by Dr. Herman G. Baity and, in 1943, by Collier Cobb, Jr. William Meade Prince, Dr. J. Penrose Harland, Judge L.J. Phipps, and John Foushee were early members. After consulting with Durham architect Archie R. Davis, who had trained in the Chapel Hill office

of university architect Arthur C. Nash, the board agreed on a unifying plan based on a Colonial-Georgian style of architecture. They then began the task of convincing property owners to accept their recommendations.

Attorney John T. Manning and his aunt Miss Alice Jones led the way by erecting the first new structure adhering to the "Williamsburg Plan" in 1940 at the southeast corner of Rosemary and Henderson, a building that served first as John Manning's law office before S.H. Basnight moved his builder's hardware business there from 102 West Franklin soon after the war, afterward enlarging the building by adding several apartments. The second female to receive an undergraduate degree from UNC, Miss Jones had retired to Chapel Hill after a career of teaching in Goldsboro public schools and at St. Mary's and Winthrop colleges. She died unmarried on 8 November 1964.

Two other buildings followed the "Williamsburg Plan" before World War II: the Carolina Theatre and the Carl Smith Building on North Columbia. Construction essentially ceased during wartime, but the post-war boom literally lined Franklin Street with 25 buildings exhibiting the colonial style, including the Farmer's Diary Co-Operative, Hazzard Motor Company, the new bus station, Fowler's Food Store and Fowler's Gulf station next door. The Jefferson Standard offices and the Western Union in midtown underwent remodeling to adopt the colonial motif. Collier Cobb, Jr. remained chairman of the planning board after a 1947 reorganization that saw Vic Huggins, Nicholas Jay Demerath, and John A. Parker become members.

The first serious move to expand the original 1851 border occurred in 1945 when the aldermen considered extending the town limits north to Bolin Creek and south beyond Eben Merritt's service station on Pittsboro Road. The new territory would have increased the current property valuation of $3,950,000 by $1,412,000; but the venture would also have cost an estimated $11,000 for street improvements, lighting, and police and fire protection, plus a prohibitive $281,000 for sewage disposal facilities.

It was not until June 1950 that the aldermen voted to extend the town limits to include the Northside School so the city could provide lights and police protection. Then on 31 July 1950 the aldermen voted unanimously to annex 275 acres, 105 houses, and approximately 355 people living on both sides of Franklin Street east of the original limits. A third annexation followed on 25 December 1951 when the city absorbed the Westwood area between Pittsboro Road and Pritchard Branch southwest of town. Thereafter, annexation became commonplace.

James and John Webb, California natives, designed many of the post-war quality homes in the Chapel Hill-Durham area after they joined other architects in forming Architectural Associates in 1949. After earning a master's degree in city planning at MIT, James Webb came to UNC

The Westwood area was officially annexed on Christmas Day, 1951, and two days later Chief Sloan (right), town manager Thomas Rose (holding the post hole diggers) and Mayor E.S. Lanier (holding the shovel) helped to erect the appropriate signs that solemnized the event.

Town officials say that under normal conditions they do not send six workers to plant one sign post. (Courtesy of Roland Giduz)

in 1947 as a professor in the Department of City and Regional Planning. His brother John joined him in 1948, fresh from working on housing projects in Birmingham, Alabama. In addition to major prospects statewide, they began to design houses tailored to the individual characteristics of the buyers. Earl Wynn was one of the first to move into a "Webb House," beginning a list that has grown to include Albert Coates and approximately 140 others.

Chapel Hill ceased to be a one-bank town in 1953, but only after a protracted struggle that pitted Bank of Chapel Hill executives and stockholders against those who wished to become their competitors. On 3 October 1950, 125 interested persons gathered at the Carolina Inn to discuss a 1300-signature petition recently submitted by Durham Bank and Trust company officials, including Chairman of the Board George Watts Hill, to the State Commissioner of Banking asking for permission to establish a second bank in Chapel Hill, the only North Carolina city with more than 10,000 population which had only a single bank. Thirty-five opponents spoke against the proposal, most of whom were stockholders in the Bank of Chapel Hill. The commissioner of banking rejected the bid, but the rejection did not stop those who were determined to open a second bank.

By 1952 it was evident that some party would soon win approval to start a new bank, although competition could hardly have benefited borrowers in those halcyon days of low interest. Of the approximately $1 million the Bank of Chapel Hill had out in loans, $100,000 was at 3%, and most of the rest at under 6%. Stockholders remained almost unanimously opposed to a competing bank, but if one had to be, most wanted it to be locally owned. Consequently, several of them signed a petition supporting George Watts Hill's offer to underwrite $200,000 in capital stock in order to get a federal permit for a new bank.

The petition was successful, and in 1953 the University National Bank opened in the Dawson Building on West Franklin Street, with Dr. Oliver K. Cornwell, an alderman and chairman of the UNC Physical Education Department, as president. The University Bank later opened a branch office on the northwest corner of Franklin and Columbia and in 1961 merged with the Durham Bank and Trust company to form Central Carolina Bank. NCNB later bought out the Bank of Chapel Hill.

By breaking the monopoly, the University Bank opened the floodgates, and by the early 1980s there were six banks with 19 local offices and branches serving the community. However, opposition to another form of bank "expansion" came from an entirely different source in 1969 when NCNB officials submitted plans for a new six-story building to occupy the space created by the razing of Eubanks Drug Store, the N.C. Cafeteria, and the old Bank of Chapel Hill. Citizens and city planners objected collectively to the proposed violation of the long-standing three-story limit to buildings in the business district.

Women floated gas-filled balloons up to the proposed height of the building and asked passersby to sign a petition protesting a structure that high on Franklin Street. A flood of signatures persuaded NCNB officials to revise their plans and erect what is now the NCNB Plaza, which stands three-stories tall on Franklin, six stories on Rosemary.

The latest entry in a crowded field is the Village Bank, which opened in the Kroger Plaza in March 1982. Charles T. Roupas, a native of Roanoke, Virginia, had grown familiar with the banking climate in Chapel Hill as an executive for NCNB. He and 26 other incorporators received permission to sell stock in March 1981, quickly

On 30 July 1948 UNC banned dogs from Victory Village. When the fall term began on 15 September, Edwin Tenny of Chapel Hill led a group to the Greensboro dog pound and brought back about 40 dogs, which they then turned loose in the village. That was followed by an impromptu parade through town, pictured here. Tenny is sitting on the left fender of the old Ford (car on right).
The Chinese student sitting on the right fender of the Pontiac is Linclon Kahn, son of the President of the Bank of China. The student holding the "beat Texas" sign was rewarded: UNC won 34-7 before 43,700 fans, a record opening day crowd in Kenan Stadium. (NCC)

Durham architect Archie Davis prepared drawings to show how the south side of Franklin Street would appear if the colonial look were incorporated into every building. Left to right, these drawings reach from the Methodist church to the Carolina Theatre. (NCC)

sold 150,000 shares at $11 per share, and obtained a charter in August 1981. The Orange Federal Savings and Loan Association received its federal charter in 1980, after 61 years of operating first as the Orange County Building and Loan Association and later as the Orange Savings and Loan Association, doing business through tellers at the Bank of Chapel Hill from 1919 to 1951 and occupying a rented house on West Franklin before moving into its present headquarters at Rosemary and Columbia in 1963.

While private enterprise and the expanding university were giving Chapel Hill a physical facelift in the late 1940s and the early 1950s, emerging religious and social problems could not be checked with superficial alterations of custom. For over a decade they would fragment the citizenry of Chapel Hill as it had never been divided before, not even during the desperate years of Reconstruction, when villagers at least had the balm of commonly shared miseries and enemies.

In ante-bellum Chapel Hill the most dramatic protest against slavery occurred in 1858 when Professor Benjamin S. Hedrick and his wife Ellen left the Presbyterian Church because their minister owned slaves and their church condoned slavery. During World War II, the Presbyterian Church was again the location of the most notable questioning of the status quo regarding race relations in Chapel Hill. This time the pastor was the leading advocate of change, this time there was a more even balance of opinion, and this time the debate left the church physically divided.

Born in Nashville in 1906, Charles Miles "Charlie" Jones dropped out of Maryville college, became interested in the ministry, attended Union Seminary in Richmond, and was serving at the Brevard-Davidson River Presbyterian church in 1940 when the elders of the Chapel Hill Prebyterian Church asked him to become their minister. Jones had established an excellent reputation by increasing his congregation from 15 to 200 in five years and by working closely with church and Brevard College youth. But like Presbyterian minister David Ker a century and a half earlier, Jones was privately developing a set of theological and political values that would place him in conflict with the conservative element in Chapel Hill.

Shortly after World War II, Jones noticed that the church steeple was 18 inches out of plumb. Carpenters discovered that rotted supports were causing the tilt, and Rev. Jones had little trouble raising $5100 to restore the steeple. But Rev. Jones' activities had created rifts beneath the steeple that could not be repaired by cash or carpenters.

In 1944, UNC students suggested that Jones invite students from the all-black North Carolina College in Durham to attend interracial Sunday morning breakfasts at the Presbyterian Church. Jones complied; six black students came, and continued to come both to the breakfasts and to services; some in the congregation protested vigorously; others, including Frank Porter Graham, defended Jones by asserting that the church should take the lead in forming better race relations in Chapel Hill; and the entire membership realized that a gauntlet had been thrown—and taken up.

In 1945, several members submitted a petition to the Presbyterian Session calling for Jones' replacement. Frank Porter Graham, W.T. Mattox, Floyd H. Edmister and others answered the petition by pointing out that under Jones' ministry membership had risen from 171 in 1941 to 242 in 1945, that his sermons were fresh and vigorous, that youth activities were increasing, and that Jones' actions had been compatible with the "social implications" of Christ's teachings. The Session responded to the petition with four formal points: Rev. Jones should have "freedom of conscientious judgement"; the church should support justice and good will between races, creeds, and classes; church doors should be open to Negroes, who need not be encouraged to attend; the church stands for progress for all people.

Jones held interracial meals at his church, joined others in calling for black policemen to patrol the black neighborhoods, and attended meetings in the AME Church. When black speakers appeared on campus, they encountered difficulty in finding places to stay. Charlie Jones, Paul Green, and others either quietly put them up

or placed them with black friends, mostly in Durham. However, the calm ended in 1948 when local police arrested four black and four white "freedom riders" after they had had a run-in with white cab drivers. The police called in Jones as a mediator. When he allowed the freedom riders to stay temporarily in the Presbyterian Manse, cab drivers stoned the home, and Jones' behavior became a matter of intense public and congregational debate.

The Rev. Jones and his adversaries maintained an unsteady equilibrium until 1952. Jones was then on a one-year leave of absence working as a consultant for the Save the Children Federation in Kingsport, Tennessee, when a 10-member Judicial Commission of the Orange Presbytery began an investigation of his ministry. In a 6000-word report submitted to church officers on 30 November 1952, the commissioners declared that they had been unable to

James Linwood Sutton (1892-1950) was educated in pharmacology at the Medical College of Virginia. He married Lucy Alderman, then opened his Franklin Street drug store in partnership with his brother-in-law, J.L. Alderman, in 1923. The store was closed for six weeks in 1931 due to the depression, but Sutton and his wife fought back and rebuilt the business. Dr. Sutton had a keen sense of humor, and used this gag photo in ads after World War II. (NCC)

assess Jones' theological convictions, which did not follow the traditional interpretations of church doctrine, and they asked Jones, all nine elders, and the 13 deacons to resign. Their report conceded that Jones was "a preacher without peer," that "he has been a fearless champion of the ideal of the brotherhood of man," and that he had followed his ideals in the face of severe criticism and serious threats.

Jones replied from Kingsport, refusing to resign. The church leaders met on 3 December and unanimously expressed confidence in and support of their minister. The next day *Daily Tar Heel* editor Walt Dear defended Jones in an editorial, crediting both him and his congregation for rising above "denominationalism." On Sunday, 14 December, by secret ballot the congregation voted 156-14 for Jones to remain as pastor. They also requested the Presbytery to withdraw the demand for his resignation. Nonetheless, the Presbytery scheduled a hearing on the matter to be held a month later in Burlington. On 20 January 1953, Frank Porter Graham took time off from his work at the United Nations as a mediator in the Kashmir-Pakistan dispute to fly back home to plead for Jones.

When Senator J. Melville Broughton died on 6 March 1949, Governor Kerr Scott appointed UNC President Frank Porter Graham to fill the vacant seat. Observers were amazed when Governor Scott appointed the state's premier liberal, and they were even more amazed on 27 May 1950 when Graham, bed-ridden with pneumonia, received 303,605 votes in the Democratic primary compared to 250,222 for Raleigh attorney Willis Smith, 58,752 for former Senator Robert "Our Bob" Reynolds, and 5,900 for two other candidates.

In one of the roughest campaigns in North Carolina history, Graham's opponents had accused him of being a socialist and a communist and of being too friendly to Negroes, but Graham had come within 11,269 votes of an absolute majority, and Willis Smith initially conceded that Graham's lead was too great to challenge in a second primary. However, in a now-famous rally at Smith's house on 6 June, friends convinced him to call for a runoff. He

Trees and flowers are the passion and glory of Chapel Hill. The young Cornelia Phillips complained of trees being cut recklessly; in 1840, miller Josiah Maddry planted oaks and elms around town; in 1889, the town fathers made it a misdemeanor punishable by a $20 fine to cut a tree in town; several streets wound around trees in the 1920-1950 era.

TOP LEFT: John "Judge" Brockwell (1845-1930s?), a Confederate veteran who at age 15 married a woman of 30, shown here in 1913 at the present-day NCNB Plaza, had a reputation for "doing nothing," but according to Robert Eubanks he planted the large oaks that today grace Columbia Street. (NCC)

TOP MIDDLE: The new saplings beind "Silent Sam" in McCorkle Place accentuate the barrenness of what is now a beautiful grove of trees. In this picture, the UNC memorial to the Confederate dead, erected 2 June 1913 by the Daughters of the Confederacy, provides the background for World War I student-soldiers Graham Davis Holding (1895-1982), later a successful Charlotte businessman, and his brother Clem Bolton Holding (1896-1968), a prominent Raleigh lawyer active in Democratic party politics. (NCC)

TOP RIGHT: In 1949, the Jaycees won a national award for a tree planting project. Pictured here, left to right, are Kenneth Putnam, unidentified, George Rettie, Wallace Williams, and Charles Phillips. (UNC Photo Lab)

BOTTOM LEFT: Rebekah Huggins (1907-1979), posing here with Chapel Hill Mayor Zebulon Council in Huggins' Hardware, organized the Chapel Hill Chapter of the American Rose Society in 1957, then in January and February 1958, she and her husband Vic promoted the sale of rose bushes with a full-page ad in the Weekly under the headline, MAKE CHAPEL HILL THE BLOOMINGEST TOWN IN THE LAND. They sold over 700 rose bushes in February alone. (Courtesy of Roland Giduz)

BOTTOM RIGHT: George Doak, a transplanted Canadian (since 1948), won several prizes in 1961 for developing lilies such as this one. Addie Williams Totten (1890-1974), a violinist in the University Orchestra, wife of a UNC botany professor, and the town's leading horticulturalist, organized the North Carolina Lily Society, and in 1961 she succeeded in getting the national organization to hold its annual convention at the Carolina Inn, where Doak won his prizes. (UNC Photo Lab)

did and defeated Graham 281,114 to 261,789 on 25 June following another gloves-off campaign. Following his defeat, Graham served six months as a consultant for the Interior Department in arranging a labor agreement for work on defense projects in Alaska, and in April 1951 he accepted appointment as the United Nations Representative for India and Pakistan in their dispute over Kashmir.

In Burlington on 20 January 1953, Frank Porter Graham admitted that Jones had made mistakes but defended him as a meek, hateless, steadfast, courageous man and insisted "this could be solved in a Christian spirit if it's in your hearts to solve it that way." After Jones stated that he did not feel persecuted and that he believed in the simple fundamentals of Christianity which needed no theologian to explain them, the Presbytery voted 54-21 to return the issue to the Judicial Commission. On 25 January, eight members of Jones' church joined 27 other Presbyterians in forming the Convenant Presbyterian Church with English Professor C. Hugh Holman as one of the elders. The new congregation met in the auditorium of the Institute of Pharmacy until the Orange Presbytery dissolved the Covenant Church in January 1954, after a new minister, Vance Barron, had been installed in the Chapel Hill Presbyterian Church.

On 10 February 1953, the Judicial Commission voted unanimously to cut off funds to the Chapel Hill church if Jones did not resign. Jones refused to resign, Frank Porter Graham defended his decision, and 150 church members met for an hour and a half on 15 February to discuss the issue. On 22 February the Judicial Commission voted 7-1 to fire Jones. The Chapel Hill congregation accepted the vote calmly and looked for avenues of appeal. In the following days the Commission dissolved the Chapel Hill board of deacons and elders and asked the Rev. Robert J. McMullen to become the church evangelist. At the annual business meeting in early April, Law School Dean Henry Brandis introduced a resolution which "vigorously protested" the dismissal of the officers, promised support for McMullen, and protested the firing of Jones.

The North Carolina Presbyterian Synod considered the Chapel Hill appeals and ordered the Judicial Commission to give Jones an open hearing. The Judicial Commission then appealed to the General Assembly of the Presbyterian Church, and on 8 June the General Assembly voted to uphold the Commission but offered to hold a trial if either Jones or the Chapel Hill church requested one. On 17 July, during the meeting of the Orange Presbytery in the New Hope Presbyterian Church, Frank Porter Graham urged Jones to "stick it out" and pleaded for a change of venue. After further debate, Jones rose, stated he was too tired to continue the matter, and resigned. In a 22-page statement, he asserted that the trial would probably not be fair or full and that it would be harmful to the Chapel Hill church and to the Presbyterian Church as a whole.

Stella Lyons came to Chapel Hill in 1940 from Wilkes County and ran the small magazine stand in the post office, shown here, until October 1955 when she moved to Memorial Hospital. She retired in 1980 and now lives in Glen Lennox. (UNC Photo Lab)

Jones and his wife Dorcas left town to relax, but he returned two weeks later as pastor of a newly formed nondenominational Community Church, which met for the first time on 2 August in the auditorium of the Institute of Pharmacy building. The 300-member congregation continued to meet in Hill Hall and other campus buildings while they were planning and building a permanent home. On 27 April 1955, chairman Ted Danziger submitted and his building committee approved plans for a church complex to be located on a 14-acre site at Purefoy Road and Mason Farm Road. The Rev. Jones dedicated the Activities Building in 1959 and remained as minister until 1967, later earning an income as a consultant for the Danziger enterprises.

On the bitter cold night of 19-20 February 1958, patrolman W.F. Hester and Gene Cozart discovered a fire in the basement of the Franklin Street Presbyterian Church at 11:30. However, the sub-zero temperature froze firefighting equipment, the flames engulfed the building, and at 1 a.m. the spire toppled. The congregation immediately began a campaign to raise $250,000 to add to the $195,000 for which the building was insured, and on 1 June 1958 ground was broken for a new church, which was dedicated on 18 October 1958.

The Baptists also had their troubles. In February 1954, the Baptist General Board asked University Baptist Church chaplain to UNC the Rev. J.C. Herrin to resign or be fired because of his liberal views. When Herrin refused to resign, the General Board fired him on 31 March. Leaders of the 1500-member UNC Baptist Student Union asked Herrin to remain as their advisor; he accepted their invitation, but said he would be busy seeking a position elsewhere "where the atmosphere is clearer." Several

Two popular places to drink beer in the years after World War II were Harry's, run by Benjamin Schreiber (above left), and the Rathskeller, owned by the Danzigers. Schreiber (1910-1976) came to Chapel Hill after World War II and bought Harry's. A few years later, Ben and his wife Syd sold the restaurant name and opened The Youth Center, a shop specializing in baby clothes. In 1948, The Rathskeller opened with 10¢ beer. (NCC)

members of the Baptist Church resigned, including former deacon Dr. Preston H. Epps, and some of them joined Charlie Jones' Community Church.

On 21 September 1958, Baptists unhappy with the current situation met in Hill Music Hall to organize a new congregation more ecumenically oriented and free from central control. They met for six years in Gerrard Hall before moving into the new Olin T. Binkley Memorial Church, located on the By-Pass and named after a former pastor of the University Baptist Church who had also served as president of the Southeastern Theological Seminary at Wake Forest.

The debates within the Presbyterian and the Baptist congregations were contemporaneous with a spate of new churches in Chapel Hill. The Episcopal Church of the Holy Family organized in Gerrard Hall on 27 January 1952 and moved into a new church on Hayes Road in Glen Lennox on Thanksgiving Day 1953. Lutherans dedicated the Holy Trinity Lutheran Church on East Rosemary on 6 January 1952. On 21 August 1955, the Right Rev. W.Y. Bell dedicated St. Joseph's CME Church on West Rosemary Street. The Rev. Kimsey King organized a second Methodist congregation which met for the first time on 21 August 1955 in the basement of the Glenwood Elementary School. On 15 December 1957, the new Methodist congregation moved into a new church on Laurel Hill Road, named Aldersgate after the London Street on which stood the church in which John Wesley converted on 24 May 1738.

On 20 April 1952, Rabbi Arthur J. Lelyveld came from

New York to deliver the dedication address at the new Hillel Foundation Building at 210 West Cameron Avenue. Rabbi Lelyveld, the national director of the Hillel Foundation returned to Chapel Hill in October 1953 to deliver another dedication address. Mr. and Mrs. George Blankenstein of Greensboro had donated a solid walnut chapel built into the Foundation building, the first Jewish house of worship in Chapel Hill.

Father William J. O'Brien of Durham celebrated the first Catholic mass in Chapel Hill in 1922, and the mission remained active with services conducted in Gerrard Hall by priests who came from the Church of the Nazareth in Wake County. A Catholic chaplain was assigned to the campus in 1934, and local Catholics began a building fund in 1942. William D. Carmichael donated a site on Gimghoul Road, and Durham contractor George W. Kane completed a $180,000 chapel built from Salisbury granite in 1956, at which time there were 310 Catholic worshippers in Chapel Hill.

The Quakers moved into the Friends Meeting House at the corner of Country Club Drive and Raleigh Road in 1960 after having used Graham Memorial for 23 years. In 1966, the Presbyterian Church of Reconciliation formed as a colonized congregation supported by the University Presbyterian Church. The Orange Presbytery and the University Church donated a spacious church site on Elliott Road, but the Reconciliation congregation met in an old house on the site, an outside place of worship called "The Dell," and the basement of the adjacent Northwestern Bank branch office until their church was ready for use on 6 March 1977. Encouraged by an increased interest in religion shown by students, some 40 worshippers met in Gerrard Hall on 1 January 1970 to organize an evangelical church, whose members now meet in the recently constructed Bible Church on Mason Farm and Purefoy roads.

The debates in the churches also overlapped a new "red scare," largely created by and centered on Junius Irving Scales. Junius' grandfather Junius Scales, the brother of North Carolina Governor Alfred Moore Scales, married Effie Hamilton Henderson, the daughter of Archibald Henderson of Granville County and the granddaughter of N.C. Chief Justice Leonard Henderson, who was the nephew of Chapel Hill merchant Pleasant Henderson. Junius and Effie Scales had six children, one of whom was born in Greensboro on 20 August 1870 and named after his uncle the governor. As a state senator, Alfred Scales the younger led early efforts for women's suffrage, for increased public welfare, and for increased appropriations to education.

Alfred Scales passed his liberalism on to his son Junius who made the leap into radicalism by joining the Communist party in 1939 while a student at UNC. Active in the campaign to organize textile workers, Junius left school to

Junius Irving Scales, pictured here in 1947, now works on the New York Times. Scales' father, Alfred Moore Scales (1870-1940) of Greensboro, led the fight for women's suffrage in the North Carolina Senate in the 1890s.

Junius descended from several illustrious North Carolina families with close links to Chapel Hill: The Pells, two of whom edited Chapel Hill's post Civil War newspaper, the Ledger; the Hendersons, one of whom, Pleasant, from 1801 to 1830 was the most respected member of Chapel Hill society.

join the U.S. Army the day after Pearl Harbor. He returned to UNC after the war, earned an AB in Comparative Literature in 1947, and revealed his ties to the Communist party in a *Daily Tar Heel* article in October 1947.

Scales directed the Karl Marx Study Club at UNC, using the auspices of that position to invite a succession of leftist speakers to Chapel Hill and the campus, one of whom was John Gates, editor of *The Daily Worker*. When administrators denied Gates permission to speak on campus, he addressed a predominantly hostile crowd in the streets of Chapel Hill. Hecklers booed, threw rotten eggs, and created a near riot. Nevertheless, Scales' report of the event in the next day's *Daily Worker* carried the headline: "1,000 Students Cheer Gates Despite Ban."

Scales lived in Carrboro, but used Chapel Hill P.O. Box #62 for his correspondence as chairman of the Communist Party, Carolina District, in the eyes of many as a guise to suggest that the university and Chapel Hill were centers of communist activity. Believing that Scales was attempting to promote a revolution of workers and Negroes, the FBI infiltrated the local communist movement. On 6 October 1951, sensing that he was in danger of arrest under the provisions of the Smith Act outlawing activities intended to overthrow the government by force or violence, Scales went "underground," using the alias "Joe Shields."

From points in hiding, Scales charged President Gordon Gray and the UNC administration with fostering racial hatred by, among other things, permitting the erection of a welcome-students sign decorated with a black child eating watermelon. He contended that Saturday classes were clothed exploitations of students by local merchants and a rightwing administration. Then on 18 November 1954, less than six hours after a Wilkesboro grand jury had

indicted Scales for violations of the Smith Act, FBI agents arrested him in Memphis, Tennessee. In a trial in Greensboro in April 1955, Scales was convicted and sentenced to six years in prison.

The U.S. Supreme Court reversed the Greensboro decision in 1957; but the Justice Department opted to try Scales once again in 1958. Scales was once again convicted, and once more sentenced to six years in prison. The U.S. Supreme Court upheld the conviction in June 1961, and on 2 October, Scales went to jail. Immediately after the Supreme Court ruling, President John Kennedy began to receive stacks of letters and petitions asking him to pardon Scales. Among the petitioners were several members of the press, nine of the 12 jurors who had convicted Scales, Frank Porter Graham, Paul Green, Richardson Preyer, and Norman Thomas. On Christmas Day 1962, President Kennedy granted executive clemency to Scales, who later went to work for the New York *Times* as a proofreader.

The contention over race that first surfaced in the churches soon spread into the secular community, and on the whole resistance to change was less rigid in Chapel Hill than elsewhere in the state and in the South, but the general spirit of moderation did not prevent the community from going through the crucible.

In January 1950 when KKK leaders threatened to organize a Klan klavern in Chapel Hill, Mayor Edwin S. Lanier promptly declared he would ask the aldermen for "any ordinances necessary to stop Klan activity." UNC became the first white university in the South to accept a Negro student voluntarily when a black entered the Medical School in March 1951, and that fall, in compliance with a court order, President Gordon Gray ordered the Law School to integrate. Nevertheless, in the spring of 1954, neither the university nor the community was eager to accept without question the implications of *Brown v. Topeka*, even though the Board of Education had

A.H. Poe and Marvin Mangum opened a DeSoto-Plymouth dealership on Columbia Street in 1938. At the end of World War II, Poe moved the business to this service station on West Franklin about 150 feet from the Columbia Street intersection, where he operated it with Watts D. and George Poe. The Poes added the service bays (right) and new car showroom (left), before moving out in 1956.

The Pizza Hut now occupies the service-bay area. Chapel Hill's oldest bar, He's Not Here, occupies the Village Green behind the building. (UNC Photo Lab)

The civil-rights activities of the 1960s hit Chapel Hill full force on 18 February 1960 when Lincoln High School students began the first local lunch-counter sit-ins. Soon afterward, they moved on to picket the Long Meadow Dairy Bar. (Photo courtesy Roland Giduz)

made a stab at maintaining separate and equal facilities by spending $238,493 in 1950-1952 to construct all-black Lincoln High School on Merritt Mill Road.

In response to the Supreme Court ruling, the School Board voted unanimously on 7 June 1954 "immediately to initiate studies and planning looking toward practicable adjustment." There were further studies, but little progress, over the next five years. Upset because the board had consistently turned down requests by black parents to transfer their children to white schools, board member Henry Brandis resigned in 1959. The next year the board voted to integrate the first grade district wide.

Meanwhile, anticipating integration movements involving society at large, city officials called for the establishment of a Bi-Racial Human Relations Committee to promote harmony. Men and women of good will on both sides of the issue continued to debate the issue with earnest passion, but little overt movement had occurred by 18 February 1960 when black students from Lincoln High School organized a sit-in at the Colonial Drug Store on West Franklin Street. Sit-ins and picketing spread quickly, and the aldermen asked for a 30-day trial integration at all lunch counters and restaurants, a plan that failed when a few owners refused to comply.

On 24 March 1960, 27 ministers took out a full-page ad in the *Weekly* announcing their support for "peaceful picketing." A week later in another full-page ad, 850 townspeople pledged their "moral support and patronage to all merchants" who desegregated voluntarily. In response

to the ads and to demonstrations directed by the Congress of Racial Equality (CORE), five restaurants integrated in April. Black alderman Hubert Robinson was in a very delicate position. Working for change inside the official political structure, he was reluctant to encourage the demonstrations or to predict a time table for official integration. Editorially, the Chapel Hill *Weekly* defended the right of the protesters to demonstrate in an orderly manner and maintained that what they were demanding would inevitably come to pass.

Protesters began picketing the Carolina Theatre in January 1961 when it was showing "Porgy and Bess," with a black-dominated cast. Enjoying solid support from the UNC faculty and students, the picketers formed the Chapel Hill Citizen's Committee for Open Movies and extended their pickets to include the Varsity. In August, manager E. Carrington Smith opened the Carolina to blacks, provided they were UNC students. Two black co-eds saw "The Dark at the Top of the Stairs," and the black community was outraged that the co-eds had attended under those conditions. Young black leaders took advantage of the theater picketing to seize de facto control of the integration movement; they demanded complete integration of the theaters within a month; the Carolina conceded before Christmas; and the Varsity followed suit a few days later. But the most difficult days were still to come.

On 20 November 1961, a group met to form a local chapter of the NAACP. Acting president Paul Dommermoth sounded the keynote when he observed, "Chapel Hill has the reputation of being the threshold of liberalism. We can use this as a lever to accomplish our goal." Realizing that they would be supported by influential sympathizers, black leaders planned to use Chapel Hill as the symbol of their success in North Carolina. A long-time resident was about to turn Chapel Hill into a counter symbol for

By 1963, civil-rights demonstrations, such as this one on Franklin Street, were attracting marchers by the hundreds, still composed mostly of young people.

In March 1933, a young Black, 24-year-old Durhamite Thomas Raymond Hocutt, sued UNC before Judge M.V. Barnhill for admission to the UNC School of Pharmacy. He was denied admission.

adherence to the status quo.

Dr. Wesley Critz George of Yadkin County earned an A.B. at UNC in 1911, an M.A. in 1912, and a Ph.D. in 1918. After having taught at the University of Georgia and the University of Tennessee Medical School at Memphis, he joined the staff of the UNC Medical School in 1920, and between then and his retirement in 1959 he became a full professor, chairman of the anatomy department, a world-famous expert on the study of blood and embryos, and the single individual most responsible for the excellence of the UNC medical library.

As president of the Patriots of North Carolina in the mid-1950s, Dr. George became a spokesman for those opposed to integration, contending that the mix of the races "would result in gradual destruction of our culture and destruction of our race, according to the best scientific evidence we have." Several of Dr. George's colleagues objected to what they considered to be exploitation of his position in the Medical School. In response, Chancellor Robert House voiced support for freedom of expression.

When Governor John Patterson of Alabama chose to refute evidence being offered by the NAACP, he commissioned the widely reputed Dr. George to prove that whites were intellectually superior to blacks. The day Dr. George released "The Biology of the Race Problem," 3 October 1962, a full-page ad appeared in the New York *Times* asking President John Kennedy to study Dr. George's findings, which in brief contended that blacks were inferior and that "integration is not Christian." In Alabama, governor-elect George Wallace said he would study the report carefully. Although his conclusions and his methodology had come under fire from several formidable sources, Dr. George expanded his study into a book-length text published in 1967, when he was 79, as *Race Problems and Human Progress*, with an introduction by Archibald B. Roosevelt, the son of President Theodore Roosevelt.

In the summer of 1962, the School Board extended classroom integration to include the first six grades. Eighty black and 70 white children crossed former barriers that fall, but the junior high and the high schools remained essentially segregated. Activity by civil rights advocates picked up nationwide in the spring of 1963, black organizations still considered Chapel Hill a symbol in North Carolina, and white participation increased locally.

The Student Peace Union, a predominantly white targeted facilities, which included Memorial Hospital and virtually every restaurant in town. Mass demonstrations began on 7 May at the Memorial Hospital and continued on 10 May at the dedication of the School of Public Health Building, with Governor Terry Sanford and other dignitaries in attendance. The great majority of Chapel Hillians agreed that the time had come to integrate public facilities. They did, however, disagree on the pace at which it should proceed. One group wanted an immediate end to official

Attorney Charles Hodson addresses the Chapel Hill Board of Aldermen as it considers a public accommodation ordinance in 1964. Seated at the table are, left to right: Hubert Robinson, Sr.; Roland Giduz; Gene Strowd; City Manager Robert S. Peck; Mayor Sandy McClamroch; Town Clerk David B. Roberts; Mrs. Harold W. Walters; Dr. Paul W. Wager; and Joe Page. (From Lefler and Wager, Orange County, 1752-1952)

segregation; another preferred a gradual approach to lessen the social shock. Both sides tried to accomplish their goals by committee, but in the end the more militant faction within the civil-rights collective came to dictate policy.

On 3 May 1963, members of both races met in St. Joseph's AME Church and formed the Chapel Hill Committee for Open Business for the specific purpose of integrating restaurants. On 18 May, 20 ministers requested that Mayor Sandy McClamroch select a committee to search for a means to end segregation locally. The aldermen accepted the recommendation, and Mayor McClamroch on 24 May composed the Mayor's Committee for Integration. The next day some 300 black and white demonstrators marched down Franklin Street, stopping to sing before segregated establishments and prompting the Chapel Hill-Carrboro Merchants Association to call for "equal treatment of ALL customers." In a 2 June editorial, the Chapel Hill *Weekly* supported the mass demonstrations.

In June, the mayor's committee conceded that an "open city" could not be achieved without a public accommodations ordinance. The state attorney general advised that the board of aldermen lacked the authority to enact such a law; Daniel H. Pollitt of the UNC Law School advised that the board had the authority under general powers extended by the General Assembly in 1961. When the board voted 4-2 against creating an ordinance, a new, more aggressive form of civil disobedience followed, accompanied by mass arrests.

Thirty-four black and white demonstrators were arrested on 19 July at the Merchants Association on Franklin Street, and once in jail they continued their protest by wrecking their cells. The Committee for Open Business collected money to pay for the damage, and internal conflict over the question of militancy caused the committee to disband later in the fall, to be replaced by the Citizens United for Racial Equality and Dignity. Meanwhile, the Chapel Hill Freedom Committee had

Roland "Sandy" McClamroch became mayor of Chapel Hill in 1961, eight years after he had founded WCHL and two years before the civil-rights movement in Chapel Hill grew tempestuous. Quietly and behind the scenes, he turned the part-time mayor's position into a full time job, calling on his broadcasting and executive experience to keep channels of communication open between the contending factions and to reduce tensions between the town authorities, including the police, and the activists.

become an umbrella organization for chapters of the NAACP, CORE, SCLC, SNCC, SLEF, and for other bodies that generally approved militancy.

In a frantic attempt to forestall further violent demonstrations, Mayor McClamroch appointed still another committee. He received some support from the demonstrators, who held no marches between 19 July and 2 August, and from the Merchants' Association, which promised not to press charges against the demonstrators. Silent marches began on Franklin Street in early August, accompanied by peaceful demonstrations on campus, but the conviction and jailing of four demonstrators in Hillsborough in December ended the calm. Over 130 demonstrators were arrested by the end of the year, and in late December over 200 merchants, city officials, university personnel, and concerned citizens met in an attempt to resolve a crisis that was rapidly becoming dangerously volatile, but they could not agree on the wording of an ordinance.

On 12 January 1964, James Farmer led 150 marchers from Durham to the First Baptist Church on North Roberson Street, where he designated 1 February as "D-Day" for an acceptable solution. That afternoon, the Chapel Hill *Weekly* endorsed the adoption of a public-accommodations ordinance, but the next day the Board of Aldermen rejected the idea, and activities by all parties to the dispute reached unprecedented levels. Street sit-downs led to the arrest of 436 demonstrators over the next three weeks; Mayor McClamroch named a Mediation Committee; the D-Day threat caused some whites to switch sides and oppose the passage of an ordinance under duress; and others opposed to the use of pressure tactics formed the Committee of Concerned Citizens and began lobbying Congress to include a public accommodations section in the federal civil-rights bill then under discussion.

The UNC student legislature adopted and some 200 faculty members endorsed "A Resolution Directed Toward the Alleviation of Tensions in Chapel Hill" which called for an end of demonstrations in their present form, for merchants to integrate, and for "our constituents" to boycott segregated establishments. However, an NAACP leader promised to continue the demonstrations, stating "It is our job to point up the problems, it is the community's job to solve them." More demonstrators were convicted and sentenced in March, but the protests continued.

It was the Civil Rights Bill of 1964 that finally ended the mass demonstrations in Chapel Hill. Following its passage on 2 July, demonstrators tested it en masse on 3 July. Four of the six restaurants still segregated served blacks, and the remaining two soon followed suit, but only after further prodding.

Chapel Hill became the center of another political controversy on 25 June 1963 when the General Assembly, after deliberating for 15 minutes in the Senate and four minutes in the House, passed the "speaker ban law." The law forbade the appearance on *every* state college and university campus of speakers who were members of the Communist party, who advocated the "overthrow of the Constitution," or who had pleaded the Fifth Amendment in response to questions regarding loyalty; but the legislators were clearly directing the law squarely at UNC. Faculty and students protested vigorously. The Southern Association of Colleges and Schools threatened to revoke the accreditation of every affected school. In late 1965 the General Assembly amended the law, returning control of campus speakers to boards of trustees, but the trustees passed the hot potato on to administrators.

UNC student-body president Paul Dickson III and other student leaders chose to initiate a court action, hoping to have the ban law declared unconstitutional. They got their opportunity in March 1966 after a joint student-faculty committee recommended that Chancellor J. Carlyle Sitterson refuse to allow the appearance on

On 29 January 1966, Governor Dan Moore asked the UNC trustee's executive committee to bar Herbert Aptheker and Frank Wilkinson from speaking on campus. Students and townspeople responded by inviting both men to speak from the sidewalk on Franklin Street while an audience stood on the campus across the low stone wall at McCorkle Place and listened. Wilkinson spoke on 2 March 1966, Aptheker a week later. This photograph was taken a few minutes after Aptheker finished speaking to a crowd estimated at 2000 persons. (NCC)

Robert H.W. Welch, Jr. (1900-1984) is pictured here at age 13 at the end of his freshman year at UNC. His adult companion is unidentified. Founder and head of the anti-communist John Birch Society, he came to the Triangle area and made a number of speeches about his organization's position on communism and the Speaker Ban Law at the same time Aptheker and Wilkinson were speaking in March 1966.

Welch was a brilliant mathematics student at UNC and as a 14-year-old sophomore helped students less gifted in the field. However, the 1916 Yackety Yack reported, "Later he decided to try a little philosophy — not with the same success he had in Math." (NCC)

campus of Herbert Aptheker, a member of the Communist party, and Frank Wilkinson, who had pleaded the Fifth Amendment in a loyalty hearing in California. Aptheker and Wilkinson came despite the ban and spoke from the East Franklin Street sidewalk bordering McCorkle Place to students *on campus*. When Aptheker and Wilkinson were again denied permission to speak on campus, the students went to court, and in February 1968 a panel of three federal judges struck down the law as unconstitutional.

When the Vietnam War began to escalate, students and faculty organized protest demonstrations that continued with increasing intensity through the buildup, the Kent State tragedy, and the bombing of Cambodia. The most visible protest in the village was the weekly peace vigil in front of the Franklin Street post office, begun on 4 January 1967 by Mrs. Charlotte Adams and other members of the local chapter of the Women's International League for Peace and Freedom. The weekly vigils, quiet and dignified, continued every Wednesday through the January 1973 peace agreement and on to "The Last Vigil" on 15 August 1973, a few hours after the United States forces ceased the bombing raids on Cambodia.

A dramatic measure of the acceptance of integration in Chapel Hill occurred on 6 May 1969 when Howard Lee won election as mayor to succeed Sandy McClamroch, the mayor since 1961. Born to a black sharecropping family in Lithonia, Georgia in 1934, Lee graduated from Fort Valley State College in 1959. In 1964 he and his wife Lillian Wesley Lee moved to Chapel Hill, where he enrolled in the UNC School of Social Work, earning an MA in 1966. Lee worked as an administrator at Duke University and taught at NCCU before he announced for the mayor's race in December 1968, setting up campaign headquarters at 413 West Rosemary Street and articulating a platform which

promised more low-cost housing, a greater involvement of youth in government, an expansion of recreational facilities, the formation of a public transportation committee, and the establishment of closer ties between the town and the university.

In late March 1969, Roland Giduz entered the mayor's race. Roland had lived in Chapel Hill since the age of two when his father Hugo Giduz, a native of Boston and a cum laude graduate of Harvard (1905), joined the UNC faculty in 1927. Hugo Giduz taught education and Romance language courses for 25 years at UNC and also taught French at Chapel Hill High School for 20 of those years.

Roland Giduz fought as an infantryman in France during World War II, graduated from UNC in 1948, picked up an MA in journalism at Columbia in 1949, embarked on a career as a newspaperman in 1950, and later attended Harvard as a Mass Media Fellow. In the 19 years before he announced for the mayor's race, Roland had worked as a reporter for the Durham *Herald* and *Sun* and the Chapel Hill *Weekly*; he had co-founded the Chapel Hill *News Leader*; he had edited the *News of Orange County*; he had served for 12 years on the Chapel Hill Board of Aldermen; he had founded *The Triangle Pointer*; and as an associate director of the UNC General Alumni Association he was editor of the *Alumni Review*. Married to the former Helen Frances Jeter of Union, South Carolina, he was the father of three school-age sons in 1969.

Very much against his will, Giduz found himself portrayed as the candidate of the white establishment. Thereby limited as an effective campaigner, he was not surprised when Lee won with 55% of the almost 4700 votes cast; and, in an effort to unify opposing factions in the campaign, he went to Lee's jubilant campaign headquarters to concede in person on election night.

As the first black mayor of a predominantly white community in the Southeast, Lee had to contend with the old, nagging problem of race relations, especially in the schools. Students and some townsfolk supported a strike by UNC cafeteria workers which raised tensions to the

Anti-war and anti-draft demonstrations occurred during and after the "speaker ban" activities. Usually, speaker ban opponents met at McCorkle Place on campus, while the anti-war forces focused on the Franklin Street area in front of the post office. (UNC Photo Lab)

Former mayor Howard Lee, pictured here on 20 April 1969 in front of his campaign headquarters on Rosemary Street, proposed and established a Charter Commission in 1973, chaired by Joe Nassif, to explore the possibility and advantages of elevating Chapel Hill from a town to a city. After about a year of meetings, the town decided against changing its status. (Photo used courtesy Howard Lee)

point that Governor Bob Scott sent in the State Highway Patrol to maintain order. Discipline and drugs became problems in the schools, intensified by racial animosities. Northside School was firebombed after the acquittal of the men charged with killing a black student during a knife fight on the UNC campus. However, Mayor Lee relied on the help of committees experienced in handling racial difficulties, and he was able to continue the progress of the 1960s. Public approval of his performance is reflected in election results: Lee received 64% of the vote when he ran for reelection in 1971 and 89% in 1973.

Lee also became mayor at a time when the board of aldermen and the city administrators were having to contend with the problems associated with enormous growth. On 28 March 1947, the General Assembly had voted to expand the UNC Medical School into a four-year program and to build Memorial Hospital in Chapel Hill. That action was the primary impetus for the massive increase in Chapel Hill property valuation and population during the 1950s. The number of UNC employees grew from 1219 to 3366 between 1950 and 1960, with a corresponding increase in payroll from $5,565,000 to $18,089,000. Property valuation in town shot upward to $23,000,000 by 1957, then slowed as the nation entered a recession to reach $28,486,519 in 1960. But the lull was only momentary, and by 1970 valuation had skyrocketed to over $100,000,000.

The growing pains were felt most by those who lamented the irrevocable evolution of "the village" into a thriving city with a healthy economy soundly based on service jobs, but the "preservationists" also had their victories. Enforcement of the three-story building restriction stopped developers from erecting a high-rise Royal Carolinian Hotel on the first block of West Franklin Street. In 1965, citizens rose united to protect the Baptist Church corner at Franklin and Columbia after Bell's Incorporated of Charlotte announced plans to build a

short-order, walk-in restaurant there to compete with the new Hardee's and Burger Chef fast-food restaurants. A Chapel Hill *Weekly* editorial entitled "Rot in the Heart of Chapel Hill" condemned the proposed restaurant as a "new affront to aesthetic sensibilities" and as a "midtown cancer," predicting that "the day can come when Chapel Hillians will have to go to Durham's festering Five Points to recapture a sense of municipal grace and charm."

However, changes on the familiar landscape were becoming many and widespread. A string of commercial structures was beginning to line the north side of Rosemary between Henderson and Columbia, facing parking areas on the south side of the street. Crowell Little spurred development of the Durham Boulevard when he established a Ford dealership a couple of miles out of town next to the Valley Drive-In Theater. Then, with the completion of the Eastgate Shopping Center in 1960, the business focus had unquestionably shifted toward the east, a shift that in the early 1970s would induce Raleigh developer Ed Richards to build University Mall nearby.

The building boom of the late 1960s picked up pace and peaked in 1971 when over $32 million was spent on construction: $3.97 million on private homes; $2.87 million on apartments; and $25.96 million on commercial and university buildings and repairs, including $7 million on the Blue Cross-Blue Shield complex and $1.75 million on the new NCNB Plaza.

Between 1960 and 1970, the population of Chapel Hill more than doubled, from 12,573 to 25,537—with students outnumbering permanent residents 18,130 to 7407 in 1970. Mayor Lee kept his campaign promise and led a determined effort to install a public transportation system to facilitate the movement of large numbers of people without destroying neighborhoods with thoroughfares and without using valuable downtown and campus space for parking. A UNC-commissioned study determined that a Chapel Hill bus system was infeasible, and opponents argued that buses would be dirty, unsightly, unsafe, noisy, and far too expensive to operate without large public subsidies.

Nevertheless, a task force appointed by Mayor Lee recommended a six-week experiment, and the city successfully applied for a federal grant to pay for a feasibility study. During the trial period, only 300 riders per day used the service, when 1000 had been predicted and expected, and on 29 April 1971 the experimental Chapel Hill-Carrboro City Coach Lines went bankrupt. Five days later, Carrboro voters rejected the proposed system by a two-to-one margin, while it lost in Chapel Hill by only three votes. However, Mayor Lee and his allies continued to lobby the public, and a feasibility study in July indicated that 68% of affected residents wanted publicly subsidized buses.

Chapel Hill and Carrboro could not start a comprehen-

On 11 July 1966, fire destroyed the old building housing Kemp's Record Bar on Franklin Street just west of the Presbyterian Church. That corner had a long history dear to booklovers: Charles P. Mallett operated his ante-bellum bookstore there; R.S. MacRae ran a bookstore-general store there for 25 years around the turn of the century, and The Intimate Bookshop occupied the building for another quarter-century before it moved to its present location in the main block of Franklin Street. (NCC)

sive system without the assurance that the university would assist by purchasing student passes, and that assurance did not come until December 1972 when trustees voted to purchase 20,000 passes at a cost of $250,000. Voters then approved a $350,000 bond issue and up to a 10 cents per $100 property tax authorization by almost a two-to-one margin on 20 February 1973. The town hired John Pappas as director of transportation in December 1973, and Pappas quickly discovered that operating costs would be far higher than earlier estimated and that the town would need an additional $310,000 to begin service.

Early in 1974, a federal grant provided $860,000 for the purchase of buses, the town bought 22 used vehicles from the MARTA system in Atlanta, and in August 1974 the buses began rolling. Even though 4.3 million riders used the system during its first two years, it was still in danger of collapse because expenses far outstripped income. Critics complained that there were too many buses, too many routes, too many runs per route, and too many hours of daily operation, all of which caused revenue-sharing funds to be absorbed by the bus system at the expense of other services and users. Service was cut 26% for the year 1976-1977 and another 27% for the year 1977-1978. But over the years, community support of the system remained firm, new buses replaced the rapidly decaying relics from Atlanta, and the system now seems secure, although service will likely be cut back as federal subsidies decline.

While still mayor, in 1972 Lee challenged incumbent Second District Congressman L.H. Fountain in the Democratic primary, losing 60,289 to 42,242 but winning Orange County by 9550 to 4849. Four years later he led the balloting in the first primary for the office of lieutenant governor, but lost to Jimmy Green in a run-off. In late 1976, Governor-elect Jim Hunt appointed Lee to head the Department of Natural and Human Resources and re-

George Spransy (1918-1976), seen here with his wife Marian in 1965, was one of Chapel Hill's genuinely loved citizens after his arrival from Durham in 1957. A Tar Heel football player in 1939-1941, George was captured during the Battle of the Bulge and later escaped from the Germans. Disclaiming any heroics, he said the prisoners in his camp simply awoke one morning to discover their guards had fled. After managing the Kenan Oil Agency in Carrboro, George bought into Huggins Hardware when Vic Huggins retired in 1968. He traditionally carried a glass door to door on Halloween, and friends traditionally encumbered him with gag gifts on his birthday. In 1963 a friend gave him 100 baby chicks. After the laughter ended, George gave the chicks to a country friend, who was so touched by the gift that she willed him two acres of Chapel Hill land. Understandably, George's motto was "Bald Is Beautiful." (Roland Giduz)

appointed him in 1980, but Lee resigned in July 1981 to put an end to the controversy surrounding the awarding of CETA contracts to union leader Wilbur Hobby. Since 1981, Lee has co-produced the record album *American Negro Spirituals*, he has worked on a movie script and his autobiography, and he lost the Democratic congressional primary of 1984, the year Second District voters elected Republican Bill Cobey.

By the time the University Mall was completed in 1973, city planners had become more alarmed than ever over the rate of commercial and residential development. The aldermen expressed hope in January 1973 that building would slow, and two months later planning and zoning director Van Opdenbrow was able to report that construction had in fact slowed, but he warned that Chapel Hill

A construction crane used in the erection of high-rise housing tower Granville West is shown here on 11 November 1965, soon after the job began.

According to Thomas E. Steahr, in 1970 there were only three rental properties in Chapel Hill that charged $300 or more per month.

Left in the photo is the old High School, and right, an elementary school. Both were razed when University Square was built on the site. (Courtesy of Roland Giduz)

must get rid of the "village" myth if planning were to be done realistically. The annual city budgets dramatically reinforce Opdenbrow's contention. The first post-war budget, for 1946-1947, was only $63,208. The budget topped $100,000 for the first time in 1949-1950, $1 million for the first time in 1965-1966, and reached a total of $12,308,361 in 1982-1983, including a $2,019,680 subsidy for the bus system.

The university got out of the business of operating the utilities in 1974. When the Consumer Utility Corporation failed to raise sufficient money to purchase the utilities, the university divested by selling the electrical system to Duke Power, the telephone service to Southern Bell, and the water and sewage operations to the Orange Water and Sewer Authority.

In the 1930s, the only stop light in town stood atop a concrete stanchion in the center of the Franklin-Columbia intersection. In response to the post-war upsurge in traffic, town governors installed a complicated collection of signals at the intersection of Henderson and Franklin that grew to include nine hanging lights and seven on an island in Franklin Street.

Of course, traffic control has been a mounting problem in the town since the late 1950s, and each new proposal for a thoroughfare plan to relieve congestion within the business-campus district and on the main surburban arteries becomes more complex and encounters increasingly difficult complications, funding being the great constant. A current long-range plan calls for major modifications in the downtown area: Franklin Street to carry traffic one-way east and to extend through Carr-

boro; Rosemary to run one-way west; Columbia one-way north; and Pittsboro Street one way south.

The expansion of the town limits, the increase in population, and a rapidly growing law-enforcement force has necessitated the provision of additional town-government buildings. Thomas Bridges of the City Planning Office worked with Architectural Associates to design a new Municipal Building which was completed on Airport Road in May 1971. The addition of a narcotics squad upped the police force from 44 in 1969 to 59 in 1971. Some law-enforcement personnel worked out of the old Town Hall, others out of the Glen Lennox fire station. Again assisted by Architectural Associates, the City Planning Office designed a revolutionary new energy-efficient building, and in 1981 the police department was able to consolidate in the William D. Blake Police Headquarters on Airport Road just north of Bolin Creek.

While Chapel Hill was growing rapidly in the 1950s and the 1960s, Carrboro was facing problems which kept property values static for almost two decades. In 1959, Pacific Mills closed its Carrboro Woolen Mills plant, the old Carr Mill #4, throwing approximately 450 employees out of work. Superior Mills, a subsidiary of BVD, took over the plant, employing some 75 workers initially and building to a workforce of approximately 200 a decade later.

Since the mid-1970s, Carrboro has been as vigorous as its adjacent sister town. Political competition between the Carrboro Coalition and the Association for a Better Carrboro has erased voter apathy; Brent Glass, Valerie Quinney, Rudolph Hardee, and others have elevated town pride by compiling oral and written histories; Jacques and

Hurricane Hazel hit Chapel Hill at 1:03 P.M., 15 October 1954, and among other havoc, it damaged or destroyed several hundred autos, over 500 trees, and, according to Louis Graves, caused S.P. Lockhart's turkey flocks to stampede. Romulus Best of Best's TV and Radio Service estimated that 3000 of Chapel Hill's 4000 TV sets were damaged.

Joseph S. Malpas, 76, was blown down on Franklin Street and suffered a broken arm, the only human injury in town. However, UNC senior Malcolm Baxter Rawlins of Charlotte was killed late in the afternoon when he was hit by a truck while filming Hazel's damage for the state highway department.

In this photo, a toppled tree and utility pole fallen from Clyde Eubanks' yard rest on a student's car. (UNC Photo Lab)

Two businesses made an impression on Chapel Hillians in 1951. The Varsity Shop, owned by Wilbur Kutz (1903-1985), held what many observers say was the longest going-out-of-business sale in local history, stretching out over 1951-1952.

Rachel Crook's fish and produce market, pictured here in 1951 and located at what is now Crook's Corner on West Franklin Street at Merritt Mill Road, had a more tragic demise. Rachel (1880-1951) inherited an 800 acre farm from her father, moved to Chapel Hill in 1930, and lived in a 7'×7' doll house on Alfred Kirkland's Ransom Street lot while attending classes at UNC. In 1943, she bought a chicken house and turned it into the market pictured here. In 1947, she opened Chapel Hill's first launderette. On 29 August 1951, someone abducted and brutally murdered her. In a sensational trial, Hobert Lee of Burlington was found innocent of the crime. (Roland Giduz)

Amy Menache (the daughter of Milton and Minna Abernethy) inspired a new level of cultural activities in 1974 when they formed the Carrboro Art School, which brought in supporters from a wide artistic radius willing to donate energy, time and money to teach a wide range of the arts and to present programs of dance, drama, jazz, folk and classical concerts, poetry readings, films, and art shows; and plans to raze old Carr Mill #4 united concerned citizens as

never before to preserve and to enhance the landmarks and the ambience that constitute Carrboro.

After the Kaiser-Aetna Company let an option to purchase Carr Mill #4 lapse in 1975, the Community Development Group at North Carolina State University studied the property to determine constructive uses and suggested that it be converted into either a care center, housing, offices, or a recreational facility. When no one

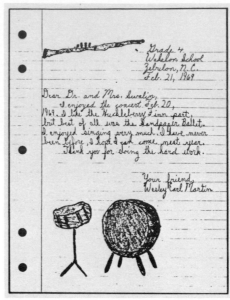

Lamar Edwin Stringfield (1897-1959), left, a Raleigh native, founder of the Asheville Symphony in 1927, Pulitzer Prize winning composer (for "From the Southern Mountains") in 1928, organized the North Carolina Symphony in Chapel Hill in 1932 at the urging of a group headed by Geologist Joseph Hyde Pratt. Stringfield left for New York in 1939, and Benjamin Swalin took over. Over the next several decades, Swalin and the symphony gave North Carolinians a rich musical education — the letter reprinted at the right is one example — and by the time of its 50th anniversary, the 68-piece orchestra had over 38,000 sponsors in the state and a secure national reputation for excellence. (NCC)

came forward to finance a conversion along either of those lines, leaving the old mill under sentence of possible razing, a group led by Ruth West formed the Carrboro Community Coalition. Then, when the Carrboro board of aldermen turned down a proposal to save the mill, the Coalition picked a slate of candidates which won control of the board.

The new board successfully solicited federal and state grants, built the 54-acre Community Park off US 54 West, constructed bikeways, repaired and rerouted streets, improved housing and water and sewer services, and won support from the community to convert Carr Mill #4 into the Carr Mill Mall it is today, which includes a 150-seat theatre used by the Carrboro Art School since 1979.

A number of well known entertainers have had their beginnings in Chapel Hill. In the fall of 1945, Andy Griffith of Mount Airy enrolled in UNC as a sociology major planning for a career as a Moravian minister. He worked as a busboy in Swain Hall, delivered laundry, did other odd jobs, and lived for over two years on the third floor of the Battle Dormitory. Griffith was very shy and decidedly not studious, but he learned he could free himself from self-doubt in front of an audience. He sang in the Methodist choir, played the sousaphone in the Tar Heel Marching Band, and won a small role in *The Gondoliers*, thereby learning who Gilbert and Sullivan were. After several shifts of direction, he settled on a music major, continuing to act in Playmaker productions and taking small roles during the summer in *The Lost Colony*.

Vic Huggins gave Griffith his first opportunity as a profes-

sional entertainer by inviting the young man to perform at the Merchants Association's Ladies Night Banquet in the Carolina Inn on 11 February 1949. Griffith's country-bumpkin version of "Hamlet" left the audience unamused, in what was an uninspiring debut, for performer and audience. After five years of study, Griffith graduated and took a job in Goldsboro as a high school music teacher, in his words "one of the worst that ever came out of the university."

After three years of teaching and performing larger roles in *The Lost Colony*, Griffith hit the Southeastern night-club circuit, with a comedy routine featuring a revised version of the Hamlet story, similar travesties derived from "Romeo and Juliet," ballet, and opera, and another rustic farce he had put together with material from several sources including a suggestion from Vic Huggins — "What It Was Was Football." When Griffith delivered the monologue for the first time before a meeting of the State Press Photographers Association, Orville Campbell was present, liked the material, and asked to record it.

Campbell entered UNC in 1939 after his graduation from Mars Hill Junior College. He edited the *Daily Tar Heel* during his senior year, joined the Navy upon graduation, and stayed on campus until December 1943 attached to the Pre-Flight School. After the war, he worked for a year as director of the news bureau at Woman's College in Greensboro before he and a partner established the Colonial Press in Carrboro to print the *Daily Tar Heel*. In 1949, Campbell wrote the words and UNC music major Hank Beebe wrote the music for "All the Way Choo Choo," a song celebrating the gridiron exploits of Charlie

Justice. Benny Goodman, Johnny Long, and others recorded the popular tune; Campbell and Beebe wrote more songs, striking another popular theme with "Way Up in North Carolina," which sold over 300,000 records.

Campbell set up the Bentley Music Company to publish sheet music and Colonial Records to distribute records, and he became sole owner of the Colonial Press in 1950. In November 1953, he pressed 500 copies of "What It Was Was Football." The record received wide play on radio, Capitol Records picked it up, and Griffith and Campbell collected royalties for over 1,000,000 sales. Campbell had other hits in George Hamilton IV's recording of "A Rose and a Baby Ruth" and Dizzy Dean's rendition of "The Wabash Cannonball," but beginning in 1954 he began to pay increasing

attention to publishing the Chapel Hill *Weekly.*

Andy Griffith's stage persona became popular and profitable, and it won him the role of Will Stockdale in a television adaptation of Mac Hyman's *No Time for Sergeants.* Griffith followed Will Stockdale to Broadway and Hollywood, and in 1957 he demonstrated a very different talent in "A Face in the Crowd" with a riveting performance that has become a classic in the great-egotist-thwarted-by-self genre. Then came nine years of "The Andy Griffith Show" on television and a lengthy series of made-for-television movies. Griffith has won two Tony Awards to go with a shelf full of Emmys.

James Vernon Taylor, the son of UNC Medical School Dean Dr. Isaac Taylor, grew up in Chapel Hill, began

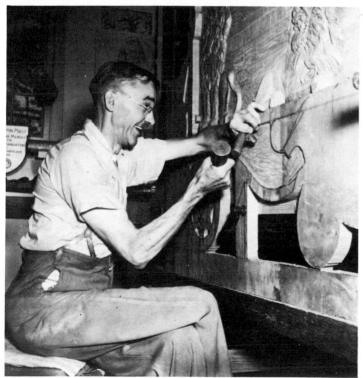

The "Circus Parade," sculpted from redwood by Carl Boettcher following a sketch by William Meade Prince, was placed in the Monogram Club in 1948. It is now permanently located in the Carolina Inn cafeteria.

William Meade Prince (1893-1951) (above right), was a renowned illustrator-writer and a descendant of a long line of Virginia Episcopal ministers, including the William Meade who visited Chapel Hill in 1819 and raised money for the American Colonization Society (see page 39).

Carl Boettcher (1886-1950) (above left), was born in Pomerania and came to the United States in 1926, eventually settling in Catawba. In 1941 at the invitation of William Carmichael, Jr., he moved to Carrboro and began work for the building department at UNC, creating a number of wooden sculptures for the university. Boettcher fought cancer for the last 10 years of his life. (UNC Photo Lab)

The actors in this scene from the 1955 Playmakers production of The Rainmaker *later established successful acting careers. James Secrest (left) of Thomasville has appeared in a large number of television productions, including the Gene Kelly series and* Rawhide. *James Pritchett withdrew from the UNC Law School and appeared on several soap operas before settling into the role of "Dr. Matt Powers" in NBC's* The Doctors. *Louise Fletcher won the Academy Award for Best Actress in 1975 for her portrayal of the "Big Nurse" in* One Flew Over the Cuckoo's Nest. *(NCC)*

playing in local combos while in junior high school, and wrote lyrics set to his own music. In 1968 at age 20, he recorded "Carolina In My Mind," the first album released by the Beatles' Apple label. Taylor used a song he had written for a nephew as the title song for his second album, "Sweet Baby James," which sold over 1.6 million copies and brought him sudden fame. After that he became a superstar, recording more albums, appearing in sold-out concerts worldwide, marrying singer Carly Simon, making the movie "Two-Lane Blacktop." More recently, he has divorced Miss Simon, kicked a drug habit, and begun to sing and record standards along with his own compositions. James Taylor's sister Kate and his brother Livingston also became popular musical entertainers.

When Mike Cross came to UNC from Lenoir on a golf scholarship in 1965, he had no interest in music. He learned to play the guitar in his freshman year, and after graduating in 1969, he kept his job as a waiter at the Carolina Coffee Shop and began to play the guitar and fiddle and to sing Irish jigs, southern folk songs, the blues, ballads, and comic songs at local clubs, such as The Endangered Species and The Cat's Cradle. After a few months, Cross happily learned he could make more money passing the hat at The Endangered Species than he could "working 50 hours at the Coffee Shop."

In the early 1970s, Cross spent two years studying law in Atlanta, then devoted himself fully to a musical career. He

enlarged his repertoire, increased the geographical range of his performances, and built a substantial local following. He cut his first album, "Child Prodigy," in 1976, to be followed by three more by 1980, the years in which he toured the United States and saw his album "The Bounty Hunter" become the best selling album in North Carolina. Cross's annual performances as the main attraction for the Kiwanis Club's Kenan Stadium Fourth of July celebrations have become a modern tradition for Chapel Hillians and UNC alumni. Cross is married to the former Cindy Gooch of Chapel Hill, also an accomplished singer.

Tommy Thompson, Jim Watson, and Bill Hicks of the Hollow Rock String Band formed the Red Clay Ramblers in October 1972, later taking on Phillip Michael Craver and Jack Herrick. Playing a wide range of music including ballads, hymns, bluegrass, and traditional fiddle tunes, the Ramblers established themselves by winning individual and group awards at several fiddlers' conventions. They then began performing on college campuses, in clubs, and in concerts set on stages as diverse as the New York Folklore Center and The Cat's Cradle in Chapel Hill.

In August 1973, Jim Wann, Bland Simpson, Mike Sheehan, Jan Davidson, and John Foley formed the Southern States Fidelity Choir, a band using electrical instruments which was also comfortable with a wide repertoire. Drawing partially from the familiar material, Wann wrote the script and with Simpson co-authored the music and lyrics for *Diamond Studs*, a play loosely based on the Jesse James legend. After a successful October 1974 trial run at the Ranch House in Chapel Hill, a cast dominated by members of the Southern States Fidelity Choir and the Red Clay Ramblers took *Diamond Studs* to New York for an off-Broadway run lasting from January to August 1975, collecting very positive reviews from the New York and national media and moving on to a booking at the Ford Theater in Washington, D.C.

Several members of the cast remain active performers, writers and composers. Jan Davidson is director of the Mountain Heritage Center at Cullowhee and also plays the small-club circuit, singing his own songs and playing percussion instruments, harmonicas, and anything with a string. Mike Sheehan is a producer-director with WUNC-TV. Bland Simpson and Jim Wann later collaborated on *Hot Grog*, a pirate tale with music set on the coast of North Carolina and performed at the Kennedy Center in Washington, D.C. in March 1977 prior to an off-Broadway run at the Phoenix Theatre. More recently Simpson has collaborated with Tommy Thompson on a musical version of Mark Twain's *Life on the Mississippi*, produced by the Playmakers in 1982; he has published a novel, *Heart of the Country*; and he currently teaches creative writing at UNC.

Jim Wann worked on two other musicals before hitting pay dirt again on 4 February 1982 when *Pump Boys and Dinettes* opened for a long run on Broadway to be followed

James Street (1903-1954), Mississippi born, came to Chapel Hill in 1945. He explained that he picked North Carolina as a home "because it's almost sinful the way I love this damn country." (NCC)

was basking in the success of *Good-bye, My Lady* on the night of 28 September 1954 when he attended the AP Broadcasters Awards dinner at the Carolina Inn, at which he passed out awards to members of the North Carolina radio medium. Prior to the presentations, Pentagon AP reporter Yates McDaniel (MA, UNC, 1929) defended the principle of "nuclear first strike" and the Pentagon's policy of releasing statements designed to mislead hostile governments. Street was shaking with anger when he followed McDaniel to the speaker's stand. "If the policy of the Pentagon is to confuse people," he uttered in a passion, "it sure as hell has confused me." He returned to his customary good humor while handing out the awards, including a "superior" to WCHL news commentator and program manager Scott Jarrett.

After posing for photographers, Street returned to his

Two of the most widely read writers in American history moved to Chapel Hill in 1963. Beulah Stowe (died 1983) married Thomas Collins (1910-1978), executive editor of the Chicago Daily News, in 1946. After they moved to Chapel Hill she wrote one-liners for "Today's Chuckle," a feature that appeared in over 200 newspapers, and he wrote "The Golden Years," and "The Senior Forum," columns that had about the same wide readership. (Courtesy of Orville Campbell and the Chapel Hill Newspaper)

by a national telecast. Wann had help on the book, lyrics and music from John Foley, John Schimmel, Mark Hardwick, Debra Monk, and his wife Cass Morgan, whom he had met when she showed up for an audition for the Ford Theatre performances of *Diamond Studs*. One of the *Pump Boys* songs, "Catfish," had been written years earlier by Wann and Bland Simpson.

Tommy Thompson, who remains with the Red Clay Ramblers, co-wrote *Life on the Mississippi* in 1982. While on a long Rambler tour in 1984, he wrote most of *The Last Song of John Proffit; a Solo Play with Music*, which traces the evolution of the banjo in the South in the mid-1800s. Thompson portrayed Proffit in a Playmakers Repertory Company production of the one-man play in the Paul Green Theatre in the fall of 1984.

The presence of Paul Green and Chapel Hill's reputation as the bastion of southern liberalism continued to attract writers after World War II. James Street had published *Look Away — A Dixie Notebook*, six novels including the immensely popular *The Biscuit Eater*, and a book of short stories before he moved from Connecticut to Chapel Hill in 1945. He said he came for several reasons — the university, the southern setting, a chance to farm, "and then, most of all, there was Paul Green." His next book was *Tomorrow We Reap* (1949), co-written with James Saxon Childers, then living in Chapel Hill. Childers had been a Rhodes Scholar at Oxford, a colonel in Air Force intelligence in World War II, and a prisoner of the Germans from September 1944 until liberated by the Russians in January 1945. He would later edit the Atlanta *Journal*.

James Street loved Chapel Hill because of its village atmosphere and because "I can argue books with Noel Houston and Betty Smith, and the same day talk local conditions with Vic Huggins at the hardware store and Y.Z. Cannon at the barbershop." Born a Roman Catholic in Lumberton, Mississippi, in 1902, when he married Baptist Lucy Nash O'Briant at age 19, he not only accepted her faith, he became a Baptist *preacher*.

Street had published five novels in the early 1950s and

table, and collapsed. Dr. Fred Patterson rushed to the Inn, checked Street, and sent him by ambulance to the Memorial Hospital emergency room, where he died from a heart attack.

Manly Wade Wellman was born in Portuguese West Africa in 1903, graduated from Columbia in 1926, worked as a reporter in Wichita, Kansas, and moved on to New York City in 1935 as a free-lance writer. He won the $2000 Ellery Queen mystery story first prize in 1946, the year William Faulkner won second prize, and he moved to Chapel Hill in 1951 to continue his craft in an office above Sutton's Drug Store. "A good half of my life has been spent here and there," he said in February 1953. "The other half of what I hope will be a long, long existence is going to be spent in Chapel Hill; for when I came here, I knew I was home at last." Still productive, Wellman has written over 70 books and 500 shorter pieces, ranging in kind from science fiction, detective tales, folklore, radio and television dramas to juvenile books, biographies, histories, and novels.

Two years after Wellman's arrival, Chapel Hill acquired a writer of extraordinary promise when Richard Milton McKenna left the U.S. Navy to enroll in UNC. McKenna was born in Mountain Home, Idaho, in 1913. After one year at the College of Idaho, he dropped out to join the Navy, in which he served 22 years, most of the time in the Pacific. When a reading of Henry David Thoreau's *Walden* convinced him that his mind had been "in a deep freeze," Chief Machinst Mate McKenna resigned, entered UNC to study English, graduated Phi Beta Kappa in 1956, and soon afterward married UNC librarian Eva Grice. He wrote several science fiction short stories, then drew on his knowledge of military life, machinery, and China to write *The Sand Pebbles*. The result was instant fame and riches, which in turn cost him the isolation and free time that had made *The Sand Pebbles* possible.

William Joseph "Billy" Arthur (b. 1911), 41" tall, described by a newspaper colleague as "a yard of fun," may well be the best liked person in Chapel Hill. A cheerleader while at UNC in 1930-1933, he later served two terms in the N.C. House of Representatives while publishing the Jacksonville News and Views, *a weekly newspaper.*

Billy writes a widely read column for the Chapel Hill Newspaper, *a column that he and his wife Edith research almost daily in the North Carolina Collection room on the fifth floor of Wilson Library. (Courtesy of Roland Giduz)*

The novel was a best seller. It won the $10,000 Harper Prize for 1962, it was the January 1963 Book-of-the-Month Club selection, and it earned McKenna an additional $200,000 for the film rights. Before its publication, McKenna was at work on *The Sons of Martha*, a "Japan novel" that would have complemented his earlier "China novel." After having written several chapters, he decided to begin anew on 30 October 1964. The next day he had a fatal heart attack. Posthumously, McKenna won the prestigious Nebula Award in 1966 for his science fiction short story "The Secret Place."

Robert Ruark attended UNC in the depths of the Great Depression (1931-1935), studying creative writing under Phillips Russell. After working his way up to becoming a highly paid columnist for the Washington, D.C. *Daily News* and the Scripps-Howard newspaper chain, he turned to writing books. The first was *Grenadine Etching*, a parody of historical novels; the second was *I Didn't Know It Was Loaded*, a potpourri relating in part to Chapel Hill. *Something of Value* made Ruark rich; *The Old Man and the Boy* and *The Old Man's Boy Grows Older* gave him literary stature. He died in Spain at the early age of 50 in 1965, leaving his papers to his alma mater.

Daphne Athas also came to Chapel Hill (from Gloucester, Massachusetts) in the midst of the Depression, an adventure she has recaptured in *Entering Ephesus* (1971). She graduated from UNC in 1943 and with the encouragement of Betty Smith, Paul Green, Jesse Rehder and others completed a novel at age 22, *The Weather of the Heart*. Miss Athas continues to write and to teach creative writing at UNC. Jesse Rehder assisted and inspired a generation of North Carolina writers before her untimely death in 1967, the year she edited *Chapel Hill Carousel*, a collection of stories, essays, and reviews by 19 writers connected to Chapel Hill — including Reynolds Price, John Knowles, Frances Gray Patton, Betty Smith, Richard McKenna, and Max Steele.

Max Steele, a native of Greenville, South Carolina, attended UNC in 1942 and returned to collect his AB in 1946. By then he had published his first short story, "Grandfather and the Chow Dog," in the August 1944 issue of *Harpers*. He won the $10,000 Harper's Prize in 1950 for his novel *Debby*, later studied painting and literature in France, where he was an advisory editor of the *Paris Review*, began teaching on the college level, and since 1967 has headed the creative writing program at UNC.

Foster Fitz-Simons began writing plays for the Playmakers before he graduated in 1934 to turn professional dancer and in 1940 to marry fellow Playmaker Marian Tatum of Raleigh (class of 1932). After the war, he signed a contract with Rinehart and Company to write a novel set in the early days of the southern tobacco industry. He said he hated every word of *Bright Leaf* (1948) because of the pressure to complete the prescribed assignment. The book sold well

and became a movie starring Gary Cooper, Jack Carson, Patricia Neal and Lauren Bacall, but Fitz-Simons was happy to abandon novel writing to spend his productive hours dancing in *The Lost Colony*, choreographing *Unto These Hills*, teaching in the Drama Department at UNC, and acting in Playmaker productions.

Doris Jane Waugh was born in Statesville in 1932. She attended Woman's College in Greensboro for two years, married Lowry Matthews Betts of Columbia, S.C., in 1952, and won a short story prize from *Mademoiselle* at age 21. While Lowry Betts was attending the UNC Law School and before he joined a law firm in Sanford, Doris worked for the Chapel Hill *Weekly*. Then, after publishing two volumes of short stories and two novels, she began teaching in the UNC English Department and continued to publish articles, short stories, poetry, and novels. In North Carolina she has won the UNC-Putnam Book Prize, three Sir Walter Raleigh Awards for fiction, and the N.C. Award for Literature. In 1983 she won the national John dos Passos Prize for Literature, two years after the publication of her latest novel, *Heading West*. Currently she is an Alumni Distinguished Professor of English and chairman of the UNC faculty.

Two Chapel Hill presses, one intentionally small and one potentially very large, offer increased outlets for North Carolina authors. After a seven year apprenticeship as editor and publisher of and contributor to *The Hyperion Poetry Journal*, in 1976 Judy Hogan founded the Carolina Wren Press, now run out of her home on Barclay Road, for the purpose of publishing new writers, primarily from North Carolina. She tries to publish four books of poetry, fiction, and drama each year. In recent years she has released volumes by T.J. Reddy, Mike Rigsby, Amon Liner, Jaki Shelton Green, Chapel Hillian Miranda Cambanis and others.

Judy Hogan is herself the author of two volumes of poetry, published by other presses; she has edited several anthologies of modern poetry; and she conducts writer's workshops and literary classes frequently. The *Library Journal* listed two Carolina Wren books among its selec-

tion of the "Best Titles of 1984": the anthology *Roadmap*, and James Cryer's translation of *Plum Blossom* by Li Ch'ing Chao, a woman poet living in China in 1084-1150 A.D.

In January 1982, Dr. Louis D. Rubin, Jr. incorporated Algonquin Books, planning to concentrate initially on works by authors living in the Southeast while molding Algonquin into a national publishing house. Rubin, who is a UNC Distinguished Professor of English, did not enter the venture a stranger to publishing. He has written or co-written two novels, some 30 scholarly volumes, and hundreds of essays; and he is the general editor of the Southern Literary Studies series published by the Louisiana State University Press, a relationship that has benefited several North Carolina authors. Algonquin Books released its first five volumes in the fall of 1982, including *My Own, My Country's Time; A Journalist's Journey* by two-time Pulitzer Prize winner and UNC alumnus Vermont Connecticut Royster, who is a retired *Wall Street Journal* editor and a current UNC Kenan Professor Emeritus in the School of Journalism.

In general the print and broadcasting media have recently fared well in Chapel Hill. After having published the *Weekly* for over 30 years, by 1954 Louis Graves was ready to sell, and he was entertaining an offer originating out of Baltimore. George Watts Hill approached Orville Campbell and asked if Campbell would be interested in publishing the *Weekly* if it were kept both locally owned and locally oriented. Campbell said he was, and Hill organized a group of stockholders that included himself, Campbell, Graves, George Watts Hill, Jr., W.D. Carmichael III, Margaret Carmichael Lester, Collier Cobb, Jr., and others. As president of the Chapel Hill Publishing Company, Inc. and as the general manager of the newspaper, Orville Campbell made plans to begin publishing twice weekly, but before that became a reality, he and the *Weekly* had competition.

Edwin J. Hamlin, Phillips Russell, Roland Giduz, and

This is the first page of a 1966 Japanese book, The Story of Chapel Hill, written by Mrs. Fumiko Seki, who lived in Chapel Hill 1955-1957 while her husband was on the UNC faculty. In the book, Mrs. Seki describes what she sees as the Chapel Hill life style. The book is highly complimentary, although it deplores corporal punishment of children and suggests that old people are slightly mistreated. Mrs. Seki became the director of UNESCO in Sapporo when she returned to Japan. (NCC)

チャペル・ヒル 物語

関 文子著

誠信書房

L.M. Pollander began publishing the Chapel Hill *News Leader* each Monday and Thursday beginning in May 1954. Business Manager Hamlin owned The News Inc. in Hillsborough, which published *The News of Orange County* and the *Alamance News* and printed the *Daily Tar Heel*. L.M. Pollander had for a time taught advertising in the UNC School of Journalism.

Editor Charles Phillips Russell was the son of Moses H. and Lucy Phillips Russell, the grandson of UNC professor Charles Phillips, and the grandnephew of Cornelia Phillips Spencer, the subject of his 1949 biography *The Woman Who Rang the Bell*. Russell left his native Rockingham at age 16 in 1900 to enroll in UNC. As an undergraduate he edited the *Carolina Magazine* and the *Tar Heel*, and after graduation he spent a decade as a reporter and a jack-of-all-trades on newspapers in Charlotte and New York City. On a bum's tour of Europe in 1914, he left Belgium a few hours before the arrival of the German army. He worked as a reporter and a free-lance writer in New York until 1920, moved to London, married Phyllis Meltzer, fathered a son, Leon Russell, handled publicity for prizefighter Jack Dempsey, published two slim volumes of poetry, divorced, and returned to New York in 1925.

After publishing a travel book, a novel, and biographies of Benjamin Franklin, John Paul Jones, and Ralph Waldo Emerson, Russell returned to UNC in 1931 to teach creative writing and to marry Paul Green's sister Caro Mae Green, who was then editor of *The Literary Lantern*, a newspaper column on books. Russell continued his prolific outpouring of books: *Harvesters* (1932), lives of great men; *William the Conquerer* (1933); a history of 18th-century Europe, *The Glittering Century* (1936); the text for *These Old Stone Walls* in 1944, published by the Chapel Hill Historical society in 1972; and a life of Thomas Jefferson in 1956. Although Russell never gave A's because "about the only one to deserve an A would be Shakespeare," he was a popular teacher and retired from UNC in the spring of 1955 only to give more time to editing the *News Leader*.

The newspaper won immediate critical recognition. The North Carolina Press Association gave the new semiweekly top honors for feature writing in its initial year, as well as a second place award for photography and an honorable mention for its editorial page. The Press Association bestowed another award for photography in 1955, and in 1956 it gave the *News Leader* more awards than any other semi-weekly in the state — a first place for feature writing, a second place for its editorial page, and a third place for photography.

However, cash flow is certainly as important as awards for keeping a newspaper solvent, and the Chapel Hill *Weekly*, which had become a semi-weekly in 1955, had the inside tack on subscribers and advertisers. The pressure to make the *News Leader* profitable resulted in management dissension leading to a lawsuit involving the partners, and the *News Leader* folded on 29 January 1959, with News Director Roland Giduz bequeathing the "soul" of the paper to the Chapel Hill *Weekly*.

Under the editorship of Jim Shumaker, 1959-1975, the Chapel Hill *Weekly* expanded its publication to five days per week in September 1972 and adopted a new title, the Chapel Hill *Newspaper*. Orville Campbell took over as editor in 1975 and began publishing every day except Saturday. Campbell and his predecessors have always had a pool of student journalists and artists to draw from, and many figures now prominent worked for the *Newspaper* during their formative years — Vermont Connecticut Royster, Doris Betts, Jeff McNelly, John Branch, Rolfe Neil of the Charlotte *Observer*, and Mark Wicker of the Philadelphia *Inquirer* are a few. That kind of talent is also responsible for many of the 100 or so national and state awards the *Newspaper* has collected since World War II.

Chapel Hill got its "voice" on Sunday, 18 January 1953 when Roland "Sandy" McClamroch's WCHL ("Where Chapel Hill Listens") went on the air at 2 p.m. with State Representative John W. Umstead, Jr. speaking on current political issues. At first limited to 1000 watts and daylight hours, WCHL expanded its program day to 24 hours in 1968 and its power to 5000 watts in 1978. Over the years, CBS newsman Charles Kuralt, singer George Hamilton IV, WBT-TV's Ty Boyd, ABC sports commentator Jim Lampley, *Sports Illustrated* assistant managing editor Larry Keith, and others have worked for the station, but Jim Heavner is the single person most responsible for turning a modest broadcasting operation into the multifaceted media enterprise it has become.

Jim Heavner came from King's Mountain in 1957 as a freshman English major. He had broken into broadcasting in a minor way in King's Mountain and at WUNC-FM, and when an announcer's position became vacant at WCHL in 1958 he rushed to apply, impressed McClamroch, and got the job. His first big break came two years later when Ty Boyd left to join WBT in Charlotte and recommended Heavner to replace him as the key

Chapel Hill Communities, Inc. Realtors and the Connecticut Mutual Life Insurance Company now occupy the original home of WCHL at 1720 East Franklin Street. (Courtesy of Roland Giduz and the Village Companies)

morning announcer and business manager. Heavner consistently took on more responsibility for programming, management, and sports coverage. He began buying stock in the company in 1967 and became the major shareholder when he purchased McClamroch's interests in 1980.

By then Heavner was president of The Village Companies, now the umbrella organization for: Village Publishing, which publishes *The Village Advocate, The Mall Advocates,* and many university directories; The Village Cable-TV System; The Print Shops in Chapel Hill's University Mall and Durham's Northgate Mall; *The Triangle Pointer* weekly guide magazine, purchased from Roland Giduz in 1978; WZZU in Raleigh and WKQQ-FM in Lexington, Kentucky; and The Tar Heel Sports Network, which broadcasts UNC football games over more than 60 stations and UNC basketball games over more than 40 stations.

In recent years Sandy McClamroch as president of the nonprofit Chapel Hill Residential Retirement Center has concentrated on the development of the 104-acre Carol Woods retirement settlement on Weaver Dairy Road. The complex now includes 230 one- and two-bedroom units, and a 60-bed health-care center. It was entirely appropriate that a luxurious retirement center be built in Chapel Hill, which by the 1970s had become popular among retirees, many of whom chose it because of its pleasant and cultured life style and because it offers a plethora of means for continuing a productive life into old age.

Luxurious accommodations are also available now to everyone — who can pay the price. Before there was a Memorial Hospital complex or a Research Triangle Park, there was little demand for hotel accommodations except for football weekends during the Charlie "Choo-Choo" Justice era. Anticipating future growth, Charles Nottingham, Sr. built the University Motor Inn on Raleigh Road in the early 1950s, and only the Tar Heel Motel and a Holiday Inn went up before 1982, when Chapel Hill got something totally unexpected — a genuinely world-class hotel.

Julius Verwoerdt, builder of over a score of European hotels, had come to the United States to study theme parks to get ideas for a facility planned in his native Holland. He liked the Research Triangle Park area, saw promise for a luxury hotel in the region, and settled with his wife Anke in Durham in 1978. After inspecting several prospective sites, Verwoerdt decided on a location on the Chapel Hill-Durham Boulevard a quarter of a mile out from Eastgate. Madrid architect Estaban Roman Marlasca helped him with initial concepts which O'Brien/Atkins Associates of Chapel Hill used to execute an overall plan. Romeo Guest Associates of Greensboro began construction in 1981 and completed the Europa Hotel a year later.

The Europa has 172 rooms, each with a private balcony, a queen-sized bed, and two original paintings done by North Carolina artists, plus the usual conveniences and fine

In 1960 the university employed student Frank Meldau to build, under the supervision of university engineer J.J. Hakan, a scale model of the campus and the business district. Meldau, assisted by John Stockard and long-time student David Kitzmiller, completed the 13-foot by 15-foot model in 1961. Here Meldau holds a replica of the Morehead Planetarium, the building in which the model is on permanent display. Meldau now designs and builds sailboats that have an international market. (NCC)

dining associated with four-star hotels. In December 1983, Verwoerdt sold the Europa for $14.9 million to Transco Incorporated, a conglomerate headquartered in Chicago.

While the growth that made the Europa a viable venture was taking place, several of the historic houses of Chapel Hill perished, but recently preservationists have succeeded in protecting many of those remaining. The ultimate fate of Miss Nancy Hilliard's Crystal Palace was sealed in 1945 when John Motley Morehead volunteered to build the Morehead Planetarium.

Morehead, the grandson of N.C. Governor John Motley Morehead and the son of James T. and Elizabeth Connally Morehead, was born in Spray, North Carolina in 1870 and graduated Phi Beta Kappa from UNC in 1891. After further training with Westinghouse, he went to work for his father in Spray, where his discoveries of new and cheaper ways to produce calcium carbide and acetylene gas provided the impetus for his father to establish Union Carbide. Working for the company, Morehead became a world famous electrochemical engineer and the choice of President Woodrow Wilson to oversee the production of gases and gas products during World War I. In 1930, Morehead capped his public career by accepting an appointment as the Hoover administration's minister to Sweden.

After Morehead had selected the site for the Planetarium, planners chose to put a parking lot on the adjacent Crystal Palace grounds and purchased the property for $35,000 from Mrs. R.B. Parker of Enfield, who had inherited it from her brother-in-law Algernon S. Barbee. The Alpha Gamma Delta sorority rented the old house until 1954, when the university razed the structure, flattened the slight prominence on which it had stood, and built the parking lot around a picturesque sundial

Gerard F. Tempest (b. 1915) surveys the 5 May 1963 opening of his Villa Tempesta. Tempest, an Italian immigrant, sold the Villa in 1969 to return to Rome and to the productive life of the artist. For a time, he designed and decorated furniture for Nieman-Marcus of Dallas, Texas. (Courtesy of Roland Giduz)

surrounded by a lush rose garden.

As the 1940s gave way to the 1950s, commercial enterprises were rapidly replacing old homes along West Franklin Street. In the summer of 1947, Mrs. Walter D. Toy sold her house on the north side of the second block of West Franklin to Mrs. Margaret Davis Haywood of Durham. Mrs. Haywood sold to the A&P, which razed the house, built a new store, and moved out of its midtown quarters, later used by Rose's Stores and now by the Rite Aid Center.

The brothers Robert Lee Fowler of Chapel Hill and Marvin Mangum Fowler of Durham moved the Model Market grocery business a few hundred yards west from their location near the Carolina Theatre to a spot in the bottom of West Franklin Street between the new A&P and the old Dr. Walter Reece Berryhill house. The Fowlers competed with the A&P by stocking exotic foods, offering fresh bread from an in-house bakery, and providing personalized services. The Berryhill house gave way to a service station and a parking lot.

Preservationists prefer to protect old buildings by putting them to use, preferably in the manner for which they were created. But "The Hill House," located behind the Baptist Church, had almost outlived all usefulness when the town installed its first public library in a ground floor room in 1958. Built in the 1890s, the house was once owned by

Mrs. Harriet Cole and later rented to students, one of whom may have been Thomas Wolfe. The school board bought the property, built the elementary school next to the house, and sold the aging residence to a Mrs. G. Bryan, who ran a boarding house there until she died in the late 1930s. Her daughter and son-in-law then ran the boarding house briefly before selling it to bandleader John Scott Trotter.

Soon after Trotter, a native of Charlotte, enrolled in UNC in 1925, he became one of the original six members of Hal Kemp's band, as the piano player. He remained with Kemp until 1936, when he went to Hollywood, wrote the score for the Bing Crosby movie "Pennies from Heaven," and then became a bandleader on his own as musical director for Crosby's radio show and later for George Gobel's television variety show. Trotter converted the rooms in his Chapel Hill acquisition into hotel-apartments, named it "The Hill House," and turned its management over to his sister and her husband, who rented mostly to students. The Baptist Church purchased the property from Trotter after World War II and continued to rent rooms to students for two decades.

Mrs. Richmond Bond led a 1950s effort to establish a public library for Chapel Hill. When the campaign won support from the town aldermen, in 1958 librarians moved their small collection from the elementary school next door into a single room in The Hill House. As the collection grew, the library spread to occupy three rooms, all of which leaked, before the new library at Franklin and Boundary Street was ready in 1968. Then the Orange-Chatham Anti-Poverty Committee razed the decaying structure, using the discarded wood to make home repairs for the needy.

Chapel Hill gained a rival to the Gimghoul Castle as a popular architectural curiosity when Gerard F. Tempest built the Villa Tempesta in 1961-1963, largely with materials taken from the Duke and Watts family mansions and a hotel being torn down in Durham. Tempest was born in Italy in 1918 and emigrated to Massachusetts in 1929. Drafted during World War II, he worked in Army intelligence and landed at Normandy on D-Day. After the war, he studied art in Boston and Rome before earning an AB in philosophy at UNC. While executing portraits, murals, and architectural designs, Tempest continued his studies at Harvard and in Rome. He then moved to Hollywood, where he painted portraits of Veronica Lake, ex-Playmaker Sydney Blackmer, and other stars. Following an illness which forced him to curtail his strenuous schedule, Tempest resumed his studies in Chapel Hill and designed the Villa Tempesta.

Using the ornate remains of the Durham mansions and relying on archaic construction techniques, Tempest built the villa himself with the help of David Kitzmiller and other common laborers. Designed primarily as an art gallery, the villa also included ample living and studio space. James Fitzgibbon of the School of Architecture at Washington University in St. Louis later wrote Tempest: "The villa was indeed one of the few buildings in North Carolina that I always felt worth a trip to see, both while it was under construction and later when you and your family lived there. It was a rich flow of pleasant and often jolly surprises that you provoked from the junk pile of old Durham houses."

Tempest opened a coffee shop in the villa, expanded it into a restaurant, and soon lamented the time it took away from his painting. Eager to return to Italy and his art, Tempest sold the villa to Bibi Danziger, who kept it open as a restaurant/art gallery/antique shop named the Villa Teo as a memorial to her late husband Ted.

With the commercial district spreading into the old residential areas to the west and north, in the mid-1960s many Chapel Hillians became concerned with preserving the threatened historical structures near the business district and on campus. On 20 September 1966, an audience of some 200 met in the Town Hall to hear talks by Phillips Russell, Mrs. John Foushee, and visitors from Hillsborough and Raleigh on the preservation of antiquities and to select committees to plan for the orderly preservation of historical buildings in Chapel Hill.

Chairman Robert E. Stipe and members Mrs. Wayne A. Bowers, John Harkness, and Mayor Sandy McClamroch made up a committee entrusted to write a statement of purpose and to choose a slate of officers. Roland Giduz, Mrs. John Foushee, and Mrs. Pearson Stewart made up another committee with an immediate goal—to raise money to stop the sale of the Presbyterian Manse, the former Charles Phillips home built by the Rev. William Mercer Green in 1849 and purchased by the Presbyterian Church in 1889. (Mr. and Mrs. Edward Yaggy erased fears that the old house might perish when they purchased it with the intent to preserve it.)

The following month, many of those who had met in the Town Hall became charter members of the Chapel Hill Historical Society. Robert Stipe organized the temporary steering committee which chose the first board of directors: Corydon P. Spruill, Mrs. Loren MacKinney, William S. Powell, Judge L.J. Phipps, Robert W. Huggins, Mrs. John Harkness, Roland Giduz, Mrs. Frederick Coenen, and John Allcott. The Society met for the first time in formal session on 2 November 1966 and selected a president, William Powell, then the curator of the N.C. Collection in the UNC Wilson Library.

At the original sale of lots on 12 October 1792, auctioneer John C. Rencher purchased the four-acre lot at the northeast corner of Rosemary and Hillsborough streets. Joseph Caldwell, Elisha Mitchell, and Jones Watson later owned the lot, and by the late 1850s Dr. William P. Mallett owned the property, which then contained a house. In the

Davie Poplar has been the focus of almost continual efforts to preserve it. Twice shattered by lightning, it remains a symbol of Chapel Hill's past and its future. This work was performed on 7 June 1961. (Courtesy of Roland Giduz)

early 1870s, Dr. Mallett sold the house and lot to Methodist circuit rider Joseph Bonaparte Martin, whose wife Clara boarded students, including Josephus Daniels while he was studying law at UNC. The house was later owned by William C. Coker, who sold it to H.G. Wagstaff, who in 1921 sold it to Romance Languages Professor William M. Dey. Dr. Dey's surviving sister Mrs. Annie Wichard sold the house to the Delta Upsilon fraternity in 1966 for $34,650.

When the Delta Upsilons sought a permit to raze the "Martin-Dey House" and a house next door in 1971 to make space for a parking lot to satisfy town codes, the Historical Society convinced the board of aldermen to halt the project by having Town Planner Harry Palmer devise a parking plan which allowed the fraternity to remain full strength and the Martin-Dey house to remain intact.

Another crisis arose in 1972 when Betty Smith died and her home went on the market. After purchasing the old Andrew Mickle house in 1944, Miss Smith added exterior bricks to the first floor, replaced the front porch with stone steps, and built a rock wall along Rosemary and

Durham native James H. Shumaker, former managing editor of the Durham Morning Herald, later general manager of the Chapel Hill Weekly from 1 June 1959 to his retirement, is the model for the comic strip character "Shoe," authored and drawn by Jeff MacNelly. MacNelly, a Long Island native, attended UNC and worked for Shumaker for about a year in 1969 as a cartoonist.

Shumaker developed a reputation as one of the South's premier journalists. In an interview with the Raleigh News and Observer, he explained how he ran the Weekly: "We just raise hell, try to save trees and try to keep the University of North Carolina from going to hell." (Courtesy of Jane Hamborsky)

Hillsborough streets. The immediate need to save the Smith house spurred Ida Friday, Georgia Carroll Kyser, Oscar Ewing and others in April 1972 to create a revolving fund for the purpose of preserving the Smith house and other historic structures. The outgrowth was the Chapel Hill Preservation Society, which bought the Smith house.

In 1973 George Watts Hill made a down payment to hold the home for Richard H. and Eliza Lamberton, the parents of Mrs. George Watts Hill, Jr. The Lambertons retired to Chapel Hill from Lake Forest, Illinois, renovated the interior of the Smith house, and decorated it with the treasures they had accumulated over the years, primarily while Richard was deputy director of the Office of Defense Transportation during World War II and a much traveled international banker afterward.

The Preservation Society also gained permission from the university to redecorate the Horace Williams House for use as a cultural center and as a meeting place for the Historical and Preservation societies. Eleven interior decorators took on the job of beautifying the six-to-ten-room house (depending upon the counter's definition of a room), which is now open to the public on a limited schedule.

The activities of the Historical and the Preservation societies were instrumental in spurring the town aldermen

A group of Chapel Hill writers gather at Paul Green's home in April 1953. They are: (seated) Mrs. Kermit Hunter, Elizabeth Lay Green (behind Mrs. Hunter), unidentified, Yoshiro Nagayo, Mrs. Manly Wade Wellman, Cliford Llyons; (standing) Paul Green, Phillips Russell, Josephina Niggli, Kermit Hunter, Manly Wade Wellman, James Street, Caro Mae Green Russell.

in 1976 to establish a historic district encompassing sections of East Franklin, East Rosemary, Hillsborough, and Boundary streets. The ordinance created a commission which must approve any major alterations or construction in the area. But the most spectacular individual success of the Preservation Society has been the relocation and restoration of the Huskey House, which in 1977 sat in a very dilapidated state at 215 East Rosemary Street, the property of the Alpha Chi Omega sorority. Julian Shakespeare Carr bought the house in a sheriff's sale in 1879 and sold it soon afterward to blacksmith John Huskey, who had joined the Orange Light Infantry with Carr in 1861 and who had left the army with Carr in April 1865, neither having risen above the rank of private.

When the Alpha Chi Omega national officers refused a request to renovate the Huskey House, the Preservation Society and the Historical Society began raising the $2000 necessary to save the structure by moving it, earning the praise of John B. Flowers III of the Historical Preservation Society of Durham for "taking the initiative to preserve something that's not grand." Mr. and Mrs. Richard Birogel gave the Preservation Society a lot on Henderson Street, the Society had the house relocated in November 1977, and architect Jon Condoret purchased the house, attached a large addition to the rear, and turned it into a decidedly fine residence for his family.

Chapel Hillians first began to lament the passing of "the village" in the 1890s. Today, even the most "devout" Chapel Hillians are reconciled to the indisputable fact that "the village" is now a thing of memory. Preservations have secured the future of the old section of town, and the next history of Chapel Hill will in all probability concentrate far more on the spread of a city across traditional borders, including the Chatham and Durham county lines, and far less on the old business and residential area that has been the prime focus of this study.

In the last two years, major shopping centers have opened on Weaver Dairy Road to the north, on Jones Ferry Road west of Carrboro, and on U.S. 15-501 to the south. Apartments and condominium construction is on a geometric rise in Carrboro, and development is a topic which arises at every meeting of the Chapel Hill Town Council. The boom of the mid-1980s will be self perpetuating for several years to come, and further expansion of the university, the medical facilities, and the Research Triangle Park is inevitable. The Chapel Hill of the year 2000 A.D. can now be only a vague vision, but it will surely have little in common with the sedate "writers' colony" that villagers envisioned a short 50 years ago.

In 1935, the Yackety Yack *presented a series of cartoons designed to chronicle Chapel Hill's development. This one envisions the William Davie visit to the wilderness that was to become the university's site.* (NCC)

Chapel Hill native John Branch, editorial page cartoonist for the San Antonio Express-News since 1981, had the same position at the Chapel Hill Newspaper from 1976 to 1980, during which time he recorded this impression of contemporary Chapel Hill. (Courtesy of John Branch and the Chapel Hill Newspaper)

Chapel Hill artist Eleanor Wiles painted "Franklin Street," the scene that adorns the dust cover of this book. John Wesley Carr, Ilia Nunn, Seaton Barbee, and several others owned the property before J.D. Webb and Herbert Lloyd purchased it and in 1900-1902 erected the buildings that now house Varley's Men's Shop, the Little Shop, Julian's, and the Carolina Coffee Shop. Webb and Lloyd sold the buildings to the Chapel Hill Insurance and Realty Company, which sold them to John Sprunt Hill, who donated them to the university.

The tree arching over the right foreground was planted in 1949 during a Jaycee's beautification program. It replaced a tree planted in the 1910s that had slowly suffocated because an iron ring, placed around it to stabilize it during its early life, had been forgotten and left in place.

A SELECTED BIBLIOGRAPHY

Asby, Warren. *Frank Porter Graham, A Southern Liberal.* Winston-Salem: John F. Blair Publishers, 1980.

Barksdale, Marcellus Chandler. *The Indigenous Civil Rights Movement and Cultural Change in North Carolina.* M.A. Thesis, Duke University, 1977.

Barrett, John Gilchrist. *Sherman's March Through the Carolinas.* Chapel Hill: UNC Press, 1956.

Bassett, John Spencer. *Anti-Slavery Leaders of North Carolina.* Baltimore: Johns Hopkins Press, 1898.

Battle, Kemp Plummer. *History of the University of North Carolina,* 2 Vols. Raleigh: Edwards and Broughton, 1907 and 1912.

————. *Memories of an Old-Time Tar Heel,* ed. by William James Battle. Chapel Hill: UNC Press, 1945.

Biographical Clipping File, North Carolina Collection, UNC Wilson Library.

Brabham, Robin. "Defining the American University: The University of North Carolina, 1865-1875." *North Carolina Historical Review,* October 1980.

Canada, John W. *Life at Eighty, Memories and Comments by a Tarheel in Texas.* Privately printed, 1952.

Chamberlain, Hope Summerell. *Old Days in Chapel Hill: Being the Life and Letters of Cornelia Phillips Spencer.* Chapel Hill: UNC Press, 1926.

Cheshire, Lucius McGehee. "Hillsborough's James Hogg," a paper prepared for delivery before the Hillsborough Historical Society, 12 March 1970.

Cohn, David L. "Chapel Hill," *Atlantic Monthly,* March 1941.

Connor, R.D.W., compiler and annotator. *A Documentary History of the University of North Carolina,* 2 Vols. Chapel Hill: UNC Press, 1953.

Cornelius, Janet D. *God's Schoolmasters: Southern Evangelists to the Slaves, 1830-1860.* Thesis, University of Illinois at Urbana-Champaign, 1977.

Crouch, Paul. "Brief History of the Communist Movement in North Carolina and South Carolina," unpublished typescript.

D.A.R. Scrap Book of Orange County; World War II Honor Roll, compiled by Edith Palmer Pell.

Freeman, Charles Maddry. *Growth and Plans for a Community: A Study of Negro Life in Chapel Hill and Carrboro, North Carolina.* M.A. Thesis, UNC, 1944.

Green, Fletcher M., ed. *The Chapel Hill Methodist Church: A Centennial History, 1853-1953.* Chapel Hill, 1954.

Habel, Samuel Tilden. *Centennial Monograph Celebrating the First 100 Years of the Baptist Church at Chapel Hill.* Chapel Hill: The Orange Printshop, 1954.

Hamilton, W.D. "In at the Death, or the Last Stand of the Confederacy," *Sketches of War History, Ohio Commandry, Loyal*

Henderson, Archibald. *The Campus of the First State University.* Chapel Hill: UNC Press, 1949.

Honeycutt, Allison W. *An Evaluation of the Chapel Hill High School.* M.A. Thesis, UNC, 1944.

Hooper, William. *Fifty Years Since: An Address Before the Alumni Association of the University of North Carolina, June 1st, 1859.* Chapel Hill: John B. Neathery, 1861.

House, Robert B. *The Light That Shines: Chapel Hill, 1912-1916.* Chapel Hill: UNC Press, 1964.

Ivey, Pete. "Chapel Hill Hostelries Rich in Tradition," *Alumni Review,* January 1936.

Johns, John. *A Memoir of the Life of the Right Rev. William Meade.* Baltimore: Innes and Company, 1867.

Johnson, Guion Griffis. *Ante-Bellum North Carolina: A Social History.* Chapel Hill: UNC Press, 1937.

Keith-Lucas, Alan. *The University Presbyterian Church of Chapel Hill, North Carolina: A History from Its Earliest Days to the Spring of 1977,* unpublished typescript.

Lefler, Hugh and Paul Wager, eds. *Orange County — 1752-1952.* Chapel Hill: The Orange Printshop, 1953.

Lindley, J.V. and J.T. Craig. "A Study of the Tax Statistics of Chapel Hill and a Report on the Chapel Hill Recorder's Court," unpublished typescript.

Love, Cornelia Spencer. *When Chapel Hill Was a Village.* Chapel Hill: Chapel Hill Historical Society, 1976.

Morphis, Sam. "The Autobiography of a Negro," unpublished transcription taken by Horace Williams.

Orange County Clipping File, North Carolina Collection, UNC Wilson Library.

The Orange Jewel, published by the Orange County Training School, 1925-1926.

Patterson, Andrew Henry. "Notes Written by Dean Andrew (Drew) Henry Patterson of the University of North Carolina at the Request of Mrs. Patrick Henry Winston, 1925," unpublished typescript.

Powell, William S. *The First State University: A Pictorial History of the University of North Carolina.* Chapel Hill: UNC Press, 1972.

Prouty, William B. *Bill Prouty's Chapel Hill.* Chapel Hill: Chapel Hill Historical Society, 1979.

Prince, William Meade. *The Southern Part of Heaven.* New York: Rinehart and Company, Inc., 1950.

Rees, Philip A. *The Chapel of the Cross: An Architectural History.* M.A. Thesis, UNC, 1979.

Russell, Lucy Phillips. *A Rare Pattern.* Chapel Hill: UNC Press, 1957.

Russell, Phillips. *These Old Stone Walls.* Chapel Hill: Chapel Hill Historical Society, 1972.

————. *The Woman Who Rang the Bell: The Story of Cornelia Phillips Spencer.* Chapel Hill: UNC Press, 1949.

Scott, Tom. *A History of Intercollegiate Athletics at the University of North Carolina.* Dissertation, Columbia University, 1955.

The Southern Historical Collection, UNC Wilson Library — Orange County merchants' books; material collected and submitted by the Chapel Hill Historical Society; and papers from the collections of the Battle family, Joseph Caldwell, the Cameron family, J.S. Carr, the Cobb family, William R. Davies, William Gaston, the Graham family, Benjamin S. Hedrick, the Henderson family, James Iredell, William R. Kenan, Jr., the Mallett family, Matthias M. Marshall, William DeB. MacNider, Elisha Mitchell, James H. Otey, Abraham Rencher, Cornelia Spencer, David Lowry Swain, Horace Williams, Norvell Wilson, and many more.

Spencer, Cornelia Phillips. "John DeBerniere Hooper — A Memorial," *University Magazine,* March 1886.

————. *The Last Ninety Days of the War.* New York: The Watchman, 1866.

————. "Old Times in Chapel Hill," a series of articles published between 1884 and 1890.

————. "Pen and Ink Sketches," a series of articles published in the Raleigh *Sentinel* in 1869.

Staples, Raymond. "Chapel Hill Is 'Our Town' in Novels," *Alumni Review,* March 1940.

Stolpen, Steven. *Chapel Hill: A Pictorial History.* Norfolk: Donning Company/Publishers, 1978.

Thornbury, John F. *God Sent Revival: The Story of Asahel Nettleton and the Second Great Awakening.* Grand Rapids: Evangelical Press, 1977.

Towle, W. Wilde, ed. *The History of James Nunn.* Chapel Hill: Chapel Hill Historical Society, 1977.

Trelease, Allen W. *White Terror; The Ku Klux Klan Conspiracy and Southern Reconstruction.* New York: Harper and Row, 1971.

Walser, Richard Gaither. *Thomas Wolfe, Undergraduate.* Durham: Duke University Press, 1977.

Wilson, Louis Round. *Historical Sketches.* Durham: Moore Publishing Company, 1976.

————, ed. *Selected Papers of Cornelia Phillips Spencer.* Chapel Hill: UNC Press, 1953.

Other sources: The microfilm copies of newspapers published in Chapel Hill — the *Harbinger,* the *Columbian Repository,* the *Gazette,* the *Ledger,* the *Chapel Hill News,* the *Chapel Hillian,* the *Daily Tar Heel,* the *Weekly,* the *News Leader,* and the *Newspaper;* UNC publications including the *Alumni Review, University Magazine,* and the *Yackety Yack.*

INDEX